Social Uses and Radio Practices

D0209771

International Communication and Popular Culture

Series Editor
John A. Lent

Social Uses and Radio Practices: The Use of Participatory Radio by Ethnic Minorities in Mexico, Lucila Vargas

The Orchestration of the Media: The Politics of Mass Communications in Communist Poland and the Aftermath, Tomasz Goban-Klas

Media Beyond Socialism: Theory and Practice in East-Central Europe, Slavko Splichal

FORTHCOMING

Human Rights and the Media: International Reporting as a Global Watchdog, Frederic Moritz

Asian Popular Culture, edited by John A. Lent

Social Uses
and Radio Practices

The Use of Participatory Radio by Ethnic Minorities in Mexico

Lucila Vargas

Westview Press
BOULDER • SAN FRANCISCO • OXFORD

International Communication and Popular Culture

Published in 1995 in the United States of America by Westview Press, Inc., 5500 Central Avenue, Boulder, Colorado 80301-2877, and in the United Kingdom by Westview Press, 12 Hid's Copse Road, Cumnor Hill, Oxford OX2 9JJ

A CIP catalog record for this book is available from the Library of Congress.
ISBN 0-8133-8886-4

Printed and bound in the United States of America

The paper used in this publication meets the requirements
of the American National Standard for Permanence of Paper
for Printed Library Materials Z39.48-1984.

10   9   8   7   6   5   4   3   2   1

To the memories of
my beloved mother, Carmen Márquez,
my dear aunt, Ana Márquez de Orozco,
and my brother, Fernando De Soto Márquez

Contents

List of Figures   *xi*
Preface   *xiii*

PART ONE
The Social Value of Participatory Radio

1   Introduction   3

Participation in Radio-for-Development, 4
Mexican Indigenous Peoples, 9
La Radio del Instituto Nacional Indigenista, 11
Conceptual Blueprint for the Book, 14
Notes, 17

2   Methodology   19

Selecting the Case, 20
Specific Aims, 21
Research Methods and Techniques, 23
Sample of the Audience Study, 25
Fieldwork, 28
Analysis, Interpretation, and Caveats, 31
Notes, 32

PART TWO
Indigenous Participation in Production Processes

3   Indigenous Peoples and Instituto Nacional Indigenista   37

Indigenous Ethnic Groups in Mexico, 37
Mexican *Indigenismo*, 41

Instituto Nacional Indigenista, 42
Notes, 47

4 The INI Network 51

History of the *Radio Cultural Indigenista,* 51
The Network in the Early 1990s, 61
XEVFS, Radio Margaritas, 66
Notes, 69

5 The Network's Staff and Other Actors 71

Stations' Staff Profile, 72
The Staff of the Network's Headquarters, 73
Station Staff , 75
Relationships and Alliances, 84
The Daily Routines of Radio Margaritas' Staff, 86
Ideology and the Everyday, 88
Notes, 91

6 The Programming of the INI Network 93

Multilingual Broadcasting, 93
Programming Profile, 95
Notes, 118

PART THREE
Audience Participation and Social Uses

7 Radio Margaritas' Target Audience: The Tojolabal Maya 123

The INI Network's Audience, 124
The Tojolabal Maya, 129
Notes, 156

8 Exposure, Listening, and Taste 161

Exposure and Differential Modes
of Involvement in Reception, 164
Patterns of Taste: Music, 170
From Live to Radio Broadcast Music, 173
Diversion Uses, 177

Radio Margaritas and the Construction of Reality, 178
Notes, 182

9 Social Impact of Radio Margaritas   185

Impact of Radio Margaritas
    on Local Information Flows, 185
Radio Margaritas as Community Radio, 194
Notes, 204

10 Radio and Ethnodevelopment   207

Tradition, 207
Improving Living Conditions, 217
Notes, 229

11 Outline of Radio Consumption Patterns   231

Limitations to Exposure, 231
Users and Consumers, 232
Uses of Radio Margaritas' Music, 233
Enhancing the Local Information Flow, 235
Radio Margaritas as Community Radio, 235
Traditions and the Reproduction of Culture
    and Society, 237
Improving Living Conditions, 237

12 Participation, Racism, and Social Uses   241

Indigenous Participation in the INI Network, 241
Unequal Participation: Project Beneficiaries, 243
Racism, 245
Collective Self-Esteem and Sustainable Development, 248
Social Uses, 250
Implications for the Use of Radio-for-Development, 251
Notes, 254

Appendix 1: Conceptual Framework   257

Concepts Drawn from Development Studies, 257
Concepts from Cultural Studies, 272
Latin American Media Research, 283
The Research on Latin American Participatory Radio, 286

Notes, 288

Appendix 2: Interview Schedules   293

Focus Groups Interview Schedule, 293
Audience Interview Schedule, 294

References   297
About the Book and Author   309

Figures

1.1   Map of Mexico Showing the INI Stations' Location   12

4.1   Radio Stations of the INI Network   62

4.2   Basic Organization Chart of the INI Radio Stations   63

4.3   Blueprint of Radio Margaritas   68

5.1   The Social Space of the INI Network   74

6.1   Sample Weekly Listings of the INI Stations   96

6.2   Radio Margaritas' Listings   97

7.1   Map of the State of Chiapas Showing
the Tojolabal Region   130

7.2   Map Showing the Location of Margaritas City,
Tabasco, and Madero   132

7.3   Ownership of Electronic Media Among the
Families Interviewed   154

A.1   Conceptual Map for Assessing Participation in
Media-based Projects   271

A.2   Sample of the Audience Study   296

Preface

This book is about the social value of participatory or community-oriented radio and stresses how the politics of race, ethnicity, class, and gender shape the extent and quality of people's participation in development efforts. It shows, ethnographically, how a number of Mexican ethnic minorities use the communication resources made available to them by a network of radio stations sponsored by the federal government through its *Instituto Nacional Indigenista* (INI).

The book includes an in-depth analysis of one of the INI stations, XEVFS, Radio Margaritas, and an ethnography of the radio consumption practices of its target audience, the Tojolabal Maya. Radio Margaritas is located in Las Margaritas, Chiapas (southern Mexico), one of the cities seized by an indigenous rebel army on January 1, 1994. Before the uprising, when I conducted the fieldwork for the book, the political situation in Chiapas was quite different from today. Although the Mexican army's presence in the region was very strong, and there were indeed many rumors of guerrilla activity in the jungle, I could not have imagined that three years after I left Chiapas, an army composed mainly of Tzeltal, Tzotzil, Tojolabal, and other indigenous peasants would declare war on the government of President Carlos Salinas de Gortari, initiating what has undeniably become the single most challenging armed rebellion in modern Mexico.

The *Ejército Zapatista de Liberación Nacional* (Zapatista National Liberation Army) launched its attack by seizing San Cristóbal de las Casas, Ocosingo, Altamirano, and Las Margaritas. The *Zapatistas*, as they have since come to be called, identify themselves as the army of a revolutionary movement, one collectively led by a committee including members of the ethnic groups of Chiapas. According to the movement's charismatic spokesperson, Subcomandante Marcos, the Zapatistas speak on behalf of the country's poor and represent a national movement seeking to redress the economic and social injustices suffered by the peasantry. Subcomandante Marcos has emphasized not only the poverty and exploitation endured by indigenous people, but also the racism of the dominant *ladino* (Spanish-speaking) society toward indigenous people. A ladino himself, Subcomandante Marcos recently commented on this same issue in an interview given to the Italian newspaper *L'Unita* (and reprinted by *Proceso* 8): "In Mexico, the entire social system is based upon the injustice of its relations with the Indians. The worst thing that can happen to any human being is to be an Indian, with its full load of humiliation, hunger and misery [my translation]."

The *Ejército Zapatista de Liberación Nacional* took its name after Emiliano Zapata, the indigenous leader of the 1910 revolution. In modern Mexico, Zapata has acquired almost mythical status among both indigenous and ladino people and has become the prototypic Mexican revolutionary hero. By identifying their movement with Zapata and his struggle, the Zapatistas have added an electrifying emotional charge to the movement's appeal for social and economic justice. Not surprisingly, the response of Mexican civil society to the uprising has been overwhelmingly sympathetic.

The government, on the other hand, first responded by mobilizing a third of the entire Mexican army to Chiapas and declaring that the events were the result of the criminal activity of a small number of people, and not a genuine, popular political movement. According to outside monitors, the federal army committed numerous human rights abuses during the first days after the uprising, including the bombarding of indigenous villages and the harassing of international and national journalists.

However, an important component of the Zapatistas' strategy has been to wage a brilliant media war, which helped to polarize public opinion quickly in their favor, despite the typically lopsided coverage of events by *Televisa*, Mexico's pro-establishment and monopolistic television conglomerate. Fortunately, the national print press, the international press, and human rights organizations were on hand to publicize the killing, torture, and intimidation being carried out by the government troops. For once, it seems, the historical struggle of Mexico's indigenous peoples against racism, oppression, and poverty has been given its share of international press coverage.

The government's bloody response was strongly condemned by numerous sectors of Mexican society and demonstrations for peace were held in many cities; the attendance at the largest demonstration in Mexico City was estimated at 150,000. Because of the negotiation of the North American Free Trade Agreement, the international community and press were closely watching Mexico, and traditional power elites found themselves suddenly in an uneasy position. Thus, nine days after the uprising, President Salinas shifted from the tactics of coercion toward a position of reconciliation, announcing changes in his own presidential cabinet and other important posts, including the governor of Chiapas. Central to the president's decision was the replacement of the *Secretario de Gobernación* (police and internal affairs), Jorge González Garrido, the authoritarian and repressive former governor of Chiapas, with Jorge Carpizo McGregor, known as a jurist, academician, and human rights advocate. President Salinas explained that with these changes his administration was recognizing its past mistakes and initiating a new strategy for peace and justice.

The first peace talks between the Zapatistas and the government began on February 21, 1994, and subsequent negotiations continue as of this writing. Particularly significant for my research are two key demands made by the Zapatistas. Along with their broader demands for land reform and social and economic justice, the Zapatistas have specifically insisted on the adoption of Mexico's first and only antidiscrimination law and for a radio station to be owned, operated, and controlled entirely by indigenous peoples.

The mediator in these negotiations has been Samuel Ruiz García, the Roman Catholic Bishop of San Cristóbal, a bishop regarded sympathetically by indigenous ethnic groups. The peace talks have shown that the two historically important actors in Mexican politics, indigenous peoples and the Roman Catholic Church, have made an important reappearance in the country's political arena. Still, the beginning of peace talks has not diminished the sense of crisis in contemporary Mexican politics, a crisis further aggravated by the assassination of Luis Donaldo Colosio, the official party's (PRI) presidential candidate in March, 1994. This crisis will very likely end Mexico's 65-year-old "one-party democracy." On the eve of the presidential election (to be held on August 21, 1994), and with three political parties running a close race, the country seems to be awaiting either another revolution or a PRI-based counterrevolution.

The Zapatista uprising, triggered by chronic injustices and by a decade of neo-liberal government policies, attests to the dominant society's indifference toward the destitution in which peoples like the Tojolabal live. Furthermore, since the uprising's epicenter was in San Cristóbal de las Casas, precisely the place where the first branch of INI (*Centro Coordinador Indigenista*) was installed 44 years ago, somber questions are now being asked about INI and the state's development policy toward indigenous populations.

Along with skepticism over the real contribution of INI's development projects to promote social and economic well-being, recent events in Chiapas also raise pressing questions for development communicators. What supporting role does participatory radio have, if any, in the growth of popular revolutions? What radio practices occur in participatory stations that might sustain or impede the emergence of political resistance and insurrection by the oppressed? What specific roles, in relation to the uprising, did Radio Margaritas and other community-oriented stations operating in the region play before, during, and after the uprising? And

PART ONE

The Social Value
of Participatory Radio

1

Introduction

Most products only derive their social value from the social use that is made of them.
—Pierre Bourdieu[1]

This book looks at the promise and performance of participatory radio for improving the living conditions and the sense of self-reliance and self-esteem of the poor. It focuses on the role played by the politics of race, ethnicity, class, and gender in media-based development projects, by examining the social practices created by a number of Mexican ethnic minorities in a network of rural radio stations sponsored by the federal government, through its *Instituto Nacional Indigenista.* By investigating these concrete practices and the relationships linking them, the book assesses the extent and quality of indigenous peoples' participation in the network and seeks to contribute to the study of the social uses (as opposed to individual media uses and gratifications) of minority broadcasting.

The book approaches participatory radio as a site where the competing demands of diverse social subjects are struggled over by inquiring, at one level, into specific questions about the concrete practices created by the participants of the radio network and by addressing, at another level, broader issues questioning how subaltern ethnic groups appropriate and refunctionalize radio, what are the social uses of radio among ethnic minorities in countries like Mexico, and what is the social value of participatory radio.

These questions have become pressing concerns not just for those interested in the study of popular communications and participatory development, but also for policy makers, development practitioners, and granting agencies committed to assisting ethnic minorities.

Since the early 1970s, the number of radio stations dedicated to minority broadcasting has dramatically increased. Populations as diverse as Mayas in Mexico, Arabs in France, and Aborigines in Australia have adopted local radio as an important communication medium for their communities.[2] In

Latin America, as in most of the Third World, minority radio broadcasting has often been linked to rural development efforts sponsored by the state, the Catholic church, and other religious and international organizations. Largely because of their sponsorship from institutions of the mainstream society, the vast majority of Latin American radio stations broadcasting for minority groups are immersed in a plethora of social and cultural contradictions and become sites where the meaning of ethnic identity is struggled over.

Participation in Radio-for-Development

Empirical research on how local people participate in these development radio projects and the creative and often contradictory ways in which communication resources are appropriated, refunctionalized, and used at the grassroots level is very scant. This book is the outcome of an empirical investigation that I presented as my doctoral dissertation at the University of Texas at Austin. The dissertation explored the possibilities and constraints that participatory radio holds for improving the living conditions, the sense of self-reliance, and the self-esteem of marginalized ethnic groups. During the course of my fieldwork, however, I became more and more aware of the importance of race as a social force and of racism itself as an ideological thread running through the participatory radio project I was studying. As my research progressed, I became more and more interested in shedding light on how racism manifests itself in this type of minority broadcasting. I need to emphasize at the onset, however, that I found that despite this racism, some ethnic minorities are using the INI stations to maintain social institutions like language, to reproduce cultural expressions like music, and to strengthen their ethnic identity and sense of community.

This book is a case study of the matrix of interactions between a network of eight radio stations sponsored by the Mexican government (through the Instituto Nacional Indigenista [hereafter INI], which coordinates government activities concerning Mexico's ethnic groups) and the indigenous peoples living under the radio network's coverage. Using ethnographic techniques I examined radio practices occurring in two settings: first, at the radio stations seen as the sites of production/transmission of messages and second in the family households viewed as the primary sites of consumption/reception. By investigating these practices, I sought to assess the extent and quality of indigenous peoples' participation in the network, as well as to contribute to the study of the social uses of minority radio broadcasting. My study thus attempts to understand how two abstractions, "popular participation" and "social uses of radio," occur in the cultural microcosm of the network's broadcasting.

In addition to my general interest in the social uses of participatory radio,

I am also concerned with the implementation of communication policies. In that vein I explore how subaltern ethnic groups attain, or might attain, access to information and radio broadcasting facilities, and how subaltern groups use these resources to improve their living conditions and strengthen their cultures. Since the explicit objective of the network is specifically the improvement of ethnic groups' living conditions through the strengthening of their cultures, my investigation necessarily contains an assessment of the network. Evaluation research into this type of radio project, one with a strategy of open broadcasting and with no structural feed back from often unorganized audiences, has been considered a challenge.[3]

I contend that the study of media-based development projects should focus on the interplay between the project and its beneficiaries, and that this interplay can be examined only by using a holistic approach addressing all three components of the process: production/transmission, cultural products/texts, and consumption/reception. Furthermore, I argue that this interplay must be observed in the practices exhibited by those flesh and blood people actually participating in the process. By *radio practices* I understand the daily routines of the people producing/transmitting messages and the network's ideology and institutional or corporate constraints framing these routines. At the audience domain, I mean by *radio practices* the customary ways in which audience members use both the radio messages and the stations' resources. It is only for analytical purposes that my investigation divides the process into its discrete parts, but I aim to treat this particular form of radio communication as a whole, and to examine this whole in its social and cultural context.

Strictly speaking, this study belongs to development communications, an interdisciplinary field between mass communications and development studies. For its conceptual framework, I draw on alternative thought in development studies and on cultural approaches to mass media. Those readers specifically interested in development communications may find it helpful to read in Appendix 1 my more systematic discussion of the investigation's key concepts and theoretical underpinnings, as well as my working assumptions regarding development processes and mass media audiences. For those readers unfamiliar with the research on Latin American participatory radio stations I have also included in the appendix some highlights of this research. Here, it suffices simply to provide a brief discussion of how I feel this study is positioned within the overlapping fields of mass communications and development studies.

Alternative thinking in development studies emphasizes that grassroots participation is the key for the success of development efforts. But I wondered initially, what exactly is "participation"? Since participation is the central concept of the investigation, I surveyed the research on the topic and found that the conceptual impreciseness of the term has allowed researchers to use it to convey very different meanings. I also found necessary to distinguish clearly the way the term "participation" is currently used (as in "grassroots participation") from its usage in the orthodox paradigm of development (as "representative participation"); furthermore, it is necessary to establish a clear-cut definition of the term that does not evade the crucial issue of power. Based on the work of critical researchers, my starting point is a twofold definition of the concept. First, participation is a means of achieving development, meaning a better life, self-reliance, self-esteem, and freedom from servitude. In this sense participation should be equated with the struggle for liberation. And second, participation implies moral and psychological empowerment, and as such, it is an end in itself.

The conceptual framework of this study also incorporates central premises and key concepts of cultural approaches to mass media. More specifically, I draw on a group of authors whose work on media is theoretically grounded in the neo-Marxist culturalism of Raymond Williams and Stuart Hall. These authors, especially David Morley, have combined this grounding in cultural studies, with its respect for experience and practice, with empirical inquiry based on qualitative methodology. By and large these investigations have targeted reception processes and are coming to be known as reception studies or as ethnographies of media consumption.[4] The authors of these studies focus on popular audiences, especially on social use and appropriation of mass media products. Like British cultural studies, but unlike more pessimistic continental understandings, such as the propaganda/mass society approach, the Frankfurt School, or Louis Althusser's focus on ideologically controlling apparatuses, these authors allow greater interpretive power to the audience when consuming, decoding, or reading mass media products. Consequently, they advocate focusing on the ways people relate to and experience mass media culture. Building upon Antonio Gramsci's theory of hegemony, they view media as a site of struggle where ideological consent is either won or lost, a perspective that orients these researchers to the social use made of media texts.

Other authors of reception studies have an acknowledged debt to the school of uses and gratifications, but they have distanced themselves from the school's orientation to the individual's psychological needs by employing the adjective "social." The phrase "social uses of media" (as used for example by James Lull) was coined specifically to distinguish the new approach from uses and gratifications research. One of the most comprehensive typologies of social uses is the one proposed by Lull who has focused on television viewing. Lull distinguishes two primary uses of television in the home, the structural and the relational. He further subdivides structural uses into environmental (e.g., background noise), and regulative uses (e.g., talk patterns). He subdivides relational uses into four categories: communication facilitation (e.g., experience illustration), affiliation/

avoidance (e.g., verbal contact/neglect), social learning (e.g., behavior modeling), and competence/dominance (e.g., intellectual validation).[5]

However, with regards to development communications, and more specifically, concerning the study of social uses of participatory radio, I found that a new dimension should be added to those uses of media heretofore suggested. Along with gratificationists and other authors of reception studies, Lull is concerned only with reception/consumption processes. But the beneficiaries of participatory radio not only consume, but many also produce and/or help to produce programs. Hence, an entirely different set of uses presents itself for analysis.

I realized that I needed to broaden the frame of reference to include not only consumption but also production processes. Consequently, I envisioned three additional kinds of social uses of participatory radio. First, at the micro level (individual and small group), I needed to account for two more uses: (1) use of the station to substitute for other communication systems, such as the use of radio for broadcasting personal announcements to substitute for telephones, or to broadcast public announcements to substitute for print media; and (2) use of the station's resources for purposes not related to radio broadcasting, for example, as a place for getting a document typed, or for getting advice on dealing with government institutions. Second, at the macro level (the ethnic group, the peasant community of a region), there are two other uses concerning the re-creation and maintenance of society: (1) use of the station as a forum for the reproduction of the group's cultural forms (language, music); and (2) use of the station as a means for generating an alternate, stronger, and more complex sense of community among members of a particular group. And finally, at both the micro and the macro level, there are the symbolic uses of radio, especially the radio receiver, as a consumer good in family politics, majority-minority relations, and other realms of social life.

Apart from the first type of uses (e.g., substitute for telephone, place for getting advice), it can be argued that most of the uses that I highlight have already been indicated either by gratificationists or by the authors of reception studies. However, there are two key differences between previously proposed uses and some of the uses that I am discussing. One difference is that both gratificationists and the authors of reception studies have examined what people do when consuming media products; the audiences studied by these two approaches, in contrast to those of participatory radio, do not participate in production processes. The second difference is that while for gratificationists the unit of analysis is the individual, for authors like James Lull and David Morley the unit of analysis is the family, and for other authors like Dick Hebdige the unit of analysis is the subcultural group, I am examining the media uses of an even larger group, an ethnic minority. Because of their particular circumstances and experiences as colonized people, ethnic minorities develop uses of media in very different ways than other groups. For example, using radio to reproduce an ethnic minority's language, a language that has been stigmatized for centuries, has an entirely different meaning than using the medium to reproduce a youth subculture's way of speaking.

Although my research focuses more specifically on ethnic minorities, it is worth emphasizing that media uses of each unit of analysis, the personal (individual), the small group (family), and the larger group (subculture, ethnic group), are not mutually exclusive, but concurrent and often simultaneous.

Since the unit of analysis is changed, so too is the methodology. Given that reception studies want to understand group uses, rather than individual ones, there has been a shift toward case studies relaying on ethnographic techniques. This combination of the case study and ethnography has often been carried out in institutions and social groups. As defined for example by Michael Real, this method is an interpretive and critical approach to people's media experience. According to Real, this method presents an ethnographic account of an influential case, situating it in its communitarian and historical context, and turning to contextualize the case in direct relation to questions of esthetic judgement, social power, conflict, ideology, and hegemony.[6]

I draw on this case-study method and rather than discussing my methods in an appendix, I go to great pains to explain in some detail numerous aspects of my methodology in Chapter 2 because I believe that methodology constitutes the governing axis of any investigation. Participation in media-for-development has seldom been examined ethnographically. Indeed I hope that a key contribution of this work may actually be a methodological one, one that orients development communications to this combined case-study-ethnographic approach. Specifically, for the study of media-based development projects, I propose (1) to focus on the matrix of interactions between the project and its intended beneficiaries; (2) to work within a conceptual framework which combines a critical perspective on development with a culturalist approach to media; and (3) to apply a holistic method that takes into account the three moments of the process under discussion (production/transmission, texts/programming, and consumption/reception) and that incorporates ethnographic techniques to examine the radio practices of subaltern groups in concrete projects. In the last analysis, the methodology of this case-study itself provides my main thesis: what I am proposing is a holistic way of doing research in participatory media-based development projects which grasps the relationships between production and consumption practices in order to ascertain the social value of these projects for their intended beneficiaries.

This way of doing research is anchored in feminist epistemologies which foreground not just a holistic view but also moral and political matters.

Feminist epistemologies build upon the insights offered by critical researchers like Paulo Freire who have developed, in opposition to positivist science with its artificial separation of questions of value from questions of fact, more participatory, and value-driven, "emancipatory" research methods to advance the struggle against various forms of domination.

This is not only a question of the way that politically-committed cultural studies, emancipatory research, and feminism align themselves against positivism's separation of facts from value, but also of the very placement of these paradigms within the social sciences. Sandra Harding, for instance, remarks that feminism incorporates many of the criticisms of positivist science raised by other emancipatory movements "while challenging the low priority that specifically feminist concerns have been assigned in such agendas of social reform."[7] Though I did not intend to undertake a feminist evaluation of a development radio project, as a feminist myself I could not help but to conduct research from a feminist perspective. My own consciousness of gender led me to view the different actors who participate in the radio project as gendered subjects, and their actions and ideologies as shaped by patriarchal social structures and androcentric beliefs.

The centerpiece of my study has to do with race and ethnicity, but rather than ignoring the intersections among race and ethnicity and class and gender, I examined precisely those intersections, considering, for instance, the emancipating impact that the radio broadcasting in vernacular languages may have had in the daily lives of indigenous women. Another important question of my research, therefore, is whether the "development" brought about by the INI stations is beneficial to indigenous women. I use feminist notions to unravel the underlying reasons for the social and cultural practices that I looked at, and I also made a concerted effort to account for women's experiences and to include female voices in my research. It is in its methodology that the study reveals more clearly my feminist stance, but before introducing the specifics of the methodology, it is necessary to delineate the salient features of the case itself.

Mexican Indigenous Peoples

Mexico, with the largest indigenous population of the Americas, has been described as two nations: one is the mainstream Spanish-speaking society and the other is composed of at least 56 minority ethnic groups. In contrast to other Latin American countries, Mexico's 1910 revolution brought about a limited number of political-economic measures to improve indigenous peoples' living conditions (e.g., the agrarian reform), as well as social policies to recognize the value of their cultures (e.g., the support for artists like Diego Rivera). Mexico became a country advocating the rights of these peoples, and as such became the only Latin American *indigenista* state.

On the other hand, just like other Latin American governments, the revolutionary government sought to establish a closed system of cultural control in the name of national unity and economic development.

Thus, although revolutionary Mexico has been an indigenista state, the country's multiethnic composition has complicated the government's task, and vernacular cultures have frequently been seen as obstacles to implementing national policies. Most of the time the contradiction has been solved by discursively positioning indigenous cultures as part of a glorious past, something very useful to the invention of traditions for the young nation. Nevertheless, progress and modernization have been given a high priority, and the rights of living indigenous people have often been ignored in the race for modernization. Today, despite their belonging to an indigenista state, Mexico's ethnic minorities remain politically and economically marginalized. Yet, they are not a small group; about one in every eight Mexicans speaks a vernacular language, and indigenous people have the highest growth rate of any population sector in the country.[8]

As I mentioned before, while I was doing the fieldwork it occurred to me that since I was examining the participation of indigenous peoples in the network, and participation is intrinsically linked to issues of oppression/liberation, I was actually doing an ethnographic account of how racism works at the micro level in Mexican society. This is indeed a complex topic heeding close consideration and analysis because Mexico, as a nation, fails even to acknowledge that the problem exists. Racism is a fact of social differences in Mexico, and the social uses of participatory radio created by Mexican indigenous peoples, by that very fact, exist within the boundaries of racist social interactions. Even so, as I argue later, many of these social uses of radio become weapons to resist racism itself.

Given 500 years of continuous mingling among native Mexicans, Europeans, Africans, and other immigrants to Mexican soil, specifying who is or is not a member of indigenous ethnic groups becomes an extremely complicated task. Numerous categories have been suggested to determine ethnicity: physiological features (e.g., dark-skin color), cultural characteristics (e.g., vernacular language), social peculiarities (e.g., *cargos*, system of organization), economic specificities (e.g., pre-capitalist mode of production), psychological distinctions (e.g., sense of self-esteem), cultural identity (sense of belongingness to a group), and more. But in addition to all of these elements, there is a key consideration at work when Mexicans determine their own as well as others' ethnic identity: a person's position on the social ladder and the likelihood that this person will be exploited, a consideration that might be thought of as a cumulative effect of the above categories. Ricardo Pozas and Isabel H. de Pozas say that "fundamentally, the quality of being an Indian is given by the fact that the subject denominated as such is the easiest man to exploit economically in the system [my translation]."[9]

This point is crucial for my study because more than any other element taken singly, it helps to explain not only the very often contradictory feelings of the radio network's staff toward indigenous people, but also many of the network's policies. Moreover it shows the significance that listening—or not listening—to these radio stations has as a cultural practice. And finally, it increases awareness of the social function that listening to participatory radio fulfills in legitimizing structural and symbolic differences.

La Radio del Instituto Nacional Indigenista

The radio network's sponsor, the Instituto Nacional Indigenista, was created in 1948 by the federal government to address the problems of indigenous peoples. Though indigenous peoples are increasingly becoming a migrant population, and many of them now live in urban settings (especially young men on a temporary basis),[10] INI is still basically concerned with rural development. The radio network is one of the numerous projects that this agency has sponsored. In the early 1990s it had eight AM stations with an estimated potential audience of about three million. One of the stations is in the northern state of Chihuahua, a second is on the Guatemalan border, a third is in the southeast, and the remaining five are in central Mexico (see Figure 1.1). The stations combine Spanish and vernaculars in their programming which includes local ethnic music, news programs, two or three hours daily of programs in which personal messages and institutional announcements are broadcast (substituting for telephone service), and series based on interviews with local people in which traditional health and agricultural practices are combined with modern expertise, as well as others.

The radio network's stated goals rely on the ideology of *Indigenismo de Participación*, the current government policy concerning indigenous ethnic groups. As with many of today's sponsors of development projects, INI's current policies have incorporated two seminal ideas of alternative approaches to development, the need for grassroots participation and the importance of the positive role played by local cultures in development. Because of this official policy and, even more, because of the effective political struggle of a number of indigenous organizations at the national level, the network's sponsor (as a federal institution) mandates the participation of indigenous people. Nevertheless, INI is a bureaucratic institution of the Mexican state, and not surprisingly, its institutional practices are derived from outdated ideologies of assimilation, with this term's racist connotations. As is probably the case with most participatory stations and their broadcasting, the INI stations are sites where opposing ideologies meet, and occasionally, even clash. They are also sites of continual struggle between the competing demands of diverse social subjects, for example, indigenous organizations versus *indigenista* bureaucrats.[11] As an

12

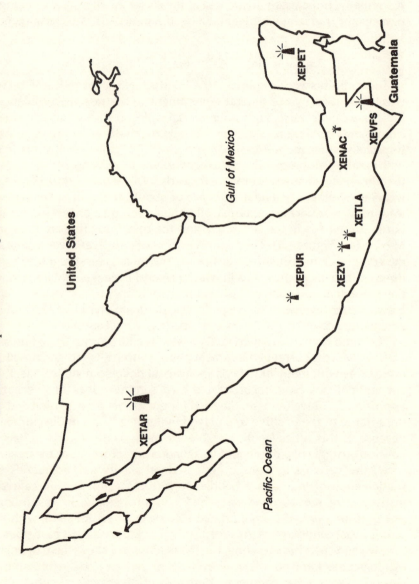

FIGURE 1.1 Map of Mexico Showing the INI Stations' Location

illustration of the potential for ideological struggle, consider the fact that complying with participatory policies, about 70 percent of the staff of the INI network are members of ethnic groups, yet the highest positions are most often held by *ladinos*, members of the Spanish-speaking dominant society. Even though I most often present the stations as sites of on-going ideological struggle and as sites where subalterns create their own uses and practices, this is not to say that the social inequalities imposed by ladinos holding the highest positions are always resented by the indigenous staff members. Here, for example, is a statement from an interview with an indigenous staff member implying that ladinos have some special, almost magical, leadership qualities that even educated indigenous station employees cannot hope to achieve. He said: "It is better to have a ladino as director of the station. Indigenous people can get an education but they cannot develop 'that something' that ladinos have. The project would fail if indigenous people were in charge."

Though I explain in more detail the reasons for the selection of the case in Chapter 2, here I should emphasize that I selected the INI radio network, rather than a self-managed station (e.g., the Bolivian miners' radio), because most participatory radio stations in the Third World are not self-managed radio, but are projects sponsored by outside agents, such as government agencies or the Catholic Church. Also, and this is especially important, I was attracted by the manner in which indigenous people have created social uses for the stations. To understand social uses further, consider for example the following quote from an interview with a Tojolabal speaker who implied that the radio is used for reinforcing the sense of community and ethnic identity:

> Some rich people [he refers to ladinos] would like XEVFS to be closed because they don't like it, because they don't understand Tojolabal, and they don't like it because they don't like for the poor people to have a medium for exchanging experiences. But for us it is very important. Our hearts get happy when we listen to the *marimba sencilla*. XEVFS is different; they speak Tojolabal, Tzeltal, Tzotzil. It's not like the rich people's radio where only *Kastilla* [Spanish] is spoken. XEVFS is different, it's our radio.

In addition, consider the ways in which people use the stations' resources. Some stations have an average of over 200 indigenous visitors per week who may want to transmit their own personal messages over the air, to play music and participate in talk shows, to get a professional recording of their music, or simply to get advice on how to deal with the dominant culture's institutions.

Some critics of the network, such as Roberto Perea de la Cabada, maintain that this kind of participation serves only to legitimize INI's other more questionable, top-to-bottom activities, both in the regions in which the stations operate and in the macro-political arena.[12] And indeed I did find some evidence that the same processes which make possible indigenous people's use of the station do provide important pay-offs to the project's sponsor, by creating a sometimes false atmosphere of cooperation between indigenous people and the federal government and by helping legitimize other INI's activities. The trade-offs between the Mexican state and the subalterns are quite complex, often contradictory, and important to delineate, but it is also important to recognize that within the context of Mexican media, which is characterized by commercial monopolization and governmental control, the network, even with these flaws, is still a rare and therefore vitally important island of participatory communication. The network offers a great deal of access to its audiences, and it may be legitimately argued that some of the stations have even struggled to realize the great potential of community radio.

Conceptual Blueprint for the Book

This book is composed of three parts. In addition to this introduction, Part One contains the chapter on methodology. Part Two (chapters 3 through 6) deals with the entire network, at both the macro and the micro levels. And Part Three (chapters 7 through 11) is an audience study of one of the stations, Radio Margaritas, plus a chapter with my concluding remarks.

Thematically, the research strategy analyzes the following five domains: (1) the institutional domain, to situate the network in its historical, social, and corporate contexts; (2) the staff domain, to investigate the employees' work practices (i.e., the daily routines of producers, disc jockeys, station director, etc.) and their ideologies; (3) the programming/texts domain, to examine general aspects of transmissions (e.g., percentage of vernacular language vs. Spanish) and to do content analysis of selected programs; (4) the users domain, to document the ways in which local people visiting the station use its material and human resources (e.g., as a local substitute for telephone service); and (5) the listeners domain, to discover patterns of listening, taste, and response to programming.

It is important to note that, as explained in Chapter 2, this research looks at the entire radio network for certain issues, but focuses on only one station, XEVFS, Radio Margaritas, for its audience study. Furthermore, I systematically sampled only one ethnic group (the Tojolabal Maya, the primary target audience of Radio Margaritas) for the reception study. Given funding and time limitations, I decided it was better to focus on reception processes as lived by a single ethnic group than to examine only superficially two or more groups/stations. Thus I conducted a qualitative study of reception (somewhat similar to Morley's studies of television viewing[13]) with a sample of 21 families selected from Colonia Tabasco and Colonia Madero, two Tojolabal villages.

I chose Radio Margaritas, located in Southern Mexico and broadcasting in four vernaculars plus Spanish, because it has a substantial number of indigenous visitors (over 200 per week), roughly 80 percent of the staff are members of the local ethnic groups, and its broadcasting is composed mainly of indigenous music, vernacular languages, and interviews with local people. Though each INI station is different from the other, I think Radio Margaritas best reveals many of the conflicts and contradictions typical of the INI stations, and thus serves better to illustrate both the possibilities and constraints of this participatory radio project. Had I chosen XEZV for example, the most participatory of the INI stations I would be presenting an overly positive picture of the network. Radio Margaritas, on the other hand, sheds light on how, despite structural constraints on popular participation, indigenous minorities make the best of the resources available to them.

In Chapter 3, I introduce the context within which the network operates. I talk about indigenous peoples in Mexico and also about the network's sponsor and its current ideology, participatory indigenismo. In Chapter 4, I narrate the network's history and, following Inés Cornejo's scheme, identify five different stages of its development: origin, constitution, transition, consolidation, and expansion.[14] I also look into issues of cost and resources and finish the chapter with a description of Radio Margaritas. In Chapter 5, I deal with the network's social space and with the people involved in radio production and their interactions. I describe their professional roles and offer a sense of who are the actual people working at the stations. Again, to provide a concrete illustration, the last part of this chapter is dedicated to recounting the daily routines of the staff at Radio Margaritas.

As I do throughout the book, in alluding to social space I used the adjective "indigenous" to refer to speakers of vernaculars, the term "ladino" to refer to Spanish monolinguals who occupy the opposite position in the social hierarchy (often middle/upper-class, and fair-skinned), and the word "mestizo" to refer to those Spanish monolinguals who are in some sense in between the two first groups. To honor a request made by a number of my informants, I do not use the word "Indian." "We have heard the word 'Indian' used so many times as an insult," one Tzeltal woman told me, "do not use it when you write your book." To refer to specific ethnic groups and their languages, I employ the terms used in recent publications in Spanish, such as "Yoreme," "Tojolabal," and "Purépecha."

In Chapter 6, I examine the network's texts and programming. I begin by looking at the specific format of the network and then go on to discuss issues related to multilingual broadcasting. Then I analyze the programming profile with its various program categories. Several charts graphically displaying programming are included, and one of them shows Radio

Margaritas' programming. The descriptions of Radio Margaritas throughout these last three chapters serve two purposes. One purpose is to shed light on how the general processes under discussion work by fleshing out the meaning of complex and subtle concepts, such as control, by depicting the way the participation of indigenous personnel is restricted by the station's ladino general manager's ability to control production and programming decisions. The second purpose is to introduce information on the possibilities of and constraints on audience participation existing in Radio Margaritas, so that the remarks and comments from audience members interviewed can be interpreted in light of this information. Still, as far as possible, the emphasis on Radio Margaritas is kept in the context of the entire network while carefully attending to those aspects in which this station's practices deviate markedly from the practices of other stations.

Given that the bulk of indigenous participation in the project occurs at the level of the audience, the second part of the book is a qualitative audience study exploring how and for what purposes indigenous audiences use the stations. Though I overview the entire network's listeners and users, I specifically focus on Radio Margaritas and its target audience, the Tojolabal Maya. The question guiding the audience study is, How does an ethnic minority group under severe material, physical, and psychological stress use available radio resources in order to cope better with socio-economic pressures and to realize basic needs?

The audience study is composed of four chapters. Chapter 7 lays out the general context of the two villages that I studied, and the remaining three chapters discuss the findings. First I present, in Chapter 7, the salient aspects of Tojolabal society and culture, then I describe two of their villages, Colonia Tabasco and Colonia Madero. Following is a brief section on the cost of day-to-day consumption of radio offerings. Then I discuss, in Chapter 8, the listening patterns and the differing modes of involvement in reception processes that I found. After this, I elaborate on patterns of taste and response to programming in a section examining the music broadcast by Radio Margaritas. I go on, in Chapter 9, to discuss the marked impact that the station has had on local information flows through airing personal messages from the audience and community announcements, and I examine the extent to which interviewees perceive Radio Margaritas as community radio. Then I address, in Chapter 10, the two explicit objectives of INI's radio project, to strengthen and preserve indigenous traditions and to improve the living conditions of the villagers. I finally summarize, in Chapter 11, the findings of the audience study and in Chapter 12 make some concluding remarks about the entire network and its social value.

This book suggests that understanding social practices and the politics of race, class, and gender relations taking place in participatory radio holds a great importance for the implementation and evaluation of participatory, radio-based development efforts. And it also stresses that exploring the possibilities and constraints of participatory radio is crucial to understanding the subaltern modes of resistance and interpretation; in addition to being sites of hegemonic processes (which indeed take place at the network level) participatory stations and their broadcasting are also sites of resistance and alternative construction of meaning. But, simultaneously, the book insists that celebrating popular resistance and the polyvocality of media texts should not yield to ignoring the ideological and/or legitimizing benefits which participatory stations might accrue to the dominant culture. As with other media institutions, participatory radio for minority populations is, naturally, a space where cultural hegemony is constructed and struggled over.

Hopefully, by examining the practices and intergroup relations that occur in the INI radio network, this case-study advances the research in the social uses of radio adopted by subaltern groups. Hopefully as well, by assessing the extent and quality of indigenous peoples' participation in a specific project, the book enhances the understanding of how diverse sectors of poor ethnic groups, such as women, attain, or at least might attain, access to information and radio resources and use them for their own purposes. Because the participation of local people in media-based development projects occurs and manifests itself in the circuits of production and consumption of its products, assessing participation necessarily means examining social and cultural practices.

Notes

1. Pierre Bourdieu, *Distinction. A Social Critique of the Judgment of Taste*, trans. Richard Nice (Cambridge: Harvard UP, 1984) 24.

2. For an analysis of non-commercial local radio at the global level see Hans J. Kleinsteuber and Urte Sonnenberg, "Beyond Public Service and Private Profit: International Experience with Non-commercial Local Radio," *European Journal of Communication* 5 (1990): 87-106.

3. See for example, Emile McAnany *Radio's Role in Development: Five Strategies of Use* (Washington: Clearing House on Development Communication, Information Bulletin Number Four, 1973) 5-7.

4. For a review of the research on the ethnography of media consumption, see Shawn Moores, *Interpreting Audiences* (London: Sage, 1993).

5. James Lull's complete list of uses is given in Appendix 1. He presents this list in *Inside Family Viewing.* (London: Routledge, 1990) 36.

6. Michael R. Real, *Super Media. A Cultural Studies Approach* (Newbury Park: Sage, 1989) 69-74.

7. Sandra Harding, *The Science Question in Feminism* (Ithaca: Cornell UP, 1986) 16.

8. According to Valdéz, census data for ethnicity in Mexico is based on language, and it takes into account only the population of those five year-olds and older; Luz María Valdéz, *El Perfil Demográfico de los Indios Mexicanos* (México: Siglo XXI, 1988) 34-35. In the early 1990s the country's total population was roughly 82 million, and

several government agencies estimated that the total indigenous population was around 10 million. See Consejo Consultivo del Programa Nacional de Solidaridad, *El Combate a la Pobreza* (México: El Nacional, 1990) 20.

9. Ricardo Pozas and Isabel H. de Pozas, *Los Indios en las Clases Sociales de México* 13th ed. (México: Siglo XXI, 1984) 16.

10. It is estimated that the indigenous population living in Mexico City is one million. See for example Consejo Consultivo del Programa Nacional de Solidaridad, *El Combate a la Pobreza* (México: El Nacional, 1990).

11. *"Indigenista"* is a term often used to designate those scholars or bureaucrats whose work centers around indigenous peoples and their cultures.

12. Roberto Perea de la Cabada, "El INI y las Radios Indigenistas," IV Encuentro Nacional del CONEICC, Colima, March, 1986.

13. David Morley, *Family Television. Cultural Power and Domestic Leisure* (London: Routledge, 1988).

14. As I explain in Chapter 4, I have borrowed this conceptual scheme from Inés Cornejo, "La Voz de la Mixteca," M.A. Thesis, U Iberoamericana, 1990.

2

Methodology

In empirical media research, qualitative methods have not been as common as those methods emerging from the North American sociological tradition. Yet qualitative techniques are well suited to my object of study because since popular participation in media institutions does not occur in a vacuum, I needed to ground my research in contextual descriptions. It was only by making use of ethnographic techniques that I could consider cultural nuances in communicative behavior and other cultural factors that are interwoven with communication processes. Moreover, I needed the methodological flexibility of the qualitative approach with its non-a priori character to study complex questions dealing with communication practices. I knew I would have to amend questions and hypotheses once the fieldwork had started, and I was also aware of the possibility of losing my initial access to the stations, so I wanted to be able to change observational settings, informants, and levels of analysis during the fieldwork.

Finally, I came to the conclusion that to shed light on how participation takes place in a radio-based development project required my examining the social uses of radio created by the intended beneficiaries of such projects. I decided these uses occur in the interplay among production, cultural products, and reception; thus, the object of study had to be approached in a holistic fashion. The case study method with its holistic approach and its openness to the use of multiple techniques and data sources turned out to be the most appropriate way to explore my questions.

As a case study of the matrix of interactions between the INI network and its indigenous audiences, my research takes into account production/transmission, programming, and consumption/reception, as well as the use of other station resources. Hence, in addition to the programming, I studied radio practices taking place at both the radio stations and the family household. For the exploration of production practices, I contrast multiple settings (six radio stations). For consumption/reception practices, I concentrated on just one station, XEVFS, Radio Margaritas, and its primary target audience, but I did compare two villages. I examined the programming basically in relation to the participatory practices that have been created in the INI stations. My exploration of Radio Margaritas can be viewed as a mini-case study used to provide contextual descriptions not only of consumption/reception processes, but also of production practices. I took Radio Margaritas as the focus of the audience research, and then used observations about this station throughout the book to illustrate particular points.

Selecting the Case

Since the 1970s, numerous participatory or community-oriented radio stations broadcasting for minority audiences have appeared all over the world. In the Third World, participatory radio has often been a component of development programs. Most of these stations have been established in marginal rural areas, and they have been directed particularly toward indigenous ethnic groups.[1] This type of radio broadcasting has prospered considerably in Latin America. Despite their similarities, Latin American participatory stations differ greatly in their degree of popular participation. Self-managed stations have often identified themselves as the media of subaltern groups' political resistance. Some of them have been clandestine stations (e.g., the Salvadoran *Radio Venceremos*), and others have operated more or less within the legal framework (e.g., the Bolivian miners' radio and the Mexican "Radio Ayuntamiento Popular de Juchitán"). Stations allowing only a limited degree of audience participation have generally been funded and operated by either the state, international agencies, or religious organizations (such as the Catholic Church, the Baha'i Faith, and several Protestant denominations), and their stated purpose has been the promotion of development, without, however, challenging the existing political system.

From the great variety of participatory radio stations operating now in Latin America, I selected the INI radio network for a number of reasons. To begin with, several social uses of radio have already been constructed by the audience itself. Second, like most participatory radio stations in the Third World, rather than being self-managed, the stations are projects sponsored by an outside agent. Third, the stations are similar enough in their institutional structure to allow a case study encompassing several stations, and at the same time are different enough to permit useful comparison. Since the network broadcasts to at least 20 ethnic groups, conclusions can be drawn both on general patterns of audience participation and on the unique features about the ways in which poor ethnic groups use participatory radio. In addition, my previous work on Mexican media and my cultural baggage as a Mexican seemed well suited for this investigation.

Lastly, although the criteria for evaluating a development program's success include many elements, longevity and enlargement are two salient indicators since projects seldom survive after their initial phase. This project was started in 1979 and has continued to expand during a time in which the nation's financial resources have greatly deteriorated. Indeed, according to the established criteria for successful projects, the network is an excellent example of participatory radio.[2] It is politically attractive (it has survived three changes in government administration); it has a sound design, which is efficiently implemented (e.g., it uses a low-cost medium, takes advantage of existing receiving technology, and involves local people); and it has incorporated current theoretical advancements (e.g., the need for grassroots participation and the importance of the positive role played by the local culture in development efforts).

Yet, there were also, of course, practical considerations for the selection of the case; as a graduate student at a time when research funding was shrinking, it was easier to conduct research in my home country, where I still have family and friends, than for instance in a country like Ecuador or Bolivia.

Specific Aims

I addressed specific questions related to five different domains of the analysis: institution, staff, programming, users (which includes audience members who visit, call, write, or participate in programs), and audience (listeners). In the institutional domain, I looked at the network's stated policies (in documents) and also at its organizational structure. Since being part of the network's staff is the most direct way of gaining access to the radio network, it was crucial to understand the role played by members of the indigenous ethnic groups working at the stations. So, I determined the mechanisms operating to promote or prevent participation by examining work practices and group dynamics occurring at the stations (e.g., who is doing what tasks?), and by looking at decision-making processes (e.g., who is making what decisions, indigenous people or ladinos?); I paid particular attention to processes concerning hiring, firing, and promotion practices.

In the network's staff domain, I focused on the nature of the employees' practices (i.e., routines of the producers, the programmers, the disc jockeys), and how these practices, first, prevent/promote the participation of the ethnic groups, and second, how they mediate between their fellow indigenous people and the sponsor of the project. With respect to this domain, I was concerned with patterns regarding (1) the type of people working at the stations (e.g., their gender, ethnicity, place of residence, and their social and educational capital); (2) the staff's opinions concerning the level of participation of members of ethnic groups at the network; and (3) the staff's perceptions of their own roles in the project.

In the programming/texts domain, my purpose was to look at those aspects of broadcasting that would illuminate the study's basic line of inquiry. Because this inquiry concentrates on radio practices, rather than on texts, I concerned myself with issues of programming only in their direct relation to radio practices. So, I addressed issues relating first to indigenous participation in the programming in general (e.g., the percentage of in-house productions versus outside recordings, music versus talk programs, transmissions in Spanish versus broadcasts in vernacular languages) and second to issues relating to indigenous participation in selected programs (e.g., local news)

Lastly, in the user and audience domains, my investigation aimed at shedding light on the key aspects of *audience uses of participatory radio*. I apply the latter expression to two different types of activities. On the one hand, I refer to audience uses of the radio broadcasts, thus focusing on listening. In this first sense the expression resembles James Lull's concept of the social uses of television. Yet I approach reception practices chiefly from Jesús Martín Barbero's formulations and understand radio reception as, to paraphrase Martín Barbero, a site where collective memories are displayed and customary ways transformed and related to new conditions.[3] On the other hand, I also, by the phrase *audience uses of participatory radio*, allude to a variety of audience uses of the station's resources. For example, the way in which the local people employ the station as a substitute telephone system, or as an audio recording studio, or simply as a place to get advice on how to deal with the dominant culture and its institutions, especially government agencies.

I found, moreover, other uses of radio that are best explained within the framework of Pierre Bourdieu's theory of consumption. For example, radio receivers are used by young Tabascan men to signify modernity, or Radio Margaritas' cultural offerings are consumed to distinguish the listener from the ladino and simultaneously reaffirm ethnic identity. Therefore, the type of social uses that I sought to detect included (1) types of listening (e.g., attentive versus distracted involvement); (2) patterns of listening (i.e., the audience's observable traits within the event of listening to the radio as regards, for example, time, location, and listener's individual characteristics); (3) patterns of taste and response to programming (e.g., indigenous music, agricultural and health programs, news programs); (4) interactions between radio listening and other aspects of family life (e.g., household chores and relaxation); (5) relation/impact of radio listening on other activities (e.g., health and agricultural practices); and (6) audience perception of Radio Margaritas (e.g., as a reliable source of information, as an attractive leisure choice, as a telecommunications medium for the local social networks, and as a means of reinforcing group identity and sense of community).

Research Methods and Techniques

I used mainly observation and in-depth, unstructured interviews with key informants. These two techniques were coupled with archival research, focus groups, a short survey questionnaire, and an instrument (called the "staff profile form") to gather information for a profile of the network's staff. For the analysis of the institution, staff, and programing/texts domains, I considered six stations (XEPUR, XETLA, XEZV, XETAR, XEPET, and XEVFS); for the exploration of the users domain, I focused on the last three stations, and for the audience domain I selected only one of the radio stations (XEVFS) for the fieldwork. I conducted focus groups with most of the stations' production employees at XEZV, XETAR, XEPET, and XEVFS, and completed staff profile forms for 71 employees from these stations. The focus groups were tape recorded, lasted between 60 and 90 minutes, and were conducted by me following a set of open-ended questions.[4] I also followed this interview schedule closely when conducting individual tape recorded interviews with both ladino personnel (who were purposely excluded from the focus groups with indigenous staff) and those indigenous members of the staff who were unable to take part in the focus groups. In addition, I used the same interview schedule for other interviews related to the audience study, such as a focus group done with Tojolabal teachers and interviews with ladino families living at Margaritas City, the place where XEVFS' facilities are located. The interview schedules used for focus groups and for audience interviews are presented in Appendix 2.

Through the staff profile form, I gathered detailed, personal data needed to support assertions regarding concepts such as ideology, social class, cultural capital, and the ethnic identities of staff members. I designed the instrument to gather, on a year-to-year basis (from the year of birth to the present), data concerning the following: family background, languages spoken, place of residence, formal and non-formal education, prior occupation(s), work in the informal economy, and community involvement (based on political, artistic, religious, and sports activities). The 71 cases from the 4 stations mentioned above comprise at least 65 percent of the entire staff of the stations, excluding headquarters staff.

For the analysis of the network's users, I conducted surveys at three stations (XETAR, XEPET, and XEVFS). They were administered to all visitors at the stations (excluding those whose only reason for visiting the station was to accompany someone else) during a selected week.[5] I used a short questionnaire that was filled out either by the stations' staff or me. The survey sought to determine (1) the number of station users during a week; (2) their reason for visiting the station; (3) their place of residence; (4) their level of education (measured by literacy); (5) their gender; (6) their ethnicity; and (7) their age group. Since I determined ethnicity by language spoken,

I was unable to make distinctions between ladinos and mestizos. I am aware that speakers of vernaculars tend to deny that they speak their native language, claiming they speak only the language of opportunity. Nonetheless, because of the particular environments of the stations, one where indigenous people are welcomed, and the fact that most members of the staff assisting with the surveys were speakers of vernaculars, I believe my data regarding language spoken to be reliable. On the other hand, my data regarding literacy is unreliable because I had no way to verify the interviewees' statements. To complement the surveys, I examined the audience correspondence of several stations.

The audience study of XEVFS, Radio Margaritas, was intended to explore the radio practices taking place at the site of reception. This investigation was concerned with actual, rather than potential, listeners. Nonetheless, I tried to complement my study with quantitative research on potential listenership that had been previously done on the network's audience.[6] My data collection technique was family interviews with a sample of 21 households from a single ethnic group, the Tojolabal Maya.

In the first stage of the research, I thought that the audience study would be more thorough and my findings more generalizable if the audience's responses from two stations were considered. However, because of budgetary and time constraints, I had to choose between conducting a broad study comparing responses from two stations belonging to the INI network or carrying out an investigation that contrasts responses from two different segments of the audience of only one station. Since I had adopted a qualitative methodological approach, it was more sound and more cogent to other aspects of the research to include as much as possible a "thick description," to use Clifford Geertz's term, of audience's uses of a single station rather than to present more sketchy findings on two stations. I likewise had to determine whether to include one or various ethnic groups in the sample. I applied the same qualitative rationale and decided to conduct the interviews with listeners from only one ethnic group, but from two different villages.

All these decisions of course made the selection of the particular station even more crucial. I chose Radio Margaritas because it was immediately obvious on my preliminary visit that indigenous people use the station. I also reflected on the urgent need for research on the Tojolabal Maya and took into account that the station was established during what Inés Cornejo, who has conducted research on the stations, calls the "consolidation stage" of the network. Thus I expected that INI's participatory approach had been more fully implemented in Radio Margaritas than in earlier stations.

A further methodological consideration was whether to conduct all interviews in Tojolabal, or only some interviews in Tojolabal and the rest in Spanish. Because of my limitations with the Tojolabal language, I was inclined to interview as many families as possible in Spanish. However, if I had done so, I would have excluded almost all women and elderly people from the sample. I decided to have all interviews conducted in Tojolabal which meant I had to sacrifice much of my control over the interviewing process. Most importantly, my interpretive power was greatly diminished because I had to work with a Spanish translation. On the other hand, the painful process of transcribing the interviews (from simultaneous oral translations) gave me the opportunity to discuss the material with my Tojolabal research assistant and to become aware of numerous cultural specificities.

The interviews were audio-tape recorded and conducted entirely in Tojolabal by Armando Alfaro, a staff member of XEVFS, and Candelaria Rodríguez, a former staff member. Ms. Rodríguez, who also helped me with the translation into Spanish, became my research assistant and the ideal key informant. She was a member of the Tojolabal community and had previously worked at Radio Margaritas for more than two years, but she now had a critical distance from the station and enjoyed more freedom than current employees to share her thoughts. The interviews followed closely a schedule with open-ended items (based in part in David Morley's research on family television viewing[7]). The interview schedule had two distinct parts. The purpose of the first was to collect factual data about the interviewees themselves and the purpose of the second was to collect opinion data.[8] The starting point of the second, or core part, was with some of the issues dealt with in the focus groups of station personnel, and it was composed of 17 sets of questions, each addressing a particular topic.[9] All interviews were complemented by simultaneous field observation done by me. In addition, I conducted interviews with three ladino families living in the station's town. Although Spanish monolinguals only seldom listen to XEVFS and are not part of the station's target audience, it was important to record their opinions and to use these interviews as a point of comparison for the audience study. What follows is a more detailed account of the sample and interpretive procedures.

Sample of the Audience Study

The households chosen were speakers of Tojolabal, who are the primary target audience of Radio Margaritas. The station also broadcasts for three other linguistic groups, but it is located in an area populated by Tojolabal speakers. The sample took into account differences among the members of this ethnic group by selecting households from two different villages. Because I was unable to spend the long period necessary to establish my own social base, I selected Colonia Tabasco and Colonia Madero, two places where my interviewers already had a social base.[10] Both were from Madero, and one of them had previously worked closely with health promoters in Tabasco. Tabasco is a village with less than four hundred people where traditional Tojolabal mores are still observed, and many people still dress in traditional costume and barely speak Spanish. It has no electricity and is relatively difficult to access by the county seat, where XEVFS is located. Madero, on the other hand, has roughly a thousand people who are changing their traditional ways. It has electricity, receives television transmission, and lies about half-an-hour by automobile from the county seat. I present a detailed description of the two villages in Chapter 7.

Rather than randomly selecting the families, I chose them based on their special qualifications regarding language spoken/ethnicity, actual listenership to Radio Margaritas, and place of residence. However, because many of the specific decisions concerning the sample were made on convenience (e.g., friendship with interviewers or previous interviewees), I took care that the families selected for interviewing belonged to various social strata. Although the sample is small, it captures much of the variability of the villages' families.

The actual number of interviews held in Tojolabal was 23, but I excluded 2 from the sample. One interview was left out because the family, belonging to a Pentecostal group, gave us only brief answers, and a second one was excluded because the senile grandfather prevented other family members from speaking. Often there were more people present during the interview than the number actively participating. Women, especially daughters-in-law (who have a peripheral role in the Tojolabal patrilocal family), frequently refused to talk, and children were not expected to do so. Even though observers played a role in the interview dynamic, they cannot be considered as interviewees. In one of the interviews, although there were several women present, only one woman did the talking. Since this particularly articulate woman seemed to be speaking for the other women present, I decided to keep this interview to compensate for the small number of female voices in other interviews.

There were 59 people actually speaking in these interviews, 36 Tabascans and 23 Maderans, 32 men and 27 women.[11] The number of participants per interview reflects the different lifestyles of the villages. In Madero, where nuclear families are common, most interviews were held with the father and the mother. By contrast, in Tabasco, where people have extended families and close networks of friends, interviews had up to six participants. In addition to the father and the mother, other people participating were usually the male relatives of the father. Attempting to include young Tabascan women's voices, we held two interviews with young couples, even though they were not nuclear families, but belonged to an extended family living at the husband's parents' residence. A detailed description of the composition of the sample is included in Appendix 2.

I sampled the same number of fathers and mothers, yet not all other family positions were evenly distributed. The sample does not reflect both communities' populations. It is especially skewed for Tabasco, where young men were eager to participate in the interviews. What the sample better reflects is those who were expected to express an opinion about the radio station. For example, note that without considering fathers and mothers, the interviews conducted in Tabasco included 11 young men, but only 5 young women. None of this reflects my numerous efforts to include women. Regarding education, only four Maderans in their twenties (three men and one woman) said they had more than three years of schooling, and all the male interviewees, but one (a bilingual teacher), worked in agriculture. Women also performed agricultural tasks in addition to their household chores.

Since I feel it is important to provide the reader with as much detail as possible about the interviews, I use a system of references that allows the reader to recognize immediately the gender and the family position of the person making a particular comment. I use the capital letter "F" followed by numbers (from 1 to 23, except for 8 and 12, since I decided to exclude these interviews from the sample) to refer to the families, and lowercase letters to refer to family position; "F3," for example, refers to family number three, and "6m" refers to the mother of family number six. (Code: f = father, m = mother, s = son, d = daughter, gf = grandfather, gm = grandmother, dl = daughter-in-law, fb = father's brother, fs = father's sister, mn = male neighbor, fn = female neighbor).

All interviews were held either on Sunday or in the afternoon, the villages' designated time for rest. Interviewees' openness was sometimes enhanced by the local alcoholic beverage that Tojolabals drink after work. The families' attitudes toward my research ranged from polite coldness to warm enthusiasm. Tabascan families tended to be more open and interested, though most Maderan families treated us quite warmly. Only the Maderans of the most educated family displayed a somewhat cynical attitude toward the interview, and the mother of another Maderan family posed the most disturbing question encountered in my whole fieldwork experience: "I want to know if *they* [she referred to INI officials] are going to take into account what we say or not," she stated. This question was deeply disturbing to me because during my fieldwork I often found myself wondering about the actual contribution of my research to social change.

More than being determined by place of residence or even gender, the revealing quality of particular remarks seems to be associated with the family's awareness of their power to influence their village's life. This awareness was overtly manifested by the father's active involvement in the village's political affairs or in indigenous organizations. There were also other factors not related to interviewees themselves that probably influenced their attitudes toward my research, such as the fact that Tabascans were aware of the greater effort involved in visiting their village and took both interviewers more seriously than Maderans. Maderans by contrast had already seen my interviewers while growing up and had often encountered ladino researchers like me. Interviewers' gender also played a key role because Mr. Alfaro either conducted or was present for seven out of nine interviews with Tabascans, though he conducted only three with Maderans. The remaining nine were conducted entirely by Ms. Rodríguez. Most Maderan women, who normally are much more assertive than Tabascan women, were not surprisingly more talkative than most of the latter.

I was particularly concerned about having female voices in the interviews, not only because I thought that most poor women are far from being assertive about their opinions, but because Cornejo's research has suggested that women are indeed the segment of the audience that listens the most to INI's radio stations, a suggestion that I contest. So my interviewing process included a number of efforts to elicit responses from women. The first challenge was to get women to take part in the interview at all, given that they are not normally expected to join in conversations with strangers. Especially in Tabasco, where most interviews involved more than one man, many women only partially participated; they would either find a reason to leave the room or would keep themselves busy with the cooking and the children. Interviewers made constant but unobtrusive and polite efforts to engage women in the conversation. Very few women would answer a question before the men, and when responding to questions directly addressed to them, women frequently covered their mouths with their hands, a gesture very pronounced among Tojolabal women and children. Women's engagement in the conversation was somehow breaking customary ways, and many times, when they allowed themselves to speak, their husbands intervened either interrupting them or preventing them from continuing. Several men not only answered first, but often used their body postures to exclude the women; one Maderan man moved and sat virtually between the interviewer and his wife, and a Tabascan covered his wife's mouth with his hand while she was talking. Notwithstanding, other men showed respect for women's opinions, and interviewers accomplished a great deal in their efforts to engage women. As a result my interviews contain moving and revealing remarks uttered by both Tabascan and Maderan women.

Fieldwork

At the time I started the research, the network was made up of seven stations. My fieldwork was done during the summer of 1989, then from June to December of 1990, and finally during the summer of 1991. In the course of my investigation, however, the network changed greatly: XENAC, the station broadcasting from Nacajuca, Tabasco, was closed down, two new stations were opened, and plans for opening as many as 22 more stations were underway. Given the time constraints and limited resources, I decided to consider only six stations for the exploration of production practices (XEZV, XEPUR, XETLA, XETAR, XEPET, and XEVFS) and only one of them for reception practices. However, my fieldwork focused mainly on four stations, XEZV, XETAR, XEPET, and XEVFS. Because Cornejo and several other researchers had already studied XETLA, I paid only a brief visit to this station. And since at the time I visited XEPUR (summer of 1989) the region was going through an unusual political moment, I also spent little time there. Though I included as much as I know about XETLA and XEPUR in my account, most of my illustrations come from XETAR, XEPET, and especially XEZV and XEVFS.

Getting initial access to the network was easy because the person who was the headquarters director at the time was interested in research efforts and provided me with valuable documents and official access to the stations. By the time I finished the fieldwork, however, I had lost official access to the stations. There are a number of things that account for this: I felt that people at managerial levels expected me to share my raw data with them, and after three years of periodically seeing some of the headquarters' employees, I became involved in their personal conflicts with one another. But most importantly, the more specific my questions or my requests for data became (e.g., the payroll), the more secretive the network's officials became. The network is a bureaucratic organization and as Gideon Sjoberg, Norma Williams, Ted Vaughan, and Andrée F. Sjoberg argue, secrecy systems are an integral part of bureaucratic life and elites are usually uncooperative with researchers. These authors say the following:

> Many social researchers lament, directly or indirectly, the fact that powerful organizational elites are uncooperative, but they fail to realize that secrecy is a fundamental means of sustaining power and influence. Cooperation with researchers in any egalitarian manner would lead elites to relinquish their monopoly on certain kinds of knowledge and thus their ability to manipulate the course of events.[12]

Access to the stations' staff varied not only from station to station, but also within every station. While some people were very open and even offered help to facilitate the logistics of fieldwork, others thought I was spying on behalf of the headquarters. But in general, I gained much more access to the first stations I visited than to the last one. Not surprisingly the greatest challenge was the general manager of XEVFS, the station at which I stayed the longest. He had been at that position since the station started and had remarkable control over the place, so my presence and inquiry into the station's daily routines were unwelcome.

Many other elements were also involved in the politics of my fieldwork in Radio Margaritas. When I went to this station, I was very dependent on the general manager. I needed him to give permission to members of the staff to work with me in the audience study and to help me with transportation to go to the villages, and I needed recording equipment because my luggage was stolen. He did as little as he could to help me and as much as he could to complicate my work. However, despite my dependency on him and the threat that he probably saw in me, I wonder to what extent the fact that during my visit to XEPUR and XEZV I was accompanied by my spouse, a North American white male, opened doors for me.

As a lower middle-class, dark-skinned Mexican woman from the barbaric northern state of Chihuahua, I had little status, and my educational capital seemed to confuse people. My gender was especially a problem in establishing my credibility as a researcher, especially with INI-employed ladinos; for instance, while general managers and other INI officials refer to each other as *licenciado*, a term implying that the person designated as such holds important educational capital, they often called me "the girl," despite the fact that I was more educated and also probably older than most of them. Concerning indigenous staff members, there was a wide range of attitudes toward me and my research. Most of them treated me with respect, and many were eager to talk to me, but a few were especially suspicious of my presence at the stations and avoided interaction with me. During the last part of my stay in Radio Margaritas, I felt that several of them feared that they would be reprimanded by the general manager if they showed too much interest in my work.

For the Tojolabals who participated in the audience study, I was obviously a ka*shlana*, a ladina, and that made my access to Tojolabal people problematic. However, since the interviews where conducted by Tojolabals associated with Radio Margaritas (an institution that many of them hold in high regard), I believe that we were able to earn the trust of most of our informants. The candid remarks uttered by many of the interviewees attest for such trust.

Finally, I should mention the issue of the network staff's use of different linguistic registers when talking to me. I found myself stymied by contradictory data, until I learned to distinguish when an informant was using a given register, especially that variety of language that is considered appropriate among Mexican bureaucrats to talk about government projects' performances, rather than another, such as friendly talk about what he or she actually thought that happens at the stations. In general, since ladinos occupy higher positions in the network, they were more prompt to speak as bureaucrats than the indigenous and mestizo employees.

Analysis, Interpretation, and Caveats

Regarding analysis, the challenge was to interpret the interviews conducted with audience members. A great deal of the interpretation of these interviews took place during the fieldwork, especially during the translation/transcription sessions. For example, I was still in the field when I realized that topics such as "news" and "avisos" should be subsumed under the theme of "information flow."

There was a clear point in the research, however, after the data collection, when I did a more systematic analysis of the interviews. I began by analyzing the explicit content of the responses given. I examined the first part of the interviews to obtain hard data on interviewees discussed above. As for the core questions, I first counted the frequency of certain answers, and then I looked at the correlation between a given response and the characteristics of the respondents, especially their gender and their place of residence. For close-ended questions (e.g., "Have you ever gone to the station?") coding was a simple procedure. But for open-ended questions (e.g., "Please describe the things you like the most about Radio Margaritas' broadcasting"), I had to find out first what were the most important themes discussed by interviewees, and then I had to develop schemes for coding responses. Though I used the results of this analysis as one of the sources for the interpretation, there were several themes/questions which did not lend themselves to this type of analysis.

I paid special attention to differences among responses. For instance, I took into account the eloquence of a given remark, the uniqueness of an answer, or the failure/avoidance to address a certain issue. Then I did a contextual analysis, examining responses in light of information on the station and its programming, as well as on data about interviewees, their village, and their ethnic group. Both observation notes on the interviewing process and commentaries made by key informants were very useful in understanding subtleties and indirect references. Likewise, interviews with XEVFS staff members, Tojolabal teachers, extension workers, and ladino families from Margaritas City helped to clarify the meaning of obscure comments. For example, there is this remark by a Maderan woman: "What I don't like is when the station airs bad words." She was talking about the open way in which women's gynecological and feminine problems are sometimes dealt with in a program about health. The same issue was brought up by Tojolabal teachers and a physician working at Madero's clinic, and my research assistant made sure I understood what this woman had meant.

To analyze the data gathered through the users survey and the staff profile, I used a computerized package (SYSTAT) to obtain a number of statistics.[13] In comparison with the rigorous analysis that I did for the family interviews, the interpretation of the interviews with focus groups was less demanding. The reason is that the focus groups were already complemented by observation, logs, institutional documents, staff profile, users survey, monitoring of transmission, and several key informants. So I had multiple sources of data and was able first to read with more certainty responses and comments given in the focus groups, and second to juxtapose information from different sources. On the other hand, for the interpretation of the family interviews I did not work with such a variety of data sources, and my own interpretive skills were severely diminished because these interviews were conducted in Tojolabal, a language in which I have no competence at all.

Both my lack of linguistic competence in Tojolabal, and the fact that this book is written in English affected the construction of my text. Because I wanted to include the voices of those who participate in the radio network, I used ethnographic techniques in my investigation. But, though I strived to write a polyvocal text, the words of my informants lost much in the translation process, especially the quotes that I culled from the audience interviews, which were initially uttered in Tojolabal, then translated by my research assistant into Spanish, and finally translated by me into English. I tried to keep as much of the original flavor of indigenous speakers as I could, for example, by retaining their use of the first person, plural subject pronoun, "we," instead of the first person, singular subject pronoun, "I."

Despite the multiple shortcomings of my translations and other inherent difficulties of translating one culture into another, I hope the reader will get a sense of why the INI stations operate the way they do and how Tojolabal audience members use Radio Margaritas as an important communication resource.

Notes

1. Hans J. Kleinsteuber and Urte Sonnenberg, "Beyond Public Service and Private Profit: International Experience with Non-Commercial Radio," *European Journal of Communication* 5 (1990): 102. For a specific example of minority broadcasting see Donald R. Browne, "Aboriginal Radio in Australia: From Dreamtime to Primetime?," *Journal of Communication* 40.1 (1990): 111-120.

2. See Robert C. Hornik, *Development Communication. Information, Agriculture and Nutrition in the Third World* (New York: Longman, 1988).

3. James Lull, *Inside Family Viewing* (London: Routledge, 1990); Jesús Martín Barbero, *De los Medios a las Mediaciones: Comunicación, Cultura y Hegemonía* (México: Gustavo Gilli, 1987).

4. I followed James P. Spradley's general suggestions for interviewing. *The Ethnographic Interview* (New York: Holt, Rinehart and Winston, 1979). And I relied on Richard A. Krueger's advice for the focus groups. *Focus Groups. A Practical Guide for Applied Research* (Newbury Park: Sage, 1988).

5. The users surveys were administered at XETAR, July 13-19, 1990; XEPET, August 7-13, 1990; and XEVFS, October 19-25, 1990.

6. Inés Cornejo, "La Voz de la Mixteca y la Comunidad Receptora de la Mixteca Oaxaqueña," M.A. thesis, U Iberoamericana, 1990; Instituto Nacional Indigenista,

¿Se Escuchan Nuestras Voces? XEVFS, La Voz de la Frontera Sur, Inés Cornejo and Silvia Luna, ts., internal document, México; and Josefina Aranda Bezaury and Verónica Valenzuela, "Investigación Sobre la Presencia Radiofónica de la Voz de la Montaña en las Comunidades," unpublished essay, 1982.

7. David Morley, *Family Television: Cultural Power and Domestic Leisure* (London: Routledge, 1988).

8. Questions 1-14.

9. Questions 15-31.

10. We tried, and failed, to interview families in another village, Bajucú. People from Bajucú were very suspicious of us; an elderly man asked Mr. Alfaro for identification showing he was employed by XEVFS. Given the social conflict that Protestant sects had created in the region, I thought they had good reasons to suspect strangers traveling in a car with U.S. plates.

11. Regarding the interviewees' linguistic competence in Spanish, only 12 of the 59 spoke Spanish fluently; 22 of them spoke some Spanish, and 25 did not speak any Spanish at all. Concerning their age, 23 were between 21 and 35 years of age, and 19 between 36 and 50 years of age; only 10 interviewees were over 50 year-old, and only 7 were under 21 year-old.

12. Gideon Sjoberg, Norma Williams, Ted Vaughan, and Andrée F. Sjoberg, "The Case Study Approach in Social Research," *A Case for the Case Study*, eds. Joe R. Feagin, Anthony M. Orum and Gideon Sjoberg (Chapel Hill: U of North Carolina Press, 1991) 56.

13. SYSTAT is a system for performing statistical analysis on Macintosh computers.

PART TWO

Indigenous Participation
in Production Processes

3

Indigenous Peoples and the Instituto Nacional Indigenista

This book provides an account of the social practices occurring in a Mexican network of rural radio stations sponsored by the government and broadcasting for indigenous populations. It highlights how and why the politics of race, ethnicity, class, and gender shape the extent and quality of popular participation in radio-for-development. Appreciating and understanding the results of the research, means learning about a number of both historical and current factors about indigenous peoples of Mexico and the workings of the government agency which exists to assist them. In this chapter, I talk about those factors necessary to situate the social practices taking place in the radio stations within the general framework of majority-minority relations in Mexico, and I also discuss the role played by the Instituto Nacional Indigenista in the making and implementation of national policies regarding ethnic groups.

Indigenous Ethnic Groups in Mexico

The nation that emerged after Mexico's 1910 popular revolution has had a dual and contradictory attitude toward indigenous peoples and their cultures. On the one hand, these cultures have been regarded as sacred roots, have been treasured as the core and source of *Mexicanidad*, and have been used to invent national traditions as well as to bolster nationalism. On the other hand, indigenous peoples have been systematically exploited, their cultures have been deemed inferior to Western civilization, and since the Conquest up to modern times, rampant racism toward dark-skinned people has been one of the fundamental threads of the fabric of Mexican society.

Since Mexico is the country with the largest indigenous population of the Americas, indigenous people constitute a large sector of Mexican society. Several agencies of the Mexican government, using language as the chief indicator for ethnicity, estimate that out of the country's total population of over 82 million, at least ten million are members of indigenous ethnic groups.[1] There are probably over 56 vernacular languages in Mexico, most of them with less than 200,000 speakers.[2] Almost two-thirds of the ten million speakers of vernaculars also speak some Spanish.[3] Many indigenous people live in remote settlements; there are about 453 *municipios* (roughly counties) with a predominantly indigenous population, and these municipios are rural areas.[4] Some indigenous people, however, like the Mazahuas from the state of Mexico, have emigrated to urban areas and have already integrated into the cities' informal economies.[5] With over one million indigenous inhabitants, Mexico City now has more indigenous people than any other single area. Since young men are increasingly becoming migrant laborers, another important demographic trend is temporary migration.[6]

Rather than seeing Mexican indigenous peoples as ethnic or cultural minorities, I should perhaps describe them as "Fourth World nation peoples." This term has been used to refer to native peoples whose land and resources have been almost completely expropriated but who still live as ethno-cultural groups in both developed and developing countries. As other Fourth World nation peoples, Mexican indigenous people live in conditions of extreme poverty. Mexico's areas with higher indigenous population, such as the states of Chiapas, Oaxaca, and Guerrero, coincide with its most economically marginalized regions.[7] The evidence for this conclusion is overwhelming; for example, while in the Federal District there are 737 people for each hospital bed, the number for Chiapas is 4,512. At the national level, the percentage of households with drinking water is 71, but for Chiapas and Oaxaca it is 44. Regarding food intake, while the country's elite (10 percent of the total population) consumes 21 percent of all food products, the large poorest sector (30 percent of the total population) consumes only 13 percent of these products.[8]

The means used by power elites to repress any attempt by indigenous peoples to change the situation have included sending them to jail, torturing them, and murdering them. To grasp the extent of human rights abuses, consider the following data published by a national newspaper: during a period of 19 months (roughly October 1989 to May 1990) 74 peasant leaders were murdered, an average of almost 4 murders per month. In that same period, 105 leaders were jailed and tortured, which is an average of 5.5 per month. The repression of peasant leaders is particularly strong in areas with large indigenous populations, like the state where I conducted my audience study, Chiapas. Out of the 74 peasants murdered, 38 were from Chiapas, as were 46 of the 105 peasants jailed and tortured.[9]

In addition to the physical violence, the countless repressive mechanisms of Mexico's dominant society include those intangible but still painfully real recourses used to stigmatize indigenous cultures. Important for this discussion is the way in which the mass media have often contributed to this multiple oppression, not only by failing to report human rights abuses but also by reinforcing racist stereotypes. For instance, *Televisa*, the Mexican media conglomerate, is said to ban faces with indigenous features from television cameras. A mere glance at Televisa's productions supports the rumor, and a more detailed examination certainly shows its unrestrained racism.

Despite almost 500 years of brutal abuse of their human rights, indigenous people in the Americas continue to resist the effects of the European conquest and colonization. Like in other parts of Latin America, in Mexico, since the 1970s indigenous resistance has especially manifested itself in the form of indigenous federations and organizations.[10] Although these countless organizations espouse distinct projects and have undertaken various political strategies, their common and comprehensive struggle is, as Miguel Bartolomé and Alicia Barabas say, "not only for political autonomy, but also for the right to cultural survival and development."[11] In my subsequent discussion about *indigenismo*, I will point out that the ethnopolitical discourse and actions of these organizations have influenced the ideological framework of the radio network's sponsor. The Mexican state, in its attempts to co-opt the indigenous discourse, has stressed the importance of cultural survival, while neglecting the need for development and ignoring the demands for political autonomy.

Adolfo Colombres, talking about the vindications sought by indigenous organizations, says that they struggle for structural changes in society, aiming at ending all forms of racial, social, economic, and cultural discrimination and oppression. According to Colombres, fundamental objectives of indigenous organizations concern political rights and rights over their lands and natural resources. These include (1) the recognition of their groups as political unities within a multiethnic state, (2) the recuperation of their ancestors' lands and resources, (3) the legalization of their properties under communal tenure, (4) the autonomous right to exploit their resources, (5) the end to the environmental destruction of their habitats, and (6) the official recognition of their languages and their cultural specificities. Particular goals related to the improvement of living conditions are formulated according to individual agendas for acknowledging each group's differences and recuperating its history. Indigenous organizations seek to advance ethnic groups' self-sufficiencies and to avoid new dependencies. Thus indigenous organizations strive for a good quality bilingual-bicultural education and for an improvement of health through measures that incorporate traditional medical knowledge. They also strive for a transference of science and technology based on each group's needs and its capacity to control and administer new resources.[12]

The best example of the Mexican indigenous movements that have integrated new communication technologies, specifically radio, in their struggle is known as the COCEI of Juchitán, Oaxaca (*Coalición Obrera Campesina Estudiantil del Istmo*). A coalition of Zapoteca workers, peasants, and students, COCEI is considered to be the most successful indigenous movement of contemporary Mexico. Founded in 1973, it has largely influenced politics in its region, especially since 1981 when it won the municipal elections for the first time and controlled city hall for two years. From 1983 to 1986 Juchitán had a strong military presence, and the official party's (PRI) candidates were imposed. However, popular protest after the elections of 1986 forced PRI to share the municipal government with COCEI in a coalition government until 1989, when COCEI's electoral victory was recognized.[13] COCEI has controlled city hall since then because its electoral victory was repeated in the 1992 elections. In more than 20 years of political strife, COCEI has resisted innumerable attempts to defeat it. Howard Campbell et al. correctly remark that "in the violent and unpredictable world of Mexican regional and local politics, COCEI has demonstrated its staying in power by surviving economic boycott, repression, and efforts at cooptation by local elites and state and federal governments."[14]

During its municipal administration, COCEI operated a truly participatory radio station: *Radio Ayuntamiento Popular de Juchitán*. This station was part of a political strategy to reclaim Zapoteca roots and to prevent the disappearance of Zapoteca culture. It included broadcasts in Zapoteca language and featured programs made by peasants, children, and neighborhood residents. It also experimented with music formats and styles and presented alternative newscasts. One of the participants of the movement, Daniel López Nelio, explains the significance of revitalizing Zapoteca culture, the political implications of making Zapoteca the dominant language in the municipality, and the role played by radio in this particular struggle:

> Control of City Hall opens up the possibility of reclaiming our culture through the radio station we now have. Today in the municipal court, matters are resolved in Zapoteca, which PRI would not accept for many years. That is, PRI forced our people to speak Spanish, whether they could or not, in judicial affairs. Today, this policy has been discarded, and Zapoteca is spoken in the courthouse, police station, and mayor's office. The previous policy meant the destruction of Zapoteca culture by forcing people to speak Spanish.[15]

Unfortunately, Radio Ayuntamiento Juchitán was jammed by the government, and its efforts to reclaim Zapoteca culture have been curtailed. Nonetheless, COCEI's station became an utmost example for popular radio. As I discuss throughout this book, the INI stations aspire to be popular radio, but they are far from being one of the projects of a grassroots movement and are instead the by-product of a particular policy of the federal government known as participatory indigenismo.

Mexican *Indigenismo*

The difficulty in specifying the meaning of the term "indigenismo" has been underscored by Raúl Reissner.[16] As Reissner points out, the adjective has been used to refer (1) to the study of Latin American indigenous peoples; (2) to a doctrine or party championing political, social, and economic rights of these peoples; and (3) to Latin American governments' policies regarding indigenous populations. I use the term chiefly in this last sense and focus on the indigenismo of the government that emerged after the Mexican revolution of 1910. In this sense, indigenismo has for the most part been a theory and political practice designed and implemented by non-indigenous elites (often anthropologists), and directed toward achieving the integration of indigenous peoples into the mainstream national culture.

The colonial (1521-1820) and independent (1810-1910) governments' strategy for dealing with indigenous peoples was ethnic genocide. Indigenous populations were drastically reduced as a result of the political domination, and vernacular cultures were aggressively repressed and stigmatized. However, with the 1910 revolution, Mexico became an *"indigenista"* state, and at the height of the revolution during President Lázaro Cárdenas' administration (1936-1942), the federal government strongly supported land reform and other actions targeting the advancement of indigenous peoples. Of special importance were the efforts to create a national agency to coordinate government policies and specific measures involving indigenous peoples: the *Instituto Nacional Indigenista,* which was finally established in 1948. The ideology structuring and sustaining official policies and actions came to be known as "indigenismo," and INI emerged as the central actor of the *"acción indigenista."*

The Mexican revolution and its populist ideology has had a decisive influence in the Latin American indigenista experience. Since for several decades it was the only popular revolution in Latin America (until the Bolivian insurrection of 1952 and the Cuban revolution of 1958), Mexico became the region's leader in state cultural and political policies regarding indigenous populations. Mexico, or perhaps better to say Mexican anthropologists, advocated indigenismo in international forums, hosting the first Interamerican Indigenista Congress in 1940 and promoting the creation of the *Instituto Indigenista Interamericano.* This key international institution, headed by Mexican anthropologists since its launching in 1940 until 1970, has influenced INI, and INI in turn has influenced it.

The profound impact of Mexican indigenismo in Latin America has also been effected through its anthropology schools and especially through INI's actions and proposals.[17] The National School of Anthropology and History was instituted to educate not only Mexican but also other Latin American students; in fact, the Mexican government granted scholarships to many foreign students. INI established a model that would be emulated, at least in part, by countries like Peru, and INI's rural development centers became the foremost places for applied indigenista projects in the region.[18] Thus, though several Latin American nations have undertaken efforts to implement indigenismo (either on their own or through the *Instituto Indigenista Interamericano*), Mexico has championed indigenismo in the region, and INI constitutes the largest and longest effort of any Latin American state to develop and implement a strategy to deal with the challenges of a multiethnic society.

But INI has been a paradoxical institution. On the one hand, at the national and international levels it has championed indigenous peoples' economic, political, and social rights. On the other hand, the institution itself has been dominated by racist ideologies and practices. (This paradoxical nature structures the history and current situation of the radio network and can be seen by contrasting the racist work practices that I describe through this book with the high status that the network enjoys at international forums such as the World Organization of Community Oriented Radio). Since later in this chapter I present the historical development of INI's ideologies as viewed by a critical anthropologist, to illustrate INI's paradoxical nature here, I would like to underscore the instrumental role that INI has played in bilingual-bicultural education.

In 1952, INI started a project that grew up to be a key agency of the Ministry of Education, the *Dirección General de Educación Indígena*. The project was based on the idea that to carry out its programs successfully, INI needed to incorporate indigenous, bilingual teachers into its staff. The first 46 *promotores culturales bilingues* had only a few years of formal schooling but had ample knowledge of the culture and social history of the people they were going to work with since they were recruited from indigenous villages. By 1963 INI had 350 promotores; one year later they became employees of the Ministry of Education, and the project was expanded to reach the national level. In the late 1980s there were over 30,000 bilingual teachers.[18] Bilingual teachers enjoy the economic benefits brought by their status as civil servants, and in their communities they are also well respected for their educational capital. Becoming a bilingual teacher is probably the best economic strategy for a young indigenous person. (As I discuss later, bilingual teachers are routinely assigned to work at the INI radio stations.)

Instituto Nacional Indigenista

Given that until the late 1980s the vast majority of the indigenous populations lived in rural areas, INI has been in many ways a rural development agency.[20] Rather than working under one of the Ministries concerned with development (e.g., Ministry of Health or Ministry of Education), INI is a parastatal of the executive branch, and its director is nominated by the President of the Republic.[21] However, INI was designed to work closely with other governmental bodies, and its board of directors (*Consejo Directivo*) includes representatives from several ministries and research institutions. During the administration of Carlos Salinas de Gortari (1988-1994), INI has been closely associated with the *Programa Nacional de Solidaridad*, the chief instrument of the federal government devoted to alleviating the extreme poverty brought on by the economic crisis of the 1980s.[22]

It is important to underscore that INI is the only presence of the executive branch in rural areas; as such it plays a key role in regional politics involving indigenous peoples and often gets involved in local political struggles with both municipal and state governments. INI has many times defied the privileges of local elites and exposed their wrongdoings, but more often than not, as a bureaucratic institution of the Mexican state, INI has served the interest of the ruling classes.

Indigenous peoples have striven to influence INI's policies and actions in numerous ways. Out of desperation, indigenous groups have often occupied INI's facilities demanding specific changes. Yet INI has never faced the kind of opposition that in 1990 the Yoreme people (also known as Yaqui) built up when they insisted that INI was interfering with their internal affairs and they decided to expel INI from their territory.[23] The events of the last few years have made INI's need for legitimizing its activities at both the local and the national levels more urgent than it used to be, and these events have also probably influenced the unprecedented expansion that the radio network has undergone during the 1990s.

In accordance with its legal mandate, INI is a research center, and that fact should be kept in mind: INI was created and has often been controlled by anthropologists. It serves as a consulting and coordinating body for other public and private institutions, and it carries out development programs in coordination with the *Dirección General de Educación Indígena* (which is part of the Ministry of Education).[24] However, because of both the shortage of government development agencies and the government's reluctance to recognize indigenous organizations officially, INI has frequently exceeded its legal functions, and it has sponsored numerous development projects. In 1988, for example, INI implemented over 1,500 projects at the national level.[25] The effectiveness of the agency's projects, however, has often been the target of strong criticism. As Guillermo Bonfil Batalla pointed out, there have been two major drawbacks in carrying out INI's actions effectively. One is the fact that INI was set up as a coordinating entity in a country where coordination among the administrative units has been, although an ad infinitum stated goal, in fact a limited if not exceptional practice. And the other is the existence of tight relations between state and federal officials and local and regional elites whose interests INI's actions will always necessarily touch.[26] In addition, one must recognize that INI has never had the resources to be the chief sponsor of the federal government's projects for indigenous peoples, a fact often highlighted by INI's officials.[27]

In recent times, INI's projects have been grouped under four general areas. The first area, which has become the primary one, is economic development. In 1988, for example, 62 percent of INI's total budget (which was over 15 million dollars) was spent on projects aimed at bolstering economic development.[28] Health and social welfare constitute the second area, which includes two basic programs, one for health and the other for scholarships and boarding centers (*albergues*). Though few resources have been directed toward the former program, the latter has received plenty; in 1988, 23 percent of INI's total budget was spent on scholarships and boarding centers, and INI was operating 1, 248 boarding centers serving 63,900 indigenous children.[29] The third area, promotion of justice (*procuración de justicia*), used to be only a small program but during the Salinas administration acquired considerable momentum. The last area, the *Dirección de Promoción Cultural y Desarrollo*, concentrates on the promotion of the cultural patrimony and includes the radio network as one of its projects.

INI's programs have been implemented primarily through its *Centros Coordinadores Indigenistas* (hereafter CCI, coordinating center) located in towns or small cities that act as the economic and political core of regions with a predominantly indigenous population.[30] The first CCI was started in 1950, and by the early 1990s INI had 84 CCIs. Mediating between the CCIs and INI's headquarters, located in Mexico City, there are state coordinating offices. Because the radio network has had a peculiar situation in INI's organizational chart, the radio stations have a great deal of independence from both the local CCI and the state coordinating office. Most of the radio stations broadcast from one of the buildings of the local CCI. The stations' staff are on the CCI's payroll, and the stations receive their operating budgets through the CCI. Notwithstanding, the stations work in a very independent fashion. Each station's general manager reports directly to the network's headquarters (or *Subsecretaría de Radio*, located in Mexico City), and rather than being a subordinate, he or she is more of a collaborator with the CCI director. In fact, the poor coordination between the radio stations and their corresponding CCIs has been one of the project's drawbacks.

Participatory Indigenismo

In his outline of the history of indigenismo, Adolfo Colombres starts by establishing the origins of contemporary indigenismo in the practice of the social anthropology initiated in Latin America by the pioneer anthropologist Manuel Gamio. Colombres says that this applied anthropology was "a comparative sociology of the structures and functions of so-called primitive societies [my translation]"[31] which aimed at improving indigenous peoples living conditions and incorporating them into the mainstream culture, regarded as civilization. Historically, this first phase of indigenismo roughly corresponds with the preconsolidation era of the postrevolutionary government (1910s-1930s). The second phase, which began in 1941 with the founding of the *Instituto Indigenista Interamericano* (the institution promoted by Gamio which preceded INI), had a pivotal moment in 1948 with the creation of INI, and lasted until the late 1970s.

During this second phase the integrationist ideology that has characterized most of INI's policies and actions was formulated and has remained deeply rooted in this institution. Colombres rightly asserts that the goal of indigenismo was the integration of indigenous peoples into the Mexican nationality or national culture, and that its means included deep acculturation achieved by paternalistic manipulation. Though condemning the ideology and practice of this indigenismo, Colombres recognizes that it prevented the continuation of genocide and militaristic domination, which were the routine ways of accomplishing national unity, and still today are the main element of the controlling strategies of other Latin American countries such as Guatemala.

By the early 1980s, responding in part to a growing Panamerican, indigenous resistance movement, INI had adopted a new ideology: *indigenismo de participación*, or participatory indigenismo, which was defined as a policy with indigenous people, instead of a policy for them.[32] But, as its critics point out, the new indigenismo has not been designed and implemented by indigenous people, but instead by INI's anthropologists. Moreover, its initial radical demands have been considerably softened. In 1982 INI's documents even indicated the end of indigenismo both as a goal and a consequence of increased indigenous participation in the institution.[33] By 1990, however, the existence of indigenismo was no longer questioned in INI's documents.

INI's participatory indigenismo has been intertwined with the complex and profound changes that Mexico has undergone in the last two decades. The economic crisis, the emergence of an unprecedented civil society, and the demands for true political participation persuaded the official party (PRI) to embrace, at least rhetorically, participatory policies in an attempt to regain the popularity they had once enjoyed among the poor. The best example of this policy is President Salinas de Gortari's *Programa Nacional de Solidaridad*. Critics of these kinds of state participatory programs have long insisted the government becomes their main beneficiary since these programs help maintain the status quo. Though they help increase production, their chief purpose is to keep the peace among those sectors that can no longer be dominated by repression.[34]

As opposed to the old indigenismo, participatory indigenismo recognizes indigenous peoples' history of domination as the principal cause of their poverty. Instead of considering native ways as obstacles for improving living conditions, it sees traditional practices as resources for constructing development. It draws on both Paulo Freire's ideas regarding popular participation and on the theses of ethnodevelopment (see Appendix 1).

The advocates of ethnodevelopment contend that the indigenous culture must be the basis for future development and that only full participation of the local people in development projects can guarantee that these projects will respond to the needs and aspirations of their intended beneficiaries. Proponents of ethnodevelopmentalist theses insist the fundamental goal of any project should be to increase the ethnic group's decision-making power over its material, intellectual, and organizational resources. Those resources include both its own resources and foreign resources that have been appropriated by the group.[35] Naturally, ethnodevelopmentalists endorse indigenous organizations' demands for the right to direct their own political affairs autonomously and to manage those government institutions concerned with ethnic groups, such as INI. Participatory indigenismo lags behind indigenous organizations' demands for political autonomy and direct participation in state institutions like INI. Not surprisingly, a former INI director has referred to the line of thought advanced by some of the advocates of ethnodevelopment as "utopian indigenismo."[36]

The participatory indigenismo of the early 1990s focuses on the "transference of functions" (*traspaso de funciones*). INI's 1988-1992 director, Arturo Warman, established a program based on three general policies: (1) to coordinate INI's work with the activities of other national and international agencies; (2) to promote indigenous peoples' participation in the planning and implementing of INI's projects; and (3) to direct such participation at achieving the transference of institutional functions to indigenous peoples and their organizations and as a second choice, to other government agencies and groups. Warman's document, notwithstanding, also specified a series of conditions for such transference of functions and clearly stated that INI's legal functions are to be exempt from this. The transference thus applies only to those functions that are not part of INI's legal mandate. The extent to which the transference will apply to the radio network is a matter of interpretation.

Setting up mechanisms for indigenous participation in INI's activities has been a leading objective of participatory indigenismo. By the late 1980s, INI had established a series of entities to allow such participation. In 1984 President De la Madrid instructed INI to create the *Consejo Consultivo de las Comunidades Indígenas*, a consulting body to INI composed of members of ethnic groups;[37] this council elects three representatives to INI's board of directors or *Consejo Directivo*. There are also representatives from the local ethnic groups in the internal board of each CCI and the boards of the state coordinating offices; direct participation of the indigenous villages is sought through community committees (*Comités Comunitarios de Planeación*). None of these bodies, however, play any significant role in the network of radio stations.

Thus, in the 1980s, INI went through a process of policy redefinition and instituted formal mechanisms for indigenous participation to match with its contemporaneous ideology. Though INI's policies, documents, and publications stress this participation, the authoritarian management practices of INI's officials are an acknowledged fact among the staff. An extreme instance of this awareness is a remark attributed to INI's former director, Warman, who supposedly equated the authoritarian stance of CCI directors to that of feudal masters. If the kind of participation occurring inside some of the radio stations is representative of the whole institution, the analogy is substantially true.

In brief, as the critics of participatory indigenismo correctly argue, the official indigenista discourse has shifted from an integrationist approach to participatory indigenismo, yet such a shift has only taken place in exceptional deeds of the indigenista practice.

Regarding the INI radio stations, overt racist attitudes are common in the network's everyday practices. Examples abound; they go from hiring policies (the best paid positions are almost entirely occupied by ladinos) to the everyday production practices such script writing (in XEVFS a ladino edits the scripts written by indigenous producers). The next three chapters are dedicated to the discussion of these practices.

Notes

1. See for example Luz María Valdéz, *El Perfil Demográfico de los Indios Mexicanos* (México: Siglo XXI, 1988) 108; and Consejo Consultivo del Programa Nacional de Solidaridad, *El Combate a la Pobreza* (México: El Nacional, 1990).

2. The few indigenous languages that have more than 200,000 speakers are Náhuatl, Maya, Mixteco, Otomí, Zapoteco, and Totonaco. Valdéz 116.

3. Valdéz estimates that 71.4 percent of the total indigenous population is bilingual and that 23 percent speaks only the native language. There is no data for the remaining 5.6 percent. Valdéz 39.

4. Valdéz 58.

5. Valdéz 58, 77-78, 110.

6. Valdéz 60.

7. Consejo Consultivo del Programa Nacional de Solidaridad 34.

8. Consejo Consultivo del Programa Nacional de Solidaridad 45, 52, 38.

9. Matilde Pérez, "Al Terror que Imponen Caciques y Pistoleros se Suma el de Judiciales," *La Jornada* 31 July, 1990, 3.

10. For a history of the Mexican indigenous movement, see María Consuelo Mejía Piñeros and Sergio Sarmiento Silva, *La Lucha Indígena: Un Reto a la Ortodoxia* (México: Siglo XXI, 1987).

11. Miguel Bartolomé and Alicia Barabas, foreword, *Zapotec Struggles*, eds. Howard Campbell, Leight Binford, Miguel Bartolomé, and Alicia Barabas (Washington: Smithsonian Institution Press, 1993) xiv.

12. See for example Adolfo Colombres, *La Hora del Bárbaro*, 2nd ed. (México: Premiá, 1984) 42-44.

13. Jeffrey W. Rubin, "COCEI against the State: A Political History of Juchitán," *Zapotec Struggles*, eds. Howard Campbell, Leight Binford, Miguel Bartolomé, and Alicia Barabas (Washington: Smithsonian Institution Press, 1993) 157-158.

14. Howard Campbell, Leight Binford, Miguel Bartolomé, and Alicia Barabas, *Zapotec Struggles* (Washington: Smithsonian Institution Press, 1993) xvii.

15. "Interview with Daniel López Nelio," *Zapotec Struggles*, eds. Howard Campbell, Leight Binford, Miguel Bartolomé, and Alicia Barabas (Washington: Smithsonian Institution Press, 1993) 234.

16. Raúl Reissner, "El Indio de los Diccionarios," *Comunicación y Cultura* 14 (1985): 5-33.

17. For a further discussion of INI's impact on Latin American indigenismo, see Oscar Arce Quintanilla, "Del Indigenismo a la Indianidad. Cincuenta Años de Indigenismo Continental," *Instituto Nacional Indigenista: 40 Años*, ed. Instituto Nacional Indigenista (México: Instituto Nacional Indigenista, 1988) 105-120; and Elio Masferrer Kan, "La Proyección del Instituto Nacional Indigenista en América," *Instituto Nacional Indigenista: 40 Años*, ed. Instituto Nacional Indigenista (México: Instituto Nacional Indigenista, 1988) 208-220.

18. Masferrer Kan 211-215.

19. Juan Larios Tolentino, "A Cuarenta Años. Experiencias y Aportaciones del Instituto Nacional Indigenista," *Instituto Nacional Indigenista: 40 Años*, ed. Instituto Nacional Indigenista (México: Instituto Nacional Indigenista, 1988) 182-3.

20. Importantly though, the political function fulfilled by INI should be noted, since the agency has often been the only presence of the federal government in remote areas.

21. INI is a *dependencia* of the *Sector de Educación Pública* of the federal government.

22. INI's director was a member of the board of this program.

23. The CCI located in Vícam, Sonora was closed on September 15, 1990. "La Tribu Yaqui Expulsó al INI de su Territorio," *La Jornada*, 20 Sept., 1990: 1.

24. "Ley que Crea el Instituto Nacional Indigenista," *Diario Oficial*, 4 Dec., 1948.

25. Raúl Villegas Ortega and Jonathan Molinet Malpica, "El Instituto Nacional Indigenista," *Instituto Nacional Indigenista: 40 Años*, ed. Instituto Nacional Indigenista (México: Instituto Nacional Indigenista, 1988) 528.

26. Guillermo Bonfil Batalla, *México Profundo. Una Civilización Negada* (México: Secretaría de Educación Pública, 1987) 175-176.

27. For instance, in a newspaper interview, the former director of INI, Arturo Warman, underscored that INI is the institute with the lowest funding. Saide Sesín, "Una Tradición Arrancada Produce Vacío," *UnoMásUno* 4 Jan., 1989: 28.

28. In 1988 INI's budget was 43,266.9 million pesos. Villegas et al. 529.

29. Children are provided food, or food and shelter, Monday through Friday. Villegas et al. 539.

30. In 1988 there were 81 *Centros Coordinadores* and 7 *Residencias*. Tolentino 7.

31. Colombres, *La Hora del Bárbaro* 18.

32. Colombres states that the first official expression of participatory indigenismo

appeared in 1977, in the inaugural speech of the new director of INI. *La Hora del Bárbaro* 21.

33. See for example Eduardo Limón Aguirre and José Manuel Ramos Rodríguez, "Indigenismo y Radiodifusión," *Mexico Indígena* 66, supplement, (1982): 4.

34. Colombres , *La Hora del Bárbaro* 41.

35. Guillermo Bonfil Batalla, *América Latina: Etnodesarrollo y Etnocidio* (San José, Costa Rica: Ediciones FLACSO, 1982) 135.

36. Gonzalo Aguirre Beltrán, "Derrumbe de Paradigmas," Seminario Permanente sobre Indigenismo, CIESAS del Golfo, Jalapa, Veracruz, México, March 30, 1990.

37. Instituto Nacional Indigenista, "El Presidente Miguel de la Madrid Definió la Política Indigenista," *Documentos* 1,1 (México: Instituto Nacional Indigenista, 1984) 2.

4

The INI Network

History of the *Radio Cultural Indigenista*

"The decision was made without making a decision,"says José Manuel Ramos Rodríguez, a key figure in the development of the INI network, when describing the circumstances surrounding the selection of the best location for XETLA, one of the stations of the project.[1] This apparently contradictory statement lucidly depicts the sui generis way in which many of the decisions about the initiation and unfolding of the project were made.

The INI network of rural radio stations originated in 1979 with the establishment of one station in Tlapa, Guerrero, a small city in southwestern Mexico. By the end of 1991, what became known as *Proyecto Cultural Radiofónico del Instituto Nacional Indigenista* was composed of eight AM radio stations, and INI officials were announcing an unprecedented expansion of the network to include as many as 22 new stations. Several reasons account for the project's growth, but its political attractiveness along with its relatively low cost for INI constitute the chief factors underlying its advancement.

In her historical analysis of XETLA, one of the INI stations, Inés Cornejo (who was the network's main researcher for several years) discerns five phases: origin, constitution, transition, consolidation, and expansion.[2] I borrowed the general elements of Cornejo's scheme to explain the history of the entire network. Though the five phases that I describe below roughly coincide with chronological periods, the last three phases overlap to a great extent, and some stations have been more prompt to conform to subsequent phases than others.

Origin

The first phase goes back as far as the 1950s and ends with the inauguration of the first radio station of the network, XEZV, which began its transmissions in 1979. INI began experimenting with radio long before the installation of

51

XEVZ. As part of the Latin American trend to use radio for education and development, INI became involved with several government agencies in radio-based projects, as well as in the production of audio material for educational purposes. One of the most remarkable experiences was a short-wave station, operated by INI and the Ministry of Education from 1958 to 1963, that was part of a project for teaching the Spanish language to indigenous peoples.[3]

The fortuitous beginning of the INI network helps explain the ambiguity that has characterized the project and also clarifies some of the striking differences among stations. Rather than being a project designed by INI, the first station was planned by the *Comisión del Rio Balsas*, a rural development program of the *Secretaría de Agricultura y Recursos Hidráulicos* (Ministry of Agriculture). Since the station was going to operate in an area with a predominantly indigenous population, INI was invited to participate in the project. According to the initial proposal, INI was to provide only the land for the station's facilities and 25 percent of its monthly expenses.[4] However, since the *Comisión del Rio Balsas* was dismantled before the actual establishment of XEZV (December of 1977), the station fell into the hands of INI.[5]

The Ministry of Education and its newly created agency, the *Dirección General de Educación Indígena* (DGEI), also became involved in the project. As I mentioned earlier, DGEI's roots go back to a project on bilingual education started by INI in 1952. The DGEI has been the agency employing the most indigenous personnel in the country, and INI and its radio network have always had strong links with it. The first station was created to produce educational programs for indigenous children, a task which INI initiated in the early 1950s and has carried out through its boarding schools and bilingual extension workers (*promotores bilingües*).[6] Since INI was handing over many of its programs related to education to the DGEI precisely during the network's first phase, and the Ministry of Education provided bilingual teachers and funding for the first station, naturally conflicts over who was in charge of the stations arose.

For several years the responsibilities of each agency over the project were ambiguous, and such ambiguity contributed to a power struggle inside the stations themselves (especially in XEZV) and to the lack of clarity with respect to the project's work and goals.[7] By the early 1990s it was clearly established that the stations are owned and operated by INI and that the DGEI's participation is limited to assigning a number of teachers to work at the stations. However, local teachers still aspire to control the stations, and new conflicts in the future are not out of the question.

The project's unfolding has been dialectically driven by two competing forces. One is the institutional force, grounded in the traditional paradigm of development and INI's old, assimilationist policies. This force requires that the stations become a communication means for other development projects and follow the radio school model. The other force is the guiding ideology of a number of key actors, people directly involved in the project who have been influenced by Paulo Freire's ideas and other alternative approaches. While the former force has conceived the network as a top-down development project, the latter has envisioned it more as community or grassroots radio. These forces have been present in all phases of the project, but it is easier to distinguish them during the first phase, particularly in two documents: the proposal of the *Comisión del Rio Balsas* and the plan elaborated by members of the first working team of XEZV (*Plan de Acción Radiofónica para la Montaña de Guerrero*).

The proposal of the *Comisión del Rio Balsas* explicitly states what XEZV's initial functions were to be the following: to promote development projects, to support formal education, to change audience attitudes toward innovations, to be a medium for villagers' voices, to contribute to the integration of the villages, and to prevent the exodus to the cities.[8] In brief, the station was expected to bolster attitude change toward innovations, yet it was also expected to become a participatory medium serving ethnodevelopmentalist purposes. This latter objective, however, was a minor element in official documents. Of the six areas that the station's programming would presumably address, only one would focus on indigenous cultural expression and local values; the rest would concentrate on customary development projects, such as support for vaccination campaigns, information for increasing agricultural productivity, and the like. Note that the current emphasis on vernaculars was definitely not a priority in this document. One of the programming areas featured literacy classes and Spanish language classes, and the only bilingual personnel included for the station's staff were three announcers, one Náhuatl, one Mixteco, and one Tlapaneco.

The expectations of the planners regarding the role of indigenous personnel in the project can be inferred from the proposed budget, which stipulated the same payment for bilingual announcers as for the janitor (1,500 pesos per month). This salary was over nine times less than the director's salary, eight times less than the researcher's, and over two and a half less than each of the three disc jockeys' salaries. Bilingual announcers were not only paid as unskilled workers, but also their work was seen as ancillary. This practice was in accord with the simultaneous understanding of the role of indigenous personnel in radio projects, which was basically limited to translating and reading scripts written by ladinos.[9]

This early role for indigenous personnel in the project has much to say about INI and other government agencies as systems of domination and subordination and is paramount for my analysis on the politics of race within the network. The view of bilingual announcers held by the project's designers reveals an unequivocal racist attitude toward indigenous people. The project's tentative budget throws light upon one of the ground rules of INI's institutional practices: a shared understanding about indigenous people as belonging to a subordinated social group, a cast of servants. The monthly budget was divided into two sections: one section itemizes the salaries of ladino and mestizo personnel (director, disk jockeys, secretary, and others); the other section lists compensations for the indigenous staff (janitor and bilingual announcers).

The second force driving the unfolding of the network springs from the work of several key actors who share a particular ideology and who have constantly lobbied on behalf of this ideology. These actors are two former directors of the network and a number of graduates from schools of communications, especially XEZV's first working team which played a decisive role. Key members of the first team were alumni of the School of Communication of the *Universidad Iberoamericana* (which is part of the Mexican ivy league), a Jesuit university immersed in the problematic posed by Liberation Theology. These people thus were familiar with Paulo Freire's theses and were searching for alternative communication models. Hence, they welcomed the participation of the locals and hoped XEZV would achieve what Luis Ramiro Beltrán and others call "horizontal communication." The most influential person of the group, José Manuel Ramos Rodríguez, continues to performed a particularly important leadership role in the formulation of a vision for the network. Ramos has worked for INI for many years and in different capacities; most recently he has been running workshops for the staff. Though at times he has worked only as a consultant for the network's headquarters, his power and influence over the project have been considerable. Worth noting is his continuous lobbying on behalf of participatory policies. In Ramos's words, rather than speaking, the network should aim to let the indigenous peoples speak.[10] During the summer of 1990 Ramos directed a seminar on "participatory research" that was attended by at least one staff member from each station.

The first team prepared INI's initial plan for XEZV. In this seminal document the language favors popular participation and ethnodevelopment, but the main traits of the *Comisión del Rio Balsas* approach are still present. Though the authors review the basic concepts of horizontal communication and participatory development, they failed to indicate how these concepts were to become operative. Therefore, the general objectives set for the project deviate little from those previously specified by the *Comisión*. The plan envisioned that XEZV would become a medium for health and agricultural extension, as well as for adult education, particularly the teaching of Spanish and literacy programs. It was also hoped that XEZV would reduce the isolation of indigenous villagers by broadcasting information on national events.

On the other hand, the plan also intended for XEZV to serve as a means to bolster local participation. The station was expected to promote the revaluation of indigenous cultures and also motivate the local population to become involved in projects, and therefore, to take an active part in their own development process. How to achieve these goals, however, was at best indefinite, and despite recommendations regarding the need for local participation, the proposed role for the station's indigenous workers was quite limited. They were not part of the station's regular staff, but rather teachers paid by the Ministry of Education. They were invited to perform essentially as translators and disc jockeys, but were excluded from the managerial positions, preventing indigenous participation in most planning and decision making. With respect to audience participation, it was proposed that the station transmit avisos, air local music, and include interviews with locals in programs about art crafts.

The first team introduced a perspective that would definitely shape the project's ideology. Their plan reveals what would become a profound contradiction of the network. This contradiction is between a discourse about horizontal communication and participatory development, on the one hand, and a racist practice that leaves little room for indigenous people's actions on the other hand.

Constitution

The second or constituting phase of the network (1980-1982) was a period of growth. Within two years five more stations were installed: XENAC (Nacajuca, Tabasco) started in 1981, and XETLA (Tlaxiaco, Oaxaca), XEPUR (Cherán, Michoacán), XETAR (Guachochi, Chihuahua), and XEPET (Peto, Yucatán) began transmission in 1982. As was the case for XEZV, two of the new stations were also started as joint ventures, but eventually INI gained complete control over the projects. For XENAC, INI was associated with the state government of Tabasco and for XETLA, with the Ministry of Education. The funding for the remaining three came from a development program of the federal government.

The stated objectives for the new stations departed little from those established for XEZV. The first goal for XETLA, for example, was to become a key media component for other development projects. The station was also expected to undertake media campaigns for specific programs and to boost audience's acceptance of innovation. A second objective for XETLA was to support the Spanish literacy campaigns and adult education programs of the Ministry of Education. However, XETLA was also expected to develop a model for radio broadcasting in indigenous regions. This last, stated objective for XETLA shows both an early dissatisfaction with the radio-school model and an effort to create a distinct and precise vision for the radio network.[11]

But by 1982 the chief elements of the network's later ideology had been laid out. In an official publication, José Manuel Ramos Rodríguez and Eduardo Limón Aguirre (who was then the network's director) insisted on the need for indigenous participation and specified horizontal communication as the model for the stations. Quoting Bertold Brecht, Mario Kaplún, and Armand Mattelart among others, Ramos Rodríguez and Limón Aguirre stated that INI radio station should aspire to become a medium for the self-expression of the local people. Four specific tactics for accomplishing this goal were discussed: (1) community service (avisos), which is notably seen not only as a substitute for the telephone but also as a supernetwork of communication for isolated villagers, a network that would foster the sense of community and would confer status and priority on local events; (2) the strengthening of local cultures, particularly through broadcasting in vernaculars; (3) educational broadcasting following Freire's thesis; and (4) organized audiences. In addition, the authors stated that the INI stations' broadcasting should counteract the impact of commercial radio and what they called "other forms of cultural alienation," a reference probably to the efforts of Protestant religious sects to convert indigenous populations.[12]

Throughout the second phase, the network's ideology started to lean heavily on the assumptions of ethnodevelopment and participatory indigenismo. In Mexico, INI has been a pioneer in recognizing the need for indigenous participation in development projects, and during this second phase INI was undergoing a questioning of paradigms in which its director, Salomón Nahamad Sitón, was leading a movement advocating true indigenous participation. Again, within the network, the sense of how to achieve such participation was vague. This uncertainty contributed to the great freedom that people working at the stations enjoyed—a chaotic freedom that characterized the third phase.

Transition

The third phase, roughly from late 1982 to 1984, was basically one of struggle, confusion, and contradictory projects. The stations were operated according to what seemed best at the time to the people in charge of each station. For example, XEZV was already implementing programs with indigenous participation, XETLA was following closely the commercial model, and XETAR was attempting to become a radio school targeting both ladino and indigenous populations.[13]

Numerous conflicts arose during the early 1980s. Personal rivalries developed among the internal staff of the stations; friction between the stations and INI, especially the local CCIs (INI's coordinating centers, its local branches), became common; and political tension between some stations and the local power elites increased. As Roberto Perea de la Cabada argues, the stations became sites of struggle reflecting not only the local political strife, but also the deep changes that INI itself was undergoing at the time. In XEZV the conflict reached extreme proportions. In addition to the power struggle occurring at the station between the DGEI's teachers and INI, an intense conflict between a political movement led by progressive teachers and the state government of Guerrero was being carried out. The station was closed for over a month, and many staff members were fired. Less extreme but similar situations evolved with XEPET, XETLA, and XEPUR. In 1983, INI's director Salomón Nahamad Sitón was forced to resign. Sitón had strongly advocated indigenous participation in INI's projects, including the stations.

By the end of the third phase, most of the stations' staff members had been replaced by new people, and INI had become the sole sponsor of the network, neutralizing the strength of the DGEI's teachers.[14] By that time at the national level, the indigenous movement had achieved recognition in terms of the need for indigenous participation in INI, and INI had officially adopted an ideology of participatory indigenismo. Ironically, the stations' indigenous staff had less control during subsequent periods than in the third phase. It is important though to note that since the network is INI's only project with a large percentage of indigenous staff, the stations continue to be sites where the meaning of indigenous participation is struggled over. Likewise, the stations continue frequently to be caught in the middle of larger political struggles.[15] The most extreme case is a more recent conflict between the Chontal people and the state government of Tabasco, which resulted in the closing down of XENAC in 1989.

Rather than being related to indigenous participation in the station or to its broadcasting, this closing down was due to a larger conflict between the state governor and the Chontal people. The former appointed a very unpopular politician as director of the local CCI, and the latter, who had their own candidate for the position, decided to challenge the governor's appointment. INI's director supported the governor's decision. The Chontal people then took possession of the CCI facilities, and in August of 1989 XENAC stopped transmissions. The Chontal had contributed labor to the construction of the station's facilities and felt the station belonged to them. For a year the staff waited in limbo, hoping the conflict would be resolved and XENAC could resume broadcasting. Meanwhile, without air conditioning, the equipment was being damaged by the intense heat and humidity of the area. In September 18, 1990, the staff was terminated, and XENAC was officially closed.[16]

Consolidation

The fourth or consolidation phase, roughly between 1985-1990, was characterized by the formulation of policies, the establishment of operating guidelines, the homogenization of the stations' formats, and the centralization of control of the stations at the network's headquarters. The trend involved attempts to achieve uniformity in programming and coordination among the stations, research efforts to understand station operations and audiences, and endeavors to centralize the production of news programs.

Also during this phase the network slowly gained recognition within INI, and it was given the status of *Subsecretaría de Radio*.[17] Before this phase the network was a sort of step-child of INI. As one of the network's former directors argued: "The stations were an isolated project; they neither appear in INI's documents nor in its directory." It is important to remember that most of the funding for the installation of the first six stations came not from INI, but from a third agency, and that the salaries for some staff members (the bilingual teachers) were—and still are—paid by the Ministry of Education, through the DGEI. In addition, since INI's projects are organized around the CCIs, the autonomy that the stations have always enjoyed from their corresponding CCIs contributed to the perception that the network was not entirely a project of INI. However, with the project's new status came more funding and support for the stations and also the possibility for the network's headquarters to play a greater leadership role. This role was necessary to guarantee that the experience gained in one station could be applied in others.

The consolidation phase coincides with the emergence of national participatory policies toward indigenous populations. These new policies, established by President De la Madrid's national development plan (*Plan Nacional de Desarrollo*) were as follows: to design and implement a policy *with* indigenous peoples; to maintain their cultures and traditions; to halt the reduction of their territories; to direct training, production, and employment programs according to community resources and traditions; to extend basic service coverage; to oppose the activities of economic brokers; and to enforce individual and social rights. Thus, during this phase INI was coming to terms with the newly emerging official ideology of participatory indigenismo. For the network, this move translated into an emphasis on those cultural forms of indigenous groups that posed the least risk of political conflict (i.e., the preservation of language, music, story-telling, and other traditional practices).

The network began to be called the *Radio Cultural Indigenista*, and the emphasis on "culture" was evident in both its name and its goals. In a document written by Carlos Plascencia, a former director of the network, 11 specific objectives were set forth:

1. To be a genuine communication service for regional ethnic groups by addressing the limitations of existing information systems;
2. To support other projects initiated by INI;

3. To support the services provided by other public agencies;
4. To promote the social expression of indigenous communities;
5. To encourage the preservation of vernacular languages;
6. To further the cultural patrimony of ethnic groups by promoting artistic and intellectual production;
7. To strengthen cultural development by spreading local, regional, national, and [sic] universal values;
8. To reinforce traditional folkways based on community organization and work;
9. To bolster the use of adequate technologies for better use of natural resources;
10. To improve, without disregarding cultural characteristics, health, food, and sanitation practices; and
11. To convey information to the ethnic groups.

Notice that out of the 11 objectives, four (numbers four, five, six, and eight) focus on tradition, and four others (numbers two, three, nine, and ten) target the improvement of living conditions, but "without disregarding cultural characteristics."[18]

By the late 1980s, then, the network had drastically changed its model, its goals, and its ideological stance. It shifted from the radio school model to community-oriented radio, and from its initial attention to education and development and the tenets of the diffusion of innovations theory to ethnodevelopment, participation, and cultural pluralism. The stations were now expected to be both outlets for development programs in which traditional local practices were combined with modern expertise, and forums for the cultivation of native cultural expressions, such as language and music. In actual practice, however, much more effort has been put into the latter than into the former. The appointment of an ethnomusicologist as general manager of the only station that was started during this consolidation phase (XEVFS, Radio Margaritas) illustrates the direction of the change.

Projects promoting such things as traditional music and language offer the advantage of being politically innocent and relatively unthreatening. To some extent, this explains the network's emphasis on those practices. There is, however, another vital reason for the network's focus, the specific position that the network occupies within its mother institution. The network belongs to the budget domain targeting the promotion of cultural patrimony. Along with the network, this area includes INI's ethnographic archive and ethnographic cinema. The official who at the time probably had the most power in planning and decision-making described the network as a "living archive."[19]

Regardless of the changes, there has been continuity in the network. This continuity is manifested chiefly in the commitment to allow access to indigenous people. Access and participation were, although vaguely envisioned, the prime goals of the first team operating the first station.[20] It took almost a decade to define what type, scope, and extent of participation were feasible for the project. The type of participation that is now sought is the participation of organized groups. The type of participation that actually occurs in the network is one of the central questions of this research.

Expansion

The last phase, still in progress in the early 1990s, involves a tremendous growth, since two more stations were opened in 1990 (XEGLO-Guelatao, Oaxaca, and XEANT-Tancanhitz de Santos, San Luis Potosí), and plans for expansion envision as many as 22 new stations. In addition, the headquarters has enlarged its staff in an attempt to enhance planning activities and, I believe, to centralize decision-making. A vital concern for the network's director at the time (Carlos Plascencia) was to incorporate evaluation research into the project, so he supported several research projects, including my own research. Although there are a number of reasons for the recent expansion, the most notable is the political attractiveness of the network in terms of the federal government's *Programa Nacional de Solidaridad,* which targets indigenous populations among its chief beneficiaries. This political attractiveness was obliquely disclosed in the comments of one of the audience members whom we interviewed, a Tojolabal man who stated that Radio Margaritas belongs to the indigenous people because it was a gift from the President of the Republic to them.

The focus continues to be on "culture," and the network has been defined as INI's "cultural radio project." There is also the idea of diversifying the activities of the project. Thus XEGLO, one of the newer stations, was conceived not as a radio station per se, but as a center involving a gallery for visual arts, a music archive, and a center for photographic production (*Centro de Desarrollo y Promoción de la Cultura*). However, as I argue throughout the book, the network's initial and fundamental goal of improving the material aspect of indigenous peoples' quality of life has apparently been overshadowed by the emphasis on culture. Specific and direct efforts targeting such things as economic productivity or health conditions lag behind the efforts focusing on storytelling and regional music.

With respect to participation, during this expansion phase there has been a trend toward developing guidelines for promoting indigenous involvement in the network. The most desirable form of indigenous involvement has been defined as the participation of organized groups, and novel strategies have been implemented to promote this participation. A remarkable example was the series of workshops held before the installations of XEANT and XEGLO for determining the local communities' expectations and needs. They were organized by headquarters, and several community groups were invited to participate in them. INI officials claim that efforts like these workshops show that more advanced forms of participation have been achieved. However, other informants say that such efforts, rather than genuinely involving indigenous people in planning and decision-making processes, serve more INI's need to comply in some way with its stated, participatory policies.

The Network in the Early 1990s

In 1991 the INI network was made up of eight AM radio stations broadcasting from towns with populations of roughly 30,000 to 60,000 people. Like Margaritas City, where Radio Margaritas is located, some of these towns are the economic and political centers of their respective regions. The stations had an estimated potential audience of nearly three million indigenous people from more than 20 different ethnic groups. Figure 4.1 presents the specifications of the seven stations that made up the network at the time of my fieldwork.[21] The two stations opened in 1990 are XEGLO-Guelatao (Oaxaca) and XEANT-Tancanhitz de Santos (San Luis Potosí). The network is under the *Dirección de Promoción Cultural y Desarrollo*, which is one of INI's four areas. The basic organizational chart of the network consists of the stations and a parent structure or headquarters. The headquarters, *Oficinas Centrales de la Subdirección de Radio*, is located at INI's facilities in Mexico City. The station organizational chart is presented in Figure 4.2. What follows is a discussion of the project's cost and resources and a more detailed description of Radio Margaritas.

The Project's Cost and Resources

INI's funding for station expenses is channeled mainly through the local CCI, but the network's headquarters has a budget of its own and constantly negotiates the resources allocated to the project. The local CCI pays the staff's salary of the station in its region and also provides a monthly stipend (*ministración*) which is controlled by the station's general manager. The amount of this stipend varies according to each station's needs and resources; a chief consideration in determining the stipend is whether the station pays electric power or it is paid by the local CCI. The way in which station's needs are perceived at headquarters, however, determines the quantity and kind of resources allocated to each station.

Though I did not obtain the exact figures for the cost of the project, an informed guess will do for the purpose of this discussion. The annual cost for operating seven stations in 1989 may have been as much as $314,647 (figures are given in US dollars unless specified). This number would have included $265,384 for the stations (an average of $37,912 each) and $49,263 for the headquarters. About five-sixths of the network's total operating

FIGURE 4.1 Radio Stations of the INI Network

Station call letters	Location	Potency (in watts)	Frequency (in kilohertz)	Coverage (in square kilometers)	Vernaculars transmitted	Year started
XEZV	Tlapa, Guerrero	1,000	800	5,027	Náhuatl, Mixteco, Tlapaneco	1979
XENAC	Nacajuca, Tabasco	500	1,440	1,257	Chontal	1980 (closed in 1990)
XETLA	Tlaxiaco, Oaxaca	700	930	2,827	Mixteco, Triqui	1982
XETAR	Guachochi, Chihuahua	10,000	870	31,416	Raramuri, Odame, Huarogio	1982
XEPET	Peto, Yucatán	10,000	740	31,416	Maya	1982
XEPUR	Cherán, Michoacán	1,000	830	5,027	Purépecha	1982
XEVFS	Las Margaritas, Chiapas	4,000	1,030	20,000	Tojolabal, Tzeltal, Tzotzil, Mam	1987

FIGURE 4.2 Basic Organization Chart of the INI Radio Stations

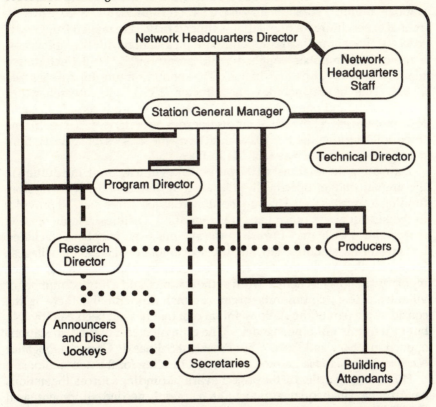

Lines linking boxes indicate lines of authority. Note that both the program director and the research director may or may not have authority over producers and other personnel; however, the program director is much more likely to have such authority.

budget is to compensate employees ($250,588).[22] Taking into account the headquarters' expenses, the total cost of running a station in 1989 was probably less than $38,000. By comparison, KAZI, the Black community radio station of East Austin, Texas, which is almost entirely run by volunteers, had an annual operating budget in 1987 of around $60,000.[23]

The headquarters may have spent roughly $50,000 in 1989. Its operating budget was about $5,263 and covered the following expenses: travel, equipment and supplies for the stations, and expenses related to the training program (payment for teachers, travel), among others. Compensation for headquarters staff was approximately $44,000 dollars, including salaries and Christmas bonuses. Monthly compensations were as follows: director ($702), three department's heads ($526 each), three coordinators ($228 each), and three secretaries ($140 each).

To operate a station may have cost as much as $37,912 in 1989. The stations' monthly stipends may have varied from $526 to $700. Thus the annual expenditure for one station's stipend may have ranged from $6,312 to $8,400. The annual staff compensations for a station with 17 employees—a rather high number—might have been around $34,073 (including a month's pay for Christmas bonus). The monthly figure for salaries was $2,621. This figure includes one director ($351), one researcher, one programmer, and one technician ($210 each); two producers ($175 each), four announcers ($123 each), four disc jockeys/secretaries ($123 each), and three building attendants ($102 each). To pay the salaries for seven stations may have cost as much as $238,511 in 1989.

Estimating the total cost of the project takes into account, in addition to the annual budget specifically allocated by INI to the network, other funding sources as well. First are the numerous resources that INI provides to the headquarters office (e.g., transportation, facilities, telephone) and that the local CCIs may furnish to the stations (e.g., telephone, facilities, housing for the station's staff, and transportation for visits to the villages). Second is the work donated to the stations by both the DGEI, which regularly assigns teachers to work at the stations, and a limited number of volunteers (e.g., community organizations). And finally, there is the considerable part of the stations' initial cost that has not been paid by INI, but by a number of other agencies. The estimated cost of the two stations opened in 1990 was $350,877, but President Salinas de Gortari's *Programa Nacional de Solidaridad* granted substantial funding for the new stations.

However, regardless of the project's various funding sources, the stations have received inadequate support. Often urgently needed equipment, such as XETAR's transmitter parts or supplies like blank audio tapes, are delayed for long periods. This is due in part to a lack of funding, and in part to bureaucratic red tape. Both network directors and station general managers complain about the lack of understanding on the part of administrators regarding the time pressure factor involved in radio broadcasting. The situation affects each station in a unique way. For instance, while XEVFS' facilities and equipment might inspire envy in many community stations in the United States, XETAR's would probably inspire pity. Coupled with frequent delays, the meager monthly stipend allocated to the stations makes it extremely difficult to perform vital tasks.

The need for adequate support, nevertheless, has seldom prevented staff members from finding ways of performing their tasks. These ways often require not only ingenuity but great generosity on the part of the staff. I found out, for example, that in some of the stations staff members regularly pay for their field trips to the villages, and that some staff members had bought their own portable recorders for field interviewing. An extreme instance of this was a formal suggestion, presented by a staff member from

XETAR and circulated among other stations: INI would buy a lot of portable recorders for the staff and then take a small monthly amount from the staff's salary to pay for the equipment. I also found that, because of the scarcity of blank tapes, producers had erased the only copy of their valuable previous productions in order to record new programs.

The major drawback regarding support is the poor compensation given to the staff. Since the best paid positions are occupied by ladinos, those who suffer the most are the mestizo and indigenous employees. Though many of the latter actually perform the tasks done by a producer, they are on the payroll as disc jockeys or even janitors. The staff's labor situation, moreover, contributes to diminish total workers gain. Mexican bureaucracy has traditionally enjoyed good labor conditions, derived from a system of tenure. The benefits obtained through the tenure (e.g., health insurance, vacations, security on the job) many times make up for low salaries. INI's employees are far from being the best paid group in the country, but they enjoy tenure benefits. It is not unusual, for instance, for tenure benefits to be a key factor among secretaries and other low-paid workers in their decisions to work or continue working for INI. Remarkably though, the status of the network's staff is *empleado de confianza*, which excludes them from tenure.

Members of the staff, especially XEVZ's workers, have repeatedly asked for better salaries and for tenure, and the administration have made some attempts to improve labor conditions. Yet my sense is that the administration is reluctant to confer tenure status on the stations' workers. Strictly speaking, the empleado de confianza status corresponds to the managerial level, and while this does not include tenure benefits, it grants other privileges like better salaries, travel expenses, and flexible schedule. However, employers in Mexico have abused this status to avoid granting tenure to workers. Ironically, the stations' staff found themselves with this status actually as part of an effort made by the administration to improve labor conditions. As empleados de confianza, the stations' workers enjoy a better situation than working on a contract basis as they had before. During my fieldwork, it was very painful to see, on the one hand, how some of the indigenous workers insisted on my being aware of this unfairness in their situation, and, on the other hand, to see the reluctance of the network's officials to redress this inequity.[24]

The consequences of the poor support for staff are numerous, especially for internal politics, but a particularly important one is the high turnover rate of station staff with its negative ramifications for training costs, experience loss, and as I argue later, indigenous participation in production processes. Since many of the indigenous employees find better employment opportunities working as bilingual teachers, there is a constant flow of skilled broadcasters up to the DGEI, and though at the DGEI they probably will not use their broadcasting skills, they will enjoy a tenured status and a better salary. A smaller group tends to go to other radio stations, mostly to those sponsored by state governments. To give the reader a more concrete idea of the INI stations, in the next section I present a description of one of the stations, XEVFS, Radio Margaritas.

XEVFS, Radio Margaritas

XEVFS, Radio Margaritas, broadcasts from Margaritas City, a small city in Southern Mexico, near the border of Guatemala. It transmits with a power of 4,000 watts, covering an area of 20,000 square kilometers, and reaches at least nine different ethnic groups. It covers 100 percent of the Tojolabal region, 66 percent of the Tzeltal, 40 percent of the Tzotzil, and 90 percent of the sierra of the state of Chiapas, where the Mam, Mocho, and Kachikel people live. It is likely that other groups, such as the Lacandón, Chuj, and Jacalteco, are also reached by the station.[25] Radio Margaritas' facilities are located about 16 blocks south and 6 blocks west of the main plaza, roughly a 40-minute walk from both the plaza and the local branch of INI, the CCI Tojolabal. XEZV, XEPUR, XETAR, XETLA, and XEPET occupy one of the buildings of the local CCI, but Radio Margaritas does not. By contrast with older CCIs which frequently have a large property with several buildings, the CCI-Tojolabal has a rather small two story building in downtown Margaritas City. Radio Margaritas' location creates logistical hardships for daily operations; for example, XEVFS lacks a telephone service when it might well share the CCI's line, as does XETAR. But these hardships are minor problems when compared to the obstacle a 40-minute walk may create for audience participation.[26] "Villagers come to Margaritas City to buy staples. Many times they pass by the CCI to arrange some affair, but the station is very far away from downtown. They don't go unless they have to," one informant told me.

The facilities for XETAR, XEPUR, and XEPET were old buildings refurnished to house the stations. Unlike the rest of the stations, Radio Margaritas has a new building that was built specifically for radio broadcasting. As shown in Figure 4.3, the building is a rectangular flat, one story construction made of brick and cement with white walls, metal window frames, and tiled and carpeted floors. In addition, there are two other small buildings; the room for the transmission equipment is next to the antenna, and a room built for one of the anniversary festivals faces the main building. The first is made in the same fashion as the main construction, and the second is constructed of wood and hay. All these buildings stand on a hill situated on a large plot surrounded by fences whose gates are closed at night.

The station's first room is a large area serving as the reception and working area for most of the staff; it has plenty of windows and six desks, some of which are shared by two employees belonging to the same ethnic group. At the first desk sits the secretary, a male Tojolabal speaker who assists visitors; in front of his desk, there are three chairs for visitors. This area also performs the function of a meeting room and is the location for the staff to meet occasionally for a chat. But they do not eat here; the indigenous members of the staff go to the wood and hay house nearby to have their lunches. One gets the impression that the station's buildings do not belong to the employees in the same relaxed way that the facilities of XEZV or XETAR do.

In spite of frequent mud in the area, XEVFS is kept spotlessly clean. "Not just because it's a radio for Indians is it going to be like a pigsty," an indigenous staff member told me, though I thought that the carpeted floor and the shiny tile can be quite intimidating to poor villagers arriving with their sandals or bare feet covered with mud. While I observed that few visitors enter further than the receptionist's desk and stay only briefly in XEVFS, in XEZV—where cleanliness standards are rather low—visitors often go into other rooms, including the broadcasting studio, and some of them even doze on the couch in the station's lobby. Space arrangements thus seem to reinforce other factors allowing/constraining indigenous participation.

The first room has access to the rest of the building, the music library, the director's office, the two restrooms, and the library. The library houses about 500 books, the best collection of useful materials that I saw in all the stations that I visited. It is a pleasant, small room with two windows, a wall with white shelves, and two desks. The ladino researcher sits at one of these, since this room serves as his office as well. The general manager's office, a small room facing the main door, has only a big desk and three chairs. The music library is a small and dark room in the center of the building, neatly organized, with a desk for the ladino program director and white shelves for the various recordings. It also acts as anteroom, and gate, for the recording studio, the editing room, and the transmission studio. The music library's door is often closed, so there is no immediate access to the broadcasting studios and the equipment. This is another unique feature of Radio Margaritas, since at other stations staff members come and go in and out of the studio and show the equipment to most visitors. Though the transmissions suffer from interruptions and noise, the priority is to make people feel that the station is open to them even at the expense of clear broadcasting. Blanca Santiago, a former producer of XETLA, explained this point nicely: "[At XETLA] we show the broadcasting facilities to all visitors and we briefly explain how the equipment works to eliminate the mysterious and the incomprehensible from technology."[27] This participatory practice is sometimes done at Radio Margaritas, but doubtless to a much lesser extent than for example at XETAR and XEZV.

FIGURE 4.3 Blueprint of Radio Margaritas

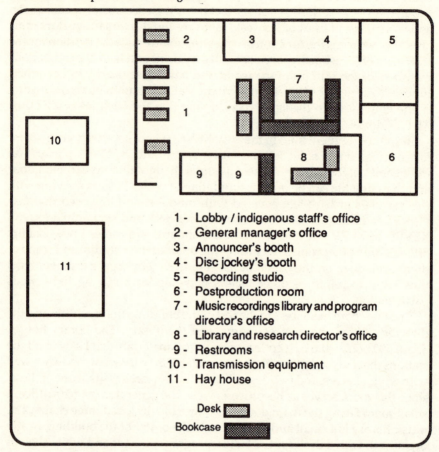

1 - Lobby / indigenous staff's office
2 - General manager's office
3 - Announcer's booth
4 - Disc jockey's booth
5 - Recording studio
6 - Postproduction room
7 - Music recordings library and program
      director's office
8 - Library and research director's office
9 - Restrooms
10 - Transmission equipment
11 - Hay house

Desk
Bookcase

The rest of Radio Margaritas' building has two medium-size rooms that
are used as the recording studio and the production room. The recording
studio has only microphones and chairs, with two interior windows to view
the editing room and the transmission studio. The production room has a
U-shaped console with a turntable, a reel-to-reel recorder, other recording
and editing equipment, and two desks. The broadcasting studio is comprised
of two small rooms which are the announcer's booth with a table, chairs, and
a microphone and the main control room with the disc jockey's U-shaped
console holding the equipment (control board, record player, tape recorder,
reel-to-reel recorder, cartridge tape player, microphone, tapes, records,
playlist). In contrast to the older stations, where most equipment and
furniture looks used (and in XETAR even the transmitter breaks frequently),
in XEVFS everything seemed to be in good condition.

Radio Margaritas, with its new building and its modern broadcasting equipment, symbolizes the recognition that the radio project gained in the late 1980s from its sponsoring institution. Also, with its precise operating procedures and its unambiguous policies, this station illustrates the everyday practices constraining indigenous participation in the radio project. And finally, with its stress on cultural revivalism and its neglect of concrete endeavors to improve the material aspects of indigenous people's quality of life, Radio Margaritas depicts the model of radio-for-development that the network envisioned during the late 1980s, its consolidation phase.

As the examination of Radio Margaritas reveals, the network has come a long way since its first station was started in 1979. In this chapter I have highlighted significant elements of the historical experience of the radio project in an effort to provide some context for the discussion of the various practices taking place inside the stations. Since these practices embody structural constraints limiting indigenous participation, it becomes crucial to understand them. In the next two chapters I talk about these practices by looking first at the network's actors, and then at the stations' programming.

Notes

1. José Manuel Ramos Rodríguez, interview by Carlos Plascencia, México City, 1989.

2. Inés Cornejo, "La Voz de la Mixteca y la Comunidad Receptora de la Mixteca Oaxaqueña," M.A. thesis, U Iberoamericana, 1990, 61-71.

3. Cornejo 62.

4. Comisión del Río Balsas, Dirección de Información y Comunicación Social, "Anteproyecto para la Instalación de una Radiodifusora en Tlapa, Guerrero," ts., internal document, n.d.

5. Instituto Nacional Indigenista, Plan de Acción Radiofónica para la Montaña de Guerrero, by Mario Chagoya Landin, Jorge Ramírez, José M. Ramos Rodríguez and Maripaz Valenzuela, ts., internal document, México, 1991, 4-5.

6. Jorge Hernández Moreno and Alba Guzmán, "Trayectoria y Proyección de la Educación Bilingüe y Bicultural en México," *México Pluricultural. De la Castellanización a la Educación Indígena Bilingüe y Bicultural*, (SEP), eds. Patricia Scalon Arlene and Juan Lezama Morfin (México: Editorial Porrúa, 1982) 86-91.

7. According to Ramos Rodríguez, the linkage with the Ministry of Education ended in 1982.

8. Comisión del Río Balsas 5.

9. See for example Alfonso Serrano Serna's article on the Ministry of Education's radiophonic system supporting educational efforts for indigenous people. Alfonso Serrano Serna, "Sistema Radifónico como Apoyo a los Programas Educativos Aplicados en el Medio Indígena," *México Pluricultural. De la Castellanización a la Educación Indígena Bilingüe y Bicultural* (SEP), eds. Patricia Scalon Arlene and Juan Lezama Morfin (México: Editorial Porrúa, 1982) 235-250.

10. Ramos Rodríguez.

11. Cornejo 64.

12. Eduardo Limón Aguirre and José Manuel Ramos Rodríguez, "Indigenismo y Radiodifusión," *México Indígena* 66, supplement, (1982): 8.

13. For information on XETAR, see for example the paper presented in 1983 by its former director. Luis Urías, "La Radio como Educación y como Conciencia Nacional," COPLADE meeting, Wachóchi, 24 March, 1983.

14. Roberto Perea de la Cabada, "El Instituto Nacional Indigenista y las Radios Indigenistas," IV Encuentro Nacional del CONEICC, Colima, March, 1986, 119-129.

15. For example according to INI officials, in 1985 the CCI located at Cherán, Michoacán, was taken over by a group of Purépechas because of a problem that originated in the commercialization of art crafts. XEPUR was closed for several weeks during this period.

16. Marta Patricia Estrada, "XENAC," unpublished essay, 1990, 1.

17. In 1990, an anthropologist, Eduardo Valenzuela, was heading this office. The *Subdirección* was part of the *Dirección de Investigación y Promoción Cultural*, headed by an ethnologist, José del Val Blanco.

18. Carlos Plascencia, "La Radiodifusión Indigenista," unpublished essay, 1986. Note that objectives number 7 and number 11 are already implied in the other objectives.

19. Eduardo Ahued, "El Archivo Etnográfico Audiovisual," *Instituto Nacional Indigenista: 40 Años*, ed. Instituto Nacional Indigenista (México: Instituto Nacional Indigenista, 1988) 544.

20. At least one of the members of the first team, José Manuel Ramos Rodríguez, has kept in contact with the project. It is my opinion that his influence has been decisive. In addition, a recent director of the network, Eduardo Valenzuela, is the brother of two women who participated in the work of the first team.

21. It should be kept in mind that my fieldwork included only six stations.

22. The rate of exchange was about 2,850 pesos per dollar at the time. My estimation of employees' compensations is probably low because I calculated Christmas bonus as the equivalent of a month's salary and this bonus actually equals 40 days' pay. Also, I did not take into account other small compensations, such as vacation pay, which employees are likely to get. There is a discrepancy in the figures for monthly salaries because I rounded numbers when doing the conversion from pesos to dollars.

23. Lucila Vargas, "KAZI, The Voice of Austin," unpublished essay, 1989, 7.

24. More than anything else, I think that the reason for my losing access to the network were my comments regarding this unfairness, which I was unable to keep from making.

25. Instituto Nacional Indigenista, ¿Se Escuchan Nuestras Voces? XEVFS, La Voz de la Frontera Sur, by Inés Cornejo and Silvia Luna, ts., internal document, México, 1991, 1.

26. In three of our audience interviews, XEVFS' listeners said that, although they have visited Margaritas City several times, they did not know where the station is located.

27. Blanca Santiago, "El Camino Andado. XETLA La Voz de la Mixteca," Memoria del 11 Seminario Taller sobre Radiodifusión en Regiones Indígenas de América Latina, Villa Hermosa, Tabasco, México, 10-15 August, 1987, 5.

5

The Network's Staff
and Other Actors

"The increasing reach and power of the large communications corporations gives new urgency to the long-standing argument about who controls them and whose interest they serve," argues Graham Murdock.[1] His point has special relevance for my inquiry because the way in which control is exercised within the INI network is a critical issue for determining the structural constraints of indigenous participation. In this chapter I describe the network's social space and its actors and their interactions, while emphasizing issues of human agency, power, and control. I begin by outlining the key positions that actors can occupy in the network, and then, to provide a sense of how actors interact with one another in their daily work and to flesh-out the discussion about the network's opportunities and constraints to indigenous participation, I describe some of the routinary activities taking place at XEVFS, Radio Margaritas. In the last section, I also comment on the workings of ideology at the everyday level by reflecting on specific work routines of the stations.

Murdock has suggested distinguishing two basic levels of control when looking at media institutions, the allocative and the operational:

> Allocative control consists of the power to define the overall goals and scope of the corporation and determine the general way it deploys its productive resources...
> Operational control, on the other hand, works at a lower level and is confined to decisions about the effective use of resources already allocated and the implementation of policies already decided upon at the allocative level. This does not mean that operational controllers have no creative elbow-room or effective choices to make. On the contrary, at the level of control over immediate production they are likely to have a good deal of autonomy. Nevertheless, their range of options is still limited by the goals of the organizations they work for and by the level of resources they have been allocated.[2]

I knew that at the network much of the allocative control is exercised by both INI officials and the headquarters director. Even so, I was concerned with the feasibility and extent of allocative control by the stations' general managers and other staff members. And because members of the indigenous staff seldom reach the managerial level, I was also particularly interested in what Murdock calls operational control. The indigenous staffers act as cultural brokers linking members of their ethnic groups to INI and other institutions of the national society. As cultural brokers they belong to a key group which might play an influential role in the politics of the country's majority-minority relations.

Stations' Staff Profile

The profile that follows is chiefly based on the information collected through the staff profile form from four stations (XEZV, XEPET, XETAR, and XEVFS); these data are complemented with information gathered through observation, interviews, and other means as well. The analysis of 71 cases indicates the following: most staff members are men (52 of 71); about two-thirds of the staffers belong to an ethnic minority (48 of 71);[3] and also about two-thirds of them are over the age of 25 years (48 of 71). Concerning education and work experience, almost half of them have less than nine years of schooling (33 of 71), and more than a third of them had been employed as domestic workers or janitors (27 of 71). Also more than a third of them had previous work experience in government agencies (35 of 71).[4] With respect to their present work at the stations and to their upward mobility, most of them occupy low-status positions (49 of 71),[5] and only about a fifth of them have climbed the occupational ladder (15 of 71). It is worth noting that only about a fifth of the indigenous staffers have reached the rewarding position of producer (10 of 48).

A central problem for the network's operations is the high turn-over rate, especially of indigenous personnel, occurring at some stations. Since labor conditions are rather poor and there is almost no upward mobility, the incentives for staying are few. Looking for job security, better benefits, and probably more autonomy in their daily work, many indigenous staff members leave the stations to work for the *Dirección General de Educación Indígena* (DGEI, Ministry of Education). Importantly though, in stations like XEZV personnel trade economic prosperity for the rewards yielded by their social positions as local celebrities. At least one person (a Raramuri) combines the best of both worlds by working for the DGEI and hosting a program for XETAR as a volunteer.

When analyzing the various actors involved in the network and their potential influence on various decision-making processes, it is crucial to keep in mind the interplay among factors such as ethnicity, place of residence, educational and other symbolic capital, and, to a lesser extent, gender. To map the network's social space and the social positions that actors can occupy in the pyramidal structure of the organization, I have heavily borrowed from Pierre Bourdieu's ideas.[6] Drawing on his work, I depict graphically the social positions that actors can occupy inside the network in Figure 5.1. The positions of the network's actors, of course, depend on the particular combination of elements and their relative weight. For example, the low prestige attached to a place of residence (e.g., the small cities where the stations are located) may be overshadowed by the high prestige attached to educational capital, as with the expertise of technical directors. A key consideration is the weight that linguistic competence in vernaculars has inside the stations. The network's social space is a distorted mirror of the broader social structure; indigenous staffers often occupy higher positions and have more social mobility inside the network than local mestizos, which is the inverse situation of what generally occurs outside the stations in the larger Mexican society.

The Staff of the Network's Headquarters

In 1987 the staff of the headquarters was composed of only four people, but in the early 1990s it was expanded to include as many as ten.[7] In addition to director, in 1989 the headquarters staff included three coordinators, three department heads, and three secretaries. None of them were indigenous people, and although all of them could be given the status of "ladinos from Mexico City," important class and gender differences existed among them. In comparison with station personnel, the staff of the headquarters enjoyed a better situation. Employees in Mexico City earn higher compensations than station personnel in analogous positions (i.e., headquarters secretary vs. station secretary, headquarters coordinator vs. station program director), and they have access to benefits unavailable at the places where stations are located, such as medical facilities and state discount stores. In fact the top position at a station, that of the general manager, is considered to be inferior to a position at the second level at the headquarters; for instance, in the early 1990s two station general managers were "promoted" to headquarters department heads. In the next section, I discuss the position of headquarters director. I limit the discussion about the staff of the headquarters to this top position because my study concentrates on station activities and also because I believe that the only person within the staff of the headquarters with real control over network affairs is the director.

Headquarters Director

The headquarters director, or *Subdirector de Radio*, occupies a position in the third level in INI's hierarchical organizational structure. The director

FIGURE 5.1 The Social Space of the INI Network

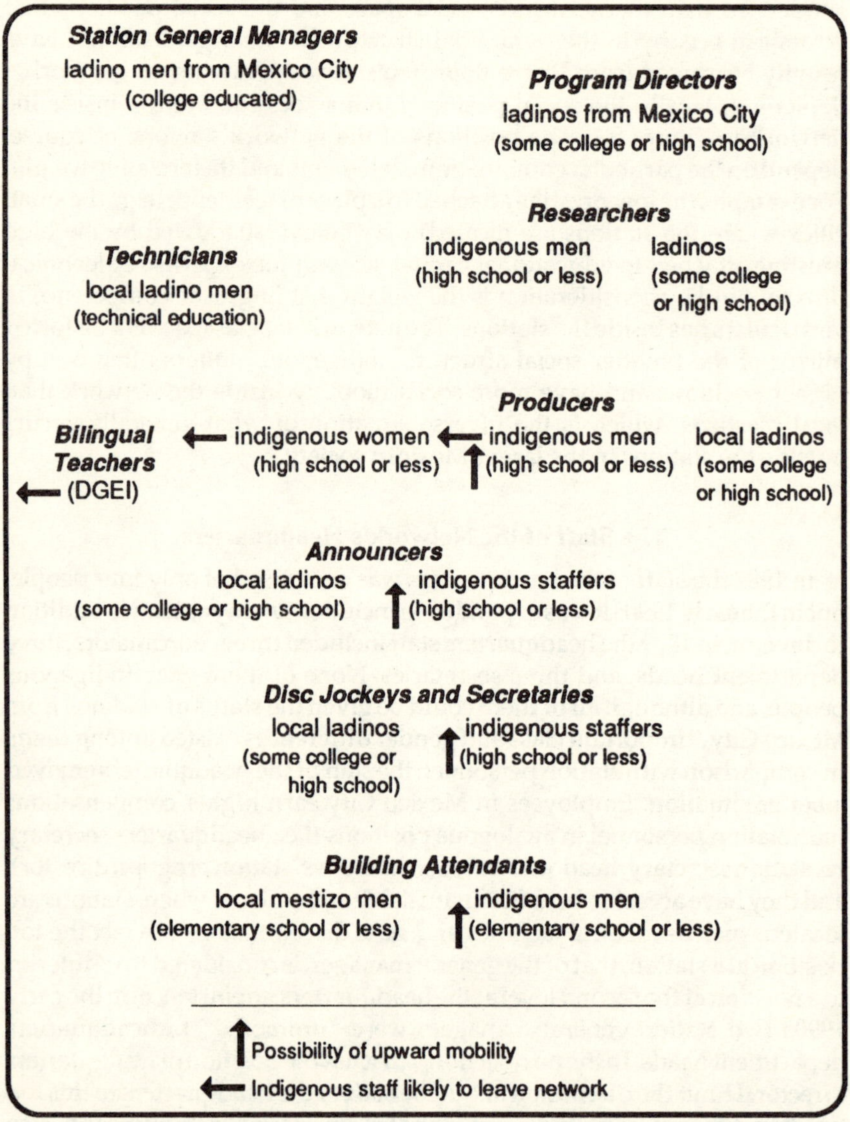

Station General Managers
ladino men from Mexico City
(college educated)

Program Directors
ladinos from Mexico City
(some college or high school)

Researchers
indigenous men   ladinos
(high school or less)   (some college
                  or high school)

Technicians
local ladino men
(technical education)

Producers
Bilingual ← indigenous women ← indigenous men   local ladinos
Teachers (high school or less) ↑(high school or less) (some college
← (DGEI)   or high school)

Announcers
local ladinos   ↑indigenous staffers
(some college or high school) (high school or less)

Disc Jockeys and Secretaries
local ladinos   ↑indigenous staffers
(some college or (high school or less)
high school)

Building Attendants
local mestizo men   ↑indigenous men
(elementary school or less) (elementary school or less)

↑ Possibility of upward mobility
← Indigenous staff likely to leave network

This chart maps the positions the stations' actors are most likely to occupy. There have been exceptions in almost every position. The vertical arrows at the left of a given group indicate the possibility of upward mobility; horizontal arrows indicate the likelihood of indigenous staff leaving the network. The words in italics refer to occupational titles. When gender or place of residence is not specified, it is assumed that the group includes men and women and people from both Mexico City and the local area, except for indigenous staffers who are, naturally, locals.

reports to the chief of the *Dirección de Promoción Cultural y Desarrollo*. But as the head of the project, he or she holds a very effective combination of allocative and operational control. It seems that with the growth of the project, the headquarters director has been gaining more allocative power. In 1990, the director was responsible for setting general policies, hiring personnel (especially station general managers), running the training program, and overseeing other headquarters' tasks, such as research, the production of a limited amount of programming, and the furnishing of supplies and equipment to the stations. Most importantly, the director acts as the liaison between the stations and their sponsor institution and leads the planning of new stations.

The director has the authority to decide on vital issues that are determined at the higher levels of INI, such as the expansion of the project or the labor conditions of station staff. Nevertheless, the director may certainly lobby on behalf of the policies that he or she would like to see implemented, and by controlling the flow of information, the director may actually limit the available options at higher levels. Because of the peculiar way in which the Mexican bureaucracy operates, the director seems to have, in some instances, more allocative control than higher officials. Based on my own experience as an insider of Mexican government institutions,[8] it appears that bureaucrats operate following a dual and apparently contradictory principle, which on the one hand establishes absolute respect for the hierarchy, but on the other hand demands respect for every actor's individual domain. Thus the headquarters director, as would station general managers, may in fact institute policies that are objectionable to his or her own boss (the head of the *Dirección de Promoción Cultural y Desarrollo*) or to other officials positioned even higher within INI's hierarchical organizational structure. The headquarters director of the early 1990s was promoted from his previous position as general manager of XEZV when the former director resigned. The former director also had a brief experience as general manager at XEPUR.

Station Staff

General Manager

A station general manager supervises the overall operation of the station at the local level and administers the station's operational budget. He or she handles personnel decisions, hires and fires employees, and negotiates staff promotions. The general manager also acts as the liaison between the station and headquarters, the local CCI, and other government agencies. In addition, he or she participates in radio work, usually producing at least a weekly program and performing as an announcer. It is important to underscore how crucial the general manager's role is as an administrator, and most of all, as a negotiator for resources. As an administrator he or she can either facilitate or hamper the staff's work, in particular can aid or restrict indigenous participation in programs, since the staff's field visits to the villages to record villagers speaking require travel expenses. His or her role as a negotiator with both the network's headquarters and the local CCI is also vital. A general manager's poor negotiating and interpersonal communication skills have in the past contributed to a station's lack of funding.

As does the headquarters director, a station general manager holds both allocative and operational control, though he or she has a much more limited range of options, and his or her allocative power operates at a lower level. The networks' organizational structure encourages the centralization of planning and decision-making processes at headquarters, but since inside the network the information flow is poor and mostly vertical, the specific combination of poor information flow, authoritarian organizational structure, and remote location may yield a higher concentration of decision-making power in the station general manager than one might expect. (Even though the network champions the idea of horizontal communication, information flows within the network are, by and large, extremely vertical. A unique channel for horizontal communication among staff members from different stations is training meetings, but these meetings are only occasionally held.)

The actual control that a general manager can exercise over his or her station depends on the combination of a number of factors. One of them is related to the station's internal politics and to the ability of the local staff to create and impose its own agenda. Closely linked to internal politics is the way in which the general manager deals with the station's organizational logistics, and also on whether or not he or she works closely with the station's program director. Another factor concerns INI's internal politics and the general manager's capacity to advance his or her own agenda by maneuvering relations with the headquarters director, with officials from the local CCI (especially with the CCI director and the CCI administrator), and with other officials at higher levels of INI. Further, the local community's perception of the general manager also determines his or her power and consequent control over the station and its impact on social change.

In accord with the prevailing racist ideology of rural Mexico, a fair-skinned, college-educated ladino male from Mexico City who belongs to elitist social networks obviously has more potential for exercising control than practically any other profile. This is one of the reasons why, with few exceptions (e.g., a Maya woman, a Mixteco man, and a Purépecha man), general managers tend to fit into such a profile. And it is one of the underlying reasons for the way in which general managers are recruited, and for the rare upward mobility from lower levels of a station to general management.

For a member of a minority ethnic group to become a successful general manager, he or she would have to overcome tremendous structural constraints on his or her actual potential to exercise control, or even just to remain in the position. It is very significant that indigenous staff members mentioned that only someone like Benito Juárez, the almost mythic Zapoteca who was President of Mexico in the 1860s, could overcome such obstacles. An extreme case throws light upon this point. XEPUR had a Purépecha as general manager for about three years; his removal from the position was probably due in part to the political turmoil taking place in the area in 1989 and in part to an apparently pervasive discontent with his administration.[9] The relationship of the Purépecha director with the local CCI director was very tense, and some staff members of XEPUR complained to me of his authoritarian management style—much as XEZV's staff members also complained to me about their former Mixteco general manager. The idea that an indigenous person cannot reach a high position without being "corrupted" by power was a common theme in my focus groups with indigenous personnel, as these comments by an indigenous staffer show:

> I have seen that our fellow people, from our race, when we reach a certain position, it happens as if we felt very big and we don't pay attention to problems any more. But when there is a ladino willing to work, it seems that things run better. If an indigenous person reaches a high position, he may be educated, but he's lacking something—a, a moral conscientization, something like saying "look, I am an indigenous person, we are indigenous people, let's struggle for our own people." But no, I bet he would look out for himself and that's it.

The Purépecha general manager expressed his desire to have had specific training for the position and his need for peer advice from other general managers. Another informant pointed out that the aristocratic director of the local CCI found it very difficult to work with "an Indian that during the day is the station general manager and at night works as a janitor in the local hospital." I thought that his ethnicity and social class prevented the Purépecha general manager from receiving peer advice because he was excluded from the social network of people holding similar positions. Actually, he had no peers. Later I realized that he could not have been more authoritarian than Radio Margaritas' general manager, or indeed more so than many other INI officials whom I encountered, and I thought that perhaps it was easier for both ladino and indigenous personnel to challenge the authoritarian management style of a Purépecha or a Mixteco than the same style of a ladino from Mexico City.

Despite the considerable obstacles to indigenous participation at the level of general management, the current situation can and should be challenged. A key element for overcoming these obstacles is the support that the station's staff needs to give to an indigenous general manager. For that support to be possible, however, the general manager would probably have to implement a democratic management style, and many members of the staff, especially indigenous personnel, would need to realize how racist stereotypes help to sustain the necessary consensus for maintaining ladino social power. In my focus groups with staff members, I inquired about the possibilities for an indigenous person to become general manager. Many staff members insisted on the need for a ladino from Mexico City to occupy the position. Their recurrent argument was that ladinos are more educated, but when I confronted them with the fact that there are many indigenous people holding college degrees, some even argued that ladinos have a mysterious and intangible "something" that indigenous people lack. "I cannot explain what it is, but they have *something* that I don't have," said a Tlapaneco staff member.

Others expressed an uneasy feeling but eloquently argued that indigenous people have been excluded from social networks of power: "How would a station general manager develop contacts, how would he connect the station with Mexico City and with other stations?" asked an indigenous staff member. An interesting contrast of opinions between indigenous staffers and ladino employees was offered by Radio Margaritas, where according to some of my informants, Tojolabals had asked INI to appoint a Tojolabal as general manager, a request that was of course denied. While several indigenous staff members agreed that the main obstacle that an indigenous general manager would face would be political (meaning especially power conflicts with the local ladino community), officials at the local CCI insisted the problem would be related to technical skills in radio broadcasting. The comment reminded me of Adolfo Colombres's argument about the way in which indigenistas have used modern technologies and the know-how accompanying them to secure their power and control over indigenous communities.[10]

In addition, the group of Tojolabal teachers whom I interviewed replied to my inquiry on the possibility of an indigenous person as general manager of XEVFS this way: "He would be crushed like a *roach*. They wouldn't allow an indigenous person to *dare* be a boss." They also pointed out that the station only reflects the general racist pattern of Mexican society: "In every place you see it, the ladinos up and the indigenous people down. Even in those institutions in which we are supposed to play an important role, like here in the DGEI, you see the same; the bosses are ladinos."

But consent is not ubiquitous at the network. Especially in XEPET, where the Mayas have a greater sense of self-esteem and considerably more participation in all spheres of the regional society than many other Mexican indigenous people, the staff even argued against ladinos from Mexico City running the station. One of the Maya producers of XEPET ridiculed the deficient cultural competence of ladinos from Mexico City who are assigned to work at the station: "They come here and spend one year getting acquainted with the area, then another year understanding what's going on here, and they're never going to learn Maya. How are they going to understand the people from the villages?"

It is only natural that staff members aspire to be promoted to general manager. To begin with, the position comes with the potential to determine the station's approach to radio broadcasting, and thus potentially to influence social change in the region, which is a key incentive for many staff members to work at the stations. The general manager may determine the specific approach to radio broadcasting taken by a station. Consider for example the extensive coverage of government activities that XEPET was doing at the time of my fieldwork and the fact that its general manager, as well as its program director, used to work for the Ministry of the Interior (*Secretaría de Gobernación*). Or consider the emphasis on cultural expressions of XEVFS and its ethnomusicologist general manager. Second, the general manager's position also confers social prestige and probably a great sense of personal empowerment. And finally, the position offers material advantages. A general manager receives twice the salary earned by a producer, and the position has flexible hours, travel expenses, and exclusive access to some of the station resources; the station's pick-up truck may become almost his or her personal vehicle (I remember that a Tojolabal announcer of XEVFS insisted the general manager personally owned the station's truck). At stations like XEZV, XEPET, and XETAR, the general manager is entitled to one of the houses of the local CCI; and he or she may on a discretionary basis use other station resources. For example, I observed that most station managers kept the station's television and video-cassette-recorder at their houses for their domestic leisure.

Another prominent issue related to the control exercised by a general manager is that since ladino control of the stations exists in the web of local politics, it is important for the general manager to operate in the local arena from a position of power. Let me illustrate this point by describing the situation in Radio Margaritas. The interactions of XEVFS with the local ladino society are almost exclusively the general manager's domain, not just because he is the station's public relations officer, but also because he is the leading reporter at XEVFS. Two extraordinary events that occurred during my stay in Margaritas City reveal how he deals with the local ladino community. The first was the visit of the Minister of Agriculture and the state governor to Margaritas City. The station dedicated almost the entire day to reporting the event, switching between broadcasts originating from the studio and remote transmission from the central plaza of the city. The general manager was the on-site reporter, and other staffers were at the station providing summaries translated into vernaculars. So, the general manager had the access that journalists often have to high-ranking officials and celebrities. Coupled with the fact that only the general manager's name is mentioned in XEVFS' broadcast, this access makes him the most important member of the local press, and certainly, an important opinion leader. Thus when acting as the station public relations person and coordinator of activities with other government agencies, he acts from a position of relative power.

The second extraordinary event was the resignation of the local *Presidente Municipal*, a result of the local political struggle among competing factions. Apparently the Presidente had had strong opposition from the CCI-Tojolabal, and the general manager was playing a part in this struggle. For instance, when the political turmoil was at its height, the general manager dedicated his weekly program (which focuses on Mexican law) to comment on municipal law and the stated responsibilities of municipal officials, especially those of the *Presidente Municipal*. Probably in an effort to secure his power, the Presidente had gone to the station a few weeks before the airing of this program, accompanied by the general of the army base at Comitán City and six other military personnel. It was a Saturday, and since I was the only ladino at the station, they naturally thought I was in charge. They entered with their bayonets, checked all rooms, took pictures, and questioned us. The intimidating purpose of the incident was evident, and the effort was successful (it was a scare for all of us present at the station). However, the outcome of the whole episode was the Presidente's resignation under public disapproval. After the resignation, the general manager aired a live interview with the new interim Presidente. These events were part of the complicated, political turmoil involving the director of the local CCI, but the point being made here is how the general manager's capacities as an influential journalist indeed play an important role in the local political arena—a role that, if played by an indigenous person, would confer symbolic power to indigenous people.

Program Director

A program director can either be the general manager's right hand person or his or her worst threat. In commercial radio, the program director is responsible for the overall programming, and he or she is also in charge of all the on-air personalities. At the INI stations, the program director or *programador* has been specifically assigned only the first function, yet depending on his or her relationship with the general manager, he or she may assume the second function as well. As his or her stated function, the program director supervises the overall programming of the station: he or she decides the schedule of programs, prepares the playlist, picks recordings, determines how often they should be played, and keeps inventories of recordings and materials such as blank tapes.

Within the limits of broad and established policies, in conjunction with the general manager the program director has control over what is actually aired by the station, and he or she has effective gate-keeping power. Take for instance something that would seem as innocent as music. The program director decides on music genres, according to his or her own assumptions about popular culture and ethnic identity, and also according to his or her own aesthetic preferences; in Radio Margaritas, for example, the program director bans popular genres such as ranchera, norteña, or tropical, but allows ladino elitist preferences such as Edith Piaf and Mozart.

The enormous operational control that the general manager and the program director can exercise together was not intended in INI's first plan for XEZV. The first team working in XEZV suggested that a board for reviewing program content and evaluating listeners' responses be created. This board would involve representatives from the local CCI, from the Ministry of Education, and from the station's staff.[11] Above and beyond all this regulation and regardless of the job description, the program director often oversees on-air personalities and may decide on matters such as on-air personnel shifts, audience monitoring, and other things. At XEPET, for instance, the program director also coordinated disc jockeys and announcers. At XEVFS, the program director was, de facto, in charge of almost everyone else.

In the network's social space, program directors are positioned one step below general managers, and more than once the program director has become the person-in-charge when the general manager either temporarily or permanently leaves the station. The people occupying this position are for the most part ladinos from Mexico City, and they are often women. They also tend to be younger than general managers and to have less educational and social capital. It is not unusual to find the general manager and the program director sharing previous work experiences. In XEPET, they had previously worked together in a supervisor-supervisee relationship, and a common arrangement is for the general manager's spouse to be the program director, despite INI's specific regulations preventing nepotism. There is a sort of symbiotic relationship between the two positions, and the extent and kind of control exercised by each of them depends on how this relationship works. If a mutually trusting relationship exists, the general manager delegates supervisory duties and is free to develop other activities that will in turn result in the greater possibility of allocative and operational control (i.e., carefully planned policies, cultivating relationships with the local CCI director). The program director expands the limits of his or her operational control and gains the possibility of effective lobbying for policies and resource allocation.

It seems that the lack of such a relationship triggers an internal power struggle within the station that negatively affects its daily operations. This can be illustrated by comparing two periods of a single station. In the early 1980s, XETAR was seen by headquarters as a station that was operating fairly well, but as soon as the aforementioned relationship ceased to exist, station operations deteriorated. By the late 1980s there was an antagonistic relationship between the general manager and the program director. The former completely relieved the latter of his responsibilities as supervisor and subsequently fired him. Months later the general manager was fired by headquarters. Analogous situations appear to have occurred in XETLA and XEZV during the 1980s.

The point that I am trying to make by discussing the relationship between the general manager and the program director is that this relationship is the axis of the potentially absolute control that a general manager can exercise in a station. Such absolute control greatly restricts indigenous participation, particularly the participation of the indigenous staff. An option would be to create democratic organizational mechanisms, such as an internal board which would allow the shared control with producers, announcers, disc jockeys, and supporting personnel.

Research Director

A position with ambiguous functions and intermediate status is the research director. In commercial radio only very large stations may have a full-time employee with this title; in the INI network, every station has this position. The research director earns as much as the program director, and depending on the relationship with the general manager, he or she may have some supervisory responsibilities as well. At XEVFS for instance, his or her work partially incorporates this role, albeit not as clearly as at XEPET. Since indigenous personnel only exceptionally reach general manager or program director positions, research director is the highest position that an indigenous person can realistically aspire to in the current structure.

A research director organizes library material and retrieves information collected during field visits to the villages. He or she is expected to conduct research directly relevant to station operation, such as audience surveys, though at most stations this activity has been limited to collaboration with projects conducted by the network headquarters' researcher. The job description also includes the coordination of field visits to the villages, but since field visits require travel expenses and the research director has no allocative control, he or she cannot really implement such a coordinating role. Hence more often than not, his or her work differs little from that of a producer.

Producers, Announcers, and Disc Jockeys

Below the management levels job titles can be very confusing. In radio in general, there is a fine line among a disc jockey, an announcer, and a producer. The specific connotation depends on the type of station and the way people see their own work. Even at the same station, people doing similar tasks may prefer to be called different titles. While some could care less about being called a disc jockey, others take offense at the term. Even so, the distinction is a reflection of different statuses, which are often reflected in salary differences. This situation is also true for INI's stations, where the salary of an announcer or disc jockey is just over two thirds of that of a producer.

Though the network's upward mobility is very low, indigenous staffers working as disc jockeys or announcers may have the opportunity to be promoted to higher positions. From the 71 cases in my staff profile survey, out of the 48 people employed as on-air personalities, 15 were recruited from lower positions. Note that all promotions occurred in either XEZV or XEPET, not surprisingly the two stations where indigenous staffers have had more control. However, once the level of a producer is reached, the odds against promotion are very high, and in stations like XETAR and XEVFS promotions seem to be a very unusual event.

Strictly speaking, a producer is expected to be a creative talent, a disc jockey is supposed to limit himself or herself to operating equipment, and an announcer is something in between. At the INI stations, the vast majority of the staff acts as on-air personalities and also operates the equipment. Many staff members also do production work of one kind or another. My data regarding job titles may not be accurate because this information is considered confidential, and also because an employee may hold the title of janitor while actually performing as an announcer or disc jockey. Even so, according to my rough estimate, at the 4 stations surveyed there were 39 employees working in some combination of producer, announcer, and/or disc jockey, but only 7 actually had the title of producer and received the corresponding pay. In addition there were 8 secretaries, most of whom acted partially as on-air personalities. Since the bulk of indigenous personnel does not reach management levels, job titles for on-air personalities are a reflection of the low status and poor monetary compensation that indigenous staff command at the stations. Regarding gender differences, I observed familiar traits: the most sophisticated equipment is operated by men, and secretaries tend to be women.

Below the management levels there is practically no room for allocative control, but as Murdock points out, people working at the level of immediate production may enjoy opportunities to make many autonomous decisions. The range of options open to on-air personalities varies greatly from one station to the next, and it is related to seniority, internal politics, and other specific structural constraints, but I found that the effective control that indigenous staffers have over production correlates with their job titles. A worker of XEVFS holding a "disc jockey" title, but actually producing his or her own series, would be amazed by the wide operational control enjoyed by an employee of XEZV doing similar work under the "producer" title, and the latter probably would be scandalized to see how little autonomy is exercised by the former.

Supporting Staff

A station's supporting staff includes a technical director and up to three secretaries; it may also include a janitor and up to two antenna watchers. Because technical directors often have a second source of income, they enjoy a very favorable labor situation. It is true that they can be called at any time when a technical problem comes up, but most of the time they work flexible hours. They tend to be local ladino men, and despite the low status associated to their place of residence, because of their technical expertise they occupy a high place in the network's social space. On the other hand, they have little control over the station's affairs because they are not involved in radio production, and so they are essentially peripheral (e.g., XEPET's technical director works as a free-lancer).

Secretaries are almost at the bottom of the payroll, next to disc jockeys and only one step above building attendants in the social space. Most of them are women, and some are local ladinos or mestizos.[12] A station usually has one or two secretaries, though XEPET had three in 1990. In addition to their normal duties as receptionists, typists, and so on, most secretaries also perform as announcers and disc jockeys. Their work concerns the broadcasting of announcements from the audience, or *avisos*; they write down/type the avisos delivered by the local population, organize them so that they will be ready to read over the air, and frequently they also participate as announcers in avisos programs. Their degree of operational control over production processes is thus limited almost exclusively to their participation in avisos programs.

Building attendants (janitors/antenna watchers) have the most unfavorable situation. They do no creative work, earn very little, and work long hours. In XEVFS, the janitor works a total of 66 hours per week (as an extreme point of contrast, consider that the XEVFS' program director works an average of 30 hours per week). Sometimes, an indigenous man takes a position as janitor hoping to combine his work with training as a disc jockey, and eventually be hired as an on-air personality. Out of the 71 cases analyzed, 5 men had taken this course. Since local mestizos have no linguistic competence in vernaculars, this possibility of upward mobility does not exist for them.

Relationships and Alliances

With respect to the patterns of staff group interaction, I should say that though there are exceptions, ethnicity is the chief overall determinant:

though there is a dynamic network of complicated relationships and changing alliances, ladinos tend to hang out with their peers, indigenous staffers with their fellow people, and the few mestizos tend to go either to one end or the other or be isolated. Interactions between groups in the two ethnic extremes are often burdened with conflict. A notable example of this during my fieldwork was XETAR, where ladinos and indigenous staffers had an openly antagonistic relationship (I noted that indigenous staffers would keep the door of the office of indigenous producers closed, and ladinos did not dare to enter).

Turning to subgroups, at stations like XEZV and XEVFS where there are several indigenous peoples represented on the staff, subgroups of indigenous personnel are formed according to language spoken. At stations like XEPUR and XEPET, where all indigenous personnel speak the same vernacular, subgroups are formed on the basis of gender and position.

Since there are few women in the personnel, I thought that women would cross the ethnicity barrier and actively interact with one another, but nothing is further from the truth. Groups are formed according to gender lines, but only within groups of similar ethnicities. At XEZV, for instance, all indigenous women make up another subgroup. Just as many indigenous men feel animosity toward ladino men, indigenous women are resentful of ladino women. The launching of radio programs targeting indigenous women provides a definite case in point. Several indigenous women expressed their resentment at the leadership role taken by ladino women in the creation of these programs. One of them said this of the meeting of indigenous women radio producers organized by the network in May 1990:

Non-indigenous women participated in the meeting much more than us because they talk more and they proposed many things. A fellow indigenous woman suggested that they should allow us to participate in the meeting, that non-indigenous women should participate less, because if it was a meeting for indigenous women radio producers, so it should be a meeting for us. There were many more proposals made by non-indigenous women than by us. I think that it was because many of us didn't talk, because we felt embarrassed. Or, I don't know, even though they gave us some minutes to participate, nobody would do it. I think that, maybe, if there had been only indigenous women, we would have been less ashamed.

An even more striking commentary was made by a second indigenous woman who told me that the station's indigenous women were discouraged by a ladino female staffer to attend a seminar on indigenous women's issues held in Mexico City: "We wanted to go, but she would tell us that people attending those seminars don't dress like we do, that people don't go to those places wearing *huaraches* [sandals]. So we didn't go. She did." Whether or not a ladino women actually made such a racist remark becomes irrelevant, the point is that indigenous women staffers believed that she thought in that way when she attended the meeting.

The Daily Routines of Radio Margaritas' Staff

To show the network's racist ideology at work, in this section I describe the daily practices of the staff of one of the stations, XEVFS, Radio Margaritas. On a typical weekday, one of the disc jockeys arrives before 5:30 a.m., turns the transmission equipment on, and the station starts broadcasting. By 6:00 a.m. the janitor and the secretary have already arrived, the station is open for business, and many people are delivering their avisos. Before 7:00 a.m. the two announcers in charge of reading the avisos are ready to start, and the researcher arrives. With the exception of the general manager and the program director, who arrive around 8:30 a.m., the rest of the staff is usually at the station by 8:00 a.m. Most employees go to lunch around 2:00 p.m., return at 4:00, and work until 6:00. Yet the program director seldom returns in the afternoon, and the general manager comes back only for a while before the station closes. Transmissions end at 6:30 p.m., but most of the time everyone but one disc jockey leaves at 6:00 p.m. On weekends, the station closes at 3:00 p.m., so the staff stays until that time.

In the morning the station has a busy environment. Most members of the staff are present, indigenous people come and go, ladinos from government institutions may arrive looking for the general manager, on-air personalities take their turns in the announcer's booth, the program and research directors work with several employees, and the general manager holds meetings in his office. In the afternoon, the station is quiet. There are few visitors, and not all members of the staff are present. It is the scheduled time for recording programs, and people work quietly in the recording studio. On weekends, a more exciting atmosphere prevails. The number of visitors delivering avisos is higher (especially on Sundays), and although few people come to attend the participatory programs scheduled, the staff is always waiting for a surprise—and also ready to have the afternoon free.

In XEVFS, except for ladinos asking specifically for the general manager, most visitors are Tojolabals wanting to air an aviso or *saludo* (greetings). Typically they sit in chairs in front of the secretary's desk while he writes down the message to broadcast. As is the case for XETLA, XEPET, and XEPUR, at XEVFS the secretary speaks the language of most visitors.[13] Visitors requesting (or rather accepting the invitation) to talk or play music over the air may arrive at any time, and whoever is available will interview them. These interviews are frequently conducted in Tojolabal and are quite unstructured. Yet interviewees do not show up very often; I observed only two interviews of this type, and my users surveys did not record any.

Audience Participation in Radio Margaritas

An indispensable activity to achieve audience participation in the INI stations is field interviewing. Even if indigenous people from the audience wish to participate in radio programs, it is difficult for many of them to visit their local stations. The staff, thereby, travels to the villages and records music, storytelling, and sometimes people's current concerns. In Radio Margaritas, however, this is a rather infrequent activity; other than on the field trips taken as part of my audience study, I did not observe any indigenous staffers going to the villages. Interviews with audience members were conducted either inside the station or during meetings (especially of indigenous organizations) held in Margaritas City and Comitán City. The monetary cost of field trips, as well as other less defined reasons, accounts for their small number. According to the books, employees should receive travel expenses when doing field trips, but the fact is that many times they do not get such payment. The money for field trips comes from the station's operational budget, which is of course a mystery to most of the staff, and they do not know how much or when they may be reimbursed. The figures for a day of travel expenses given by my informants varied between $21 and $6;[14] the variation depends on how travel expenses are defined (either as *viáticos* or as *ayudas alimenticias*). It also depends on the staffer's perception of his or her right to a reimbursement and his or her personal relationship with the general manager; I had the sense that staffers feel that asking for such reimbursement constitutes asking for a sort of personal favor from the general manager, and some opt for not doing so. Other reasons for the low number of field trips are the hardships of the fieldwork itself noted by several indigenous employees, and the fact that when one member of the staff takes a trip, other employees have to cover his or her air shifts or the traveler has to prerecord them in advance.[15]

Then how, in light of the few field visits I observed, is Radio Margaritas' sound devoted to voices from indigenous audiences? To begin with, interviews recorded in a single field visit, once edited and combined with the producer's comments and music, may supply a series for weeks. Then, on their own trips to visit their families, staffers record people from their own villages and social networks (these trips are not considered field visits, and staffers receive no reimbursement). And finally, many times staffers find their reception by villagers rewarding in itself: "This is what I like the most, when we come to the villages and the people are so nice to us," said an on-the-air personality. A significant element sustaining the prevalence of indigenous voices in the network's programming is, thereby, the dedication of the indigenous staff.

Ideology and the Everyday

A close look at the routinary activities of the INI stations discloses underground workings of the strong authoritarian strands of the network's ideology. For example, the physical neatness of Radio Margaritas corresponds to the orderly manner in which daily routines are performed, and it also reveals this station's general manager's authoritarian style. Logs are kept for the most minimal chores, strict schedules are set, and activities are meticulously organized. Initially I thought that such logs and strict records were kept for evaluating the station's performance; on second thoughts, and facing myself the management's secretive attitude toward the station's affairs, I realized these routines contributed more to the control of the station's staff than to the evaluation of the station's performance. I found a somewhat analogous situation at XEPET, while at XETAR I got the impression that daily routines were performed in a chaotic manner, and at XEZV I felt that people got an excellent job done while keeping a relaxed and not-terribly-organized ambiance.[16]

The stations' routinary activities also speak for the ethnic conflict and discrimination taking place inside of the network. A case in point is maintenance work. By contrast to other stations, Radio Margaritas and XEPET employ a man exclusively for maintenance and security.[17] At the INI stations it is not unusual for announcers and disc jockeys to do maintenance work (e.g., sweeping and mopping the floor), and probably since many of the indigenous employees have previous work as domestic workers, this does not seem to be an issue. But it was a critical issue for XETAR's ladino announcers, and indeed a high point of controversy with indigenous announcers who fail to understand ladinos' outrage at being expected to mop the floor.

But especially revealing of the prevailing racist ideology of the network are the activities of XEVFS' on-air personalities. At XEVFS, the disc jockey's role is quite limited. As a general rule, in commercial stations the tasks involved in disc jockeying may be limited to operating equipment, cueing discs, airing the songs specified by the playlist, giving the time, and making brief comments. In public and community radio, the disc jockey may have a great deal of freedom to choose the songs to be aired and may spend long periods chatting with the audience. In fact, underpaid and voluntary disc jockeys at such stations often see their work as a performance and point out how rewarding it is to be able to organize the music on the program, to have the opportunity to surprise the audience, to set listeners' moods with music, and to display creativity by blending songs and words.[18] This wide range for creativity and operational independence is absent at XEVFS, where disc jockeys' roles resemble those in commercial stations.

Differing from other INI stations, XEVFS' disc jockeys and announcers are not allowed to give their names over the air, a liberty that today only the disc jockeys of FM automated stations do not enjoy. Naturally, the restriction of this liberty is a question of control. I cannot help quoting Joseph Dominick, who in reviewing the history of radio in the United States, says:

> Odder still, announcers didn't give their own names over the air, they used code names instead. (Evidently, early station managers were afraid that announcers would develop personal followings, ask for more money, and generally become hard to handle).[19]

I should emphasize that this restriction is far from being common at other INI stations, where actually some announcers have become local celebrities. I overheard the uneasiness expressed by INI officials about the possibility of the latter announcers using their status as media celebrities to become political leaders. A brief look at the history of international communications would tell that such possibility has been indeed frequently realized in both highly industrialized and developing countries.[20]

Reflecting upon announcing routines I also spotted another manifestation of a racist and non-participatory ideology at Radio Margaritas. At this station, announcing (*locución*) specifically refers to the programming, including music and spoken word transmitted in the morning (8:00 a.m. to 12:00 p.m.), Monday through Friday. Usually four people, one for each indigenous language, act as announcers during this time. Every one has two 30-minute air shifts, and his or her job is to talk on diverse topics.

The indigenous announcers have prepared the copy for these topics in advance. They have written it in Spanish (even though the broadcast would be in vernaculars) and have presented it to the ladino research director, who checks form and content. The ladino program director keeps a record of these topics in a book which announcers sign in on every time before beginning each air shift (every 30 minutes). Once they are on the air, announcers simultaneously translate their topics from their notes written in Spanish into their vernacular languages. As far as I can tell, this strict announcing procedure is not followed at the other stations, though at XEPET announcers often read prepared notes.

The procedure has its advantages and disadvantages. On the one hand, announcers are forced to study and prepare their topics, and also they have to practice their written Spanish. Moreover, having a prepared topic keeps them from spontaneous talk which may be uninteresting or even frankly stupid (as I observed at one of the stations). On the other hand, why do they have to write in their second language something that is going to be broadcast in their mother tongue? Again, the reason seems to be more an issue of racism and control: either ladinos do not believe indigenous employees are capable of doing their work by themselves, and/or ladinos fail to trust indigenous announcers to talk freely over the air.[21]

An important aspect of the mechanisms of ladino control over the stations is the way in which indigenous employees contribute to it. I was told at Radio Margaritas that supervision is not exclusively localized at the management level, but rather joined with and dispersed among the chores of lower levels. One of the announcers is in charge of preparing the air-shift schedule and directing the meetings held to discuss topics and evaluate the announcers' performance; however, I noticed the ladino researcher is usually present at these meetings. One of the producers is responsible for dispensing equipment to the staff, though the ladino program director has the final word. And the disc jockeys are encouraged to supervise the announcers' performance. I copied some of their petty comments from the playlist: "The announcer didn't warm his voice up," "the announcer arrived at the booth three minutes late," and "the announcer was not prepared." Rather than illustrating how indigenous staff members share the control of the station, what this kind of supervision shows is how effectively indigenous staffers police each other. Far from enabling the staff's involvement in station management, these practices are part of the subtle mechanisms settling the boundaries for indigenous participation.

Production activities at the INI stations also disclose the way in which work practices are used to maintain or improve individual and group positions in the rigid structure of the network. Disc jockeying and the announcing described above are not considered production (*producción*) at INI radio, but announcing (*locución*). Although staffers do not have a common usage for the words *programa* and *producción*, the last term is most often used only to refer to a series having a script and being kept on tape. Most of the time these programs are produced by a single person. Using the word in this sense, production involves an elaborate, multi-step process: a number of preproduction tasks (writing a proposal for the series, developing a script, interviewing, and many times taking field trips to the villages), production (taping), and postproduction work (editing). These series are highly valued; they not only confer status on their authors but are often used to evaluate the overall operation of a station. "Such and such station is not operating properly; their production is minimal," was a comment that I often heard at headquarters.

Only a handful of staffers produce series. At Radio Margaritas only three indigenous employees, plus the ladino program director and the ladino research director, participate in this especially rewarded type of production. On the other hand, as usually happen in the other INI stations, except for the janitor and the technician, the entire staff at XEVFS is involved in a simpler type of production which entails neither field work nor an elaborated script. Examples of this type are the following: first, avisos and newscasts, which at XEVFS are the responsibility of a team; second, other programs produced by only one or two people (these programs are on the borderline, and getting your program to be defined as a "production" will bring you a secure compensation); and third, spots and production aids such as jingles. All of these production tasks constitute the "invisible work" that keeps the stations working but receives little recognition.

In brief, my exploration into the roles played by the network's actors and their work routines led me to believe that there is a pervasive ladino control of the radio project. However, despite this control, the stations' programs reflect an unexpected degree of indigenous participation in the network and suggest that indeed the project is helping its intended beneficiaries. In the next chapter I will examine the most salient aspects of the network's programming and will talk about the predicaments encountered by the staff when doing their work. I will highlight how radio production processes and the stations' programs display the elusive but nonetheless effective operational control exercised by some indigenous staffers.

Notes

1. Murdock talks specifically about media corporations and discusses issues of ownership and shareholding that are irrelevant to my study. However, his distinction between allocative and operational control is a useful concept for the present analysis. Graham Murdock, "Large Corporations and the Control of the Communications Industries," *Culture, Society and the Media*, ed. Michael Gurevitch, Tony Bennett, James Curran and Janet Woollacott (London: Metheun, 1982) 121.

2. Murdock acknowledges that R. Pahl and J. Winkler initially proposed this distinction 122.

3. I thought that since I included XETAR in the sample but excluded XETLA and XEPUR, my estimation of the percentage of speakers of vernaculars would be considerably skewed. Nonetheless, excluding XETAR from the sample does not significantly change the result.

4. Note that the last two variables are not mutually exclusive.

5. They are either announcers/disc jockeys or members of the supporting staff. The sample included 32 disc jockeys/announcers, 10 producers, 17 members of the supporting staff, and 12 management employees.

6. I review Pierre Bourdieu's work in Appendix 1. Pierre Bourdieu, *Distinction: A Social Critique of the Judgement of Taste*, trans. Richard Nice (Cambridge: Harvard UP, 1984).

7. The actual number has been constantly changing. In the summer of 1989, there were ten people.

8. I was a faculty member for over six years at the Universidad Nacional Autónoma de México.

9. In 1989 the leftist movement led by Cuauhtémoc Cárdenas had enormous popular support in the area, and there were rumors inside of INI of XEPUR's support for the *cardenistas*.

10. Adolfo Colombres, *La Hora del Bárbaro*, 2nd ed. (México: Premiá, 1984) 112.

11. Instituto Nacional Indigenista, "Plan de Acción Radiofónica para la Montaña

de Guerrero," by Mario Chagoya Landin, Jorge Ramírez, José M. Ramos Rodríguez and Maripaz Valenzuela, ts., internal document, México, 1991, 88.

12. The exception was XEVFS' secretary, who was a Tojolabal male.

13. At XEZV, which is often visited by Náhuatl, Mixteco, and Tlapaneco speakers, Náhuatl and Mixteco producers have to play a larger role in reception, given that neither one of the two secretaries speaks those languages. At XETAR, where the two secretaries are ladinos, Rarámuris visiting the station may have to leave their messages in their broken Spanish if none of the Rarámuri employees is present at the moment.

14. The specific amounts in pesos were 60,000, 45,000, 40,000, 30,000, and 17,000.

15. Conversely, I kept hearing from ladinos: "It is difficult for you to go to the villages because you were not raised in a village, but for indigenous people it's natural."

16. To be fair, I should say that my visit to XETAR was concurrent with an extraordinary event, the firing of the general manager. On top of this, XETAR was understaffed, and the transmitter often had to be shut down because of thunderstorms, which are common in the summer. So the high number of visitors kept employees very busy, while the weather kept them guessing.

17. At XEVFS indigenous and mestizo, but not ladino, personnel do maintenance work the day the janitor rests.

18. See for example Diana Ríos, "KUT 90.5 FM: A Case Study of Public Radio Disc Jockeys," unpublished essay, 1989; and Lucila Vargas, "KAZI, the Voice of Austin," unpublished essay, 1989.

19. Joseph R. Dominick, *The Dynamics of Mass Communication*, 3rd ed. (New York: McGraw-Hill, 1990) 183.

20. There are many examples about media personalities becoming politicians; some of the most remarkable include Evita Perón in Argentina, Julius Nyerere in Tanzania, and Ronald Reagan in the United States.

21. Fortunately, XEVFS' announcers have some opportunities to talk more freely, either when they carry out live interviews with visitors who have just arrived or when visitors do not show up for the participatory programs scheduled on weekends.

6

The Programming
of the INI Network

The INI network has a distinct format aiming for an audience defined by its ethnicity. It specifically targets the traditional sectors of the indigenous populations reached by its stations. This format offers a variety of news, music, features, and participatory programs. In a general way, the network resembles the United States public radio format; most of the morning hours are devoted to music and the afternoon hours to features. But the INI stations are restricted to daytime operation; most of them broadcast an average of 12 hours on week days and 8 hours on weekends. A typical hour is divided into two, 30-minute parts, each with a segment allotted to two or three spots.

Strictly speaking, the INI network has little to do with what is usually called network radio, which is the kind of arrangement existing between, for instance, Columbia Broadcasting System and its affiliates. A major difference is that the INI network is not an important source of content for its stations. The only programs that have been regularly furnished to the stations are soap operas produced by the federal government's *Radio Educación*. Importantly though, we should note that in the early 1990s the headquarters was trying to provide news, and that it had also made efforts to create a system of exchange for musical recordings among its stations.

Even though I found significant differences in the particular ways in which each station treats the network's format, I also found common patterns in programming. In this chapter I discuss the salient features of these patterns and provide a detailed description of the weekly programing of Radio Margaritas.

Multilingual Broadcasting

Since encouraging the preservation of vernacular languages is one of the network's objectives, the stations give prime importance to broadcasting in vernaculars. Broadcasts are divided between Spanish and at least 15 vernacular languages: Náhuatl, Mixteco, Tlapaneco, Triqui, Rarámuri, Odame, Huarogío, Maya, Purépecha, Tojolabal, Tzeltal, Tzotzil, Mam, Pame, and Tenek. The broadcasting time for each language, however, varies greatly. For instance, while Maya is the only vernacular used in XEPET, Tzotzil shares XEVFS' time with three other vernaculars. Further, the number of speakers of each language employed by the network—and thus that vernacular's variety and uses—also differs very much. Two dialects of Mixteco, for example, are spoken by both male and female speakers (Guerrero Mixteco in XEZV and Oaxaca Mixteco in XETLA), but Odame is spoken by only one male announcer in XETAR.

Multilingual broadcasting requires careful program planning which depends on the availability of human resources. In those stations like XEPUR and XEPET where there is only one ethnic group in the area, the broadcasting is limited to Spanish and that particular vernacular. But the rest of the stations face the challenge of doing multilingual broadcasting with more limited human resources. XETAR offers a noteworthy example of this point. In the summer of 1990, the station's staff was composed of 15 people, but included only five speakers of vernaculars (three Rarámuris, one Odame, and one Huarogío speakers). Furthermore, the three Rarámuris each spoke a different dialect, and there was only one Rarámuri woman. The network has a severe shortage of female speakers of vernaculars because of the relative scarcity of educated, indigenous women. The shortage of bilingual workers naturally results in an unbalanced treatment of the languages transmitted.

The network's best multilingual broadcasting is probably done by XEZV, which includes broadcasting in three vernaculars. In 1989, with the exception of two antenna watchers and the technician (Spanish monolinguals), all the staff members were participating in broadcasting. Four of them (the general manager, the programmer, a producer, and a secretary) were Spanish monolinguals; three men and two women spoke Náhuatl; three men and one women spoke Mixteco; and two men and two women spoke Tlapaneco.[1] In addition, six bilingual teachers under DGEI (two for each vernacular) were working at the station. This makeup of the staff helped make it easier for programming to be arranged so that the same languages were broadcast each hour of the day in the same sequence. The sequence was Spanish, Tlapaneco, Mixteco, and Náhuatl. The same language sequence was observed within programs, across the daily schedule and across the weekly schedule. And this logic also guided production. For example, the daily transmission of avisos followed the same sequence, and the transmission of the four versions of the news program *Resonancias* did likewise.

When and where to place broadcasting in a particular vernacular language in the station's schedule is a crucial decision. I found that among XEVFS' listeners one of the very few reasons for turning the radio off or switching stations is broadcasting in a vernacular listeners are unable to understand. Inés Cornejo also reports similar findings for XETLA.[2] Nonetheless, the network has no specific policy for programming decisions regarding multilingual broadcasting. As a result, guiding principles that have been developed in some stations are not used in others. Consider, for example, the airing of avisos. In speaking of the trial-and-error phase of XEZV, the first station (early 1980s), José Manuel Ramos Rodríguez mentions that at the time every aviso was aired in all four languages broadcast by XEZV. The staff realized that multilingual airing of the same aviso was pointless and even counterproductive when their audience research found that listeners felt very dissatisfied at having to listen to a message personally addressed to them in a language that they were unable to understand.[3] However, Radio Margaritas had yet to benefit from this lesson since at the time of my fieldwork, every aviso was still aired in three languages.[4]

What is the percentage of broadcast time in vernaculars? Even for a station in which the treatment of languages is fairly structured, it becomes almost impossible to estimate this accurately. Consider the following: songs in Spanish are often played during time slots designated for vernaculars, spots do not necessarily match the language of the framing announcement, many programs are bilingual productions, and announcers often code-switch (Spanish-vernacular) when doing their work. However, I can fairly say that with the exception of XETAR, where the percentage of broadcast time in vernaculars is considerably lower, the stations use vernaculars at least in half their transmissions. A teacher assigned to work at XEZV estimated that vernaculars are spoken during 65 percent of the station's daily broadcasting.[5]

Programming Profile

I grouped the programs aired by the stations into nine categories: (1) music programs, (2) avisos or messages from the audience, (3) programs on tradition, (4) newscasts, (5) programs on development, (6) programs for special segments of the audience, (7) programs on government institutions and Mexican law, (8) vernacular language classes and language workshops, and (9) programs produced by members of the audience. Figure 6.1 gives an idea of how a station's weekly listings might look, and Figure 6.2 provides a more accurate illustration of the programming for one of the stations, Radio Margaritas.

Music Programs

Music programs make up about two-thirds of the stations' listings. In a typical hour, an average of 5 songs are programmed, and a station may play as many as 95 songs a day. Much of the music aired by most stations is local

FIGURE 6.1 Sample Weekly Listings of the INI stations

	Monday	Tuesday	Wednesday	Thursday	Friday	Saturday	Sunday
6:00	Music *(XEVFS & XETLA*)*						
6:30	Avisos						
7:00	Series on health and agriculture				Music		Participatory program for local music
7:30							
8:00	Indigenous music						
8:30							
9:00							
9:30							
10:00	Regional / Mexican / Indigenous music				Participatory program for children		
10:30							
11:00							
11:30							
12:00	Write-in programs		*(XEPUR*)*				Week in review
12:30	Music		*(XETAR*)*			Music	
1:00	Music		*(XEVFS*)*				
1:30	Music		*(XEPET*)*				
2:00	Music						*(XEZV*)*
2:30	Avisos						
3:00	(Series on health and agriculture)						
3:30	(Programs featuring civic education)						
4:00	Music						
4:30							
5:00							
5:30	Avisos		*(XEZV*)*				
6:00		AA program		AA program			
6:30	Soap opera						

Since the stations constantly change their programming, this chart provides only an approximate idea of how the stations' listings may look. Parentheses indicate that programs are likely to be aired at certain time slots. Note that XETAR does not end transmissions early in the afternoon on weekends.
*Italics indicate newscasts regularly aired by the particular station noted in parentheses. Some of the stations' newscasts are not recorded in this chart.

indigenous performance.[6] The stations highlight this music in response to one of the network's objectives, which is to further the cultural heritage of ethnic groups by promoting their artistic and intellectual activities. But the abundance of music in the programming also results from at least three other factors: the network's ideological shift from the traditional, radio-school model to participatory radio; its growing emphasis on the traditional elements of indigenous cultures; and the fact that in contrast to features which require time-consuming production tasks, music programs are much easier to put together. One can give graphic expression to the music programing as a series of concentric circles: local productions at the center,

FIGURE 6.2 Radio Margaritas' Listings

	Monday	Tuesday	Wednesday	Thursday	Friday	Saturday	Sunday
6:00	Marimba music						
6:30	Health (2)	Agric. (1)	Health (1)	Agric. (1)	Health(2)	Agric. (1)	Wk in rev.
7:00	Avisos						
7:30	Marimba music					Women's	(Series)
8:00	Locución Tojolabal & traditional music					Children's	Traditional
8:30	Locución Tzeltal & traditional music					program	music
9:00	Locución Tzotzil & traditional music						
9:30	Locución Mam & traditional music						
10:00	Locución Tojolabal & Mexican music					Music	(Partici-
10:30	Locución Tzeltal & Mexican music					Headquart.	patory
11:00	Locución Tzotzil & Mexican music						program)
11:30	Locución Mam & Mexican music					Traditional	
12:00	Write-in (1&5)					music	
12:30	Avisos						
1:00	Newscast						INEA
1:30	Series or music (AA[5]) (AA[5])						Health (1)
2:00	Mam language classes					INI's prog.	Wk in rev.
2:30	Music (e.g., Nueva canción)				Write-in,5	Avisos	
3:00	Marimba music						
3:30					Music (4)		
4:00	Law (5)	Music	Forest (5)	Music	Forest(5)		
4:30	Series or music						
5:00	Health (2)	Women's	Health (1)	Women's	Health(2)		
5:30	Avisos						
6:00	Soap opera (5)						
6:30	Music	Agric. (1)	AA (5)	Music	Music		

Since the station constantly changes its programming, this chart provides only an approximate idea of the listings. Numbers in parentheses indicate language: (1) Tojolabal, (2) Tzeltal, (3) Tzotzil, (4) Mam, and (5) Spanish. Participatory programs on weekends may combine all languages, though Tojolabal and Spanish are most often used. Avisos programs combine all languages, except Mam, in every program. Newscasts are done in a different language every week. Women's programs include Spanish and Tzeltal.

surrounded by the music of ethnic groups from other regions, then Mexican music, and finally the Latin American *canto nuevo* and other genres.

Along with the broadcasting in vernaculars, the transmission of local musical expression has become the core of the network's strategy to revaluate ethnic groups' cultures. Even so, the portion of the music programming dedicated to traditional forms varies from one station to the next. This is probably due to the great differences among the stations' listenerships, especially to those differences related to the role played by indigenous productions in their societies, and the extent to which they have appropriated ladino genres. XEPUR, for instance, schedules local *pirecuas*

(Purépecha songs) in more than half of its weekly music programming, but XEPET only programs one hour a week for the traditional Maya music or *Mayapax*.[7] For most of XEPET's audience, the traditional Mayapax has long ceased to be part of their daily lives, but for XEPUR's Purépecha listeners, a people of musicians, pirecuas are a vital part of their everyday experiences.

The stations also dedicate between 10 and 20 percent of their music programming to Mexican ladino genres, or Mexican music. As a general rule, misogynist songs and songs about drinking are banned, but beyond these general guidelines, the limits are ill-defined. All stations include the national hits of the 1940s and 1950s (which owe their popularity to the Golden Age of Mexican Cinema) and some contemporary creations in the same genres. They may also air regional hits of the same era; XEPET, for example, regularly broadcasts *boleros*. A major discrepancy, however, exists among stations concerning more contemporary Mexican hits that are very popular with the network's audience. Genres such as contemporary *ranchera* and *norteña* music are seen by some staff members as "commercial" music, which in this context has a sense of "corrupted" or "corrupting." XEVFS and XEPUR ban these genres, while other stations do not. Both XETAR and XEPET include programs of norteña music, and XEZV was even experimenting with a rock program run by teen-age mestizo volunteers. These discrepancies chiefly result from the relation of at least three factors: the commitment that a particular station has to serving the mestizo sector, its staff's attitudes toward cultural appropriation, and judgements of musical taste.

In contrast with commercial radio where programming decisions are to a great extent based on perceived audience needs and local competition, in the INI stations these decisions are based on the staff's taste. This practice is the only explanation for those programs that feature *canto nuevo*. Canto nuevo emerged from the urban Latin American counterculture of the late 1960s and is certainly one of the favorite genres of many indigenistas, but it is entirely alien to the audience that the network caters to. While norteña music is seen by some general managers and programmers as being in bad taste, canto nuevo is considered to be in good taste. Such classification of music reveals clearly the pervasive and deeply rooted racist and classist attitudes among the ladino staff.

Music programs involve a good deal of audience participation. Villagers are encouraged to participate as both listeners and performers, though they are not expected to have a voice in programming decisions. As listeners, people become actively involved in write-in programs, where letters from the audience, or saludos (greetings) are read over the air. These letters request musical selections for friends and family. Audience requests are honored to the extent they comply with the station's programming standards; other requests are discouraged (e.g., norteña music). The write-in programs run usually around noon Monday through Friday, and at most stations they are very popular.[8] Radio Margaritas' program *Aquí les Mando mi Saludo* receives about 30 letters per day, and XEZV's *El Correo de los Amigos* about 10, remarkable numbers considering rural Mexico's low literacy rate and inadequate mail service. Importantly, these programs provide villagers with a channel for phatic communication. Keeping in touch with family and friends is especially necessary for migrant workers; among the Purépechas from Michoacán (central Mexico), for example, it is not uncommon for young men to work for long periods in places as far away from their communities as the United States. The following quote is an extract from a letter received by XEPUR, the station serving Purépechas:

> Dear announcers of the well-liked XEPUR:
> We send you this letter from the city of the big buildings that is New York, if you can be so kind with we the absents, we work in a Japanese restaurant and we don't forget the radio station's *Cultivando Amigos* [XEPUR's write-in program], we are from here, from Cherán, and well we wanted to see if you can please us with a pretty *pirecua* [Purépecha song] of the band *San Francisco*. We Jorge and Héctor are neighbors of the station. Well, we hope you can dedicate this song to the following people.[9]

The letter continues with a list of 22 names, including the name of a local band. First on the list are the names of one of the senders' wife and children. Dedicating a song over the radio, a communication practice that might be trivial in other settings, acquires a novel significance in this context. Purépechas make the best of XEPUR's write-in program using it as a means to keep in touch with their beloved ones, and at the same time, to reproduce the musical production of their people.

It is also interesting to note that these letters, as cultural texts/artifacts, evidence the existence of a collective experience shared by rural Mexican dwellers. Despite the physical distance among the senders to the various stations, most of the letters have almost exactly the same formal characteristics and often include the same words; also frequently they incorporate old popular verses in Spanish. These verses, archaic for most urban Mexicans, come from a tradition which origins go back to colonial times (probably the eighteenth century) and they constitute an old and distinct form of popular communication in rural Mexico that has found a new expression in radio.

A more active form of audience participation is achieved through the broadcasting of local musicians' performances. Practically all the indigenous music aired by the network has been recorded by the staff, either at the station's facilities or during field visits to the villages. On weekends, the stations schedule participatory programs featuring live music, and musicians from the villages come to the stations to perform and record their music. INI officials often emphasize that the network's music archive has over 16,000 musical selections. Though the exchange system among stations is far from being adequate, the stations exchange a fair amount of music to fill out programs featuring music of indigenous ethnic groups from other regions.[10]

Avisos Programs

Avisos are by far the single, most popular programs. This use of radio as a substitute for the telephone and other means of communication is a worldwide practice, and it has also certainly been a source of revenue for commercial stations serving rural and urban-rural populations. Like other community-oriented stations directed to ethnic minorities, the INI network airs avisos in vernaculars, and free of charge. People from the audience either go personally to the stations to deliver their messages, or send them through fellow villagers visiting the city where the station is located. Others use the telephone and/or the postal service to send their messages to some stations.[11] Many of the latter are temporary migrants working in places as far away as the United States.

Most INI stations air three avisos programs a day: early in the morning (between 7:00 and 8:00 a.m.), early in the afternoon (between 12:00 and 3:00 p.m.), and in the evening (between 5:00 and 6:00 p.m.). They are usually scheduled for 30 minutes; though in those stations having a high demand for the service, programs often run over the assigned time, and urgent avisos are broadcast during other programs as well. These programs feature two kinds of avisos: personal and non-personal messages, the latter including community announcements (generally from traditional indigenous authorities and community organizations), as well as institutional announcements (generally from the local CCI, other government agencies, and municipal governments).[12]

An avisos program aired on the morning edition of Radio Margaritas on November 28, 1980 is a typical example. As usual, the program was introduced first in Spanish, then in Tojolabal, Tzeltal, and Tzotzil. Avisos were divided into two categories: personal and institutional (which includes all non-personal avisos). Since most of the station's users are Tojolabals, all avisos were read first in Tojolabal, then in Tzeltal, and finally in Spanish. In all there were 38 avisos aired, and 25 of them were personal messages. This is the list of the remaining 13 non-personal avisos: six were sent by the municipal government to the general public or to specific villages, three were from organizations to their members (two by a organization of coffee growers, UNCAFESUR, and one by the local teachers' union), one was by the DGEI to a group of students, one was from a village's authorities calling for a meeting, one was from a community organization inviting the public to a festival, and the final one from a man looking for three lost horses.

The vast majority of the senders (22 of 25) and addressees (20 of 25) were men, and most personal avisos were related to travel (19 of 25).[13] For instance: "Mr. Ranulfo Campos Santis from the Colonia El Porvernir tells Caralampio López García from Santa Margarita Aguazul that he will arrive today." Most personal avisos aired over the INI stations—and probably over most radio stations providing this service—are sent to family members, though the explicit content does not always reveal this. In this program there were 11 avisos actually indicating a sender-receiver family relation, five of them involved women.

With respect to audience participation, avisos programs outnumber all other programming by far. With the exception of XEPUR (where many people visit the station to record music) and XEPET (where most of the station's few visitors want to send a saludo), it is probable that the vast majority of visitors to the INI stations are there to air an aviso. Also, in stations like XETLA and XEZV, a considerable part of the correspondence and telephone calls received are requests to air an aviso. Rather than being a service envisioned by the project's planners, avisos were imposed by the audience itself at XEZV.[14] The planners, nonetheless, were perceptive enough to understand the great importance of the service to isolated linguistic minorities. Avisos then became the most concrete form of audience participation established in the seminal document produced by the first team at XEZV, and this service is the network's objective specified first in current documents.[15]

The number of avisos aired by some of the stations is remarkable. Based on official documents, I estimated that from January to April 1989, XEZV broadcast about 5,000 distinct avisos.[16] Of these avisos 2,544 were aired in Spanish, 1,419 in Tlapaneco, 1,318 in Mixteco, and 541 in Náhuatl. The weekly average comes to 625.[17] According to my users surveys, XETAR had 291 visitors wanting to send avisos during a given week, and XEVFS had 164. However, the broadcasting of avisos is far from being such a general practice at all stations. By the early 1990s headquarters had recommended that all stations offer this service. Still, despite the efforts made, the number of avisos requested in some stations was rather low. On the week surveyed in XEPET,[18] there were only 17 people wanting to send avisos, and Teresa Niehus reported that in 1988 XENAC was airing about 5 avisos per week, and XEPUR aired none at all.[19]

The disparate number of avisos aired by different stations reveals how audience use of radio responds not only to the availability of resources, but also to audience needs. XEPUR's and XEPET's audiences enjoy far more communications means than XEZV's and XEVFS' audiences. In addition, while the latter stations are located in cities that are political and economic centers of their respective regions, the former are not. On the other hand, XETAR speaks for the case of the availability of resources. Of the 473 people visiting XETAR in a given week, 60 percent were Spanish monolinguals (most likely, ladinos). The vast majority of the avisos aired by XETAR are sent by, and addressed to, ladinos. I observed how an indigenous authority, a *Gobernador* Rarámuri, asked to send an aviso to convene a meeting of his fellow villagers. He specifically requested that the aviso be aired only in Rarámuri so that members of *Antorcha Campesina* (a national leftist political organization) would not be informed of the meeting. Yet, since none of the staff members present at the moment spoke Rarámuri, the aviso was left in Spanish, waiting for a Rarámuri speaker to read it over the air. The Gobernador Rarámuri looked frustrated, and I no longer wonder why Rarámuris, who live in remote and isolated villages, do not use XETAR's aviso service more.

Avisos are also the most concrete way that the stations support other development projects. According to its own documents, XEPET broadcast 12 avisos from development agencies in January, 1990, and 23 in April of the same year.[20] By contrast, from the 411 non-personal avisos aired by XEZV in April, 1989, at least half were sent by development agencies; the Ministry of Education alone sent 86, the rural bank 39, and the local CCI sent 14.[21] These differences have to do with a number of factors. One is again related to the availability of other media and the efforts made by a particular station to support other development agencies' projects. But perhaps the most important factor is related to local politics because the specific relations between the station general manager and other government officials (especially the local CCI director) determines to a great extent the use of the station as a telecommunication means for other development projects.

The broadcasting of avisos in vernaculars free of charge is probably the major immediate contribution by stations like XETLA, XEZV, and XEVFS to indigenous populations. This service has enabled villagers to expand and facilitate information flow in their social networks. Consider, for example, that XETLA and XEZV are used in combination with the telephone and the postal service by indigenous people working illegally in the United States to keep in-touch with their families. In Chapter 9, I discuss how the Tojolabal use this service and the importance that members of the audience ascribe to it. Here I must limit myself to pointing out that the Tojolabal are far from being unique regarding this use of radio; the broadcasting of avisos has been a widespread practice not just among people living in remote areas all over the world, but also among Third World nations' urban poor. In my previous study of this use of radio among urban-rural and rural populations in the state of Chihuahua, Mexico, I found that most avisos broadcast over a commercial AM station located at Chihuahua City concerned either health or travel.[22] Because of the shortage of medical facilities, rural dwellers travel to urban areas to meet medical needs; the reason for traveling thereby often involves health problems.

Linked to the avisos service is the fact that the telecommunications infrastructure furnished by the stations can and has been used in relief efforts for natural disasters. The way in which XEZV assisted its audiences in the devastation created by hurricane Cosme speaks for this crucial function of the stations. From June 20 to 22, 1989, the hurricane devastated the region under XEZV's coverage, destroying bridges and telephone lines and leaving Tlapa City isolated. According to Félix Dircio Melgarejo, a Náhuatl producer, because of the failure of electric power, XEZV was unable to broadcast for two days, but on June 22 at 4:00 p.m., transmissions were resumed, and the station started to air all kinds of avisos: avisos from people telling their families either that they were safe or that they needed help because their house had collapsed; announcements giving advice for sanitary prevention, such as vaccination against tetanus; and announcements asking the general public for help for the most devastated villages. The local CCI and the station became a center for relief efforts, people slept in the CCI facilities and talked about the devastation over the station's microphone, and others brought whatever they could to assist the injured.[23] Months later, I observed how both the staff and indigenous villagers were still using the station to make the best of the meager relief.

Programs on Tradition

The stations air programs featuring interviews with indigenous people who talk about their traditional festivals, music, customs, and the like. I cluster these programs under a single heading, "programs on tradition."[24] Much of the interviewing for these programs is done during the staff's field visits, in fact a chief purpose for these visits is to record interviews for these programs. I should emphasize that although these programs focus on tradition, many times the local people take the opportunity to talk about their current concerns. This type of program is best illustrated by a series produced by XEZV, *Nuestros Pueblos* (our peoples). The production uses real sound and voices and is done in the three vernaculars broadcast by XEZV.[25] The series is part of the network's revivalist crusade. A producer of *Nuestros Pueblos* described his work this way:

> Usually we deal with the foundation of the village, how it was established, when it was established, where the grandparents came from, the number of people living in the village, issues of land ownership, land tenure, traditional festivals, costumes, music, dance—it's very important to keep our dances alive because here there's no other form of diversion but the people's festivals. But many times people don't know, they don't know many things about their villages, about the grandparents.

XEZV's staff, then, gathers information about the problems of the villages, and particularly about how villagers organize themselves to deal with their problems. The recordings are made so that other villages learn not only about each village's history, but also about its current concerns. The series thus acts as a medium for sharing this kind of information with other villages. The staff members, with no training as historiographers, are actually recording oral history. They remarked upon the villagers' great need for information concerning themselves and also about the tremendous difficulties encountered in finding information about the local villages. Most importantly though, the staff highlighted the predicament confronted when villagers want the station to be their advocate:

> When we go to the villages to record, people approach us and tell us, "Look, we, we have a problem. The *presidente municipal* [ladino municipal official] came here to promise things and he hasn't fulfilled his promises. Now we would like you, at the station, well that you make public that he hasn't fulfilled his promises." So they want the radio to work as their *lawyer*, as their *interpreter*. They want the station to advocate for them [original emphasis].[26]

Through these and other programs, as well as through many other tasks in their everyday work, XEZV's indigenous staff indeed plays the role of advocate for the villages. Consider the topics discussed in two consecutive programs in the series, focusing on a Mixteco village and aired in June, 1989. The topics were the village's current problems with the municipal government, marriage customs, communal land arrangements, problems with a nearby village over property lines (a major problem within the indigenous peoples community), establishment of the village, lack of state government support for public services, lack of drinking water, the village's first *Comisariado* (indigenous local authority), changes being brought about in the village's internal government, and again, problems with the ladino municipal government.

In airing programs like *Nuestros pueblos*, XEZV acts as a crucial information source for its audience, yet the rest of the network's stations fail to do this to the same extent. XEPET, XEPUR, and XETAR air a very limited number of this type of programs, and XEVFS concentrates on elements of tradition and generally disregards current concerns. Nonetheless, as I discuss in Chapter 9, my interviewees from XEVFS' audience greatly appreciate the exchange of information among the villages fostered by the station. Rather than through newscasts, it is mainly through avisos and programs on tradition that the network meets its listeners' information needs.

Newscasts

The network airs four types of newscasts: in-house programs aired several times during the week, in-house weekend reviews, newscasts produced by headquarters, and newscasts produced by state governments.

In addition, the stations also transmit the live coverage of special events (e.g., the presidential address on the state of the union, a governor's speech). For these transmissions, the stations usually get linked to the state radio system, and only on rare occasions cover such events live. With respect to the language of the broadcast, many in-house productions are either produced or translated into vernaculars, while outside productions are aired only in Spanish.

Apparently newscasts produced by state governments fail to attract indigenous listeners because they mostly feature stories about the state government and, as several staff members said, people know these newscasts are political propaganda. Headquarters' newscasts deal with issues related to ethnic groups and their organizations, are produced in Spanish, and include notes from newspapers and stories sent by the stations. They were started in 1990 and constitute an effort to improve interconnection among the stations. Though at the time of my fieldwork it was too soon to assess their value, programs produced using the Mexico City dialect of Spanish are not expected to attract indigenous listeners.[27]

Although all the stations regularly produce a newscast with three segments (international, national, and local news), the news content and production values of these programs vary greatly from station to station. For instance, whereas XEVFS' newscasts rely entirely on newspapers and fail to include any local reporting, XEZV's news magazine *Resonancias* features mainly local reporting. XETLA's *Viernes Informativo*, XETAR's *El Reportero Serrano*, and XEPET's *Voces de mi Tierra* use both sources. What is the significance of non-local news for the station's target audience? Probably little, since most journalists agree that newsworthy events are characterized by proximity, either physical or psychological (cultural affinity). In my audience study of XEVFS, only one family mentioned that they like to know about other places. Cornejo found that XETLA's audience shows little interest in national news.[28] And Josefina Aranda and Verónica Valenzuela mention that XEZV's listeners often said, "We do not find out what's going on in other parts of the world because it's very far away and we never travel there, and that's why we don't care."[29]

The best newscasts produced by the stations combine three elements. They are in-house productions concentrating on local events, so they rely on local reporting, and include interviews with local people, using both the local dialect of Spanish and vernaculars. Second, they are the responsibility of one single producer. In the network's station organization chart, there is no news director (news comes under programming), and many people participate in the production of newscasts. However, in stations like XEPET and XEZV, only one of the producers is the person in charge of the newscast, and this has probably made possible the development of the necessary expertise. And finally, rather than being produced five times a week (and necessarily being limited to an in-brief look of non-local news gathered from the newspaper), the best newscasts are produced less frequently. A less frequent production frees the producer to perform the required time-consuming tasks of treating topics in-depth and focusing on local reporting.

Though XEPET and XETLA also produce excellent newscasts, XEZV's *Resonancias* is probably the most successful effort in covering local issues (in the focus groups held with the XEZV's staff, the program was rated second, only after avisos). *Resonancias* is produced by Ubaldo Pantoja, a local mestizo, in Spanish and broadcast on Sundays at 2:00 p.m. and Wednesdays at 5:30 p.m. Summaries of the program are translated into the three vernaculars broadcast by XEZV and aired throughout the week in the afternoon.[30]

Resonancias is an hour-long program combining 30 minutes of in-depth reportage with 30 minutes of headline news. The latter segment often follows up previous reportages and outlines future stories. The announcer's way of delivering the news is repetitive and has a slow pace and a clear enunciation, vital elements for a listenership whose first language is not Spanish. It is interesting to note that this way of speaking seems to be very popular among the rural listenership. Cornejo found that some of XETLA's listeners complained of announcers' fast speaking, and also of not understanding what announcers were talking about.[31] Their failure to understand announcers' speech may be due not just to the lack of linguistic competence on the part of indigenous listeners, but also to fast speaking on the part of the announcers.

Resonancias covers local issues, taking care to discuss problems, but also solutions that villagers have come up with. It includes a wide variety of voices and presents them in a very democratic way; both the state governor and peasants are given voice, often side-by-side. According to its producer, the program aims to be a mirror that reflects reality from the most diverse aspects, and to help members of the audience to educate others. Speaking of the difficulty of reporting on local issues within the restrictions imposed by the network regarding politics, the staff pointed out that the program has overcome the problem by giving the microphone to the people and, as Pantoja said, "by letting them be the ones who inform." In this way the station staff avoids blame if a local politician complains about a story (and keep in mind that such complaints have reached INI's highest officials more than once). "The program is basically made up of the testimonies of the peasants, of the village leaders, of the public, of government employees, of housewives who send their message in their own words and in their own voice," said the producer.

One of the *Resonancias* programs aired in the summer of 1989 provides an example of the type of issues which are ordinarily dealt with by this newscast. The issues, in their actual order, were the general hospital at Tlapa, the function of CONASUPO stores (the government agency buying and distributing staples throughout the country), the national vaccination campaign, junk food, mail service in Tlapa, the problem of paternalism in government agencies (interview with the CCI director), the new municipal library (where it is located, how it works), the general hospital (a complaint made by a lady who came by the station), migration in the region (interview with temporary migrants to the state of Sinaloa in Northern Mexico, where they live in Sinaloa, the conditions they live under while there, how they get there), alcoholism, and Holy Week in Tlapa.

During my fieldwork in Tlapa, I had the opportunity to observe the treatment of a particular story aired on *Resonancias*. The story was about a man robbed of his entire herd (36 goats and 7 cows) by masked and armed bandits. For me, the story began when three Náhuatl peasants who, after walking eight hours, arrived at the station from the village of Acotequila. Only the youngest, a nephew of the robbed man, spoke Spanish. Rather than going to their own county seat, they had come to XEZV because they knew that officials at their seat would not pay attention to their grievances. They came to the station in the hope that the staff could do something about the robbery: "I have heard on the radio in *Resonancias* that if one has any problem, one may go to the station because at the station they speak *Mexicano* [synonym for Náhuatl] and they may help you there. In *Resonancias* they always invite us to come here, they say they can help us," said the youngest man in a broken Spanish.

On their arrival at the station, everyone gathered around, Náhuatl staff members translated, and the staff held a discussion about the whole matter. They decided to run an aviso describing the animals and asking anyone who saw the animals to report to the police. After this they recorded the story. Two staff members suggested that the three men accompany them to the local *Procurador Social de La Montaña* (a justice agency recently established to help indigenous people): "We can help you with the translation, but we cannot solve your problem. You have to go there," they said. Then they accompanied the group to see the agency's chief who sent the group to another agency (*Ministerio Público*) where a formal grievance was taken. The peasants returned to their village to get the brand mark, which is required by the Ministerio. Three days later, the producer interviewed and recorded the chief of the Ministerio (about the incident in general, their procedures for handling things, etc.). The Ministerio assured him that the report had been forwarded to the police, and the producer went to the chief of police (recording the interview) who said that he had not received anything. The producer returned to the Ministerio who asked his assistant to track down the report and send it to the police. Everybody knows that the police pay no attention to these grievances, but the staff hoped to pressure public officials by airing the details of the officials' irresponsible treatment of the matter.

In the actual newscast, the producer used the incident to talk about how the region as a whole has been suffering from these kinds of robberies. The young peasant's comments were embedded in the story, so that the incident served as an illustration while still retaining its force as a particular denunciation/grievance. As the incident was being presented, formal procedures were also taught (i.e., here is what you can do, and what is likely to happen at the institutional level, the run-around, etc.). Thus the program aimed at playing an educational role by presenting the names of the institutions to be dealt with (and, without saying so, implying the unlikelihood of anything being done), and the need for documents on hand (brands) for formal grievances. Using a previously recorded speech by a local politician, the program also talked about how the source of the problem itself was tied to unemployment and poverty, and how the difficulty of prosecuting was tied to the lack of communications infrastructure. Lastly and most importantly, the program presented alternatives: the producer also interviewed a Mixteco staff member who knew about how a Mixteco village had successfully organized to deal with this kind of problem.

Sadly, the remarkable strengths of *Resonancias* are rare in many of the network's newscasts. It says much about the network that this resourceful way of doing a newscast has generally caused its producer not praise but reprimands by headquarters. Since events happening close to people's lives concern them the most, reporting local news has proved to be the most challenging to produce. Although several elements account for the challenge posed by newscasts, the network's sponsorship poses a major dilemma. As a government institution in a country that has been described as a one-party democracy, INI occupies a very sui generis and contradictory position: it is an institution of the ruling political elite, but at the same time it is supposed to be the advocate of a social sector that suffers the most from the oppression imposed by precisely this elite. The network thus faces contradictory demands from different social subjects. On the one hand, the ruling political elite expects the stations to work for the preservation of the status quo, and on the other hand, the indigenous audience and many staff members believe the stations should support indigenous resistance efforts. Thus, while network officials often complain of pressures from politicians to favor openly certain policies and actions, distressed staff members comment how they are torn when against their journalistic ethic and their emotional loyalties, they have to remain silent. "We keep our mouth shut and still the rich ranchers say that we're a bunch of communists," said one staff member of XEZV. Even for the most savvy newscaster, true reporting becomes a nightmare when local politicians steal the election, as was the case in XEPUR in 1989.

The network's policy regarding hard news on critical political events has been to accommodate the ruling class' expectations, but nonetheless, a very real struggle between the two tendencies takes place within the institution. An extraordinary event, the case of XETAR during the 1987 gubernatorial election illustrates how in the last instance the stations support the status quo. For the first time in the history of the state of Chihuahua, the gubernatorial candidate of the official party (*Partido Revolucionario Institucional*, PRI) was at risk of losing the election. As a general rule, the INI stations do not air political spots, but it just so happened that XETAR had not been transmitting for several weeks because its transmitter was broken, and the PRI candidate got the transmitter fixed, responding of course to a request from the local ladino population. Hence XETAR broadcast political spots supporting his candidacy.

The accommodation to the ruling class' expectations, however, generally takes the form of embracing the self-censorship strategy of mainstream Mexican media, which involves limited and selective coverage of local events and reliance on uncontroversial sources (established news agencies) for non-local news. At the end of 1990, the network began to subscribe to NOTIMEX, the Mexican wire service. This innovation has effectively minimized the stations' pervasive problem regarding timely access to non-local news, yet my sense is that the reason for the innovation relates more to politics because it in effect demotes and discourages the coverage of local events.

Newscasts also present other types of challenges. Like all programs focusing on local issues, newscasts pose problems related to the internal control of the stations. Since broadcast journalists tend to develop a very emphatic and personal relationship with their audiences, staff members can turn into local celebrities, and this can put the station's delicate power structure in jeopardy. Take, for example, the acquiescent behavior of XEVFS' staff and this station's poor coverage of local public affairs. Then compare XEVFS' reporting style to the defiant attitude of XEZV's staff and the latter station's emphasis on local investigative reporting. Moreover, consider the power struggle between XETLA's acting general manager and a popular producer, which resulted in the resignation of the latter and the cessation of an extremely successful series involving grassroots participation (*El Camino Andado*, which I discuss below). Though numerous other factors (e.g., gender, ethnicity, and seniority) account for the intricacies of the interpersonal relations inside the network, the threat posed to the established hierarchy by the possibility that staff members become local celebrities unquestionably shapes the coverage of local events, and it also shapes the kind of grassroots participation that is achieved in programs.

Radio Margaritas' Newscasts. Perhaps nothing is more poorly done at Radio Margaritas than newscasts. The station produces two news programs; one is aired on week days, and the other on Sundays (see Figure 6.2). The format of both programs is the same: news items are read by one person, according to an order that goes from regional to international news, passing through state and national news. The main news sources used are newspapers, although the station was connected to NOTIMEX in November 1990. Since there is very little reporting done at XEVFS, the source of regional news is limited to local newspapers and the few news items provided by the station's visitors. Sunday's program is a week-in-review produced only in Spanish. The only newscast accessible to those without linguistic competence in Spanish is the daily 30-minute program, which is a bilingual production. However, the vernacular of this program changes every week; for instance, one week it is Tojolabal, the next week Tzeltal, then Tzotzil, and finally Spanish (the program is not produced in Mam, the fourth vernacular broadcast by the station). This curious way of broadcasting news favors speakers of Spanish and does not serve monolinguals of vernaculars very well. Tojolabal monolingual women, for instance, only understand the news broadcast during one week of the month. So, the segment of the audience that has little or no access to other news media is in fact the least served by XEVFS' newscasts.

Mary Jill Brody, an anthropologist who has conducted research on the Tojolabal language, pointed out to me the linguistic difficulties involved in producing newscasts in indigenous languages, like Tojolabal, using news sources in Spanish.[32] Brody says that these sources pose a real challenge for translation, not just because of the inherent difficulties faced by the Tojolabal staff, whose competence in Spanish is rather low, but also because the news items from Mexican newspapers and wire services contain many acronyms and also numerous words for which there is not a concept in the Tojolabal language. These news items often pertain to the coverage of the activities of the government and political institutions of the Spanish-speaking society. How does the announcer say, for example, *"Tribunal Supremo de Justicia"* (Supreme Court) or *"enmienda constitucional"* (constitutional amendment) in Tojolabal?

Programs on Development

By "programs on development" I mean all those programs whose content aims at making an immediate contribution to the improvement of living conditions and economic productivity. These include series on health and agriculture as well as spots on the same topics. The stations air both in-house and external productions on these topics.

External productions are either full programs or shorter segments developed and supplied free-of-charge by government agencies (mostly from the federal government). They usually have high production standards and uniformity of sound—resembling somewhat the BBC style—but they lack the local appeal and flexibility of in-house productions and are done only in Spanish. In the focus groups with indigenous staff, most of this programming was rated rather negatively. XEVFS' listeners interviewed did not even mention it, and Cornejo found some evidence of audience's dissatisfaction with it.

This programming may be divided into three categories: soap operas (*radio novelas*), spots, and other programs. Soap operas are done by Radio Educación, cater to a rural non-indigenous female listenership, and often deal with family planning. Since a soap opera frequently has over a hundred (30-minute) programs, soap operas run for weeks. Spots are short recordings featuring either announcements on specific campaigns or short talks on issues such as vaccination or history. They are provided by the Ministries of Education (especially through the DGEI) and of Health, as well as by other federal and state agencies. Other external productions involve the programming done by the DGEI, the *Instituto Nacional para la Educación de los Adultos, Radio Educación,* and the *Instituto Mexicano de la Radio* (some of the programs made by the latter agency have been coproduced with INI[33]). Most of this programming is series dealing with history and literature; many of them are designed as pedagogic support for bilingual teachers and literacy campaigns.

Turning to in-house productions, given that the network is a development project I expected the stations to dedicate great resources to this kind of programming, but most of the stations have paid strikingly poor attention to these programs. According to Cornejo, only three percent of XETLA's broadcasting time involves these programs.[34] I estimate that the figure for XEPUR and XEVFS is less than seven percent, for XEPET less than two percent, and for XETAR zero. Even if one takes into account that in some stations development issues are also dealt with in programs not specifically targeting health and agriculture problems, the percentages are still quite low.

I hardly need to point out that the people served by the network have an urgent need for this kind of programming. If their overwhelmingly poor living conditions were not enough evidence of this need, I can easily find voices from the audience asking specifically for programs on development. I found these voices in our audience study on XEVFS (see Chapter 10), and also found them in the network's documents. For example, in the internal diagnostic study carried on by headquarters in 1988, stations like XEPET, XETAR, and XETLA stated that villagers had requested programs on issues such as agribusiness, health, vegetable gardens, and control of forest fires.[35] And a more instructive example is a paper presented by a peasant leader at the symposium organized by XEZV in October, 1989. The paper's author was explicitly requesting two types of programs: one on land tenancy law and farmers' legal rights and another on agricultural development.[36]

Why has the network failed to produce more programs on development? One reason is that producing these programs is a laborious and demanding task. Another crucial reason has to do with the staff's disheartened and well founded feeling that information by itself will hardly solve any problem when what is needed are resources. "I tell the ladies over the microphone to boil the water, but I know they're not going to do it, because they have no fuel, they have no wood," a female producer told me. But a further reason concerns the network's governing ideology and its emphasis on cultural revival. I am inclined to believe that many programming decisions respond to a crusade for cultural revival that often disregards the everyday survival of the people creating indigenous cultures.

XEPUR, XEVFS, XETLA, and to a limited extent, XEPET produce series on agriculture and on health. Most of these are produced in vernaculars. Since XEPUR and XEPET broadcast only in one vernacular, they produce only one series on each topic. XEVFS, however, produces one series on each topic for Tojolabal speakers, plus another series on health for Tzeltal speakers (I give more detailed information on these series on Chapter 10). XETLA produces a series on health for Mixteco, Triqui, and Spanish speakers, and a second series on agriculture only for Spanish speakers. The series are the responsibility of a single producer, who generally does a 20 or 30-minute program once a week. The same program is transmitted two, three, of even four times during the week, usually in the early morning and in the afternoon. The content combines modern technical expertise with traditional native practices, and the format is chiefly based on interviews. For example on a health series both medical doctors and traditional healers are interviewed.

XEZV is once again the exception. It pays more attention to development problems, and it treats these issues in a more holistic fashion. It broadcasts a series on indigenous medicine three times a week, but instead of retransmitting the same program, each program is produced in a different language. Thus the series attempts to reach all the ethnic groups targeted by the station. Health issues are also systematically addressed on women's programs, and all development issues often appear in programs dedicated to folk ways such as *Nuestros Pueblos*. In addition, this station also conducts specific campaigns that, though more often involving only spots, have also included series.

One of these campaigns targeted the diffusion of information on the African or killer bee. In 1987-1988 the staff produced spots in vernaculars and a special series of 10 programs in Spanish called *La Guerra de las Abejas* (the war of the bees). According to XEZV staffers, the series was quite successful, and because of popular demand, the station retransmitted it twice. Furthermore, INI placed the series on commercial stations. The series had three main characters: Don Quirino who like many of the local villagers keeps bees for honey production on a small scale, his son, and an apiarist with modern expertise from Tlapa's CCI. The plot starts with Don Quirino listening to a program on the killer bee aired by XEZV and his subsequent discussion of the program's content with his son and his friend. After this the group goes to Tlapa's CCI for more information and to arrange a meeting at the village with the CCI's apiarist. Later, father and son invite villagers to the meeting, pass on what they have learned about the killer bee, and propose forming a committee to deal with the problem.

Unfortunately, this type of series is more the exception than the rule at INI stations. And unfortunately as well, only XEZV and to a lesser extent XEPET regularly produce spots targeting development problems.[37] In the summer of 1989, XEZV's list of active spots included 40 in Spanish, 17 in Náhuatl, 19 in Mixteco, and 16 in Tlapaneco. In contrast to the rest of the network's stations, many of XEZV's and XEPET's spots in vernaculars address development issues. The spots in vernaculars aired by other stations were only jingles, station identifications, and promotional announcements for the station's programs. Moreover, although all stations transmit the spots supplied by government agencies, most fail to translate the content into a format and language suitable for their audiences.

I mentioned before that at some stations development problems are also addressed in programs not specifically targeting development issues. I discuss these program in the next two programming categories, programs for special segments of the audience and programs on government institutions and Mexican law.

Programs for Special Segments of the Audience

The network broadcasts some programming for two special segments of the audience, children and women. Women's programming has received much more attention than children's programming, which is basically limited to live entertainment programs featuring children's songs and involving the participation of local (mostly ladino and mestizo) children. Children's programs are often conducted in Spanish and broadcast either on Saturday or Sunday morning. Stations like XEPET also air short programs featuring short stories and lullabies.

Women's programs are a more serious matter. In the last few years, expanding these programs has become a vital concern, and the network organized a special meeting of women producers for this purpose (May, 1990). However, only XEZV has actually produced a woman's program for several years. *Nosotras las Mujeres* (we women) is produced by the indigenous and ladino women working at XEZV. It is broadcast in the morning (10:30 to 12:00), Monday through Friday and is divided into three half-hour parts, one for each vernacular. Each day is dedicated to a given topic: indigenous medicine, food, health, organization, or vegetable gardens. With the exception of a special, pre-recorded section on medicine, the program is a live production. The host usually combines information and commentaries with music and short (pre-recorded or live) interviews in which folk practices are discussed with local women. According to one of the producers, the program's purpose is "to change the conception of women about themselves because women don't see themselves as human beings; they don't believe they are capable of doing things by themselves when actually they do many things all the time." The program also attempts to voice indigenous women's concerns, though engaging the participation of these women has proved to be a great challenge: "Most of the ladies are afraid of the microphone, they don't want to participate," said one of the producers.

XEZV's program illustrates a successful attempt to coordinate a station's efforts with other government projects. It has played an important role in encouraging and assisting women in creating organizations (ranging in size from 12 to 60 women). There has been a trend in government policy, and more recently in network policy, to support grassroots organizations rather than individuals; though for an organization to be legal, certain formal requirements have to be satisfied. The first is to establish legally the organization and a directorate by holding a meeting with local authorities and taking minutes at the meeting. All requests for funding or services require documents. Since most indigenous women in the region are neither literate, nor fluent in Spanish, these formalities are an unsurmountable obstacle to getting support. On the radio program, producers talk about the alternatives that women from the villages—often illiterate and monoglot— have in overcoming these obstacles. Customarily XEZV's staffers help villagers with the writing of documents and orient them on how to deal with the institutions of the dominant society. The program has tried to encourage more women to make the best of this assistance.

In 1987, the radio program promoted women's organizations with a project supporting vegetable gardens. Small packages of seeds were provided free to groups of women. The program's producers visited several villages and recorded the experiences of a number of groups that relied on these seeds for growing vegetables. The recordings were used later in subsequent programs. Although the station lacked resources for following up on all the groups that requested seeds, as a result of this project two remarkable developments took place. One was the formalizing of an already existing women's organization in Xochapa, Alcozauca; the other was the creation of a new organization in Crucero de Oztocingo, Copanatoyac.

The organization in Xochapa originated mostly as a group of old widows. They requested that the station's staff help them obtain fertilizer from one of the government agencies. According to the staff of the station, in 1989 this organization was the only group of women in the region working with the rural bank (BANRURAL). The women from Crucero de Oztocingo, working closely with a village teacher and one of the program's hosts, successfully set up a pig raising project. For their project, they got suckling pigs from the

Secretaría del Desarrollo Rural and other necessary items (pig food, veterinary equipment, and medicines, as well as construction materials) from INI. The producers told me that they did not believe that the women have become organized as a result of the broadcast, but rather that they are using indigenous forms of organization in combination with the services provided by the station. One of the producers said, "We're not organizing the ladies through the radio; they are already organized. But they do not know it. They are very organized for the collective work in the villages, and especially for the festivals. We only tell them how they can use their own ways of organization to make the best of government programs."

The network's headquarters has promoted the production of similar women's programs in other stations. For example XEVFS has been airing its own program since 1990. However, it is unlikely that other stations will achieve the success of XEZV's program in the near future. The main reason is that the only station in which members of the staff customarily act as cultural brokers for the people being served is XEZV. Reaching more women through *Nosotras las Mujeres* has been only an enhancement of this cultural brokerage service.

Programs on Government Institutions and Mexican Law

At least two of the stations (XEZV and XEVFS) air a weekly 30-minute program on government institutions and Mexican law. These programs are produced by the general manager who discusses issues relating to agrarian reform, human rights, social organization, and the like. The host may read and comment on laws and regulations or may interview local politicians and officials from government agencies. These programs are broadcast only in Spanish and probably fail to reach the vast majority of the network's target audience. This situation is unfortunate since in the last few years INI has carried out an outstanding effort to assist indigenous peoples with the numerous problems arising from their inability to deal with the national legal system. Most CCIs now include a bilingual lawyer on their staffs.

I would expect that INI would take advantage of the stations to bolster its efforts and that the stations would diligently disseminate information about the legal system in vernaculars. I would also expect the stations to work with this type of problem since it is exactly the type of problem that radio is best suited to solve. One of the important lessons derived from the international experience on the use of radio for development is that radio projects are often ill-suited to solve the typical problems of developing regions because the solution to such problems frequently demands resources that radio projects cannot provide like land, credit, and health care facilities. However, development communicators have also learned that radio can indeed assist with those problems whose solutions lie in the dissemination of specific knowledges, such as the statutes and workings of a legal system.

The present programs on Mexican laws and public institutions are quite important. In the focus groups conducted with the indigenous staff of XEZV and XEVFS, the present programs produced by these stations' general managers were given a high rating. The reason is not difficult to understand because the position of general manager is in many ways a political post. Since one of the network's objectives is to be a medium to diffuse information about government agencies, stations are compelled to collaborate with local politicians and federal and state agency heads. These programs give the general manager some power to deal with local dignitaries, a power that may be vital for the attainment of the station's goals. In the web of complex negotiations between local dignitaries and the station's general manager, the latter has the power to hold the former accountable over the airwaves. It was no coincidence that XEVFS' general manager was discussing in his program the legal duties of a *Presidente Municipal* (county head) precisely one week before the firing of the local *Presidente*.[38]

Vernacular Language Classes and Workshops

During the first phases of the network, the spread of the Spanish language constituted a prominent objective of the network. With the advent of ethnodevelopmentalist and participatory policies, the emphasis on Spanish language was replaced by a focus on vernaculars. Hence, more recently the programming has included language classes and workshops whose purpose is to counteract the influence of Spanish on vernaculars. During my fieldwork only XEVFS was airing language classes. There were five hours a week of classes in Mam, a Maya language which has been declining among Mayas living on Mexican soil.

Language classes on vernaculars showing clear signs of decline and extinction are a controversial issue in the network. While XEVFS' general manager believes these classes should receive more support, the network's highest official sees them as "futile efforts to save the California condor." What do the speakers of these vernaculars think about this? My audience study, as well as Cornejo's research, failed to include speakers of Mam, but it is fair to say that badly done radio classes on a declining language probably attract few listeners.

Indigenous peoples are struggling for two issues regarding language. One concerns a political movement to give vernaculars the status of official languages, and the other is a popular demand for learning Spanish, the language of opportunity. For example, a group of researchers working on a literacy campaign targeting monolingual speakers of Náhuatl in the state of Puebla in the early 1990s found that these people, rather than wanting to learn more about Náhuatl, demanded the teaching of Spanish. As happens with the vast majority of indigenous people, extreme poverty forces them to complement their income with temporary migration and thus they have an urgent need to learn Spanish.[39] Aranda and Valenzuela found the same reaction among XEZV's audience.[40] At the beginning of my fieldwork, I was astonished at indigenous staff members' requests to help them learn English.

Productions by Organized Groups from the Audience

The network's ultimate goal is to include in its programming a large number of programs produced by grassroots organizations. Aside from numerous plans and a handful of programs that have actually been on the air, the only grassroots organization regularly broadcasting programs on the stations is *Alcohólicos Anónimos* (Alcoholics Anonymous).[41] The six stations that I examined were airing talk programs produced by the local chapter of AA. The programs are usually produced in Spanish and cater to an urban and urban-rural male audience. They are aired once a week, last between 15 and 30 minutes, and are produced at the station's facilities with the technical assistance of a disc jockey. The participants, most of them working class mestizos, talk about their personal experiences regarding alcoholism, their struggle to quit drinking, and the support they have received from the organization. They also explain how the organization works and encourage people to join.

It remains to be explained why, despite the steady presence of AA groups in the network and the fact that alcoholism is rampant among indigenous people, both network officials and many staff members seem to be unaware of the significance of AA programs.[42] One way to explain this puzzle is to point out that the network's ideology condemns any kind of assimilation, and that, instead of coming from indigenous traditions, AA is an organization with alien (United States) origins, and AA groups attract mostly mestizos and indigenous men highly assimilated into mainstream society.

A second program incorporating people from the audience in its production was *El Camino Andado* (the walked path). It was a weekly series of 30-minute programs broadcast by XETLA from 1986 to 1990. It started under the initiative of a group of Triquis from San Andrés Chicahuaxtla, Oaxaca, and was produced by villagers assisted by a Triqui female producer, Blanca Santiago. According to Santiago, 10 Triqui villages participated in the series. The villagers' initial idea was to produce a program to disseminate their culture and way of thinking. During the series' first stage, the focus was on music. Yet many times the music was a springboard to discuss a village's past and present situation and to share the village's experiences with other Triquis. On November 30, 1986, an unprecedented meeting of Triqui musicians was organized through the series. During its second stage, the series became a forum for a cooperative of women huipil weavers. These women talked about the folk lore of the huipil, the weaving process, and the problems related to its commercialization. Subsequent topics were traditional authorities and legends of the Triqui people.[43] However, with the unfortunate departure of Santiago from XETLA, the series lost its attraction.

I was told that Santiago, a very charismatic and intelligent Triqui woman, left the station because of quarrels with some of the ladino staff members. It seems to me that more than mere personal rivalries, what was at stake in the dispute was the challenge that an outstanding indigenous woman posed to the network's racist and sexist hierarchy. Furthermore, apparently among the people participating in the series were leaders of the Triquis, an ethnic group who have sustained a very active political struggle for their rights, and it was of some concern that the series might turn into a means for this struggle. *El Camino Andado* illustrates the network's ideal regarding programming and sheds light not only on the intricate power struggle taking place inside the INI stations but also on the dilemmas surrounding popular participation in state projects.

Notes

1. Note that the gender ratio is eight male versus five female speakers of vernaculars.

2. Inés Cornejo, "La Voz de la Mixteca y la Comunidad Receptora de la Mixteca Oaxaqueña," M.A. thesis, U Iberoamericana, 1990, 94.

3. José Manuel Ramos Rodríguez, interview by Carlos Plascencia, México City, 1989.

4. My sense is that this practice has to do more with the station's internal power structure than with audience needs.

5. Odilón Castañeda Peñabronce, "Las Lenguas Indígenas en la XEZV," XEZV Foro, Tlapa, Guerrero, México, March 1989.

6. According to Cornejo (77), XETLA's programming includes 68 percent of music programs. Internal documents on XEPET talk of 72 percent, and I estimated either similar or higher percentages for other stations.

7. According to XEZV's programmer, between 65 and 70 percent of XEZV's music programming is filled with local productions.

8. Aranda Bezaury et al. found that, along with avisos, *El Correo de los Amigos* was XEZV's most popular program. My findings on XEVFS suggest similar conclusions. Josefina Aranda Bezaury and Verónica Valenzuela, "Investigación Sobre la Presencia Radiofónica de la Voz de la Montaña en las Comunidades," unpublished essay, 1982, 41.

9. Instituto Nacional Indigenista, "Cartas del Auditorio," internal document, ts. México, 1988.

10. XEPET programs two and a half hours a week (about three percent of its total broadcasting time).

11. Especially XETAR and XEZV.

12. Different stations use different terms to refer to non-personal messages. What in XEVFS is called *"aviso institucional"* in XEZV may be seen as a *"convocatoria,"* and in XEPET as an *"aviso comunitario."*

13. The content of the remaining six avisos was either travel (four avisos) or keeping in-touch with family members (two avisos).

14. Ramos Rodríguez .

15. Carlos Plascencia, "La Presencia de la Radio," *México Indígena*, Número Extraordinario, Otoño (1988): 37-41.

16. The exact figure was 5,848, but I estimated that about a quarter of the avisos in Spanish were also aired in one vernacular, thus some avisos were actually counted twice.

17. Though I was unable to conduct a users survey for XEZV, I noticed that this station has much more audience participation than the other four that I visited. So, these figures seem to be reliable.

18. XEPET's researcher reported 67 avisos for January, 1990. Instituto Nacional Indigenista, XEPET, "Informe," by Filemón Ku Che, ts., internal document, 9 February, 1990.

19. Instituto Nacional Indigenista, "Diagnósticos de las Radiodifusoras del Instituto Nacional Indigenista," by Teresa Niehus, ts., internal document, México, 1988.

20. Instituto Nacional Indigenista, XEPET, "Informe," by Filemón Ku Che, ts., internal document, 8 May, 1990.

21. Instituto Nacional Indigenista, XEZV, "Informe," ts., internal document, 12 July, 1989.

22. Lucila Vargas, "The Radio broadcasting of Messages from the Audience," M.A. thesis, U of Texas at Austin, 1987.

23. Félix Dircio Melgarejo, "¿Cúal es la Verdera Cara de la Voz de la Montaña ante los Desastres de la Naturaleza?" Unpublished essay, 1989.

24. This grouping includes two programming categories: programs on indigenous ethnic groups and those on history.

25. The series is not done in Spanish.

26. Some of the Tojolabals that I interviewed for the audience study also took the opportunity to complain about their *presidente municipal*.

27. Neither staff members nor the listeners of XEVFS who participated in the audience study mentioned this newscast, but it would be unfair to assess this program on this basis alone.

28. Cornejo.

29. Aranda Bezaury et al. 41. Cornejo's studies emphasize that members of the audience said they listen to the stations for information purposes. However, these studies fail to distinguish between newscasts and avisos programs.

30. The program in Tlapaneco is aired on Mondays at 2:00 p.m., the program in Mixteco on Tuesdays at 3:00 p.m., and the program in Náhuatl on Thursdays at 4:00 p.m.

31. Cornejo 94.

32. Mary Jill Brody, personal communication.

33. For example the series *Un viaje, una Historia*.

34. Cornejo 75.

35. Instituto Nacional Indigenista, "Diagnósticos."

36. Fernando Cruz Merino, "Mejoramiento de Transmisión y Calidad Noticiera," XEZV Foro, Tlapa, Guerrero, México, March, 1989.

37. XEPET is a special case regarding spots. It produces spots on development topics and also on national heroes. During my fieldwork, it was also producing a

large number of spots on a major local event done by the federal government taking place at the time (*Semana del Programa Nacional de Solidaridad*).

38. This was part of a larger conflict involving also the local CCI.

39. Ana Lydia Flores,"Prioridad en Comunidades Indígenas de Eloxochitán, el Aprendizaje del Español," *El Universal* 15 July, 1990, 2.

40. Aranda Bezaury et al. 36.

41. For example, in 1989 XEPUR was broadcasting a program produced by a local ecological organization, the ORCA.

42. The most remarkable exception is XEPET's technician, who belongs to the local AA group and participates in its programs.

43. Blanca Santiago, "El Camino Andado. XETLA La Voz de la Mixteca," Memoria del II Seminario Taller Sobre Radiodifusión en Regiones Indígenas de América Latina, Villa Hermosa, Tabasco, México, 10-15 August, 1987; Cornejo 106-108.

PART THREE

Audience Participation and Social Uses

7

Radio Margaritas' Target Audience: The Tojolabal Maya

How do ethnic minorities under severe material and psychological stress use available radio resources in order to cope with socio-economic pressures and to realize basic needs? This is the question that I extensively explore in the remaining chapters of the book. In this second part of the investigation I concentrate on the Tojolabal Maya, an ethno-cultural group from the state of Chiapas, Southern Mexico, who are the primary target audience of XEVFS, Radio Margaritas, the station that I singled out for a more in-depth analysis. Here I describe the specific ways in which a segment of XEVFS' audience uses radio, and I also shed light on the social value of participatory radio by examining the type and extent of audience participation in XEVFS. I look at the radio practices of Radio Margaritas' listeners and deal with other topics related to media consumption.

Since I was interested in the specific radio practices of actual indigenous listeners rather than in potential listenership, I conducted a qualitative investigation based on group interviews with 21 families. The core of the second part of the book is, then, an ethnographic account of radio reception practices among the Tojolabal Maya. To contextualize the responses of my my Tojolabal informants, in this chapter I offer a general introduction to the Tojolabal world.

However, before introducing the reader to the Tojolabal, I discuss the audience of the entire network. This discussion is partially based on my own fieldwork but also relies on previous quantitative audience research on the network. The first few pages of this chapter, then, are dedicated to provide a broad view of the entire INI network's audiences because it is crucial to learn about these audiences to understand the social value of the stations and, further, because this broad view of the network's audiences, based mainly on quantitative research, sets the stage to grasp the meaning of the qualitative interviews that I conducted with Tojolabal families.

The INI Network's Audience

I see the network's audience as comprised of three groups: (1) the largest group, or potential audience, is made up of all those people who live under the coverage of the INI stations; (2) the second group, or listenership, is made up of actual listeners who regularly tune their radios to one of the stations; and (3) the smallest group, or users, are those people who in addition to regularly listening to one of the stations also use its resources in a variety of ways. I have no reliable data regarding the number of people in each group. Network documents refer to three million people but fail to distinguish between potential audience and listenership.

Under Inés Cornejo's direction the network has conducted a number of audience studies, but they do not provide a reliable estimate of the number of people involved in each of the groups mentioned above. Since the samples of these studies were not randomly selected, their findings are not generalizable to the total population. Nonetheless, these studies provide comparative data. The samples for these studies were taken from several *municipios* (counties) under the coverage of each of the stations and included men and women as well as ladinos/mestizos and indigenous people.

What follows is a summary of Inés Cornejo and Silvia Luna's study on Radio Margaritas: the sample included 51 men and 49 women, 53 Spanish monolinguals, and 47 speakers of vernaculars.[1] The latter contained 24 Tzeltal speakers, 10 Tzotzil speakers, and 13 Tojolabal speakers. Only 12 of the 100 interviewees live in the municipio Las Margaritas, where the station as well as the two Tojolabal villages where I conducted my own audience interviews are located.[2] The findings of Cornejo and Luna's study are particularly skewed because XEVFS' personnel decided to sample only those villages in which they had reason to believe the station's ratings were much lower than in other areas. This was a circumstance over which the main researcher, Cornejo, had no control whatsoever. Thus they found that from the potential 100 listeners sampled, 73 said that they listened to the radio but, only 35 said that they preferred Radio Margaritas. Nonetheless more than half of the indigenous interviewees who listened to the radio said they preferred XEVFS.[3] I should underscore that nine people said they listened to XEVFS despite the fact that their homes are not equipped with radio receivers, and that six of these nine were indigenous interviewees. My own audience study validates this finding. I also found that lacking a radio receiver does not prevent Tojolabal people from participating in radio listening. In fact, there were enough receivers in Tojolabal villages for most people to have at least limited access to XEVFS' offerings.

Regarding consumption of electronic media, 64 respondents said they own a radio and 38 a television (11 out of the 47 indigenous interviewees). As far as radio use and listening practices are concerned, nearly half of the total sample indicated that the radio is their primary source of news. About half of the 73 people who said that they listen to the radio specified that they listen mostly in the morning, and 71 percent said they listen less than two hours a day (19 of the 30 indigenous interviewees). I discuss other relevant findings of this study throughout the next three chapters, but I should point out that regardless of this study's flaws, it was Cornejo's previous research on other INI stations and the numerous conversations held with her that supplied the basis for my own research.

The main findings of Cornejo and Luna's research on XEZV, XEPET, XETAR (which I believe are more reliable than their findings on Radio Margaritas[4]) suggest that the vast majority of the people under the coverage of these three stations listen to radio and that most of them listen to these INI stations. In the questionnaire, Cornejo and Luna included an intriguing question, "What do you use radio for?" Most listeners of XETAR and XEZV responded that they use their stations either to send avisos/saludos (38 percent for XETAR and 25 percent for XEZV) or to get information (51 percent for XETAR and 19 percent for XEZV). In stations like XETAR and XEZV, these two uses overlap because, as I argue in Chapter 9, the most valuable information aired by the stations is broadcast during the avisos programs rather than during newscasts. These responses hint at uses of the stations to satisfy practical needs that in the modern world are met by other communication systems such as telephone, print media, post service, and electronic mail.

Based on my own research, like Cornejo I also estimate that a large sector of XEZV's and XETAR's listeners use the hardware and human resources of these two stations for sending avisos and for other practical purposes, but only a handful of XEPET's listeners use their station in a more comprehensive way. Only less than five percent of the listeners of XEPET interviewed by Cornejo said that they use this station to send avisos. The popularity of a particular station, of course, is linked to the number of uses it is put to by its audience; XEZV and XETAR thus probably have a larger listenership than XEPET.

Turning to indigenous participation, it is important to distinguish three segments of the audience according to ethnicity: ladinos, mestizos, and indigenous people. While in stations like XEZV and XEVFS, only a handful of ladinos and probably some mestizos living under the coverage of the station actually listen to it; in XETAR ladinos and mestizos are an important segment of both the listenership and the users' group. The network's documents and officials insist that the stations should not serve ladinos, yet the issue of the inclusion of mestizos into the target audience remains to be addressed. Meanwhile, the issue is decided within each station, often by the general manager. As early as 1983, members of XEZV's staff suggested that the station's target audience should include three sectors: the traditional indigenous sector, the transitional indigenous sector, and the semiurban mestizo-indigenous sector. This distinction is based on mode of production and provides the best typology so far.[5]

A fairly good indication of indigenous participation in INI's radio project is the local ladinos' view of a particular station. When they appreciate having the station in town, it is naturally because it serves their interests. By the same token when they are concerned over the money spent on the station or are even openly antagonistic, it is because the station may be benefiting the indigenous people. "Frankly, we dislike Radio Margaritas; we want to become civilized and they bring us a radio station broadcasting in Tojolabal!" said an educated ladino member of XEVFS' potential audience. Many of these ladinos dislike seeing an important communications resource assisting the Tojolabal. "Of course," a prominent ladino in Margaritas City said to me, "Radio Margaritas is useful for the Indians. I would say that it is too useful for them."

XETAR, on the other hand, is regarded with respect and interest by ladinos living in Guachochi, the town where the station is located, and other ladinos visiting the town make sure to drop by the station and get acquainted with its facilities. Raramuris (the indigenous primary audience of XETAR) also come by the station, but they, especially women, tend to stay outside the facilities, sending a young boy or a man in when delivering an aviso. XETAR, located at the heart of the Tarahumara Sierra, is indeed the station airing most avisos, but the users of the avisos service are mainly ladinos.

Users

I use the term "users" to refer to all those actors who either visit, call, or write to the stations requesting a service. In addition to the data provided by documents, I conducted users surveys at XETAR, XEPET, and XEVFS (see Chapter 2 for the methodology of these surveys). I found that while XETAR had 476 visitors during a given week, and XEVFS had 203, XEPET had only 66. Though XETAR had the highest number of visitors, 60 percent of them were Spanish monolinguals, which indicates that this station serves to a great extent the needs of the local ladino/mestizo community.[6] On the other hand, most of the visitors to the two other stations surveyed were speakers of vernaculars; the figure of speakers of vernaculars was 65 percent for XEVFS and 93 percent for XEPET.[7]

I also found remarkable differences in radio use between men and women, and a strong correlation between ethnicity and gender. In XETAR, a station used mainly by Spanish monolinguals, 48 percent of the visitors were women, but in the stations used more by speakers of vernaculars, the percentage of female visitors was very low; only 9 percent of the visitors to XEVFS and 17 percent of the visitors to XEPET were women. Apparently fewer indigenous women use these stations, and then only for limited purposes. For instance, out of the 203 people visiting XEVFS, only 12 were Tojolabal women wanting to send an aviso or saludo. Hence, most visitors to XEVFS and XEPET are members of ethnic groups and are men; in contrast, most visitors to XETAR are ladino/mestizo, and this station receives almost equal numbers of male and female visitors. Further cross-tabulation showed that many ladino/mestizo women use XETAR, but few indigenous women use these three stations.

Regarding visitors' ages, I found that the vast majority of the people visiting these three stations were young adults and older adults and that neither gender nor ethnicity correlated with users' ages. In XETAR, 23 percent of the visitors were 13-20 years old, 39 percent were 21-35 years old, and 36 percent belonged to other age groups; note that by contrast to other stations, XETAR regularly received many children as visitors. In XEVFS, 20 percent were 13-20 years old, 53 percent were 21-35 years old, and most of the remaining 26 percent, who belonged to other age groups, were over 35 years of age. In XEPET, 26 percent were 13-20 years old, 29 percent were 21-35 years old, and a high percentage, 42, fell into the other age groups category; like in XEVFS, most of the visitors in this age group were over 35 years of age.

Finally, concerning visitors' reasons for going to these stations, the surveys disclosed the importance of avisos for the local population of XETAR and XEVFS. In XETAR, 61 percent of the visitors wanted to send an aviso, 34 percent wanted to send a saludo, and 34 percent visited the station for other reasons, such as to see what the station was like or to use the telephone. The picture for XEVFS was even more striking; 81 percent of the visitors to this station wanted to send an aviso, 15 percent wanted to send a saludo, and only 4 percent had another reason for their visit. XEPET was, again, the exception because only 26 percent of its visitors wanted to send an aviso, but 51 percent of them wanted to send a saludo; the remaining 21 percent went to XEPET for other reasons. It is worth mentioning that in the three stations surveyed, only a small number of visitors went to participate in the radio programs.

There are four different types of senders of messages: individual members of the audience, villages' traditional authorities, government agencies, and indigenous organizations. Individuals use the stations to broadcast two different types of messages, first, saludos, which lack informational value per se, but are used as phatic communication to keep in touch with family and friends, and second, avisos, which are brief messages often pertaining to travel and health. Villages' traditional authorities employ the stations to invite other villages to festivals and celebrations, as well as to publicize other activities. Government agencies use the stations to make announcements and to spread both general information and specific information on development projects. Indigenous organizations make use of the stations to air announcements for their members, as well as to broadcast information about the organization in general.

People also use the broadcasting of avisos in combination with other means of communication. Stations like XETAR and XEZV receive a large number of letters addressed to audience members living in villages with no postal service. These letters are sent from an addresee's family or friends now living in places where postal services are available (such as temporary migrants in the United States). The station airs the aviso to the addressee requesting him or her to come by the station to pick up the letter. People also use a station's telephone in the same way, calling initially to request the airing of an aviso like this one: "To my wife Adelaida Alvarado, please wait for a phone call at XEZV on Sunday at noon, I will call you there." It is important to point out that Radio Margaritas' audience does not use the station for these purposes. The station has no telephone line, but it could well be used in combination with the postal service. Both the station's location and audience's little need for the service probably explain the absence of this use.

In addition to using the stations for airing avisos, many individual members of the audience also broadcast saludos, or greetings. There is a correlation between users' ethnicity and the airing of saludos. It seems that ladinos seldom use the station to send saludos, since few XETAR's users wanted to send saludos. On the other hand, half of XEPET's visitors, almost all of them Maya speakers, requested the airing of saludos. The same station, which hardly ever broadcasts avisos, nonetheless did air saludos, 473 in the months of March, April, and June of 1990. This use of the stations is particularly popular during special celebrations such as Mother's Day. Looking at the stations' documents, for example, I found that the number of saludos aired by XEZV was much higher in May than in other months; for example, the average monthly number from January to April 1989 was 283 while the average monthly number for May and June was 420.

Though most people ask the stations to broadcast messages, I also identified other creative ways in which people use the stations' resources. I discussed above the reasons that people visit the three stations that I surveyed. Note however that I conducted users surveys in only three stations and that the frequency of two important uses, recording music and seeking advice, is probably much higher at other stations which I did not survey (e.g., XEPUR and XEZV). I did observe many Purépecha musicians asking for their performances to be recorded at XEPUR, and I also observed a large number of Nahuas, Mixtecos, and Tlapanecos coming by XEZV to get advice from the staff on how to deal with government agencies, to chat with the announcer over the microphone, or to record their music.

In sum, according to the users survey of XEVFS, the profile of a typical user of Radio Margaritas would be a young, adult male, Tojolabal speaker who does not live in Margaritas City. In the remaining part of this chapter, I draw a picture of the target audience of Radio Margaritas, the Tojolabal Maya.

The Tojolabal Maya

The *Tojol winik'otik*, the right people, as they call themselves, live in the highlands of Mexico's Chiapas state (Figure 7.1 is a map of Chiapas showing the Tojolabal region). Although they share Maya cultural roots with many other indigenous peoples of Middle America, including their neighbors the Tzeltal and Tzotzil, they are quite distinct linguistically and culturally. The Tojolabal Maya have suffered from the effects of a two-pronged strategy of exploitation that Mexico's dominant society has historically inflicted on indigenous peoples: the exploitation of their material resources and the stigmatization of their ethnicity. The Tojolabal also have a high rate of population growth and have been subject to the repercussions of the civil war in neighboring Guatemala. In the early 1990s these effects included not only immigration of refugees to the Tojolabal region but also a strong military presence that added a new dimension to the usual harassment suffered by indigenous peoples. For example, there were new prohibitions about the use of gunpowder for the traditional fires of religious celebrations and restrictions for religious pilgrimages across the border between Mexico and Guatemala. Any real or alleged violation of these restrictions may have resulted in verbal and physical abuse, incarceration, and even death. In addition, the Tojolabal have been facing land shortages, which in turn have increased non-permanent migration and high morbidity as well as mortality rates, the latter contributing to this people's profound preoccupation with disease. Needless to say, such circumstances make Radio Margaritas' role in the region's social change crucial.

Previous Research

Probably the Tojolabal are one of the most dispossessed peoples. They live not just with remarkably few material resources but also with scarce knowledge about their history, their culture, and their current socio-economic conditions. The research on the group goes back no further than the 1930s, making them the least known ethno-cultural group of Middle America.[8] In contrast to the vast research focusing specifically on the Tzeltal and Tzotzil, and on the Maya in general, little is known about the Tojolabal. Mario Humberto Ruz says that the "spectacularity" of the cultural forms of an ethnic group often plays an important role in its selection for research, and consequently that the lack of interest on the part of anthropologists and other researchers in the Tojolabal is explained by the fact that their culture is far from what is considered "spectacular." Its archaeological sites are of minor importance, and present Tojolabal culture lacks the special appeal of many cultural expressions of the Tzeltal and Tzotzil, such as the carnival of Chamula Tzeltals and the healing rites of Tzotzils from Larrainazar.[9] Whatever the reason for the lack of interest in the Tojolabal, the result of the

FIGURE 7.1 Map of the State of Chiapas Showing the Tojolabal Region

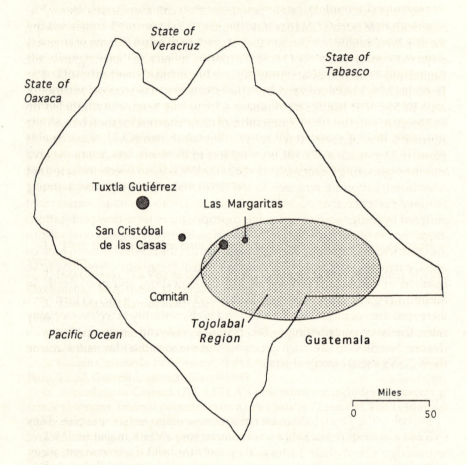

scarcity of scholarly works, coupled with the few and often unreliable governmental sources, is a fragmented picture of these people. With the exception of their language, most aspects of their society and culture have been insufficiently recorded.

Research on the Tojolabal Maya is chiefly concerned with issues of linguistic anthropology. A number of researchers have, however, contributed to the study of other aspects of their culture and society. The most important ethnographic work has been done by Ruz, and there are two publications that should not be overlooked, given that they have been written for Tojolabals: a two-volume Tojolabal-Spanish, Spanish-Tojolabal dictionary by Carlos Lenkersdorf and a bilingual (Tojolabal-Spanish) book by Arturo Lomelí.[10]

Demographics and Health

Using language as the sole criterion for ethnicity, it is still difficult to determine the number of Tojolabal people. The 1980 census (which is the most recent reliable report available, since the 1990 census had many reliability problems) counted 22,331 Tojolabal speakers. More recent estimates give figures of 46,200[11] and 50,000.[12] Given the group's high population growth (it has been suggested that its annual growth rate is about 1.71 percent[13]), these figures are probably conservative for the 1990s.

Despite living in a state with fertile valleys and an abundance of natural resources, the Tojolabals are stricken by what has been called "diseases of poverty," which include malnutrition, as well as infectious and parasitic diseases such as acute respiratory infections, diarrheal disease, and mange. They also suffer from some of the so-called "diseases of affluence," which are associated with poor dietary balance, lack of physical exercise, tobacco use, abuse of alcohol and other drugs, and stress. Their life expectancy (at birth) is estimated to be between 35 and 50 years. Some research indicates moreover that Tojolabal adults and children are smaller and lighter than those of other Maya groups; the reason for this is probably their poor diet.[14] As to morbidity, here are the data provided by the local health center of one of the villages of my audience study, Madero: in 1989, at least one member of every family in the town visited the local health center because of intestinal parasites, about one in every three families reported suffering from mange, and several cases of tuberculosis and malaria were reported as well. I suspect that these data probably fail to reflect the actual health of Maderans, since many Maderans do not report their illnesses to the local health center. The Tojolabal have little confidence of the benefits of Western medicine, due in part to traditional beliefs and in part to the fraudulent practices of merchants, pharmacists, and health workers.[15]

The Tojolabal Land

The majority of Tojolabals live in nucleated settings (colonias) which occupy an area of over 6,000 square kilometers on the east side of Chiapas state, an area which borders Guatemala (roughly between the latitudes 16° north and 16°45' north and the longitudes 91°15' west and 92°15' west).[16] Much of this area is under the political jurisdiction of the municipio of Villa Las Margaritas, itself located in the eastern part of Chiapas. Figure 7.2 presents a map of this region showing where the two villages of my audience study are located. There are at least 412 settlements in this area, most of them small villages. Beyond the county seat, only 14 towns are mentioned in government sources as important settlements. Madero is one of them.

With subhumid climate, a median temperature of 18°C, three rivers and

FIGURE 7.2 Map Showing the Location of Margaritas City, Tabasco, and Madero

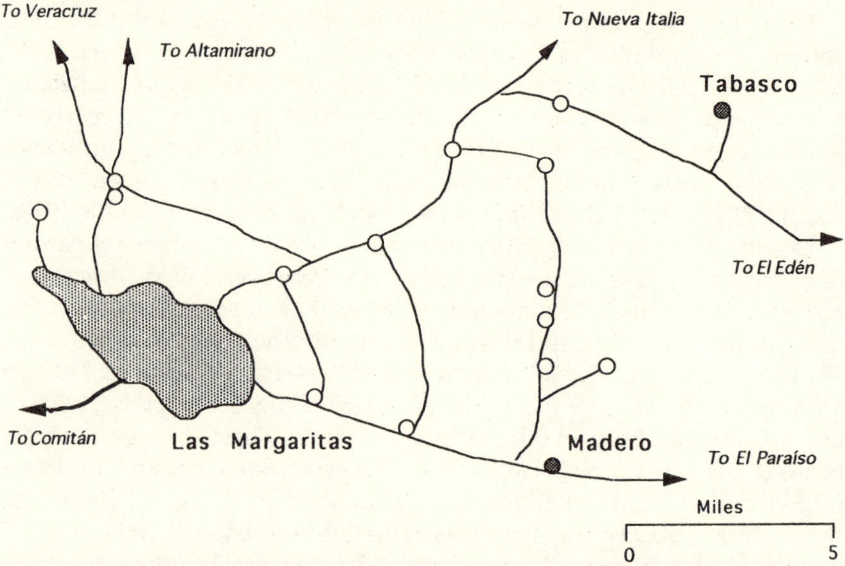

four lakes, as well as extensive highlands (only 10 percent in plateaus), most of the municipio's 4,250 square kilometers are not well suited for agriculture. Only about 30,000 hectares are arable land, and of this figure just 2,200 hectares have irrigation. The tenure of the total municipio land is mostly ejidos; the rest is either private property (20 percent) or communal lands (10 percent).[17] Often translated as "communal holding," the ejido is land belonging to the nation but held in common by a group of peasants which has the usufructory rights. This Mexican unique way of land tenure is the outcome of the long struggle of indigenous peoples for the restitution of their ancestral communal lands.[18]

The municipio's urban population is about 14 percent of the 86,365 people registered by the 1990 census. The rest of the population is loosely connected with the main settlements. There are three roads in the municipio (Comitán City-Ocosingo City, Margaritas City-El Edén, and Margaritas City-El Paraíso), but only the 18 kilometers between Margaritas City and Comitán City are paved. Many Tojolabals travel by commercial buses and trucks operated by ladinos, though in the last few years several _Uniones de Ejidos_ (federations of ejidos) have acquired their own trucks, assisted by INI. Postal, telegraph, and telephone services are available only in the county seat. Nevertheless, many radio as well as television stations reach the area. A small number of Tojolabals have access to television while probably all of them have access to radio.

None of the studies on the Tojolabal deals with their use of electronic media, but when talking about the Guatemalan smugglers, some authors indirectly shed light on the wide availability of transistor radios in the Tojolabal area. These authors mention that for centuries the Guatemalan smugglers (Chujes, Jacaltecos, and Kanobales) have traveled throughout the area selling consumer goods. Ruz says that Japanese radios have replaced earlier consumables such as the salt and textiles that the Guatemalan smugglers, or *Chapines*, used to trade with the Tojolabal in Colonial times.[19] Louanna Furbee-Losee, describing the relationship between the Tojolabal and indigenous Guatemalan groups, states: "...all good things of commerce come via the Guatemalan smugglers, from marimbas to transistors radios to the prettiest rebozos."[20]   Thus radio receivers have probably been a popular consumer good among Tojolabals for at least two decades. The oldest Mexican radio station in the area is XEUI, Radio Comitán, established in 1963, but evangelical radio stations have been transmitting from Central America as early as the 1950s. Radio Margaritas started broadcasting in 1987, long after the introduction of radio in the region. Rather than introducing a new communication technology, Radio Margaritas' impact has more to do with the station's format, its emphasis on traditional cultural forms, and its potential for new social uses.[21]

With regard to the number of Tojolabal-speaking villages, Lomelí says that the Consejo Supremo Tojolabal has identified 184. There are 114 in the municipio of Las Margaritas, and the rest are in the municipios of Comitán (8), La Independencia (7), Trinitaria (8), and Altamirano (47).[22] Ruz's list agrees with these numbers.[23] John Stephan Thomas and Mary Jill Brody estimate about 219 villages. These villages are mostly in the highlands or valleys; a few recently established villages in the tropical forest share the area with Tzeltal and Tzotzil speakers who have immigrated to the Tojolabal region during the last few decades. Based on Thomas and Brody's estimates, about 210 people live in an average village which has 35 households (the medium household size is six persons).[24] I believe these figures are a low estimate for the 1990s.

As are most indigenous villages, Tojolabal *colonias* are connected with urban settings dominated by ladinos, and these in turn are the center for most of the economic, political, and religious activities of the region.[25] The core of the Tojolabal region is comprised of the cities of Margaritas, which has a population of about 30,000, and Comitán, with about 90,000. Many Tojolabals live in these two cities, and it is probable that more will immigrate in the near future because of the continuously increasing hardships in their villages. Most migrants, however, do not leave their villages permanently, in part to retain rights of land use.[26]

The Collective Experience

Until the 1930s and 1940s, the Tojolabals were attached to the *fincas* (ranches) owned by ladinos. That was the time known as the *baldío*, because the Tojolabals had to work two weeks of every month *de balde* (for free) for the *patrones* (landlords) in exchange for a place to live and a small plot of land. According to the older Tojolabals, they lived under conditions of virtual slavery. The Mexican Revolution, and the subsequent agrarian reform, made it possible for the Tojolabals to establish their own ejidos by petitioning the federal government for either parts of the finca land or the national forest land. Today the Tojolabals strive to make a livelihood by farming their ejidos, though many still work for the modern fincas, either permanently by exchanging their labor for the right to use small plots, or as wage laborers on a temporary basis. The slavery of roughly half a century ago has been transformed into new forms of oppression sustained by the current web of social and economic interrelations between the Tojolabals and the ladinos.

The Economic Strategies

Tojolabals have been traditionally subsistence farmers who use slash-and-burn techniques to grow corn, beans, squash, and chilies. In some areas, especially in the rain forest area, they grow coffee as well. In addition women keep a family garden in which fruit trees (oranges, limes, lemons, bananas) and herbs are often grown. Most families cannot live on their own crops and often have to complement their precarious economies by taking in cash through wage labor and marketing livestock (chiefly pigs, chickens, and turkeys) and forest resources. Thus the economy of Tojolabal villages is far from self-sufficient; it is in fact closely tied to the ladino economy. The Tojolabal's economic relations with the ladino world follow the pattern of most neocolonial situations, with the Tojolabal providing cheap labor and raw materials (e.g., livestock and coffee), as well as a market for products (e.g., sugar, powder milk, bread, cookies, and meat), manufactured goods (e.g., clothes, radios, drugs, and tools), and services (e.g., transportation).

The Tojolabals' economic dependency has been encouraged by the ladinos, who use every means to maintain the status quo. There is for example the case recorded by Ruz of the 1980 municipal prohibition to have home stills, which made production of local alcoholic drink (*aguardiente*) illegal except for the factory in Margaritas City. After home stills were confiscated, the price of aguardiente went up by 400 percent.[27] There is also John Stephen Thomas and Michael Robbins's account of the actions taken by owners of a bus company serving the villages to stop the Tojolabals in their effort to be less dependent on commercial transportation; these actions extended from appealing to state transportation officials, to declaring illegal the creation of a bus cooperative planned by Tojolabals, to the threat of physically blocking any buses operated by indigenous peoples.[28]

As with other *ejidatarios*, insufficient arable land is a major economic problem for the Tojolabals. This problem stems first from the particular way in which the system of land tenure was set up, and second from rapid population growth. The ejido land, which belongs to the nation but is held by a group of peasants, may be individually or communally worked. In Tojolabal *colonias* (which are a variation of the ejido), the land was reapportioned to heads of households for each household's use. Thomas and Brody point out that the Tojolabals do not farm communally, and that the basic unit of production is the family, keeping in mind the existence of social networks whose members help each other in production activities (*mohalhel*).[29] Since ladinos kept the most fertile valley lands, the ejidos were often relegated to mountainous and less fertile lands. The ejidos were granted neither the same quantity nor the same quality of land. Ruz underscores the substantial difference between the ejidos by mentioning that some ejidos obtained the entire finca (e.g., ejido Jonatá received more than 3,400 has.) while others received almost no arable land at all (e.g., ejido Allende received about 300 has., mostly forest).[30] And while many ejidos applied for additional allotments or *ampliaciones*, still the actual arable land gained may have been only 30 percent of the total land granted (as in the case of the village studied by Thomas and Robbins),[31] and the plot held by every ejidatario may be only between two and three hectares (approximately between 4.94 and 7.41 acres). According to the best data that I was able to obtain, Madero was granted 2020 hectares of which only 400 are suited for agriculture; Tabasco originally received 635 hectares, and an additional allotment of 659, of which only 160 hectares are arable.

The Changing Conditions

The Tojolabal are presently facing extreme conditions; as Furbee Losse and other authors note, arable land and disease are these people's two main preoccupations.[32] Their small plots do not yield enough crops for subsistence farming, and their opportunities for employment in the ladino world are significantly limited. An alternative for the young used to be the establishment of new ejidos, especially in the rain forest. But immigration of other people to the same land, including over 100,000 refugees from Guatemala, and the official lapsing of the Agrarian Reform in 1978 have greatly reduced this opportunity, which makes disputes over land even more likely to increase.[33] In addition, there are the changes brought on by oil exploration in the region as well as the consequences of the political unrest in Central America, a strong military presence and an environment of fear.

The Tojolabal live in a rapidly changing environment. Added to their material hardships are the negative impact that Protestant sects operating out of Guatemala have had on their minds and communal solidarity. Though the situation in Chiapas has not reached the level of village disintegration that these sects have brought about in numerous Guatemalan villages, it cannot be said that Protestant missionaries have had no impact on Tojolabal communities.[34] It is estimated that in the 1980s the protestant population of Chiapas tripled.[35] Multiple forces are thus pushing or inviting Tojolabals to "become modern," to leave behind their traditional religion and mores. Many Tojolabals choose not to speak their own language, prefer not to dress in their traditional costume, and are determined not to participate in traditional festivities. Radio Margaritas was established in the region with the specific purpose of counteracting the influence of such modernizing forces, specifically Protestant sects.

The Social World

Ruz has suggested that the social space of the Tojolabal can be divided into four levels: the family, the village, the ethnic group, and the national society.[36] All interactions of the Tojolabal among themselves belong to the first three levels, and the relations the Tojolabal have with the ladino world and its various institutions belong to the last level. I borrow Ruz's scheme but add another level, indigenous peoples, which is the social space where the interrelations of the Tojolabals with other indigenous peoples, especially those living in the area (i.e., Tzeltals, Tzotzils, Mames, and Lacandones), take place. I see these levels as concentric circles but give special attention to the family, which contains the immediate family and the mohalhel or extended family, first because it is within the family that most of the social uses of radio are constructed and second because the social space of many Tojolabal women is restricted almost exclusively to the family. Likewise, since the recent increase in the number of immigrants to the Tojolabal region and the fact that XEVFS not only broadcasts for the Tojolabal but also for the Tzeltal, the Tzotzil, and the Mam, I also pay special attention to the level of indigenous peoples.

The Family. The Tojolabal family is patrilocal. When a young couple get married, they are expected to live for a number of years with the husband's parents before establishing their own home. The youngest son takes care of the old parents and inherits their house and the status of ejidatario, but the other property is usually divided equally among the sons.[37] Women have no property rights, although small animals such as chickens and pigs as well as the family garden are their domain. Most families include a couple and their children. The typical household matches the nuclear family, yet households with extended families (i.e., having more than one nuclear family) are not unusual.[38] Thomas found that in a Tojolabal village having 40 households, there were 28 with nuclear families, and the rest were other types of families.[39] In Madero there are many households with nuclear families but in Tabasco most households have extended families.

It has been suggested that the most important social unit for the Tojolabal is the *mohalhel*, which is an extension of the family, a network of relatives and friends who exchange labor and other resources. The daily routines are done with other members of the mohalhel, and a number of families may share a house compound called the *sitiyo*. When they migrate, either temporally or permanently, Tojolabals are likely to go with people of the same *mohalhel*. This level of the social space is especially important for women because they are excluded from most of the activities at the more comprehensive levels.

The Village. The village is the level of the social space in which most of the political activity takes place. In contrast to the Tzeltals and Tzotzils, who have at least a nominal role in municipal politics, Tojolabal political activity is limited to the village level. Indeed, as Furbee Losee remarks, in this respect "their situation is closer to that of their Guatemalan than their Mexican counterparts."[40] Since the late 1980s, however, the Tojolabal have made stronger efforts to gain political power through the electoral process; a Tojolabal, Antonio Hernández Cruz, was a candidate for *Presidente Municipal* in 1989. Also there are some Tojolabal men who are very active in indigenous organizations (both grassroots and government-funded) and/ or political parties.

The political activity inside the village takes place within the framework of the nation's system (the ejido, the municipio, the state, the federal government) and is largely determined by factors beyond the reach of the Tojolabal. However, this system also has an extensive communal dimension which allows the group a certain degree of self-government. The communal meeting, or *junta*, constitutes the Tojolabal political arena, in which affairs are discussed and decisions are made by consensus. The authority established by the junta can act on a wide range of issues: from those that concern the village as a whole (e.g., religious festivals, land distribution) to those involving members of a single family (e.g., divorce, inheritance). In accordance with traditional mores, women and, to a lesser extent young men, are excluded from this indigenous political system. Adult men may hold political positions only when they have the ejidatario status, and the number of non-ejidatarios who live in Tojolabal communities (*avecindados*) often far exceeds the number of ejidatarios. In Madero there are 81 ejidatarios to 193 avecindados; in Tabasco there are 33 ejidatarios to 42 avecindados.

The most important official in the village is the *komisariyado ejidal*. He is elected by the junta every three years and is recognized by the municipal government. He represents the village to the outside world, is the speaker of the junta, and organizes collective work. Thomas maintains that he is not necessarily a significant political leader,[41] but Ruz has pointed out that he has a twofold power which may allow him to exercise a strong leadership role: he has, on the one hand, the power given to him by the junta, and, on the other hand, he has the delegated power given by the municipio.[42] Nevertheless, the village has a number of ways of controlling individual power, such as not allowing the komisariyado to appoint his own assistants.

The Ethnic Group. The Tojolabal people constitute a distinct ethnic group, and its members share both a culture and a social status. Yet politically they do not act as a people or as a nation. This is true not only for the Tojolabal but also for many ethnic groups in Mexico. Rather than by entire ethnic groups acting as nations, the political struggle of indigenous peoples in the country often has been characterized by individual villages acting independently.

Ethnic identity is closely linked to speech.[43] The particular way in which an ethnic group perceives its own language is in turn associated with the group's self-perception and self-esteem. As opposed to Spanish, which is the lingua franca and the language of opportunity, the Tojolabal language has a minority status, especially since Tojolabal speakers feel they are in a subordinate social position to Spanish speakers. The Tojolabals' perception of their language suggests low self-esteem regarding their ethnicity. Thomas and Brody found that within their villages, Tojolabal speakers feel very comfortable with their language, but that they will avoid being heard speaking Tojolabal in ladino settings. These authors claim that "many Tojolabal speakers have themselves come to regard Tojolabal as inferior in some way to Spanish."[44] Furbee Losee also highlights Tojolabal feelings and attitudes toward their language and their ethnicity:

> to speak Tojolabal is a stigma in many places and situations and is the ultimate mark of Indian identity to be erased. When a Tojolabal travels away from the colonias, he often changes his dress to a ladino style for the trip. In town, he frequents only certain places, the markets, certain stores, and so forth. Except for fiestas, he intrudes very little on the ladino atmosphere of the urban centers; he often tries to speak Spanish when there. When he returns home, however, the entire situation reverses.[45]

Most Tojolabals have had contact with Spanish, but a person's gender greatly determines his or her individual competence in the second language. Men are usually bilingual because of the activities that require dealings with ladinos (*kaxlanes*, as Tojolabals say) and which are usually in the masculine domain. Women, by contrast, have very limited opportunities to hear and speak Spanish. Furbee Losee underscores that women's monolinguism corresponds to the role assigned to them as carriers of traditional culture. "For the Tojolabal women," points out Furbee Losee, "to be a fluent Spanish speaker is a threat to the culture in a way that men's bilingualism is not."[46] So, in addition to being the language of opportunity in the highlands, Spanish is also a predominantly masculine language in the villages. It is not surprising that Tojolabals' feelings about their own language are, if not negative, at least ambivalent.

In addition to the detrimental impact of conflicting feelings about their language, the Tojolabals' low social status compared to other ethnic groups of the highlands adds to their low self-esteem. There are numerous factors that indicate that the Tojolabal occupy a very low social position in the region. Evidence of this includes objective indicators, relative income, characteristic labor, education levels, housing, and health, each showing the Tojolabals are often worse off than their indigenous neighbors. Other factors may also contribute to the low social status of the Tojolabal. Among these are the subordinate role played by Tojolabals in some of their own religious festivities, which are directed by Tzeltals[47] and the fact that history does not record a Tojolabal golden age or glorious past, as is the case for Tzeltals Chamulas, for example. The plainness of their rituals and the simplicity of their artifacts may contribute to the group's low social status and sense of worthlessness.

The *Pobres*. The Tojolabals are socially distinguished from other ethnic groups, yet all indigenous peoples share a common place in the social space. At this level, the Tojolabals are differentiated as *pobres* (poor people) or indigenous people, as against *ricos* (rich people) or ladinos. The Tojolabals interact with other pobres (either Tojolabal or, for example, Tzeltal) for example when visiting Margaritas City or Comitán City. They interact with the Guatemalan smugglers and, in some places (Altamirano), with the Tzeltals who share the same area. They interact with Tzeltals and Guatemalan groups during the romerías or religious pilgrimages (which have greatly declined).[48] More recently, they have been interacting with members of the local organizations, such as *Uniones de Ejidos* and organizations of the coffee growers.[49] Radio has added a new dimension to interactions among villages. As I show later, a frequent comment made by the families interviewed regarding the service provided by XEVFS is that the villages now have a way to communicate with each other.

The *Ladino People and Their Institutions*. In the last level of Tojolabal social space, the group's interactions with the national society take place. These interactions include the economic relations with the ladino world that were discussed above and the interactions with the Mexican government and its institutions. The ideology structuring social interactions between pobres and ricos is naturally imbedded in Mexico's history of conquest and domination and comprises the following: the profound racism of Mexican society toward dark skinned people; the widespread belief that indigenous cultures are ontologically inferior to European culture, known in Mexico as *malinchismo* (a feeling of contempt for indigenous and mestizo cultures coupled with Mexicans' admiration for Europe); and the prevalent classist attitude among Mexicans which views peasants and poor urban workers as somehow deficient and inadequate (indigenous peoples constitute the vast majority of the lowest class in Mexico, and particularly in Chiapas). Thus racism, malinchismo, and classism mutually reinforce each other and create a threefold source of prejudices perpetuating the economically and socially disadvantaged position of indigenous peoples.

Among the Tojolabal themselves, individuals are usually the actors in economic relations while the principal actor in interactions with the government is the collectivity. The villages have to maintain links with the municipio, the state, and the federal government. The municipal government could act as a channel for the Tojolabals to reach state and federal governments, but John White notes that this is not the case, and Tojolabals deal with the municipal, state, and federal governments separately. White says that the municipal government, dominated by segregationist ladinos, is first unwilling to act on behalf of the Tojolabals, and second unable, because of its inefficiency, to do so.[50] I would underscore that the success of any action taken by Tojolabal villages (e.g., land litigation, infrastructure projects) is likely to be directly proportional to their success in evading the local power structures. Although one should not underestimate the role of federal institutions in maintaining this oppressive status quo (especially the military's role), the more direct oppressors of the Tojolabal are the local ladinos. They immediately benefit from cheap labor and the locally skewed distribution of resources. Moreover, most governmental actions to improve living conditions for the Tojolabal have originated with the federal government; the Tojolabal were able to emancipate themselves from the fincas thanks to the Agrarian Reform, and most of the assistance they have received, though insufficient, has come from the federal government. INI best illustrates this point.

It should be noted that the interactions of indigenous Mexican villages with the national society's government and institutions occur within the web of unofficial alliances, negotiations, and conflicts among the diverse social sectors of ladino society. The frequent confrontations between officials of federal institutions (like, indeed, INI) with local politicians should be kept in mind as well. Indigenous villages sometimes find ways to use these conflicts to their advantage, though more often they are caught in the middle.

Tojolabal interactions with government agencies are usually for health reasons (*Instituto Mexicano del Seguro Social, Secretaría de Salubridad y Asistencia*), agricultural credit (*Banco de Crédito Rural*), and the commercialization of their products (*Instituto Mexicano del Café*). In addition, many ejidos work closely with the *Centro Coordinador Indigenista Tojolabal* (CCI-Tojolabal) for a number of developmental purposes. The CCI-Tojolabal was established in 1975. Indigenous participation in the CCI was channeled through a body institutionalized toward that end, the *Consejo Supremo Tojolabal*. This body acts in accordance with guidelines established by INI ("Bases para la acción 1977"), and its president holds office in the CCI and receives a salary from INI. Sonia Toledo Tello claims that the Consejo helped to solve some of the Tojolabals' problems, especially those dealing with land tenancy, but that the Consejo has also became bureaucratized.[51] According to Ruz, the Consejo has been a source of conflict between villages; the indigenous peoples themselves complain of their lack of opportunity to participate in the elections of Consejo's members who are nominated by INI's officials.[52] This practice is in line with the authoritarian style of most of INI's officials.

Last but not least are the Tojolabal's interactions with the national society's most important institution of control, the military. Historically, the Southern border has been characterized by polical instability and by a strong military presence. First there is the courageous resistance struggle carried out by the local ethnic groups, especially the Tzeltal and the Tzotzil, which has included two instances in which indigenous peoples have launched war against ladino rule, one in 1712 and another in 1869. Second, there are the long standing border conflicts with Guatemala due to the fact that in the Colonial period Chiapas was not part of the Nueva España, but of the Provincia de Guatemala. It was annexed by Mexico in 1824, after Mexico's war of independence. Moreover, the last two decades of civil war in Central America have caused a considerable increase in the military presence and also brought a flood of refugees to the region. In addition, land shortages (a consequence of both migration and population growth) has increased inter-village land disputes, as well as disputes with ladino ranchers. For the Tojolabal, the military presence has resulted in both anxiety and downright fear.[53] Radio Margaritas operates within this context of strong military presence.

The Area of the Audience Study

Margaritas City. Margaritas City lies at the heart of the Tojolabal region. It was founded as the county seat in 1871 and received the status of city in 1981. Situated on the west side of the municipio (16° 18' 4" north latitude, 91° 59' 1" west longitude), it is 1,512 meters above sea level. It shares many of the characteristics of Mexico's main population centers in interethnic regions: it is the political and economic core of the area, concentrates regional services and infrastructure, and represents the unequal relations between ladino and indigenous peoples.

Like other political and economic centers of rural Mexico, Margaritas City is connected to the surrounding villages and in turn is linked to a larger city (Comitán City). It is connected with the surrounding villages by three unpaved roads; one goes to El Paraíso, a second to El Edén, and a third to Altamirano. It is linked to Comitán City by a paved 18-kilometers road, which also links Margaritas City to the Chiapas road system (carretera internacional Cristóbal Colón). This road was built in 1961 by the timber companies and was paved a few years ago. Margaritas City also has two small airports, which are used mainly for coffee commerce.

The subordinate position of the Tojolabal on the local social ladder can be seen not only in the social life of Margaritas City, but also in the spatial arrangements of its architecture and services. Ladinos, mestizos, and Tojolabals live in Margaritas City, but the downtown area is predominantly ladino. Most Tojolabals live in the barrios (San Sebastián, Los Pocitos, Saksalún, La Pila, Guadalupe y Yalkoc), where few of the services available downtown are enjoyed. Electricity was introduced in 1968, but in the early 1990s large areas of the barrios were still without service. Some parts of the barrios as well were not supplied with drinking water, or with a sewage system. Telephone service was established in 1971, but at the time all the lines (about 200) were concentrated in the first square (three or four blocks around the plaza). Likewise, educational and health facilities were mainly located in downtown. The city has three kindergartens, four elementary schools, one secondary school (sixth to ninth grade), one high school, a public library, a cultural center (*Casa de la Cultura*), a health center (*Centro de Salud "C"*), and a medical dispensary.

The downtown area also has a Tojolabal section which is located, as is the Tojolabal culture in the region, not on the main street but behind the church. The downtown is organized around a plaza with its kiosk. To the north side of the plaza is the church, and next to the church stands a government building housing public offices (the *Presidencia Municipal*, the telegraph and postal services, the state radiotelephony, and others.) The remaining three sides are occupied by stores, restaurants, a local branch of Bancomer Bank, and a small hotel. Ladinos have opened their stores and offices on the main street (Avenida Central norte-sur), which is paved with cement like a few other streets in downtown. Tojolabals shop in ladino stores, but they hang around behind the church where the municipal market, the *Casa Ejidal*, and the bus and truck terminals are located. INI's CCI-Tojolabal used to be in this area but was moved about three blocks west from the market. Radio Margaritas is situated in the barrio San Sebastián, about 16 blocks south and 6 blocks west of the main plaza, which is to say a 40-minute walk from both the market and INI's CCI-Tojolabal.

From the relatively large number of stores and pharmacies downtown, one can easily see how Margaritas City constitutes an important commercial center for the people in the surrounding villages. Commercial activity gives the city its two main rhythms: one, running from Monday through Saturday, when activities are at a slow pace, and the other, on Sundays when a large number of Tojolabals visit the city and a busy, festive, market environment is created. Villagers come to buy medicines, batteries, clothes, needles, thread, salt, sugar, soap, candles, matches, bread, cookies, cigarettes, coffee, beans, and audio cassettes. They may also buy dresses, hand lamps, ammunition, radios, and cassette players from the Guatemalan Chapines who are in charge of the local black market dealing in manufactured goods. But not all commerce is done in Margaritas City since both Chapines and ladino animal buyers travel throughout the villages, and Tojolabal women also exchange goods (art crafts, some agricultural products and animals).

Colonia Tabasco. Tabasco, one of the two Tojolabal colonias that I selected for the audience study, is a place where Tojolabal customs and mores are zealously kept. To go to Tabasco people travel the road going northeast from Margaritas City to El Edén and drive for about one hour. Then they turn left and continue on a dirt road for about another ten minutes before arriving at the river's bridge. If there's no mud, people can drive up to the village, but if it has been raining, they have to walk through the muddy hills. Both roads are narrow, in very poor condition, and the dirt road has a gate across it with two big, old Chinese locks. So, when visitors arrive at this point, they have to walk to the colonia and see if the komisariyado will allow the door to be opened. I thought that the spatial separation from the main road of Tabasco resembles Tabascans' cultural distance from mainstream Mexican society.

Tabascans actively participate in one of the local federations of ejidos (*Unión de Ejidos Tierra y Libertad*) which coordinates the efforts of several local villages to obtain credit and infrastructure. Rather than becoming part of the dominant political party (PRI), Tabascans favor the national democratic movement led by Cuauhtémoc Cárdenas. "It is very difficult to deal with them," I was told by a municipal government official, "They are very leftist." Tabascans have also strengthened the village's authority and enforce it even over religious practices and affairs that are legally under the jurisdiction of the municipio. As one of Tabasco's leaders put it:

> Before, people had to go to Margaritas City for every little problem; now we take care of everything among ourselves. If someone gets drunk, we have a jail, or if someone doesn't respect our agreements, for instance, we don't allow anyone to have pigs because they cause much damage in the colonia; we have also prohibited religious practice (protestant sects) in the colonia; religion creates division, that's why we do not allow it here.

The ejido is situated next to an old finca that, according to a Tabascan, "used to belong to a gringo," and that is still private property. The dirt road lies along the finca, and the locks on this road are the result of grievances between Tabasco and Chiapas, its neighboring ejido. In order to prevent their Tojolabal neighbors from using the dirt road, Tabascans installed the locks. Thus people from Colonia Chiapas lack a good way to transport their products in trucks and have to carry them on their backs up to the main road. As is often the case in conflicts involving indigenous communities, the

Tabascans' grievances with their neighbors have to do with land boundaries.

Tabasco received 635 hectares in 1959, and according to the records of the *Secretaría de la Reforma Agraria*, ten years later the ejido was granted another 904 hectares.[54] According to my Tabascan informants, however, the ejido received only 659 more hectares, and several ejidos (including Chiapas and Tabasco) are still claiming the remaining 245 hectares. These hectares are timberlands, but a current environmental restriction prevents anyone from exploiting them. Tabascans say they have a total of roughly 160 hectares of arable land, which is about a quarter of the initial 635 hectares. In Tabasco 33 *ejidatarios* (head of households with ejidatario status) and 42 *avecindados* (head of households with a non-ejidatario status) make a living by farming about 160 hectares. Another quarter of the first land grant of 635 hectares is suitable to raise cattle, but Tabascans do not make a significant income from husbandry because usually a family cannot afford more than two cows and a few chickens. Cows are used to help with agricultural work, but dairy products, which are foreign to Tabascan diet, are not consumed.

The colonia lies in a beautiful small canyon, very green and surrounded by hills covered in winter with yellow flowers. Not far off are the mountains partially covered with clouds. I was able to determine only one short street, around which the houses of roughly 60 families are established. Except for the school, all buildings are made of wood. During my fieldwork, a large room made of brick and cement was being built: "It's going to be the kinder garden," I was told. There is neither electricity nor drinking water, but people have plenty of water nearby.

Houses are built with lumber and have roofs with two slopes made of either tin, tile, or hay. People no longer care for hay because insects will thrive in the roof; when they can afford it, they invest in tin roofs. Most families have two buildings, the kitchen and the "house," which is the place where people sleep and relax. In extended families, a young couple may have their own house but will share the kitchen with the husband's family. The typical house has a rectangular floor plan of about 11 by 6 yards; kitchens tend to be smaller, with a square shape. In the region, structures often had no windows at all, and even those made of brick frequently have either no windows or only very small ones. Houses in Tabasco have neither bathrooms nor latrines (the only latrines, in deplorable condition, are in the school). Buildings are surrounded by large fenced-in sitiyos (yard-gardens). In some sitiyos three or four structures stand together forming a house compound. The sitiyos are full of greenery and have many fruit trees, lemon, orange, coffee, and banana.

In the center of the kitchen, and often burning the whole day, is the *fogón* (fireplace). It is either placed directly on the floor or on a low platform. Next to the fireplace, and often against the wall, stand one or two long tables where women cook and place dishes. Since the fireplace has no chimney, the smoke stays inside the room, escaping through the open triangular space between the roof and the walls, the spaces between the lumber of the walls, or the door. Usually there is no eating table, but a few chairs and benches may be in the kitchen. Other objects usually kept here are dishes made of pewter and clay, a large number of baskets, a hand grinder for the cooked corn, a wooden press for making tortillas, a *chiwte'* (a long stick with three ends on top, which serves as the base for a water container or a basket) and several *tajab'al* to carry loads on the back (also known as *mecapal*, a pre-columbian instrument). The corn is stored either in the kitchen or in the house.

The house is often divided into two small rooms with one or two beds in each. Beds resemble long, low tables, with no mattress, and all the furniture (beds, tables, chairs, and benches) is very small. There is also an altar in this building, which may carry an image or two of saints or of the Virgin, with candles and flowers. I had the impression that though the Catholic altars were there, people did not take extremely good care of them, since they had no fresh flowers or lighted candles. Tabasco's patron is the Virgin of Guadalupe, and her church, a building like the rest of the town's architectural structures, was made of wood with tin roof. The only signs indicating that it is the church are the two bells and the modern speaker placed outside. I was told that a priest visits Tabasco every two weeks.

Usually placed on the same table as the altar is the radio receiver, next to a bottle of *posh*, a local alcoholic beverage. The radio is often covered by a plastic bag and cassettes may be also on the table. In addition to radios, the only other electric device are flashlights operated with batteries. In two houses I saw mechanical sewing machines; I was told that there are about six sewing machines in the colonia. Tabasco has access to the same radio stations that reach Margaritas City.

According to the 1990 census taken by the local teachers, 365 people live in Tabasco, 188 women and 177 men. Two-thirds of Tabasco's population (230) is reported to speak Spanish, and only 56 adults are declared to be illiterate. I believe, however, that these figures are quite misleading. With the exception of young men, most Tabascans are not fluent in Spanish. In the teachers' census, 29 people said they reached the fourth grade, and only one man said he reached the fifth grade. This means that 117 out of the 147 who are said to be literate reached at the most the third grade. With very poor educational resources and little demand for literacy and numeracy skills, it is very unlikely that they have kept the few skills learned in school. Most the interviewees of my study stated themselves to be illiterate, and numeracy is definitely not one of the Tabascans' strengths (for example, one lady insisted she was 120 years old).

Men, especially young men, look more ladino than women. They speak some Kastiya (Spanish), and most wear ladino pants and shirts. Many go barefoot, but frequently men wear black plastic boots (the kind American janitors use to wash floors.) Only a few old men still dress in their traditional knee-high pants and shirt, both made of white cotton fabric. Women, on the other hand, often speak only Tojolabal and wear their traditional costume, which has been "heavily influenced by medieval European peasant style."[55] This is made up of a white blouse with rich embroidery and a colorful skirt (orange, blue, purple). Women go barefoot and their long hair has colorful ribbons, and many women, especially the young, wear long earrings and several necklaces made of colored plastic. Like the boys, girls wear ladino clothes until they are seven or eight years old, after which they start wearing the traditional costume. Most people and their clothes look dirty, yet young men wear clean clothes, bath often, and take care of their hair. Some wear wrist watches and even white tennis shoes and white socks, which, to me of course, seemed very inappropriate for the muddy ground of the region.

The ladino attire of the young men, however, has proved to be a helpful component of their economic strategy. Young men migrate seasonally to work in the modern fincas, and this provides an important source of income for the family. They are likely to receive better treatment when their ethnic identity is concealed. Many of the interviewees talked about the ethnic harassment that they have been subjected to. In one instance, a father told us how the *patrones* (finca landlords) harass them because they observe their traditional customs: "Our traditions are being lost because the patrones scold us, and because we only understand a little Spanish we get scared of the patrones and we do what they say, that's why we do it and we lose our customs." Since Tojolabals need to earn some income outside of their villages, the challenge, especially for young men, is how to continue being faithful to their native culture while at the same time developing a sense of security for advancing themselves in the modern ladino world. They have appropriated radio to respond to this challenge. Like the wrist watch, radio receivers are used by young men to signify modernity, and more importantly, participating in Radio Margaritas seems to offer an opportunity to reconcile their Indianness with their desire for becoming modern.

Now I will turn to their daily routines. Tabascans awaken about 4:00 a.m., and by 6:00 a.m. most of them have left for the *milpas* (corn fields). Some take a yoke of oxen with them. In November, men, women, and children are either *tapiscando* (picking-up) corn or preparing the land for the new sowing. During the morning and early afternoon, only women (most of them old), young children, and some girls stay in the colonia. The grandmother has a definite role in housework: she is in charge of preparing the food and supervising the children. Grandmothers and young girls spend a lot of time together. They take care of young children and do the household chores; they prepare the food so that it will be ready when the others come back from the milpa; they go together to the nearby creek to do the laundry, wash coffee beans, and fetch water on their backs or their heads.

At 9:00 a.m. children go to school and take classes until 11:30 a.m., when the school day ends. In Tabasco's school, the only structure built according to ladino standards, bilingual lessons are given. Officially, but not in actual practice, the first three grades of elementary education are taught. During my fieldwork there were two Tojolabal teachers, and the possible enrollment was 81 children. Teachers often fail to be present (a common regional practice is to leave town on Thursday afternoon and return next Tuesday morning), and parents do not complain because they need the children's help. Students in Tabasco seemed to me very young; I thought most of them were under four years, but the teacher said that the youngest were five. I felt that the place was more a day-care center than an elementary school.

By 2:00 p.m. Tabascans come back from the milpas, and the colonia becomes quite lively. Some people carry large bags with corn-on-the-cob on their backs; others carry fire wood. After eating, they finish the day's chores: feeding the cows, taking care of the coffee beans drying in the sun, grinding the corn, shelling the beans, milling the nixtamal, cooking. In the afternoon, especially on Sundays, the day dedicated to rest, people spend time in their sitiyos relaxing and socializing with neighbors. Sunday is also the day to take a bath in the river, get a haircut, and wear clean clothes. About 6:30 p.m. the village starts to get quiet again; by 7:00 p.m. it is completely dark, and Tabasco prepares for sleep.

Tabasco has a health center (*Centro de salud*) which is a pair of small rooms with a little table, three little chairs, and a medicine case. These rooms are part of the building that houses the local co-op store. There are four health extension workers (*promotores de salud*) in Tabasco, and one of my interviewers had done some recordings for Radio Margaritas with them. One of the promotores told me that they have attended training classes outside the town, and that they prescribe medicine and send people to the hospital. He said that they mainly prescribe dehydration therapy for children. The medicines in the Centro were packages for dehydration therapy, anti-inflammatories, condoms, aspirin, penicillin, and cough tablets. At night I was able to hear half the town coughing.

The store is open every day from 5:00 to 7:00 p.m. It is managed by the co-op composed of 48 men. It is the local place to hang out for young men. They get together there, drink soft drinks, and smoke cigarettes. Women also go to the store, but they do not stay for long. The store sells soft drinks, candy, packages of potato chips (and other like food), soap, batteries, candles, bread, cans of chiles and sardines, salt, cigarettes, and matches. One of the managers, a man in his early twenties, told me that these products are brought from Margaritas City, and added: "We opened this store recently, after the store started by the nuns (*Hermanas de Asís*) failed because of bad management."

Next to the store is the garage for the *Unión de Ejidos'* brand new, three ton truck. "We bought the truck supported by INI," said the young driver. The truck has a legend on its doors that reads: "*Unión de Ejidos Tierra y Libertad. INI, Fondos Regionales.*" This truck, with trips scheduled on weekends, provides transportation for people and products. Driving is a skill highly appreciated, and although there are two drivers in Tabasco, only one man drives now. The other is afraid because another truck (also belonging to the Unión) was involved in an accident. One of Tabascans' diversions is going out of town on weekends. On one of my field trips I rode back to Margaritas City on the truck. There were about 20 other people as well, going either to the county seat or to villages nearby. Several bags of corn were also transported, and we stopped before Margaritas City to sell the corn.

My audience study includes nine interviews conducted in Tabasco. Since Tabascans keep extended families and they were more willing to talk about Radio Margaritas than Maderans, the study ended up having more interviewees from Tabasco than from Madero (36 versus 23). The study also has more Tabascan men than women (21 versus 15) because young men were particularly eager to participate in the interviews; whereas, the women were openly discouraged by their families. The geographic isolation of Tabascans, combined with their strong sense of ethnic identity, is helpful in understanding why they treasure Radio Margaritas in a way that seems to be alien to most Maderans. The next section introduces Madero, the second village selected for the study.

Colonia Francisco I. Madero. Whereas Tabasco is enclosed and separated from the main road, Colonia Francisco I. Madero is open, crossed by one of the region's main roads. Madero typifies a Tojolabal settlement undergoing a rapid process of acculturation to the ladino society. On the one hand elements of the traditional culture are clearly seen: nearly all people speak Tojolabal, most houses are built according to the region's customary way, inherited agricultural and medical practices are employed, and ancestral customs regulate many aspects of the social life. Yet, on the other hand, significant changes can also be noted: many people also speak some Spanish, several buildings are made of brick or adobe, television antennas and electric wires are part of the town's scenery, few women (and hardly any men) wear the traditional costume, innovations such as fertilizers and pharmaceutical products are widely used, and people are opting for values foreign to their parents.

One cannot say that Madero, with a population of over a thousand,[56] is a classical Tojolabal village (which a few years ago was estimated as having an average of 210 people[57]). However, one cannot deny that the living conditions of an increasing number of Tojolabals resemble those of Maderans. Madero leads a group of large Tojolabal villages whose people are adopting new life styles.[58] Its proximity to Margaritas City (a 20-minute drive) has brought infrastructure, social services, and other innovations to the colonia. About 70 percent of the colonia has electricity, and one of the three main roads from the county seat to the villages (Margaritas City-El Paraíso) passes through Madero. It has a health center (with a physician and a nurse) and several educational facilities: a kindergarten, an INI boarding school, a complete primary school (first to sixth grades), and a *Telesecundaria*.[59] Madero also has a number of public buildings and recreational facilities: a Catholic church, a *Casa Ejidal*, a basketball court, and a CONASUPO store. A note of interest is that INI seriously considered installing Radio Margaritas in Madero.

Electricity has made it possible to install a public *nixtamal* (cooked corn) mill, and furthermore, to receive television. Radio listening habits have also changed with the introduction of electricity, since people can afford to have the radio on for longer periods. Madero is covered by the same radio stations as Margaritas City, and it also receives the same television channels. There have been, moreover, other very important agents of change in the ejido since the Presbyterian and Pentecostal missionaries have made a few converts among the villagers.

The ejido accounts for 2020 hectares, but only 400 of them are arable land (200 *temporal* and 200 *pulja*). Five hectares are used for cattle raising, and there are no forest resources to exploit. The soil quality is much worse than in Tabasco, and the land has became insufficient for the number of people trying to make a livelihood from it; there are 81 ejidatarios básicos and 193 avecindados (a total of 274).[60] "For more than 20 years, we have been asking for more land, but we haven't achieved anything," said one of my informants. Other Maderans said that every ejidatario, with his children, works between two and three hectares (considering only temporal) and owns two cows.

The colonia's landscape contrasts sharply with Tabasco's. Madero sits on an eroded plateau with only a few trees; along with herbal and ornamental plants, family gardens may have orange and lemon trees, but they have no banana or coffee trees. The architecture is also different from Tabasco's; the church and the Casa Ejidal are old buildings resembling those of ladino towns, streets follow straight lines, and many dwellings show elements of ladino house-building (e.g., tiled roofs, windows, adobe and brick walls) and tend to be isolated as opposed to being a part of a house compound.

Are Maderans better off than Tabascans? Regardless of what I would like to argue concerning the loss of traditional values and the sense of community, most Maderans believe they have better living conditions than Tabascans. But although Maderans have greater access to modern services than many Tojolabals, they still live under very poor conditions. The following data were the best quantitative information available; it was gathered by a survey conducted by the local health center physician.[61] One can easily imagine the numerous flaws in such research (e.g., people reporting having a latrine to the same person who has told them before about the need for having one). I use these data as rough indicators; however, from the perspective of my own observations, the situation seemed worse.

The colonia has 278 rooms for 153 families, which means that 28 families may either live in a single room or share the kitchen with another family (this does not take into account that a handful of families have more than two rooms). The vast majority of the rooms have dirt floors, 206 houses have no windows, and 70 kitchens have the fireplace directly on the floor. All of the houses are infested with rats, mice, roaches, fleas, and bedbugs, and 15 families have cattle or poultry living inside the house. There is no running water, only 16 families have latrines, and none of them burn nor bury the garbage. These conditions, coupled with a very low income, could only result in high morbidity and mortality rates. In 1989, 175 children younger than five years of age were diagnosed with malnutrition; since about half of the population (e.g., roughly 500 people) is less than 15 years old, practically all small children lack an adequate diet. Also all 153 families visited the local health center with symptoms of intestinal parasites, and 49 families had symptoms of mange.

However, according to Tojolabal standards, Maderans are quite educated. Although roughly half of the adult population (223 people) is illiterate, 163 people have had some schooling, 86 have completed the sixth grade, 13 have attended secondary school, 35 have graduated from secondary school, and 11 have had further education. Most people make a livelihood farming, and 47 complement their income raising cattle. The exceptions are 10 merchants and 11 people employed as teachers or public servants (at least four of them work for INI). The population's schooling and competence in Spanish are linked with a trend toward integrating into the political mainstream. Maderan leaders have been members of the official party, PRI, and of INI's *Consejo Supremo Tojolabal*. Ruz notes that Madero has received infrastructure and social services because of the associations of local political leaders with the *Consejo*.[62]

Since they farm like Tabascans, Maderans' daily lives are structured by similar routines. Still, remarkable differences exist. Men often spend the night in the milpa's temporary shelters or arrive home late (after 5:00 p.m.) because many of their plots are located far from the colonia. People do not go to bed as soon as the sun sets. Many of them have electric power, and some have television. Maderans travel frequently, and there are also many outsiders in town because of their proximity to Margaritas City and the road crossing through the colonia. Children attend school for longer periods, so they have became more of an economic burden than a help to their parents. A combination of these dissimilarities with Tabascan life explains what is probably the major contrast: women cannot work in the milpa every day, they have to take care of the children's needs, they need to apply themselves to house chores previously performed by their daughters, and they must keep an eye on the house to make sure strangers are not around.

I selected Madero as the second village for the audience study because, as I mentioned before, increasing numbers of Tojolabals do not live in small and remote villages anymore, but in settlements similar to Madero. Although we interviewed 14 families in Madero, I only included 12 of them in the sample for the audience study. In contrast with Tabasco, usually where other people in addition to the father and the mother participated in the interviews, in Madero most interviews were conducted with only the father and the mother. The exceptions were three interviews: one with a father and son, a second one with the father and his sister, and a third with only the mother. In the latter, two other women, her daughters, were also present, but their participation was meagre, so I did not count them as interviewees.

My sample then is composed of 23 Maderans, 11 men and 12 women. Maderan women tend to be more talkative than their Tabascan counterparts, a fact in part explained by their higher acculturation to ladino culture (including changes in their everyday activities), yet also explained by elements directly related to my research. Regarding the interviewing process, most interviews held in Madero were conducted by a Tojolabal woman, Candelaria Rodríguez, rather than a Tojolabal man, Armando Alfaro. Both interviewers, moreover, were from Madero. As for the object of study, radio has lost much of its meaning as a signifier of modernity since television, and even the video casette recorder, has already been introduced. So I suspect that in Madero, radio belongs less to an exclusive male domain, and women can talk about radio. Most importantly, as I will show, Maderan women have far more opportunities for radio exposure than Tabascan women.

Media Environment

Tojolabals have a number of listening options in Spanish, but only XEVFS transmits in their own language. These options are a wide range of non-local stations plus three stations broadcasting from Comitán City. The former include commercial stations (e.g., XEW which transmits from Mexico City, and T de Monterrey), religious broadcasting from Guatemala, and external services available on shortwave (e.g., The Voice of America, and Radio Habana Cuba). Two out of the three stations airing from Comitán City were set up quite recently and do not represent competition for XEVFS; XEMIT, an AM affiliate of the *Instituto Mexicano de la Radio*, was started in January 1989, and XHCTS-FM in August 1990. This FM station targets the ladino audience, though its general manager said that he is trying to attract rural audiences, programing ranchera and marimba music from 5:00 to 7:00 a.m.

The real competition for XEVFS is XEUI, Radio Comitán, an AM commercial station established in 1963. Radio Comitán conforms to the monopolistic scheme of an industry that has been properly described as a "family industry."[63] The license was granted to Ms. Partida Amador, a relative of José de Jesús Partida; the latter holds shares not only in this and other radio stations in the state of Chiapas, but also in stations located in the state of Veracruz and Chihuahua. XEUI transmits with a power of 1,000 watts and targets both ladino and indigenous audiences. In a study conducted in April 1988, Florence Toussaint found that XEUI enjoyed great popularity among local audiences. This study focussed on Comitán City, and its sample included probably few, if any, Tojolabals. Thus its findings are representative of the ladino rather than the Tojolabal population. According to Toussaint, roughly 92 percent of the sample indicated that they listen to the radio, and 77 percent of them said they prefer XEUI.[64] To attract Tojolabals XEUI broadcasts avisos and popular music (e.g., ranchera music). Cornejo and Luna found that XEUI is the second listening choice of Radio Margaritas' target audience.[65] My own investigation supports this finding, and it also shows that when talking about their radio listening, Tojolabals often mention XEUI and compare this station with XEVFS. I discuss this comparison in more detail later.

In addition to radio listening, some Tojolabals have access to television. In places like Margaritas City and Madero, people can watch Televisa's channels 2 and 5, as well as the government-owned channels 7 and 13. Toussaint also found that in 1988 most people in Comitán City watched channel 2, which has been the most popular channel throughout the country for many years; it features mainly Mexican productions such as the newscast *24 Horas* and telenovelas (the program with the highest rating was the telenovela *Rosa Salvaje*).

With the exception of a handful of educated people, most of them men, Tojolabals do not read newspapers. Even among the ladino population, local newspaper readership is very low. According to Toussaint's study 74 percent of Comitán City's population did not read any newspaper, and only 8.3 percent of those who read the newspapers bought the newspaper each day. What is striking, though indeed common in Mexico, is that local and political news concerned readers the least. While over a half of the readership was primarily interested either in sports news (34.4 percent) or in news about social events (17.7 percent), only 12.5 percent was interested in political news. Local news, likewise, appealed only to 14.6 percent of the readership; whereas, national (40.6 percent) and international news (40.6 percent) were seen as equally important.[66] It follows that the newspaper most chosen by readers was not a local but a national daily (*Excelsior*), and that the second and third choices were dailies published in Tuxtla Gutiérrez, the state capital (*Número Uno* and *La República en Chiapas*).

The lack of readers' interest in local and political news suggests that the audience attributes low credibility to these news items. It is well known that local journalism in Chiapas, like in many other regions of the Third World, operates within an environment of press censorship and control. To take an extreme example, consider that in 1988 a journalist from Comitán City's recently installed newspaper *El Mundo* was murdered. Therefore, it is not surprising that Chiapas journalists' writing fails to meet U.S. standards of objectivity (in the sense of factualness) and that investigative reporting on current local affairs is rare in Mexican dailies. Though the vast majority of indigenous people do not relate to the print media, it is important to keep in mind that assumptions and practices originating in print journalism permeate radio broadcasting. Radio Margaritas operates within a media environment characterized by censorship and control, and as my research suggests, does not escape the working assumptions of Mexican journalism.

Availability and Cost of Reception Technology. Since radio uses low-cost and widely available reception technology, and since transistor radios also can receive signals in places without electricity, the consumption of radio offerings seems to be a media experience within the reach of the rural poor. For the Tojolabal, however, consuming radio offerings costs more and is less feasible than might be thought. As in other rural areas in Mexico, radio consumption in Tabasco and Madero is characterized by the poor quality and the extremely high price of radio receivers. Likewise such consumption is distinguished by the relatively high cost of operating receivers with batteries. In Margaritas or Comitán City, a radio receiver costs about three times as much as in Mexico City's black market or in the United States. But despite the inflated price, the receiver has extremely low quality. It is not surprising then that in Margaritas City radio-repair shops abound. The owner of one of these shops said he repairs an average of 40-50 receivers per month. The ownership of electronic media among the families interviewed is given in Figure 7.3.

As figure 7.3 shows, at the time of the interviews, almost a quarter of the families sampled had broken receivers, and there were four families with no receivers (two had no working receiver at that time and another two, old Maderan couples, had never had a receiver at all). It is worth comparing the situation regarding the ownership of media technology in the two villages. Tabascan families share a similar level of ownership of electronic appliances; they either own a radio cassette recorder or a simple radio receiver, but sharp differences exist among Maderan families, because in Madero some families have only radio receivers and other families own television sets. These patterns naturally mirror the general pattern in the distribution of wealth in the two villages.

The cost of owning a radio receiver can be a substantial expense for a poor Tojolabal family. It includes not only the initial cost, but also the cost of repairs and consumed energy. The initial cost depends on the type and quality of the radio set, as well as where it is bought.[67] At the time of my fieldwork, an AM-FM, made in the United States, radio cassette recorder sold in Comitán for about $70 dollars, and a simple AM receiver, Chinese-made, sold for about $21 dollars. As a point of reference, bear in mind that

FIGURE 7.3 Ownership of Electronic Media Among the Families Interviewed

Family			Media			
I.D. number	Village	Parents' age	Simple radio receiver	Radio cassette-recorder	Stereo system	TV
1	Tabasco	31-40	Broken			
2	Tabasco	41-50		Working		
3	Tabasco	30-40		Working		
4	Tabasco	+60		Working		
5	Tabasco	41-50		Working		
6	Tabasco	51-60		Working		
7	Tabasco	31-40		Working		
17	Tabasco	31-35		Working		
18	Tabasco	21-25		Working		
9	Madero	26-30	Broken	Working		B&W
10	Madero	31-35	Broken	Working		
11	Madero	21-25		Working		
13	Madero	21-25	Working	Working	Working	B&W Color
14	Madero	51-55				
15	Madero	51-55	Working			
16	Madero	26-30	Broken	Working		
19	Madero	61-65				
20	Madero	51-55		Working		
21	Madero	46-50		Working		B&W
22	Madero	31-35	Working	Working		B&W
23	Madero	31-35	Broken Working			
Total			5 Broken 5 Working	15	1	4 B&W 1 Color

Note that the total number of families interviewed was 21.

the minimum daily wage was at the time about $3.48 dollars. Thus, assuming that a Tojolabal earns the minimum wage, which only a handful of them do, to buy an AM-FM radio cassette recorder such a person would have to invest the earnings of 20 work days. In addition, this person would have to invest in repairs because receivers come with no guarantee and are of very low quality.

The monthly expenditure for keeping the receiver operating with batteries comes roughly to the earnings of a half-day of work. The type of batteries needed by almost all the families' receivers ("C" type) in Madero or Tabasco sold for $0.42 each. Radio cassette recorders need four batteries, and simple radios need two. A frequent answer to the question, "How often do you put new batteries in your receiver?" was, "Once a month." So the monthly cost of batteries may reach $1.68 dollars. It is important to note that, in addition to Tabascans, some Maderans also use batteries to run their receivers either because their houses have no electric outlet, or because their receiver works only with batteries.

Ownership of Reception Technology and Social Uses. In her ethnography of Nahuas of Guerrero, Mexico Catharine Good Eshelman describes how stereo systems have become the most widely sought consumer goods among these people because stereos promote social gatherings and can also be used as any other good or service, for reciprocal exchange.[68] Though naturally Maderans and Tabascans use radio for such purposes, I suspect that their uses of radio include not only a dimension of sharing and cooperation, but also of family conflict and gender domination. At another level I also suggest that the consumption of Radio Margaritas' offerings is a signifying practice challenging both the conventional meaning of listening to radio and the established definitions of Indianness. I mentioned above that a striking use of the radio set, and most importantly of radio listening, is as a commodity consumed to acquire the status of being modern.[69] The radio set, as well as the wrist watch, seems to be used by young Tojolabal men to signify their participation in modern life. This point finds support in the patterns of ownership and control of the receiver.

Most families claimed that the radio receiver forms part of the household and that it is used as such by all family members. Three families specified that "as a property itself, the radio belongs to the father."[70] I must interpret their answers in the light of property rights in the Tojolabal society, which grants only limited rights to women. Women do not inherit from their parents and seldom acquire the ejidatario status (in Madero two widows have ejidatario status), but they may own cattle, chickens, and household items such as pots and even sewing machines.[71] As a household item, the radio receiver could well be part of women's domain. However, I found that more often radio receivers belong to men, a fact consistent with the history of technology and indeed with the history of radio. Shaun Moores, for instance, in his historical study on the incorporation of radio technology into the life of U.S. families, found evidence that "it was mainly young men, caught up in the play of experimentation, who were listening to broadcast transmissions" in the 1920s.[72]

The number of radios per person is higher in Madero than in Tabasco,[73] and gender differences concerning ownership of receivers vary little from what feminist historians of technology have found in other places. In Tabasco, where the radio receiver itself acts as a signifier of modernity and higher social status, it belongs to men's domain, particularly to that of young men. In Madero, where people have already moved to more advanced technology, it is probable that property rights over the receiver have lost importance. Nine young Tabascan men were named either as owners or main users of the receiver.[74] Even more revealing was the remark made by a 32-year old Tabascan father, who said: "The radio [receiver] belongs to all of us, to all the family. Since I don't have grown-up children, it belongs to us. If there were grown-up sons, the radio might belong to one of them" (17f).[75] Yet in Madero, where people have already moved to more advanced technology, radio has lost some of its meaning as a signifier of modernity. Among the Tojolabal, teachers are the most modern people; the Maderan teacher's family in my interviews owns a stereo system, a radio cassette-recorder, a black and white television set, and a color television set. Another Maderan teacher (who was not part of the audience study's sample) owns the only video cassette recorder in town. Also, it is important to consider that in contrast to women, young men have the possibility of earning cash either in the fincas or in other occupations and thus buying consumer goods.

Ownership and control of electronic equipment may also play a part in the power dynamics inside the family. The role played by electronic technology in these dynamics has been studied by feminist researchers interested in soap opera audiences and by other critical authors like David Morley. Morley's study on television viewing highlights how home video and television equipment is used to reinforce the father's authority in the family power dynamics.[76] Although less conclusive than Morley's, my research suggests that radio may be used inside the Tojolabal family to reinforce male authority. I explore the role of radio in family and village politics in the next four chapters.

Notes

1. Instituto Nacional Indigenista, *¿Se Escuchan Nuestras Voces?* XEVFS, La Voz de la Frontera Sur, by Inés Cornejo and Silvia Luna, ts., internal document, México, 1991. I should underscore that probably most of the Spanish monolinguals sampled by this study do not fit my use of the term "ladino." I use this term to refer to the members of the local elite and their culture. Some authors use another term, "mestizo," to refer to those people who, although they do not speak an indigenous language, have a strong indigenous heritage, which includes physiological and cultural features, and seldom belong to the economic elite. The Spanish monolinguals sampled by Cornejo and Luna better fit the definition of mestizos.

2. Interviewees from other municipios were 24 from Altamirano, 18 from Venustiano Carranza, 18 from Trinitaria, 16 from Huistán, and 12 from Independencia.

3. It is important to note that Cornejo and Luna's findings on radio listening are based on the responses from these 73 interviewees and that only 30 of them were indigenous people, including Tzeltals, Tzotzils, and Tojolabals.

4. I excluded the findings on XETLA and XEVFS because they cannot be compared to the findings for the rest of the stations. XETLA's study was done in a

very different manner and the sample for XEVFS was very skewed. Since I am not discussing these studies in detail, I prefer to omit their findings because a brief summary of these findings would, rather than cast light on this topic, mislead the reader. This discussion is based on Cornejo and Luna's findings presented in ¿Se Escuchan Nuestras Voces? XEVFS, La Voz de la Frontera Sur.

5. Roberto Perea de la Cabada says that this proposal emerged about 1983 in XEZV; "El Instituto Nacional Indigenista y las Radios Indigenistas," IV Encuentro Nacional del CONEICC, Colima, March, 1986, 124-25.

6. I was unable to distinguish between ladinos and mestizos because I determined ethnicity by the language spoken.

7. Please note that there are missing data for all the values of the users surveys.

8. Mario Humberto Ruz, *Los Legítimos Hombres. Aproximación Antropológica al Grupo Tojolabal*, II, (México: UNAM, 1982) 13.

9. Ruz 13-14.

10. Arturo Lomelí González, *Algunas Costumbres y Tradiciones del Mundo Tojolabal* (Chiapas: Gobierno del Estado, 1988). Carlos Lenkersdorf, *Diccionario Tojolabal-Expañol* (Comitán, Chiapas: Carlos Lenkersdorf, 1979). For a literature review see Ruz 23-47.

11. See John Stephen Thomas and Mary Jill Brody, "The Tojolabal Maya: Ethnographic and Linguistic Approaches," *The Tojolabal Maya: Ethnographic and Linguistic Approaches. Geoscience and Man 26*, eds. Mary Jill Brody and John S. Thomas (Baton Rouge: Louisana State University, 1988) 3.

12. Lomelí González 4.

13. John Stephen Thomas and Michael Robbins, " The Limits to Growth in a Tojolabal Maya Ejido," *The Tojolabal Maya: Ethnographic and Linguistic Approaches. Geoscience and Man 26*, eds. Mary Jill Brody and John S. Thomas (Baton Rouge: Louisana State University, 1988) 10.

14. Louanna Furbee Losee, John S. Thomas, Harry Keith Lynch and Robert A. Benfer, "Tojolabal Maya Population Response to Stress," *The Tojolabal Maya: Ethnographic and Linguistic Approaches. Geoscience and Man 26*, eds. Mary Jill Brody and John S. Thomas (Baton Rouge: Louisana State University, 1988) 22-24.

15. Teresa Campos, "El Sistema Médico de los Tojolabales," *Los Legítimos Hombres. Aproximación Antropológica al Mundo Tojolabal*, ed. Mario Humberto Ruz (México: UNAM, 1983) 195-223.

16. As described by Louanna Furbee Losee, *The Correct Language: Tojolabal. A Grammar with Ethnographic Notes* (New York: Garland Publishing, 1976) 10.

17. Gobierno del Estado de Chiapas, *Las Margaritas, Memorias Municipales* (Tuxtla Gutiérrez, 1988).

18. Strictly speaking, like many other Tojolabal communities Madero and Tabasco are not ejidos but *colonias*. Indigenous communities in Mexico are communal societies which may be legally constituted in either *comunidades, ejidos, colonias,* or *pueblos*. Each of these community organizations has different forms of land tenure and are regulated by specific laws; the differences among them respond to the everlasting tension between the two opposing views concerning property rights that has characterized Mexican history, communal versus private property. Comunidades, which are the closest to the ancient communitarian organizations of indigenous peoples, enjoy more autonomy from the national government and a

better legal situation. Today's ejidos were legally created by the 1917 Constitution and came from the long struggle sustained by indigenous peoples to keep their communal lands and communitarian land tenure system during both the Spanish colonization (1519-1810) and the independent times (1810-1910). Colonias were established in the 1940s and are a hybrid form of land tenure; as in the ejido, the colonia's land belongs to the nation but *colonos* are given private (rather than communal) usufructury rights over their parcels. Pueblos are the result of the multiple redefinitions of the ancient forms of communal tenure and admit an even higher degree of private property rights. Gustavo Esteva, *La Batalla en el México Rural*, 6th ed. (México: Siglo XXI, 1987) 150-56.

19. Mario Humberto Ruz, *Los Legítimos Hombres. Aproximación Antropológica al Grupo Tojolabal* II (México: UNAM, 1982) 238.

20. Furbee Losee 13.

21. The media environment of the Tojolabal region is presented in Chapter 5.

22. Arturo Lomelí González, *Algunas Costumbres y Tradiciones del Mundo Tojolabal* (Chiapas: Gobierno del Estado, 1988) 4.

23. Ruz 298-300. There is the possibility that Ruz is the source for the Consejo Supremo Tojolabal. John Stephen Thomas and Mary Jill Brody note that "Ruz does not indicate how he arrives to these figures." *The Tojolabal Maya: Ethnographic and Linguistic Approaches* 3.

24. Thomas and Brody 3.

25. As I mention in Appendix 1, Mexican sociologists and anthropologists have explained the dependance of indigenous communities on ladino settings as internal colonialism. See Pablo González Casanova, *La Democracia en México*, 17th ed. (México: Era, 1987) and Rodolfo Stavenhagen, *Problemas Etnicos y Campesinos* (México: Instituto Nacional Indigenista/Secretaría de Educación Pública, 1989).

26. Furbee Losee 19.

27. Ruz 257-9.

28. Thomas and Robbins 9.

29. Thomas and Brody 4.

30. Ruz 87.

31. Thomas and Robbins 11.

32. Furbee et al. 23.

33. Thomas and Robbins 14.

34. See for instance, Michael Dodson, "Failed Development and the Rise of Fundamentalism in Central America," Unpublished essay, 1990.

35. Gilberto Giménez, "Sectas, Religión y Pueblo," *El Nacional*, 21 Sept. 1989, Suppl. Política, 3.

36. Ruz.

37. Ruz 169.

38. John Stephen Thomas, in his study of a Tojolabal community, defines a household as a group sharing a common kitchen and regularly eating together. "Determinants of Political Leadership in a Tojolabal Maya Community," diss., U of Missouri, 1978, 26.

39. Thomas 27.

40. Furbee Losee 1.

41. Thomas.

42. Ruz 192.

43. For a discussion on minority languages see Ronald Wardhaugh, *Languages in Competition* (Oxford: Basil Blackwell, 1987) 29-35.

44. Thomas and Brody 5.

45. Furbee Losee 35.

46. Furbee Losee 4.

47. Ruz 223-32.

48. Ruz 219-32.

49. INI has been instrumental in some of these organizations, but neither the development of the organizations nor INI's role has been adequately documented.

50. John Standridge White, "Lexican and Cognitive Aspects of Tojolabal Semantics," diss., U of Texas of Austin, 1979, 109.

51. Sonia Toledo Tello, "Estudio de la Organización Social del Grupo Tojolabal," Unpublished essay, 367.

52. Ruz 255.

53. Thomas and Robbins 9-10.

54. Secretaría de la Reforma Agraria, Resolución Presidencial (April 8, 1969).

55. White 107.

56. According to the 1990 census taken by the local health center, Madero's population was 1076; the Las Margaritas municipal government's figure for 1989 was 990.

57. Thomas and Brody 3.

58. Among these are Bajucú, Vicente Guerero, Guadalupe El Tepeyac, El Porvenir, Chiapas, El Edén, San Antonio Bahuitz, Palma Real, Nuevo México, González de León, Plan de Ayala, and Realidad Trinidad.

59. Telesecundaria is a distance education project sponsored by the federal government. It combines television lessons with classroom teaching. Madero's telesecundaria is not operating according to the project's design because the school has no electricity.

60. Data from the Secretaría de la Reforma Agraria and from the Municipio Las Margaritas are conflicting. The figures given here were obtained from the komisariyado ejidal; other interviewees from Madero agreed with these figures. I use them here because, though they may not be accurate, they do reflect the villagers' opinion.

61. IMSS-Solidaridad, Unidad Médica Regional Número 56, Internal document, México, 1989.

62. Ruz 255.

63. Oscar Morales, "La Radio Comercial Regional: Anatomía de un Poder," *Perfiles del Cuadrante*, eds. María Antonieta Rebeil Corella, Alma Rosa De La Selva and Ignacio Rodríguez Zárate (México: Editorial Trillas, 1989) 59.

64. Florence Toussaint Alcaraz, Recuento de Medios Fronterizos (México, Fundación Manuel Buendía, 1990).

65. Cornejo and Luna (51) found that roughly 48% of their sample prefer Radio Margaritas, but 12.33% prefer listening to XEUI the most.

66. Toussaint Alcaraz 28-29.

67. I was not able to obtain data on the prices of products sold by the Guatemalan Chapines. Although several authors (cfr. Ruz, 238) report that Tojolabals buy radios

from Chapines, the practice seems to have diminished.

68. Catharine Good Eshelman, *Haciendo la Lucha. Arte y Comercio Nahuas de Guerrero* (México: Fondo de Cultura Económica, 1988) 63-65.

69. I am speaking of status in Max Weber's sense of attribution of social distinction based on consumption or lifestyle.

70. Families 1, 5, and 18.

71. Sources are not clear on the ownership of household items. Some of my informants said that when a married couple get separated the woman keeps the furniture.

72. Shaun Moores, *Interpreting Audiences* (London: Sage, 1993) 77.

73. My conservative guess for Madero is about one radio per four persons, and for Tabasco about one per six persons.

74. F3 named three men, F4, F6, F7, and F18 named two.

75. "17F" means the father of family number 17.

76. David Morley, *Family Television: Cultural Power and Domestic Leisure* (London: Routledge, 1988). I review the literature on reception studies in Appendix 1.

8

Exposure, Listening, and Taste

Interviewer: At what time do you listen to Radio Margaritas?
Tojolabal informant: We listen when we have time and when we are at home; we also listen when we like the broadcast.

To find out what the patterns of listening to Radio Margaritas are in Tabasco and Madero, I thought that I should begin by inquiring into the times when the listening event takes place. Rather than specifying time slots, most interviewees indicated the following three circumstances: "We listen to the radio when we have time," "We listen when we are at home," and "We listen when we like the broadcast." Since of course they can only listen when the station is broadcasting, the best response must account not just for three but for four circumstances. These circumstances center on the station's broadcasting schedule, audiences' daily routines, and listeners' programming preferences. I discuss programming preferences in later sections of this chapter; first I concentrate on audiences' routines and XEVFS' schedule, then suggest that there is a lack of correspondence between them, and finally argue that 40 percent of the total, potential prime time of XEVFS is not put to use.

Tabascans and Maderans are most likely to be at home and have time for radio listening during three time slots. One is on Sundays because Tojolabals rest on Sundays. The second is in the early morning (4:00-7:00 a.m.) since in both villages people get up around 4:00 a.m., go to work about 7:00, and rarely come back before 3:00 p.m. And the third is in the late afternoon and early evening, probably between 3:00 and 9:00 p.m. Tabascans return from the milpa about 3:00 p.m. and go to bed around 7:00 or 8:00 p.m., while Maderans may arrive home after 5:00 p.m. and stay up later than those in Tabasco. This quote by a Tabascan man illustrates how interviewees talked about these three periods:

Since we go to work at six thirty in the morning we listen for a while in the morning and after work, at about three in the afternoon, then we listen again

because we come back from work at that time. So we listen for awhile in the
morning and for awhile in the afternoon because we have no time due to our
work. We go out to work almost all day, but when we do not go to work [on
Sunday], then is when we listen to the radio! (7f)[1]

These three periods have different potential audiences. In their audience
study on XEVFS, Inés Cornejo and Silvia Luna found that almost 60 percent
of the indigenous people sampled reported to listen most in the morning.[2]
Mornings are likely to have far more listeners than afternoons and Sundays
considering that the station's signal reaches the remote areas only, or better,
in the early morning hours. We must also take into account that all families
interviewed said that they usually listen to XEVFS in the morning, but
references to afternoon listening were less frequent: only seven Tabascans
and one Maderan pointed out that they generally listen after work,[3] and
four Maderans stated that they have the radio on all day.[4] In addition, two
women (one Tabascan, one Maderan) made clear they listen in the afternoon
only if they have time,[5] a remark consistent with observed routines. Naturally,
the work has priority over radio listening, but a young Tabascan mother
said that she sometimes inverts these priorities: "I like the talk shows
because sometimes they are very nice, when we hear the talk shows we like,
even if we have important tasks to do, we stop doing them to listen to the
radio" (2m).

Do people listen to the radio before six o'clock in the morning, when the
station begins transmitting? Most families (17 of 21) stated they begin to
listen to XEVFS around 6:00 a.m. However my interview schedule failed to
address directly the possibility that they listen to other stations before 6:00
a.m. The daily routines of both villages suggest that people listen to other
stations before XEVFS begins broadcasting. In fact I found support for this
point in the interviews: "We turn on the radio at four o'clock in the morning
but since at that time Radio Margaritas is not yet broadcasting, but it began
transmissions about five thirty, at that time we start listening to it" (11f).
And another Maderan man said: "I get up at two, at three, at four, and at that
time I turn the radio on and listen to it, about six I tune to radio Margaritas" (16f).

Radio listening represents an important leisure alternative on Sundays.
Even though Sunday is the preferred day for diversions outside the house
(e.g., going out of town, bathing in the nearby rivers), many people,
especially Tabascans, stay at home and enjoy listening to the radio. And
they may choose XEVFS over other stations, as a Tabascan young women
put it when she commented on the hypothetical closing of the station:

I think it would be very sad for us if they closed Radio Margaritas because on
Sundays we do not go out of town and we listen to the radio, but if they closed
the radio we would not be able to send our avisos, we wouldn't even listen to
the pretty music, perhaps this is also transmitted by Radio Comitán, but that's

something else, and you have to pay, in our own radio you don't have to pay for the services offered to us (2d).

Thirteen interviews explicitly indicated that people listen to XEVFS on Sundays.[6] Further, one of the few criticisms expressed by my informants concerns XEVFS early close of transmission on weekends. A Tabascan young father offered the following objection:

We always listen to radio Margaritas, and sometimes it happens that when on Saturdays and Sundays, because the radio stops working at three, after work we come and turn the radio on to listen to Radio Margaritas and we see there's nothing, but then we remember that on weekends it stops working at three in the afternoon, and we disagree with that, to stop working at that time (18f).

Early morning, late afternoon, and Sunday are XEVFS' potential prime time. Assuming that people are likely to spend time listening on Sunday from 4:00 a.m. to 7:00 p.m. (15 hours per week), and other days in the morning from 4:00 a.m. to 7:00 a.m.(18 hours per week), as well as in the afternoon from 3:00 p.m. to 7:00 p.m. (24 hours per week), then the potential weekly prime time would be 57 hours. Yet this time is greatly reduced because of the lack of correspondence between XEVFS' schedule and its listeners' daily routines. The station transmits from 5:30 a.m. to 6:00 p.m. on weekdays, and it leaves the air at 3:00 p.m. on weekends. Thus the station fails to employ one and a half hours every day in the morning, at least one hour in the afternoon Monday through Friday, and four hours in the afternoon on Saturday and Sunday.[7] All this comes to 23.5 hours per week, which means that the station may not be taking advantage of about 40 percent of its potential prime time. Over and above this, XEVFS fails to put to use half of its valuable morning hours (4:00 to 5:30 a.m.).

This lack of correspondence between the station's schedule and its potential prime time is due in part to legal constraints, and in part to operative reasons. The station holds a license to transmit from 6:00 a.m. to 6:00 p.m. XEVFS begins broadcasting half an hour before six o'clock, but since it is not officially on the air, it transmits only music for 30 minutes during this period. Apart from legal constraints, the reasons for the present schedule are related to station management. To adjust the station's schedule to its potential prime time would bring about a variety of difficulties in terms of labor availability, work schedules, and supervision. Such difficulties, however, could be overcome, and perhaps INI may find a way to obtain a license for more transmission hours.

But what lies at the heart of this misfit between broadcasting schedule and potential prime time seems to be a question of technology transfer. In communication research it is commonly argued that when a new technology is introduced to a different setting, what is transferred is not only the technology itself, but also a set of assumptions and practices regarding the particular technology and its use. Despite the efforts made by the INI stations to adjust radio to indigenous populations, this argument still finds strong support in the case of Radio Margaritas, since its broadcasting schedule fits better U.S. urban audiences than Tojolabal listeners.

Most people in the United States listen to the radio when they are getting ready for and driving to work, and when they are driving back home. Thus in the United States listening prime time—"drive time" as it is called in the U.S. media industry—is made up of two main periods: from 6:00 to 10:00 a.m. and from 4:00 to 7:00 p.m.[8] Since North Americans have plenty of diversions available, on Sunday they are exposed to radio much less than during weekdays. Not only is Radio Margaritas' schedule better suited for the drive time of North Americans than for the daily routines of Tojolabals, but also the station's Sunday programming ignores the potential of Tojolabal Sunday listening. On Sundays XEVFS ends transmission earlier than during week days, it broadcasts its weekend news review produced only in Spanish twice (6:30-7:00 a.m. and 2:00-2:30 p.m.), and it dedicates four hours (9:00 a.m. to 1:00 p.m.) to poorly attended participatory programs. Rather than treating Sunday as an important segment of its prime time, on Sundays the station conducts its business in a casual style (see section on Radio Margaritas' daily routines, Chapter 6).

One last point regarding exposure time to radio. Exposure occurs only in certain settings, and even though my schedule failed to include this issue, the interviewees often said that they listen to the radio when they are at home. It follows that listening usually does not take place in the other major setting of their daily life, the corn field or milpa. This reasoning is consistent with Inés Cornejo's study on XETLA, which found that 29.5 percent of the sample admitted to listening to the radio only at home.[9] Yet four of the Tabascan families of my sample talked about taking their receivers to the milpa occasionally,[10] and a Tabascan man explained that they only carry the receivers when they go to work on the milpas near the village.[11] Because most milpas in Madero are much farther from the village than the milpas in Tabasco, his comment explains the fact that no Maderan talked about listening to the radio at the milpa.

Exposure and Differential Modes of Involvement in Reception

Listening to Radio Margaritas broadcasting is the most widespread way of participating in the station. Thus, differential modes of involvement in reception processes were a crucial concern for my study. I began tackling this issue in the first question regarding the amount of exposure time to radio, but I also included in the interview schedule another set of questions regarding exposure.[12] Specifically, I asked which family member listens to

XEVFS the most and which member the least. When I compared interviewees' answers to these questions with information about both their daily routines and other factors determining preconditions for radio exposure (e.g., the cost of batteries and the access to a receiver), I found that age is a clear indicator of exposure because regardless of their gender and their place of residence, children and the elderly seldom listen to radio offerings. I also found that gender and place of residence, on the other hand, are more complex indicators and have to be considered together. Maderan women are heavier consumers of radio than Maderan men, but the situation appears to be reversed in Tabasco. Especially in Tabasco, XEVFS primarily appeals to a similar demographic group that all-news stations reach in the United States.[13] Interestingly enough, the profile of Tabasco's heaviest consumer of XEVFS' offerings somewhat resembles the profile of the prime reader of daily newspapers in the United States: young and middle age, educated men.

Listening time is directly linked to daily routines that are, in turn, tied up with the division of labor. Often, the network's staff and other extension workers (e.g., INI's employees, doctors, and teachers) state that the segment of the audience listening the most are women, because they stay at home while men go to work outside. Cornejo also concurs with this opinion; though in her study about XEVFS she found only a slight difference between men's and women's time of exposure.[14] In my interviews people seem to support this assumption because they often stated both that the people staying at home listen to the radio the most and that people working at the milpa listen the least. These comments, however, may not necessarily mean that regardless of their place of residence, women outnumber men as consumers of XEVFS' offerings. I found that the opposite may well be true. Josefina Aranda Bezaury and Verónica Valenzuela reached a very similar conclusion in their investigation on XEZV.[15]

In Tojolabal communities farming is far from being exclusively a male activity. With the exception of tasks requiring the use of male strength (e.g., plowing), women and children often do all kinds of agricultural work.[16] But there is, of course, a division of labor among the Tojolabal which varies according to the particular circumstances of every village, and whose distinctions are based on gender and age. Hence the division of labor differs in the two villages. In Madero occupations are more clearly divided along gender lines than in Tabasco. In both communities adult and young women carry out agricultural tasks in the milpas, but in Madero women dedicate more time to housework (which is exclusively a women's domain) than to agricultural activities. In Tabasco, on the other hand, with the exception of elderly women, women do agricultural labor every day.[16] While most women from Tabasco go to the milpa on a regular basis, women from Madero tend to perform tasks closer to their homes. Thus if Tabascan women do not regularly stay at home, they cannot be heavy radio consumers. Conversely, if Maderan women spend more time at home than in the milpa, they may be frequent listeners.

This conclusion is consistent with interviewees' responses. When asked, "Who is the family member who listens to the radio the most?" most families (16 of 21) indicated that it is a female family member. However, there was an important difference between Tabascan and Maderan families; while almost all Maderan families (11 of 12) told us that the person listening to the radio the most is a woman, only five of the nine Tabascan families said the same. Here are two examples of Tabascans' responses:

Interviewer: Who listens to the radio the most?
Mother: All of us listen.
Father: Well, nobody, because of the work we have, only on Sundays is when all of us listen.
Interviewer: Which of you listen to the radio less frequently?
Father: All of us listen only a little since we all go to work, men and women (F4).

And another Tabascan family:

Interviewer: Who listens to the radio the most?
Father: Well, everybody, men and women, because we do the work together, those staying at home, only the elderly, and they also like to listen when pretty music is broadcast, and also because the broadcasts are in Tojolabal, they understand better. Those who like taking their radios to the milpa, there they listen while men and women work, but if we don't take our radio to the milpa, in the afternoon we listen together. But those who listen the most are those women staying to take care of the house (F1).

Now compare Tabascans' comments with responses from Maderans:

Interviewer: Who listens to the radio the most?
Mother: We women because men go to work and they are seldom here. They only listen for a while in the morning and in the afternoon after work (F14).
Interviewer: Who listens to the station less often?
Mother: Well, if we don't go out, we all listen.
Interviewer: Sir, do you have time to listen several hours every day?
Father: No, I only listen to the avisos program at seven, after that I go to work and when I leave I tell my daughters to listen to the radio because there may be an aviso for me.
Mother: Well, we are the ones who listen to the radio because we stay here, he goes out to work, if they call my husband for a meeting [she refers to indigenous organizations sending avisos], we tell him where and what day it's going to be (F21).

There are several preconditions for radio exposure which may not be fulfilled by some women, particularly Tabascan women. One of them is time: "We women also like to listen," said a Tabascan mother, "but we have a lot to do and for that reason we do not have time to listen to the radio" (3m). These women often work in the milpa side by side with men, but unlike men, they do not spend much time at home relaxing; for them the house is also the work place.[17] A second precondition is accessibility to the radio receiver. Women (even those not going to the milpa) perform most of their chores either in the kitchen or outdoors, and the radio receiver is usually not kept in the kitchen, but rather in the "house" (bedroom-living room). A third and only partial precondition is fluency in Spanish. Few women are bilingual, and XEVFS dedicates less than three hours a day to Tojolabal programming.[18] The fourth precondition has to do with financial resources. In all Tabascan and some Maderan households, the radio receiver is run with batteries and listening time has to be discretionary because of cost; thus even those women staying at home may have to limit their exposure time. Finally, more subtle preconditions for exposure are related to the ethnic group's assigned roles and expectations regarding gender. Gender roles and expectations may discourage women from consuming XEVFS' offerings. The interviews provided some evidence concerning these subtle preconditions:

Son: We could say that of all family members the one who listens the most is myself because I am "weird" and I like the talk shows.
Father: After work is when my son turns the radio on and this is when he listens and all of us also listen.
Son: Yes because they also like to listen to what is broadcast by the radio when I turn it on, either the programs or other talk shows, but the station that we like to listen to the most is the one from Margaritas, but we could say that the one who listens more is myself.
Interviewer: Then, who listens to the radio the least?
Son: Well, we could say it is my mother because she is the one who works in the kitchen and she is the one who has less time to listen to the radio, because she has many chores.
Mother: Yes but when the work is finished and when we heard that the radio is broadcasting pretty music, then we come to listen (F6).

These remarks were made by a Tabascan family. Note how the young son, not the mother, indicated that he is the one who turns the receiver on. Aranda Bezaury and Valenzuela also found that often women are not the ones turning the radio on. They suggested that since women belong to the most traditional and isolated sector of the population, their possibilities for appropriating a new medium may be more limited.[19] Examples of this point abound in my interviews. There is this remark from another Tabascan woman:

Mother: When my husband goes to the milpa, sometimes he leaves late and turns off the radio at nine o'clock in the morning, but since I have an unmarried son, he turns the radio on again because my kid likes to listen to the station's music, he went to play once [to Radio Margaritas] but they haven't aired his music yet (5fn).

The hypothesis that women are light consumers of Radio Margaritas' offerings becomes harder to sustain when we consider, not Tabascan, but Maderan women (especially young and bilingual) because the latter fulfill more preconditions for exposure than the former. However, even if Maderan women are exposed to radio more than men, there is still the issue of the kind of attention given to the broadcasting (attentive versus distracted listening). Discussing the research on this issue, Denis McQuail argues that "we can expect attention to what is close, familiar, positive, unthreatening, equal or subordinate in social power and we can expect avoidance of objects with reverse characteristics."[20] Do Tojolabal women find XEVFS' programs unfamiliar and/or threatening? The following two quotes from interviews with Maderan families might help to explain this point more fully:

Interviewer: Who listens to the station less time?
Father: I listen for a while in the morning, the one who listens the most is she [his wife] because she stays at home, and also because the station broadcasts in Tojolabal we understand what it is said, but when I go to work she keeps listening to what is said, she listens but what happens is that *she does not pay attention to what is being said because it has no importance for her* [emphasis added] (F19).

Interviewer: Who listens to the radio the most?
Father: Well, since we always go out, the person staying here is our daughter-in-law.
Mother: Yes, but *I think she doesn't like to listen a lot because I see that she also— like all of us—listens only two hours and then she turns off the radio*. Now, if all of us are at home, then we all listen [emphasis added] (F15).

Note how these informants imply that radio listening is not an important element of Tojolabal women's culture. Moreover, one Tabascan associated radio listening with literacy, as if literacy were a precondition for radio exposure: "The kids are the ones who listen to Radio Margaritas the most, because they know how to read and write and that's why they like it," said a father (3f). More than meaning literacy by itself, what this man probably meant was cultural literacy in the dominant culture, and Tojolabal men surpass by far Tojolabal women in this type of literacy. In addition, one must consider that most XEVFS' programs are produced by men and appeal to men.

A further reason to believe that radio may not belong to Tojolabal women's culture lies in Tojolabal traditions. Radio touches two areas in which women's participation has been limited in Tojolabal society. These areas are information and the performing arts. Women have been excluded from many activities in which people exchange information. Although women are in charge of a particular type of commerce (*chona jas kosa*),[21] they are excluded from the village meetings, and they travel far less often than men. Women have also been excluded from the performing arts. They do not play music, and very often, they are not storytellers.[22] Women only participate in festive occasions in which live music is performed by dancing with men. Playing music has been a masculine domain, though listening to music has been enjoyed also by women.

The analysis of interviewees' responses fails to show any significant difference between the genders; both men and women said they like listening to the music broadcast by the station (see next section in this chapter and Chapter 10). However according to a Tojolabal male teacher, Tojolabal women are not frequent radio listeners because they do not enjoy music as much as men do:

> Always men have had more fun than women, since the moment in which a woman gives herself to the marriage, she takes that responsibility, and the man, even though he also takes that responsibility, he has more fun, and man's greatest diversion has always been music, music... I have tested this, I have told my wife, I have asked her, "let's see, why don't you play music?" She doesn't like it, because "I don't have time," she says, that's true, but if she doesn't have time that's another thing, she doesn't like to listen to the music because the person who likes music, even if he's locked in, he listens to music.

Aside from gender, a person's age may also indicate how much he or she participates in radio listening. According to my key informants, neither children nor the elderly are very interested in what the station has to offer. Radio Margaritas attracts young adults and middle aged listeners.[23] Although children were not allowed (by their parents) to take part in the interviews, there are several commentaries, made by adults, that suggest radio listening is not a preferred activity for children. A Maderan mother stated that children are the ones who listen the least because they go to school (22m); a young Tabascan man said that children seldom listen because "they are children, you see, they go out to play, that's why they seldom listen to to the radio" (6s1). But there is one exception: a Maderan family pointed out their children like to listen to the Saturday morning children's program (16f). This program features children who go to the station to sing and talk, and although it includes Tojolabal, a substantial part of the program is in Spanish. Since most of the children participating are from Margaritas City, it is probable that children from Tabasco do not identify themselves with the participants. On the other hand, children from Madero probably do.

Likewise, the interviews also bring up the elderly's low interest on radio.

"Since my wife and myself are old we do not like to listen to the radio that much," said an elderly Maderan man (15f). A Tabascan grandfather stated that "usually the young people at home are the ones who turn the radio on" (3gf). In addition, one must consider that the only two families not having a radio receiver are old couples (one of them with no young family members living with them), and that particularly in Tabasco radio receivers are used by young man as signifiers of modernity.

Patterns of Taste: Music

One of the most important forms of indigenous participation that has been achieved in XEVFS has to do with music. Indigenous people participate by performing a high percent of the music aired by the station, and they also participate by listening to this music. They are excluded, however, from making decisions about the music aired and promoted by Radio Margaritas. Despite indigenous informants' caution in expressing criticisms, some of the interviewees made their awareness of this exclusion clear. Interviewees talked about music extensively; they talked about music when explaining their preferences regarding XEVFS' programming, when describing how live music used to be played in their communities many years ago, and when discussing their past and present entertainment choices. Some of their remarks are directly related to Radio Margaritas' role in preserving traditional Tojolabal customs. I discuss these remarks in a section dedicated to this question in Chapter 10. Here I deal with three issues: programming preference and patterns of taste, XEVFS' impact on Tabascans' and Maderans' musical experience, and the prime importance of audience uses of XEVFS for diversion.

Since Radio Margaritas' music has enabled the creation of a variety of social uses of radio related to music, it is not surprising that interviewees spoke of this programing. With the exception of one Maderan woman (23m), all Maderans spoke of one or several topics on music; by contrast only about two-thirds of the Tabascans did so (23 of 36). Women mentioned music probably more than any other issue; 20 of the 26 women interviewed talked about music. This finding represents a reversal of a pattern that I had found in other issues because generally speaking, men and Tabascans tended to talk more in the interviews than women and Maderans. The reversal of the pattern may suggest that in fact women and Maderans do prefer XEVFS' music to other types of programming, but given that many remarks on music are rather vague, the reversal is probably due to the likelihood that non-frequent listeners only remember what is transmitted most of the time. Regarding gender differences this reversal may allude to the point I hoped to make before about women's distracted (as opposed to attentive) listening.

As for the patterns of musical taste of Radio Margaritas' potential audience, Cornejo and Luna found that 18 of their 47 indigenous interviewees said they prefer ranchera music, and 6 regional music (most of them mentioned marimba music). By contrast, in addition to regional music and ranchera music, their 53 Spanish, monolingual informants also included other genres such as romantic music, tropical music, religious hymns (Protestant sects), and contemporary music. It is important to highlight that the percentage saying they prefer ranchera music was higher for indigenous people than for Spanish monolinguals, and that 13 of the latter 53 indicated they prefer regional music against 22 of the former 47. These 13 interviewees meant by "regional music" only marimba music. But the 22 indigenous interviewees also included under this term several of the instruments traditionally played by their ethnic groups.[24]

Programming Preferences

A note about my analysis of interviewees' remarks on music. I developed a coding scheme to select meaningful remarks and attempted to group them into mutually exclusive categories. The remarks on music nonetheless did not lend themselves to this kind of manipulation. Thus the following headings should be understood not as categories but as topics around which the conversation on XEVFS' music revolved. These topics and the number of families mentioning them are the following: (1) four Tabascan and one Maderan families talked about general remarks on XEVFS' music programming; (2) five Tabascan and eight Maderan families made remarks on traditional music, either remarks on local instruments or remarks on "music from the local villages"; (3) two Tabascan and three Maderan families talked about marimba music; (4) six Tabascan and three Maderan families specifically mentioned the program *De la Marimba al Son*; (5) one Tabascan and four Maderan families said they listen to XEVFS' music as a leisure choice; and (6) two Tabascan and three Maderan families expressed criticisms about XEVFS' music programming.

When explaining their preferences regarding XEVFS' programming, all families stressed that they enjoy the Tojolabal music broadcast by the station. Rather than indicating specific types of music, they mentioned specific instruments: marimba, *tambor* (drum), violin, *carrizo* (indigenous flute), guitar. All these instruments have been played in the Tojolabal region for many years, though the marimba is the most recent appropriation. Tambor and carrizo, which are considered the most traditional Tojolabal instruments, are played in religious rites, while violin, guitar, and marimba are secular instruments.[25] Interviewees made a distinction between the marimba and the other instruments. Their categories for the local music played by XEVFS are "traditional music" (tambor, carrizo, violin, and guitar) and "marimba music." They also distinguished between marimba *sencilla* (simple marimba, which may be placed in both categories), identified as legitimately Tojolabal, and marimba *buena* (good quality marimba), which is a more elaborate instrument and is identified as the ricos' musical instrument.

At least 20 interviewees (from 13 different families) mentioned they like XEVFS' traditional music. Their preference for this music was associated with the pleasure of listening to members of their own ethnic group—that pleasure that a collectivity feels when it looks at itself in a mirror. This remark by a Maderan man shows how such pleasure comes not just from listening to Tojolabal musicians played over the radio, but also from other forms of indigenous participation:

> Interviewer: What do you like the most about Radio Margaritas?
> Father: Well, what we like the most is almost everything, for example when marimba and programs about our work are broadcast or when other fellow people participate in the radio and tell us how they do their work, whoever plays marimba in the old way (F11).

Note how interviewees' preference for traditional music is linked with local people's participation in XEVFS. "We think everything Radio Margaritas airs is fine because it airs music from the colonias," said a Maderan woman (16m), and almost identical remarks were stated in three other interviews.[26] Interviewees' affinity with the Tojolabal music broadcast by XEVFS intertwines with their fondness for local participation.

Marimba was the instrument most often mentioned. In fact, at least 18 interviewees said they enjoy XEVFS' marimba programming, and the only single radio program that 9 families indicated by either its title or its scheduled time was *De la Marimba al Son*. This one-hour program is aired at 3:00 p.m., Monday through Thursday, and as one of our interviewees said, "everybody likes it (16f). From the nine families talking about the program, six are Tabascans while only three are Maderans. Two-thirds of the families from Tabasco talked about the program, while only a quarter of the families from Madero did so. This difference, however, may be better explained by daily routines and gender variations, for many Maderan men return home after the time scheduled for the program. I had argued before that afternoon listening seems be an unusual practice for women, an argument confirmed by the fact that 9 of the 10 remarks on the programs were made by men.

Marimba music makes up a high percentage of XEVFS' playlist, and it is the only local music regularly aired by Comitán City stations.[27] XEVFS transmits marimba music during two periods coinciding with what I contend is the station's prime time. It broadcasts marimba everyday for about an hour in the early morning (5:30 to 6:30 a.m.) and also in the afternoon during the time scheduled for the program *De la Marimba al Son*. Since marimba is played by the four ethnic groups targeted by XEVFS, scheduling marimba music at prime time was necessary. In addition to the ten comments on the afternoon program, there were four more people stating they enjoy listening to marimba music.[28]

Criticisms About Radio Margaritas' Music

Naturally interviewees revealed that they listen selectively to XEVFS' music programming. Yet most interviewees talked about the station's programming in a sympathetic way, and only four Maderans (surprisingly two women, though one of them very educated) and two Tabascans ventured brief criticisms.[29] A woman put the following in a typical Tojolabal way: "When the music is pretty we like it, but when it's not our hearts get sad" (11m). A Maderan man pessimistically replied to the possibility that the station might air different music: "Yes, I would like Radio Margaritas to air other kinds of music. I would like it, but they won't do it" (23f). And a young educated woman expressed a feminist view: "What we like the least is when men sing badly, in such a way to offend the woman, and what we like is when they sing nicely" (13fs). And another Tabascan man told us: "The only thing that we don't like is when the music is not pretty"(3f).

At first glance the interviews failed to disclose what music offered by XEVFS the families disliked. However, many sympathetic remarks shed light on the programming content disliked by our interviewees. Two very frequent comments were: "We like to listen when the station broadcasts pretty music," and "We like to listen when the station broadcasts the music we like." In a broad context these comments may mean that interviewees dislike all music aired by XEVFS which is neither "traditional" nor "marimba." Apart from classical Mexican music (the music that became famous during the 1940s and 1950s, the golden age of Mexican cinema), most of this music is mainly *nueva canción* (Latin American folklorist music), a genre popular among the members of an urban subculture attracting university students, artists, and intellectuals, a group of people who often find work interesting at institutions like INI.

From Live to Radio Broadcast Music

Interviewer: When you come back from work, what type of music do you play?
Father: We don't play music anymore, but we listen to it on the radio (F3).

One of my aims was to find some clues regarding the impact of XEVFS on its listeners' daily lives. So I included an item in my interview schedule asking interviewees to describe how music was played and heard in their communities a long time ago. Informants were also asked to relate what changes they have witnessed in the local music experience. These changes have been more dramatic in Madero. In their lifetime, the older generation of Maderans has witnessed important developments. Local musicians appropriated a new instrument, the marimba; villagers stopped celebrating weekly parties and many festivities in which live music was played; people began to listen to broadcast and recorded music regularly; adults became attracted to ladino genres such as ranchera music, and youngsters to electronic music; and the village's musicians died without passing their knowledge on to the younger generations. In addition, as have Tabascans, Maderans have also witnessed the revival of traditional Tojolabal music promoted in part by Radio Margaritas, since today many villagers can listen to traditional music everyday.

To lift their spirits, some years ago Maderans and Tabascans used to enjoy live music. Besides playing for religious pilgrimages, holidays, and other important occasions, Tabascan and Maderan musicians used to get together every week, usually on Saturday afternoon, and play for their families and neighbors. Yet these weekly gatherings are no longer held either in Madero or Tabasco. People remember a time when violin and guitar were played, and a more recent period when marimba was used. The evolution of local music can be seen in Tabascans' descriptions of these parties. A Tabascan man in his sixties said:

> Before, every Saturday we used to play violin and guitar music, we used to nominate who was going to play every Saturday but now it's not done in this way anymore. Every group of musicians used to play for two months, now if there were another group the second used to play for another two months and that's how we used to do on Saturdays before (3gf).

And another Tabascan man in his late thirties added:

> Before, to make our hearts happy, on Saturday after work we used to go to the place where marimba was played, because before, every Saturday they played the marimba and we danced, they also played the tambor and in that way we used to get happy (1f).

Although Tabascans no longer hold these weekly parties, a few local musicians still play from time to time. Maderans on the other hand have completely lost this practice, and today they hire professional musicians for their festivities. A Maderan man explained that today they need to hire professional musicians because of the large number of people attending their festivals. Today he said, "over a thousand people live in Madero and many people from the neighboring villages also attend the festivals" (22f). The disappearance of the weekly parties has affected many aspects of village life. For women who did not (and do not) play music but used to dance in the weekly parties, it meant that their opportunities for dancing were greatly reduced. A woman in her forties stressed this change:

Before, every Saturday we used to get happy because they used to play the marimba here, but now they don't play because the marimba sencilla doesn't exist anymore. Every week we had dances, now we don't dance every Saturday but only every festival, for example on December 12 [Virgin of Guadalupe's Day, Madero's patron]. Before, if there was no one who played marimba music, the tambor and the violin were played and with that music people used to dance and this happened not only here but also in other villages, Colonia Veracruz[30] and Colonia Nuevo México, people used to dance with those instruments too (21m).

Tabascans are also ceasing to produce music. It is worth noting that tambores made in Tabasco are locally famous, and that among the interviewees there was a tambor maker, as well as tambor, marimba, and guitar players. However, most local musicians have stopped playing. There were five musicians in the families interviewed,[31] but only one Tabascan (5f) still plays the marimba. A frequent comment was: "The people who knew how to play, those people do not exist anymore, and we haven't continued playing." Instead of playing musical instruments, villagers play their audio cassettes and listen to the radio. Responding to the question about the kind of music played in Tabasco, a man said: "We don't play music anymore, but we listen to the radio."

Maderans and Tabascans began to listen to broadcast music long before Radio Margaritas was established. Many stations have reached the area for decades. Radio Comitán started its transmission 24 years before Radio Margaritas did, and religious broadcasting originating in Guatemala has probably been trying to reach the Tojolabals for years. Interestingly, one of the Maderan families mentioned the Guatemalan stations: "Before, we used to listen to the stations from Guatemala, that radio also belonged to indigenous people. But people speaking other languages, we didn't understand what they were telling us but we only listened to the music" (23f). However radio receivers were not as widespread as they are today. Interviewees often underscored that radio listening was not an entertainment choice available to everyone but only to those few with access to a receiver: "We didn't listen to the music in the radio before," said a Maderan woman, "only those having a radio set used to listen to the music, those not having one didn't listen to the music" (19m). Tabasco and Madero differed in the rate of adopting radio receiving technology.

New technologies of course were first adopted in Madero. While only one young Tabascan family (F17) stated that they used to listen to Radio Comitán before the introduction of Radio Margaritas, five Maderan families cited Radio Comitán as a past leisure choice.[32] Often interviewees pointed out they did not like the broadcast because it is a radio station for ricos:

Interviewer: What did you do before to make your hearts happy?
Mother: We were sad because there was no music.
Father: When Radio Margaritas didn't exist we were sad because we didn't listen to the music.
Father's brother: There was Radio Comitán but we didn't listen to it because it's a radio station for ricos, but now there's Radio Margaritas! (F1)

I will come back to this point about Radio Comitán being "the ricos' radio." What I want to highlight now is that radio broadcasting has probably been an element in bringing about social change in the region, but one cannot say that radio has wiped live music out. In addition to radio, numerous agents of change (e.g., protestant sects, merchants, government agencies) have simultaneously acted in the region, and the communities have also undergone important endogenous transformations. It is safe to say that to a great extent radio has taken the place that used to be occupied by live music in the villages. And most importantly Radio Margaritas has opened a channel for some local musical expressions that were not likely to be broadcast by other stations. Numerous informants (e.g., ladinos from Margaritas City, station staff members, Tojolabal interviewees) indicated that many Tojolabals began buying radio receivers and batteries shortly after the installation of Radio Margaritas. Or as a Maderan man put it: "Many young people have bought their radio-recorders in order to listen to Radio Margaritas." Having a station interpellating them and perhaps also an alternative medium suiting their taste, many Maderans and Tabascans began to listen to the radio more often.

Music has always been one of the most important diversions for Tabascans and Maderans. But their way of enjoying music has undergone a considerable shift, from live music to mainly broadcast and recorded music. Although in Madero people sometimes have the opportunity to listen to out-of-town musicians who play marimba buena and electronic music, the occasions for playing and listening to live music have been greatly diminished for both Maderans and Tabascans. The religious pilgrimages or *romerías* are declining, the carnival is no longer observed, and the old weekly parties brightened by the local musicians are seldom held in Tabasco and no longer in Madero. Against this scarcity of music availability, listening to radio broadcast music has emerged as a new, popular practice. One of the consequences of these changes is that as villagers have become less involved in playing music, the gap between producers and consumers of music has widened. A further consequence is the magnitude that consuming radio offerings has acquired, not only as a signifying practice, but also as a source of joy, of sheer pleasure.

Diversion Uses

Because Radio Margaritas' music fills most of Maderans' and Tabascans' free time, there are several closely-related uses that can be grouped under the general heading of "diversion uses." I have borrowed this term from the uses and gratifications school (see Appendix 1), specifically from Denis McQuail, Jay G. Blumler, and J. Brown, who use it to refer to personal uses of media for escaping routines and problems as well as for attaining emotional release.[33] But I also allude with the term to at least five of the interpersonal uses of James Lull's typology for television, which are companionship, entertainment, family relaxant, conflict reduction, and relationship maintenance (as Lull says, the distinction between the personal and the interpersonal uses of media is somewhat arbitrary).[34] Rather than proposing or subscribing to a typology, I wish to delineate a prime dimension of audience uses of radio that tends to be highly underestimated by both staff members at the INI stations and INI officials.

The central significance of having time for relaxation and spiritual regeneration has been emphasized by virtually all peoples. For the Tojolabal, a people under great stress, the need for diversionary activities is even greater, and the psychological relief offered by music is likely to be one of their most effective alternatives for dealing with stress. Like other indigenous peoples, the Tojolabal are facing many hardships, from economic exploitation and ill health to racial, ethnic, and class discrimination and low-self esteem. What can they do to prevent themselves from becoming seriously distraught? As for many other marginalized minorities, alcoholism has been a choice:

> The only way to make our hearts happy was drinking, that's the way to let tiredness and sadness go, but listening to or playing music, we didn't have a way to do it, sometimes they aired pretty music in Radio Comitán, then we listened to it but that happened only seldom (16f).

Maderans and Tabascans recognize the problems brought about by alcoholism. Maderans have taken strong measures to control it, such as banning the sale of alcoholic beverages in the village, but it is still a considerable problem in both communities. I am not suggesting that listening to radio may prevent people from drinking—the opposite may well be true.[35] What I am saying is that Tabascans and Maderans find an important gratification in listening to Radio Margaritas and that this gratification may help them to cope better with everyday hardships. A Tojolabal teacher described these hardships and the gratification derived from music:

> The worker goes to the milpa, arrives there and suddenly there's something bad in the milpa that he doesn't like, or the milpa didn't produce anything. He

gets sad, and he doesn't have anything to go to but music, oldies, that's what helps him forget his hardships (teachers' interview).

Many interviewees underlined how they use radio listening for family relaxation and to reduce family conflict. A Tabascan man explained his use of radio listening for emotional release: "Sometimes we came back angry from work, but when we listen to the pretty music our hearts get happy" (3f). And another young Tabascan man talked about his family's afternoon listening:

> After work we listen to the music, we have time to listen to the afternoon program where marimba is played, at that time we come back from work, we turn the radio on, we listen to it and sadness is gone, because many times my wife and I fight in the milpa but later with the music our hearts get happy again (18f).

They also said that they enjoy listening to the music broadcast by Radio Margaritas while they work. As you may recall, sometimes Tabascans and Maderans take their receivers to the milpas. A Tabascan mother also talked about her radio listening for companionship: "One gets happy when one listens to the radio broadcast's pretty music because when I am working, either milling the *nixtamal* or making tortillas, I get happy" (2m). Indeed, the Tojolabal need diversions to forget their numerous hardships; radio broadcast music is today a suitable alternative for the entertainment that used to be provided by live music. The importance of having a suitable entertainment choice should not be underestimated.

Radio Margaritas and the Construction of Reality

The station reflects the communities, but simultaneously the station also creates a representation of the communities and their music. Tojolabal music broadcast by XEVFS comes from recordings of local musicians' live performances. The station's staff (usually two ladinos, the general manager, an ethnomusicologist, and the program director) edits and selects these recordings. The staff also determines which recordings are aired and which are not, which recordings are retrieved and which are erased. The program director chooses the frequency in which recordings are placed on the playlist. So the station broadcasts an image of Tojolabal music which is more than a mere reflection of the music played by local musicians. It is a selective image of Tojolabal music. This image may well be the only representation that some communities have of each other's music, because many Tojolabals do not have frequent and direct contact with people from other villages. There is this remark by a Tabascan man: "We know that other ejidos haven't lost their way of playing music because it sounds very nice on the radio" (7f). Four more families stated they like the station's music programming because "it airs music from all the colonias."[36]

XEVFS' selection of music constitutes a form of censorship. The station's staff not only censors popular genres, but also performances of traditional Tojolabal music. These performances are censored on the basis of aesthetic judgements made by some members of the staff (more often than not, ladinos). Does the audience agree with this judgement? The station lacks the mechanisms to input audience participation in this area, but our informants offered some clues. Several Tabascans asked why a program featuring interviews with the village's health workers included music from other places rather than music played by Tabascans. They specifically requested that Tabascan musicians' performances be aired with the interviews with Tabascans. A Tabascan mother also bitterly complained, stating her son's recording had not been aired (5fn).

Concerning genres I found conflicting opinions. My interview schedule only asked about the music broadcast by XEVFS and failed to inquire specifically about other popular genres, such as ranchera music, but two informants advanced a strong argument for including more ranchera music in XEVFS' playlist. Two, young, educated Maderan men (13f, 20s) argued that XEVFS should transmit more ranchera music because the Tojolabal have already appropriated this genre. However other informants strongly disagreed with this argument. Notable illustrations of these opposite views were provided by a Tojolabal teacher and by Tabasco's komisariyado. The teacher said:

Although ranchera music is not ours—to tell the truth, it is not our music—people have appropriated it, well the elderly, now, as it's said, that the young people want only modern music, they don't want ranchera anymore, but the old people sing ranchera music, they reminisce with that music. And really, I have always remarked, I have said, well, we, this music is not ours, there's so many things that aren't ours, but yes, we have already appropriated them, they belong to us, they're now ours, and by the same token, ranchera music can be our music as peasants.

But the Tabascan komisariyado did not mirror the teacher's view:

What I believe is that all that is heard over the radio is what we know, and the way the station is working is very good because from what we listen to we learn other fellow people's music, maybe there's something that should be changed because to tell the truth we are very accustomed to the music aired by the UI [Radio Comitán], which airs only ranchera music and the music talks about many things regarding the ricos' ways, poverty or drunkenness. Then many times the rancheras aired, even if a person doesn't want to drink, but since it's heard all over that's where the person is invited to drink through the music and what happens when a person drinks is that he loses everything. What I see from the radio "La voz de la frontera sur" is that it is airing everything about our customs and it also airs music made by our own fellow people, they sing about the work, the life, or the poverty, and by doing that they are telling us what's happening in their lives, and those who know how to write songs talk about what they harvest and how customs are in their communities. That's what I see that is lacking a bit, we should have more people writing music, but the communities' participation is needed too, so that it would talk about our customs, through a *corrido* [Mexican musical form of storytelling] or another form. And that's how I see that the station's work would be complemented, by the communities participating more. My view is that ranchera music shouldn't be aired, it talks about the *patrones*, we need to have more participation so that songs about ourselves are made, through more participation (1f).

Both informants recognized the high consumption of ranchera music by Tojolabals, but while the teacher sees cultural consumption as legitimate appropriation, the komisariyado does not; he stressed that ranchera is the "patrones' music," while the music aired by Radio Margaritas talks about pobres, about indigenous peoples. Since Tojolabals refer to indigenous people as pobres, perhaps *pobreza* (one of the numerous loans from Spanish that have acquired a new meaning in Tojolabal language) should be most properly translated here as the indigenous people's *weltanschauung*.

Evidently the opposing viewpoints of these two quotes reflect informants' profound differences regarding lifestyles and ideologies. The komisariyado's ideology understands ranchera music as an expression of the oppressive ladino culture. Vividly, the komisariyado argues that musical forms are media for disseminating specific ideologies and influencing people's attitudes and behavior. Ranchera music, he says, leads indigenous people to the circle of poverty, alcoholism, and oppression, while vernacular Tojolabal songs can play an important liberating role. Furthermore the komisariyado makes a very good argument for the need to encourage people's participation. A related point was raised by a Maderan woman who was worried about the loss of self-reliance that the use of new instruments has created in Madero: "Before when marimbas sencillas were used, it didn't cost anything because they were ours, but when it's looked for other marimbas buenas, as now it's done, it costs very much" (11m).

By contrast, the teacher's ideology sees ranchera music as part of the Tojolabal life. His point is that Tojolabals have been consuming this music extensively for many years. Along with norteña and tropical music, ranchera (widely available in rural Mexico and probably in most of rural Latin America) is broadcast by local commercial stations and is sold in local music shops. Take the list of best sellers of a popular shop located in Margaritas

City, which included (1) four groups playing ranchera music, *Las Jilgueritas*, *Bertín y Lalo*, *Las Vecinas*, and *Las Abajeñas*; (2) one group playing norteña music, the nationally famous *Los Tigres del Norte*; and (3) two recordings of local celebrities who play tropical and norteña music, *Los Angeles de Fuego* from Comitán City and *Filiberto Remigio* from Ocosingo City, who plays the synthesizer. Or consider the audio cassettes owned by one of the families interviewed (F3): *Conjunto Alma Purépecha, Conjunto Michoacano, Justiano Buc V, Las Palomas, Los Cumberos del Sur, Las Jilgueritas, Los Gabilanes del Norte, Los Serranos de Hidalgo, Los Michoacanos,* and *El Dueto Castillo*. Apart from *Justiano Buc V* (a recording of religious protestant music made in Guatemala), all these recordings are either ranchera, norteña, or tropical music. Moreover, one of the few volunteers working at the INI network, a Raramuri who produces a daily program featuring chiefly norteña music in XETAR, argued many Raramuris enjoy listening to this music. And Aranda Bezaury and Valenzuela, in their study about XEZV, found that ranchera music was the most liked genre among Mixtecos, Tlapanecos, and Nahuas; it especially appealed to women and to men in the 25 to more than 50 year-old age group.[37]

Norteña and tropical music are not broadcast by XEVFS. Even so, ranchera makes up for a small percent of its programming. Yet the station only airs "classic" ranchera music (e.g., José Alfredo Jiménez), and it excludes regional best sellers. Only two interviewees said they like the ranchera music played by the station (15f and 6f). The station goes further in its efforts to encourage certain cultural expressions while discouraging others. At XEVFS it is specifically prohibited to air avisos promoting festivals in which non-traditional music is performed. A young Maderan man has this to say about XEVFS' ban on these avisos:

I would like to know why they don't air some announcements, when the community comes to deliver an announcement for the community's sake and arriving at the station they refuse to air them, as I say, I don't know, it may be because they refuse or because they have orders not to air them, we don't understand why. Last December the 12th we tried to air those types of announcements, but on arriving at the station, they didn't air them, and what we wanted was for the nearby villages to know, to know which musicians are coming. Of course it is not marimba music from the village but out-of-town musicians, sometimes those musicians come from around Trinitaria, or from Independencia, of course we found it difficult to understand because why if in Margaritas City there's a radio station did we have to go up to Comitán City to deliver those announcements? In *Radio Balún Canán* [state sponsored radio, IMER], they don't charge us a penny, but in radio UI [Radio Comitán] they do charge, but as I say, to let the people know we had to air those announcements there (20s).

He was talking about the festival held honoring Madero's patron, the Virgin of Guadalupe. This is the most important holiday observed in Madero. Planned by the ejidatarios in a communal meeting, organized by the komisariyado ejidal, and attended by hundreds of people, the festival is definitely a community affair. Nonetheless, since electronic music is performed in the festival, XEVFS refused to support it. Thus the station selects only those components of the Tojolabal society which fit best a certain view of Tojolabal life.

In the next chapter I argue that the station's working concept of the Tojolabal corresponds to a romantic view of their culture and society. I also describe how, despite its distorted image of the Tojolabal, the station has had a tremendous impact on the local villages' flow of information, and it is perceived by both Tabascans and Maderans as a community station serving the Tojolabal people.

Notes

1. I use a code to identify the families interviewed. The capital letter "F" followed by a number refers to one of the families, for example "F4" refers to family number four. Numbers followed by lowercase letters refer to family members. For instance, "6m" refers to the mother of family number six; "6f" refers to the father of the same family; and "6gf" to the grandfather. The complete code is presented in Chapter 2, page 27.

2. Instituto Nacional Indigenista, ¿Se Escuchan Nuestras Voces? XEVFS, La Voz de la Frontera Sur, by Inés Cornejo and Silvia Luna, ts., internal document, México, 1991, 34.

3. 1fn, 4f, 4m, 6s1, 6m, 7m, 18s, 13fs.

4. 9f, 10f, 13f, 22m.

5. 6m and 14m.

6. 1fn, 2m, 3f, 4f, 5f, 6s1, 7f, 9f, 10f, 13f, 17m, 16m, 22m.

7. In the case of places like Madero, where many people go to bed after 7:00 p.m., it may well be more than one hour.

8. Joseph R. Dominick, *The Dynamics of Mass Communication*, 3rd ed. (New York: McGraw-Hill, 1990) 461.

9. Inés Cornejo, "La Voz de la Mixteca y la Comunidad Receptora de la Mixteca Oaxaqueña," M.A. thesis, U Iberoamericana, 1990, 37.

10. 1f, 6s1/f, 7f, 18m.

11. 7f.

12. Question #16 of the audience interview schedule.

13. All-news stations in the United States appeal to a male audience in the 25 to 54 year old category. XEVFS also attracts younger men (18 to 24 years old). The difference, however, becomes irrelevant when one takes into account differences regarding life expectancy and social roles in both societies.

14. These percentages refer to the 34 women and the 39 men who said they listen to the radio (including XEVFS and other stations) out of the 100 people sampled in this study. Cornejo and Luna 26.

15. Josefina Aranda Bezaury and Verónica Valenzuela, "Investigación sobre la Presencia Radiofónica de la Voz de la Montaña en las Comunidades," Unpublished essay, 41-46.

16. Mario Humberto Ruz, *Los Legítimos. Aproximación Antropológica al Grupo Tojolabal*, II (México: UNAM, 1982) 171-2, has also reported that it is common for women to do agricultural work.

17. Inés Cornejo and Silvia Luna (33-34) found that considering indigenous as well as mestizo interviewees, men outnumber women in afternoon listening; about 15 percent of the women said they listen in the afternoon against roughly 35 percent of the men.

18. See XEVFS' listings in Chapter 6, Figure 6.2.

19. Aranda Bezaury and Valenzuela 43.

20. Denis McQuail, *Mass Communication Theory* (London: Sage, 1984) 167-68.

21. Ruz 236.

22. Are Tojolabal women storytellers? I have not found any evidence indicating that they are. On the other hand, sources like Lomelí include tales told by males. Lomelí goes so far as to include an explanation of childbearing given by a male informant. Arturo Lomelí González, *Algunas Costumbres y Tradiciones del Mundo Tojolabal* (Chiapas: Gobierno del Estado, 1988) 141.

23. There are some relative similarities between XEVFS and the United States talk format. The talk format appeals to listeners in the 35 to 65 year old age group.

24. Cornejo and Luna 43-49.

25. See for example the descriptions of festive occasions given by Lomelí 89-135.

26. 4s2, 3s2, 20f.

27. Some members of the staff of XEVFS believe the station has influenced the programming of other local stations, which, according to them, now air more marimba music than they used to.

28. 5mn, 5m, 11f, 14m.

29. They were: 2f, 3f, 11f, 11m, 13fs, 23f.

30. She refers to Tojolabal villages. Many Tojolabal villages have taken their names from other places.

31. F2, F4. F5, F11, and F16.

32. F9, F10, F16, F22, and F23.

33. Denis McQuail, Jay G. Blumler, and J.R. Brown, "The Television Audience: A Revised Perspective," *Sociology of Mass Communication*, ed. Denis McQuail (Harmondsworth, England: Penguin, 1972).

34. James Lull, *Inside Family Viewing* (London: Routledge, 1990).

35. A great challenge for Radio Margaritas is finding ways to discourage high alcohol intake, which is often seen as part of Tojolabal traditions. Alcoholism is probably a problem in most, if not all, sectors of Mexican society, including, of course, the bureaucracy.

36. F4, F3, F16, and F20.

37. Aranda Bezaury and Valenzuela 48.

9

Social Impact of Radio Margaritas

Impact of Radio Margaritas on Local Information Flows

Ah! In the old times! Nobody would communicate with you, nobody would send you an aviso, we couldn't communicate because there was no radio in Margaritas City.
—A Maderan grandfather

What impact may XEVFS have had on the information flows of the Tojolabal people? I was particularly interested in shedding light on the specific ways in which marginalized people react to the presence and availability of new communications resources. I also wanted to know if the INI stations might serve as catalysts for the development of more complex and rapid information flows. Thus I paid attention to this issue within several aspects of the research, including focus groups with staff members and in the audience study. The results of my inquiry reveal the tremendous impact that XEVFS has had on the local information flows. Furthermore, they suggest that the station, particularly through its broadcasting in Tojolabal, may have had a democratizing effect, especially for women, on the local communication practices.

Since problems related to the impact of media should compare a present situation with its past, I developed two sets of questions. First interviewees were asked to recall how people used to find out about both the things going on in the village and events happening in other places. Then they were asked about current information flows, and the role played by Radio Margaritas in the change experienced in local communications. Interviewees' responses to these questions, coupled with their numerous remarks concerning avisos, detail various aspects of XEVFS' impact on local information flows. I present these responses by discussing two types of information flows, internal (or intravillage) and external; the latter includes intervillages flows and flows between the villages and ladino settings, mainly Margaritas City and Comitán City.

Impact on Intravillage Information Flows

Intravillage flows involve the interpersonal communication taking place through the closed social networks of family and friends, as well as through the *ejidatarios* network. I mentioned before that the ejido is a unique Mexican way of land tenure drawing on the communitarian traditions of indigenous peoples. The ejido also embraces ancient forms of self-government which depends to a large extent in the sharing of information about the community. Most interviewees mentioned the ejidatarios network when explaining how they find out about the village's affairs. Composed of the male adults of the village (i.e., ejidatarios and avecindados), the ejidatarios network has an important formal channel which is the communal meeting or junta; it has also designated messengers (i.e., *agente municipal, comisiones*) and speakers (e.g., komisariyado), and it serves to circulate important information directly concerning the community. A Maderan man explained how this information moves from the ejidatarios network to the family network:

> We get together at the end of every month, then is when we find out about the things going on in the village, or, if a celebration is going to take place, we also have to get together and reach agreements. Only we the men get together, then we come home to tell to our wives what was discussed in the meeting, that's the way we all find out what's going on (22f).[1]

Intravillage information flows thus include a two-step flow which runs from the ejidatarios network to the family network. Since women and youngsters are excluded from the former, they have to rely heavily on the latter. An occasion for intravillage information exchange indicated by one of the male informants was the communal tasks in which women also participate (16f). It can be argued that women may also take advantage of their role as merchants to gather information. Mario Humberto Ruz says that women are merchants (*chona jas kosa*) who sell groceries bought in Margaritas City; however, in Tabasco the cooperative store is managed by men, and in Madero there are several mom-and-pop shops managed as family businesses.[2]

None of our interviewees indicated that women's role as merchants gives them the opportunity for gathering information; on the other hand, some women interviewed pointed out the ejidatarios network as an important channel for intravillage flows (15m). This network, rooted in old traditions, has probably changed little over the last few decades. One of the interviewees even insisted the network works in the same way it used to during the *baldío* times (19f). The only difference noted by a Tabascan grandfather concerned the old use of the *cacho* (bull horn) to call for the communal meeting (3f).

But, although the two networks of intravillage information flows apparently have not changed, the profound changes that have occurred in external flows have greatly affected internal communications. Increased traveling opportunities and radio broadcasting in Tojolabal have probably diminished the importance of the ejidatarios network, since information coming from outside the village now comes to many people simultaneously. Years ago, external information flows had more formal and centralized receiving points, usually the village authorities. Changes in external flows may have had a democratizing effect too. The broadcasting in Tojolabal has introduced an alternative source of social knowledge for women, who have been geographically isolated in their villages and have been excluded from the ejidatarios networks of their own villages. "I like Radio Margaritas because we all listen to it," said the daughter-in-law of a Tabascan family (3dl). The significance of this remark becomes unmistakable when remembering that daughters-in-law occupy a peripheral position in the Tojolabal patrilocal family.

Impact on External Information Flows

By "external information flows" I refer to both intervillages flows and flows between the villages and the ladino settings, especially Margaritas City and Comitán City. The ejidatarios network counts on established ways to communicate with other villages and with the county seat. These are elected officials whose responsibility is to be messengers; the agente municipal is the messenger between the village and the county seat, and there are six other people (comisiones) under him who may also deliver messages. In addition to these formal channels, the indigenous communications system is comprised of a number of gatherings for religious, work, or commercial reasons. Gatherings at the market constitute a foremost, indigenous means of communication. Ruz has observed that Margaritas City's Tojolabal market constitutes the space where a great deal of the communication among people from different villages occurs:

> the market is a place for something else but selling, buying, or exchanging products. This secular grouping mechanism allows Tojolabals to reaffirm their solidarity links with other members of the ethnic group who are as poor as they are. While they drink a beer or get together to ask for Santa Margarita's protection ... they interchange experiences, news, and regards in a language that makes them be part of a world which is different from the world of the mestizos [ladinos] around them [my translation].[3]

Other important gatherings are the romerías, or religious pilgrimages. Yet, in spite of the premier role that they used to play in intervillage information flows, they have greatly diminished. "We used to walk from our community," said a Tabascan grandfather, "up to Trinitaria, we were playing tambor, the whole way we were playing tambor, and when we arrived there, we talked with the other people who were also arriving" (3gf). None of the interviewees spoke of romerías as present opportunities to exchange information.

In the course of the last few years external information flows have undergone a profound transformation in Tabasco and Madero. Radio has been a determining factor in this transformation, but another medium, the automobile, has also been very influential. The greatest impact, however, has come from the unprecedented convergence between these two media. The roads to the villages facilitated transportation, which in turn expanded and accelerated information flows. Villagers traveling more often needed not only to expand their social networks, but also speed up the flow of information in such networks. Simultaneously, their frequent trips to Margaritas City made available their use of communication resources that were previously beyond their reach. Villagers turned to radio to fulfill their telecommunications needs, and began to use radio to expand their village's external information flows.

Roads and local radio stations are a recent development in the area. The main road in Las Margaritas county (Margaritas City-Comitán City) was opened in 1961 and was paved only a few years ago. The dirt roads connecting Tabasco and Madero are much more recent. A small bridge, making automobile traffic possible to Madero during the rainy season, was constructed in 1986; Tabasco's bridge was built later, and the route to Tabasco was made as a dirt road in 1990. Radio stations are recent too. Radio Comitán was established in 1963 and Radio Margaritas in 1987. An elderly man related how Madero was about three decades ago:

Madero didn't have anything, now we have electricity; we have the service of this radio [he refers to Radio Margaritas], there are also cars transporting passengers, but when we were children there were only two cars in Margaritas City, they belonged to a man called Hidalgo, now, thousands and thousands of cars, trucks, and station wagons, everything we see now didn't exist before. We had to walk from here to Comitán City or to Margaritas City, and we would come back very late at night, because there were no cars. We were not able to return quickly, there were no roads, the one who built the roads was the president Luis Echeverría[4] and he gave us everything, that's why there are roads (19f).

Maderans improved their external information flows before Tabascans, and at present the former enjoy much better communications than the latter. However, the time when Maderans lacked all means for rapid, external, information flows is still very recent. A Maderan man in his early thirties described how slowly information flowed when he was a child, even when crucial information was at stake. "Many times we didn't find out anything," he said, "sometimes we would find out, but only after many days, for example if there was someone in jail, or someone was killed, we would find out but only after many days" (23f).

Thus before the advent of roads and radio, external information flows were slow and sporadic. To establish intervillage contact was an arduous and time-consuming activity: "There were no roads," a Tabascan man remarked, "there was nothing. To communicate with each other we would have to walk, there was no radio, when we had a family member far away we had to walk an entire day to arrive there" (5mn). The comisiones had to endure such hardships when the village wanted to invite neighboring villages to festival and celebrations. Now they broadcast the invitation by radio. Likewise, the agente municipal would spend considerable time in his frequent trips to Margaritas City. Not surprisingly this position is regarded, not as an honor, but more as a disciplinary measure.[5] According to a telling anecdote that has become part of the network's lore, villagers would respond to the question "What do you use the radio for?," which was posed by one of the stations' staff, in an unexpected and direct way; villagers simply said: "We use the radio for not walking."

The poverty of external information flows that prevailed in Tabasco and Madero a few years ago is illustrated dramatically by a frequent replay to one of my questions. We asked our interviewees: "Do you recall how people in Tabasco/Madero used to find out what was going on in other villages?" The answer was succinct: "We didn't find out." Many of them explained their reply by comparing the past to the present situation. A Tabascan man said:

Well, before we didn't communicate with each other because we didn't have radio, we didn't find out when problems were occurring in other ejidos, but now we have our radio [he refers to Radio Margaritas] and through this radio they inform us of the problems in other ejidos, so, that's the way we communicate at present. But before we didn't find out, now that the radio exists we can easily communicate with other ejidos (7f).

And a Maderan man mirrored the Tabascan's remarks:

Before we couldn't find out what was going on in other villages, for example if there were problems or they were celebrating festivals, we didn't find out because we had no radio, but at present we find out what is going on in other villages, we find out by means of the radio and that's why we really like to listen to the radio because we know what is going on in other villages (10f).

It is not difficult to see that Tabascans and Maderans have indeed appropriated radio to improve intervillage information flows and that Radio Margaritas has greatly contributed to this. But there is an apparent contradiction between these last remarks and the station's failure to produce news programs that are truly relevant to Tojolabal villages. I have already discussed the numerous shortcomings of Radio Margaritas' news programing in Chapter 6. The point I hoped to make regarding the news programs is that they fail to fit the needs of indigenous listeners. The interviews confirm this, though one Tabascan man favorably mentioned the news broadcast by the station: "We like the news, the music, since that's aired we find out the problems happening in other nations and that's the most important thing of the radio" (1mn). Inés Cornejo and Silvia Luna's research also suggest that indigenous listeners have no interest in the station's news programs. In their study on Radio Margaritas' potential audience, they found that from the 56 people in their sample who said they listen to XEVFS, there was only 1 out of the 19 indigenous interviewees who said the station is useful for news listening against 12 of the 37 Spanish monolinguals who said the same. Cornejo and Luna emphasize that XEVFS' news programs, rather than serving the indigenous population's needs, respond to ladino and mestizo demands,[6] an observation that certainly corresponds to my own conclusions.

When carefully considering interviewees' comments, I realized that when they talked about the information service provided by Radio Margaritas, they were not referring to news programs. Indeed their silence regarding the station's news programs eloquently revealed that the news programs broadcast by the station are irrelevant to most Tojolabals.[7] What interviewees were talking about when they referred to the information provided by the station were avisos and programs with audience participation.

The radio broadcasting of avisos has probably been a practice throughout the world among people who either lack other telecommunications means (e.g., remote areas) or cannot afford those available (e.g., migrants). Maderans and Tabascans began sending avisos before the establishment of Radio Margaritas. I have already pointed out that both Tabascans and Maderans listen to Radio Comitán and Maderans also air avisos on this station. However, interviewees often said they prefer to broadcast avisos in XEVFS and gave a number of reasons for their preference. One of them concerns social distinctions and boundaries as well as group identification. While Radio Margaritas is seen as their radio station, Radio Comitán is perceived as "the ricos' radio." Other reasons are practical considerations: Radio Margaritas is closer, it broadcasts avisos in Tojolabal, it gives urgent avisos preferential treatment over other programming, and most importantly, it airs avisos at no cost. Cost was the single reason most often given by interviewees, in virtually all interviews there were remarks like this one: "We like Radio Margaritas because it doesn't charge us for sending avisos."

The use of the station as a telecommunications medium constitutes the most obvious use of radio developed by Tojolabals. This practice has had an extraordinary impact on the villages' external communications flows.[8] XEVFS has helped enhance and speed up interpersonal communication among villagers. It has also eased the burden of the villages' messengers and has facilitated the spread of information from government agencies (like INI) and indigenous organizations. Therefore the station is not only used as a substitute for the telephone but also as a mass medium to reach a highly illiterate and disperse population. In the last sense, avisos fulfill some of the needs met in many areas by the postal service and the print media, such as newsletters and classified ads.

As a substitute for the telephone, XEVFS provides communication resources to deal with immediate problems, and one of Tojolabals' most urgent problems is their ill health. Virtually all interviewees mentioned avisos as the best service offered by the station, and many of them specified how crucial it is to have a fast communication medium when people's health is involved. In interviewees' responses to one of my questions which posed the hypothetical closure of XEVFS, there were several, pertinent descriptions of how the station is used by villagers as a telecommunications link when a family member is ill. Here is one of such descriptions:

Interviewer: Some people do not like Radio Margaritas and they would like the station to be closed, what do you think about this? Do you agree with them or do you prefer that Radio Margaritas continue broadcasting?

Father: To close Radio Margaritas? Ah no! It should continue working because we listen to the avisos, about an illness for example. We can notify a family member quickly, but if it were in Comitán City, it's very far away and also you have to pay when you air an aviso. In this station it's a free service, it wouldn't be ok if the station were closed, on the contrary, it should be improved because if this station is lost we are going to miss it a lot, because it's useful to us in many ways. We easily communicate with each other, but if the station were closed we will miss it a lot, because there are many people who get sick and live far away from their family, but since there's this radio they quickly communicate with each other and the family members show up. But if there were no radio, the news is going to arrive anyway but meanwhile the sick person might die, but having the station, avisos are aired very quickly (F11).

This remark, made by a Maderan man, shows that Maderans use XEVFS' avisos service, but Tabascans, who have less access to health and communication resources, have an even more pressing need for this kind of service. Tabascan interviewees spoke of their need for the radio station. One of them said:

When we listen to the radio, we listen to the avisos, we listen to the urgent avisos, it might be an aviso about a sick person in our own family, about someone who just passed away, or about other villages' problems. Since we have radio, we can find out about all of this, but before when we didn't have radio we couldn't learn anything (3f).

Avisos have become a prominent means for external (especially intervillage) information flows because by listening to the avisos programs villagers pick up individual messages, and they also can get a general sense of what is going on in other communities. By listening to the avisos, people find out if an aviso has been sent to someone belonging either to their immediate social network or to their village. They also hear when information is directed to the ejidatarios network (e.g., from the municipal government or other corporations) and to the village as a whole (e.g., invitations to festivals from other villages). Likewise, people find out information directed to other places because regardless of its destination and original language, every aviso is broadcast in Tojolabal as well as in Spanish (and also in Tzeltal and in Tzotzil). As a result, Tojolabals are exposed to enough information about other villages to realize, for instance, when an unusual number of people have become ill, or what the specific actions of a certain government agency are. Therefore, the linkage established by the avisos service works at a different level than the telephone, linking the Tojolabal speech community in somewhat the way a specialized publication links people with similar interests.[9]

Providing the infrastructure for this communication system is XEVFS' best contribution to the Tojolabal community's information flows. Nonetheless, other aspects of the programming have also extended information flows. In fact, it is probably the station's participatory approach to radio broadcasting that has facilitated the development of information flows. For a community subject to discrimination, extreme poverty, and pressure to assimilate to the mainstream culture, a radio station boosting an ideology of participation must be a valuable communication resource. This point was explained clearly by a Tabascan young man when he was confronted with the hypothetical closing of XEVFS:

> For those who dislike Radio Margaritas to be working, we the people from this community disagree with the idea of closing the station because we know that this radio is helping us with free services. It's really helping the poor, because we also see when they invite us to air avisos or saludos or to tell stories, in this case we have open doors, but if we were to have only Radio Comitán, it costs either 500 or 1000 pesos, but you have to pay to air an aviso, in Radio Margaritas there's support for us because in general it is working for this region, that is to say that it's ours and I would disagree if the radio were going to be closed because it's helping us, if we have urgent avisos, even if it is not the scheduled time for avisos, the station airs them, the station airs them because the people working there [at Radio Margaritas] are also poor [indigenous people] (6s2).

Radio Margaritas' participatory ideology favors audience participation in the programming, which in turn has probably strengthened the bonds among Tojolabal villages. As I showed in Chapter 6, interviews with members of the audience are a major component of the programing dedicated to development topics such as health and agriculture. These programs then are also a means for intervillage information flows. A frequent comment made by the interviewees was that they like to listen to these programs because they are a way of "exchanging experiences" with other villages. "Why we say that what the radio offers us is beneficial?" asked a Tabascan man, "Because we find out about the work done by other communities, or when the indigenous healers talk over the radio, we exchange experiences" (1f). Four other men made similar comments.[10]

Another aspect of the programming that contributes to strengthening the bonds among Tojolabal villages is the phatic (tele)communication enabled by the broadcasting of saludos. Regardless of the low informational value of saludos, this specific way of social (tele)interaction indirectly furthers intervillage information flows by keeping open the channels of social networks. Extending this argument, I contend that all aspects of the programming that focus on local matters, including music, facilitate intervillage information flows.

On the other hand, because of Radio Margaritas' policy toward news programs, the villages are in need of a broadcasting alternative for much important local news. For instance, while information on traditional festivals is openly aired, political news is only obliquely broadcast. Local political news was an issue raised by the network's staff members, Tojolabal teachers, and other indigenous leaders, but the participants in the family interviews declined all opportunities to discuss it. Only a Tabascan man, who was somewhat drunk, risked saying that the station should broadcast information concerning a specific political problem involving Tabasco and the municipal government (5f). I have already talked, in Chapter 6, about the difficulties that the INI stations encounter in producing alternative news programs.

The point I am aiming at in this section is that despite the station's lack of relevant news programs, Radio Margaritas has definitively modified the form and the amount of local information flows. It has provided a telecommunications infrastructure, it has opened a radio channel in Tojolabal, and it has introduced Tojolabal concerns into local radio discourse. By doing so, the station has not only broadened Tojolabals' information sources, but has also enabled the Tojolabal speech community to improve it communications bonds. A Maderan woman underscored this aspect by saying: "What I like the most about Radio Margaritas is the way in which the villages have a means to keep in touch with each other."

Radio Margaritas as Community Radio

With our radio the indigenous villages are happy, because before the ricos' radio didn't make our hearts happy (2f).

Comparing Radio Margaritas with the classic model for community radio, the Pacifica Radio model, none of the INI stations are community radio because they are not owned and operated by the community but by a government agency. The Pacifica Radio model, however, does not take into account Third World conditions. Leif Lønsmann proposes a model which is more realistic for poor regions; rather than seeing sponsorship as the key element, it focuses on the relationship between the radio station and its listeners. Lønsmann argues that a community radio station is characterized by interacting with the community, encouraging audience participation, and reflecting local ways of speaking, living, and thinking.[11] Taking Lonsmann's view of community radio as the starting point, I explored how the interviewees perceive the relationship between the Tojolabal community and Radio Margaritas.

Tackling a subject so elusive required more than a simple and direct question. Thus I developed several sets of questions directly addressing the issue,[12] and another set of questions presenting the hypothetical closing of XEVFS.[13] First interviewees were asked about their visits to Radio Margaritas, their awareness of the station's annual festival, and their opinions about the station's claim of being the voice of the local people. Then they were presented with the hypothetical closing of XEVFS. This last set of questions elicited valuable responses and provided important details regarding the Tojolabals' symbolic use of Radio Margaritas to reaffirm social distinctions and to create group solidarity. I discuss here findings concerning all these questions and also deal with the comments about Radio Comitán (XEUI) that are interspersed throughout the interviews.

The One Who Has Gone to Radio Margaritas Is My Son

As one of the most immediate forms of people's participation, audience visits to Radio Margaritas' facilities uncover patterns of participation and uses. Audience perceptions of these visits may also clarify the extent to which the Tojolabal community feels that XEVFS is an integral part of the community. Audience visits to XEVFS follow two different cycles: a daily cycle for which the purpose of the visit is mainly to send avisos and saludos and an annual cycle for which the purpose is to attend the station's anniversary festival. I included two related sets of questions in the family interviews; the first set[14] concerns everyday visits to the station, and the second set pertains to XEVFS' anniversary festival.[15] Given the proximity of Madero and Tabasco to Margaritas City, it was not surprising that in all families interviewed there was at least one person who either had gone to XEVFS or who knew someone who had. Who visits the station and for what purpose, however, appears to be determined not only by proximity to the station, but also by the relationship of place of residence and gender.

During the daily cycle actual proximity to the station does not account by itself for audience visits. Despite the fact that Madero is closer to Margaritas City than Tabasco, Tabascans go to the station more often than Maderans. The reason must be Tabascans' more urgent need for telecommunications (most visitors to the INI stations are trying to broadcast an aviso). But we must consider also the possibility that Tabascans may feel more welcomed at the station than Maderans. There was for instance the question raised by a Maderan man regarding the station's refusal to publicize Madero's festivals. While two-thirds (6 of 9) of the Tabascan families stated that a family member had visited the station, only half (6 of 12) of the Maderan families claimed to have gone to XEVFS. Notwithstanding, the number of visitors is higher for Madero than for Tabasco. There were 6 Tabascan visitors from 6 different families, and 11 Maderan visitors also from 6 different families. All Tabascan visitors were young men, yet Maderan visitors included 3 men under 25 years, 4 men older than 37 years, and 4 women.

Proximity to XEVFS, on the other hand, does explain the annual visits. From the seven interviewees who said they had gone to the station for the purpose of attending the anniversary festival,[16] six are Maderans. The only Tabascan (a rich man by Tabascan standards) stressed that he only made a short visit; "I only went for a song, I didn't stay long," he said (3f). Undoubtedly, annual visits reflect both communities' traveling practices, but they also indicate that Tabascans visit XEVFS to fulfil telecommunications needs and Maderans to satisfy a desire for diversion.

Gender is a prominent determiner in visiting the station. As the users survey shows, few women visit XEVFS during the daily cycle. Several women interviewed explained why they do not visit the station. Five women said that they have no time because of their laborious work.[17] Other reasons given by women were that they have to watch their houses[18] and that they do not know XEVFS' location[19] (only two Tabascan men explained their reasons for not visiting the station; 4f said it was because of his work, and 7f said he does not know XEVFS' location). When both men and women were asked about the possibility of visiting the station, men were much more assertive than women. Compare the statements made by the father of a Tabascan family with those made by his wife:

Interviewer: Have you ever visited Radio Margaritas? Do you know any person that has gone to Radio Margaritas? Had you ever thought about visiting Radio Margaritas?

Father: I haven't gone to the station, I go to Margaritas City sometimes but I haven't gone to the radio station. The one who has gone is my son, but some day I'm going to go there because I know some stories, I'm going to participate there since I would like to talk over that radio sometime.

Interviewer: Madam, have you ever thought about visiting the station?

Mother: Yes, I have thought about it, but since I live alone in my house I cannot leave the house alone and even though I want to go, because I don't have anyone to watch the house, that's why I don't go.

Interviewer: Do you think you may visit us later?

Mother: Yes, but because I have too much work, I don't know if I could (F6).

Note how this Tabascan woman implies that it is difficult for women to visit the station because their family role demands that they stay at home. Among the Tojolabal this role includes not only those tasks associated in the Western world with women's work, but it also includes watching the house (which I thought may be an indirect way to keep them at home). In addition, more compelling reasons for visiting/not visiting the station are insinuated in the previous quote: there is the conviction concerning the worthiness of one's knowledge. Note how the father feels that he knows something worth being said over the radio, while the mother only talks about her work, politely declining the invitation. Remarks similar to the previous quote led me to believe that, especially in Tabasco, people see radio primarily as part of the masculine domain. Moreover, the custom of daily visits to XEVFS has the antecedent of broadcasting avisos from Radio Comitán. The local people have used Radio Comitán to send avisos probably since 1963 (for about 24 years prior to XEVFS' beginning in 1987). Radio Comitán,"the ricos' radio",is an institution of the ladino society and in Tojolabal communities dealing with institutions of the dominant culture has traditionally been a male domain. Thus those in charge of delivering avisos to Radio Comitán, and in turn to XEVFS, are men. A further illustration of this point is found in a Tabascan young mother's remark: "The one who goes more often is my brother-in-law, because he's the one who goes to run errands to Margaritas City and he's the one who goes to deliver the avisos" (18m).

On the other hand, three of the seven interviewees who claimed to have attended the anniversary festival were women. This is explained because of their place of residence, Madero, and their individual characteristics. These three women hardly fit into the traditional stereotype of the Tojolabal woman. One of them (15m) is a 50 year-old mother who displayed a stunningly assertive role during the interview. The second one (13fs) is a young woman highly educated by local standards (she studies telesecundaria). And the third (21m) impressed me as one of the most assertive woman taking part in the interviews. The last two enjoy a high socio-economic status. Moreover, in contrast to Tabascans, Maderans,including many women,often travel to Margaritas City and can afford to enjoy the festival. Tabascans cannot. As a Tabascan mother argued: "We cannot go to the festival because the work is very important, and also to go to Margaritas City we have to spend money because the trip fare is very expensive, we need money to go there" (5m).

Place of residence thus affects people's reasons for visiting XEVFS, and in turn, their ways of participating in the radio station. Maderans may seldom visit the station to send avisos but are more likely to attend the festivals. Tabascans often send avisos and saludos from XEVFS, but their principal way of participating in the festivals is listening to the broadcast. A Tabascan man described the way Tabascans take part in the festival:

> Even though we were not there, we listened to all programs aired and to where the musicians who participated came from, and we liked the way in which our brothers from other municipios talk, we see that it's very pretty how the anniversaries are celebrated and we had noticed all the anniversaries celebrated by our radio (1f).

Radio Margaritas Is Our Radio

The interview schedule included the question, "Radio Margaritas says that it's the voice of the Southern Border. Do you think that the station is really the voice of the people from the Southern Border?" This question often required long explanations on the part of the interviewers, but it was a revealing question. After more than four years of airing the station's identification, *"La Voz de la Frontera Sur,"* many interviewees did not understand the term "Frontera Sur" (southern border). However, I decided to keep the term precisely because it is Radio Margaritas' identification. The interviewers used the Spanish expression "Frontera Sur," but also rephrased it to "the people from the state of Chiapas." In several interviews the question needed further explanation; "the Southern Border," said a Maderan man,"where's that located?" (16f).

From the 21 interviews, 19 families agreed that Radio Margaritas is the voice of the local indigenous people, and most of them underscored that XEVFS encourages their participation. They expressed this in many different ways: five families talked about the broadcasting in Tojolabal,[20] four families highlighted the indigenous ethnicity of staff members,[21] while two women focussed on the way the station reflects the nuances of Tojolabal everyday life.[22] But the most striking finding was their recurrent reference to Radio Margaritas as "our radio."

Importantly, these comments disclose that most interviewees feel XEVFS reflects indigenous cultures. A Maderan mother stated: "Everything that is aired is the life that we live here in our houses" (14m). And a Maderan man said: "We like the station's programs because we know how to do the things they talk about. For example the *zahojeo* [cleaning the milpa]" (15f). Second, Tojolabals believe the station encourages their participation. To illustrate this point, there is this answer given by a Tabascan family:

Interviewer: Do you think that the radio airs the voice of the people from here, the state of Chiapas, the voice of the people from the Southern Border?

Son: Yes, because everyday our voice is aired, and also what was seen when the station started was that they gave us the opportunity to participate, whether in the Tojolabal language or in other languages, and that's why we like it, and also because they aired saludos.

Father: Yes, because the radio is ours and everything we say there is clearly heard [understood] in our communities.

Interviewer: And yourself Madam, do you think that those talking over the radio are the Southern Border people?

Mother: Yes, because we like what is broadcast over the radio, and also because even if people from other places talk, we understand (F6).

As an interesting gender contrast, the son and the father stress the possibility of actively participating in the radio, while the mother only talks of reception. There is a common thread, however, in their answer: the broadcasting in Tojolabal language. "Yes," replied a Tabascan woman, "it is we who talk [over the radio], because our voice and *our way of speaking* are broadcast [emphasis added]" (7m). Language, so closely related to ethnicity among the Tojolabal, is also closely associated with the opposition between "us" and "them." This opposition was implied in many responses, but it was specifically mentioned in these two comments made by Tabascans: "Yes, XEVFS is the voice of our people," answered a mother, "because we the peasants speak there in the radio, because it's a radio of us, it's not a radio of the ricos" (2m). "Yes, XEVFS is the voice of our people," replied a father, "because it's an indigenous people's radio station and it's not a ricos' radio" (3f). Likewise, an active participant in indigenous coffee-growers organizations associated the vernaculars spoken by members of these organizations with the indigenous languages broadcast by the station and concluded that XEVFS is the voice of all these people (19f).

A commonplace throughout the interviews is the reference to Radio Margaritas as "our radio." I found this expression, or a similar one, in two-thirds of the interviews (14 out of 21), used by 20 different people.[23] Although all families conveyed a positive perception of XEVFS, there is some indication of Tabascans' greater identification with Radio Margaritas; 7 of the 9 Tabascan families interviewed used the expression "our radio" as compared to 7 of the 14 Maderan families. Similarly, gender differences are also clear: men seem to identify themselves closer with XEVFS than women; 15 of the 32 men of the sample used the expression as opposed to 5 of the 27 women, but men also spoke more than women.

But there were also dissenting remarks. Only two Tabascan fathers openly disagreed with the question about XEVFS being the voice of the local indigenous people. One man replied: "Well, in my opinion, the radio's name is not written in Tojolabal but in Spanish" (18f); and the other stated: "They [indigenous people] listen to it, but I don't know if it's truly their voice" (4f). In addition, though all other families agreed with the statement, a number of them qualified their answers. There are these two examples: "Yes," said a Maderan father, "the radio says so, and it is almost as if all of us were there because when our language is aired, it is as if we were personally speaking there" (10f). "We know," a Tabascan man told us, "that the radio comes from INI, and according to INI the radio is for the indigenous race, it's not for the ricos" (5f). Significantly, the Maderan implied that XEVFS is only metaphorically their voice, and the Tabascan pointed to the claim made by the station's sponsorship.

It's Already a Radio of the Indigenous Peoples

One question elicited especially heated responses. The question was: "Some people do not like Radio Margaritas and they would like the station to be closed down. What do you think about this?" Most interviewees reacted strongly to the idea of closing down the station. They assumed the "ricos" were the proponents of the hypothetical closing, and they interpreted the speculative situation as quite real. Their reaction, by itself, tells something important about the position of the station within the web of antagonistic relationships of the Tojolabal with the ladino population. It also confirms the hypothesis that Tabascans and Maderans perceive the station as belonging to their own group's domain.

All families emphatically stated that XEVFS should continue broadcasting. The two chief reasons given were that XEVFS is very useful to them and that listening to the station has become a part of the Tojolabal everyday. While women tended to emphasize daily practices and listening pleasures, men argued more strongly for the utility of the station. These findings are consistent with my previous point regarding the genders' different modes of participation in radio. Women participate almost exclusively in reception; men participate in more active ways. I discuss remarks regarding the utility of XEVFS for the Tojolabal in the section devoted to development programs. Here it will suffice to present a brief summary.

There were 19 different people[24] belonging to 14 families making 28 remarks about the usefulness of the station.[25] Half of the 28 remarks concerned avisos, especially the fact that the station offers this service for free. The rest of the remarks were related to the general idea of service (e.g., "the radio is useful to us"). Interviewees also argued that XEVFS should continue operating since it has become a part of their everyday lives. The argument is presented well by this comment by a young Tabascan mother:

> I disagree with the idea of closing down the radio because we like very much everything that it airs and throughout the years it has been working we have become used to the radio. We are already accustomed to listening at certain times, if that [the closing down of Radio Margaritas] happened, we would feel sad and very different" (18m).

Nine people from four Tabascan and three Maderan families maintained that Radio Margaritas should not be closed down since it is already a part of their daily lives.[26] Interestingly enough, four of these five Tabascans and three of these four Maderans were women. Taking into account that in general men were more assertive than women, and that the number of men interviewed was higher, it is important that seven women stressed that XEVFS should continue operating because it has become a part of their daily lives. Furthermore, these women's remarks were extended and eloquent. There are, for example, these remarks made by two Tabascan women who offered persuasive reasons for keeping the station in operation:

> Interviewer: Some people do not like Radio Margaritas and they would like the station to be closed, what do you think about this? Do you agree with them or do you prefer that Radio Margaritas continue broadcasting?

> Daughter: I believe Radio Margaritas should not be closed down because if it were closed down we would be sad, because when we're at home we start working and we listen to the radio and our hearts get happy, and they shouldn't close it down because it's already a radio of the indigenous peoples.

> Interviewer: And what do you think madam?

> Mother: I believe that those who say that are not our people; if the radio were closed we are going to be sad, because if the radio is closed our communities are going to be sad, our ejidos are going to be sad, but when the radio is working there is a happiness inside our homes, but if it's closed our hearts are going to get sad, because when the radio is working it tells us the time very frequently, it tells us how many hours we have been working ...

Daughter: I also believe that it would be very sad for us because on Sundays we don't go out and we listen to the radio ... (F2).

Note how these Tabascan woman argued that listening pleasures attained from XEVFS' broadcasting constitute a substantial benefit for Tojolabal villages. They argue that listening to XEVFS has became a daily practice which contributes to the psychological well-being of the Tojolabal. Since Maderans have much more entertainment choices than Tabascans, I expected the latter to value XEVFS' broadcasting more than the former. There is a slight indication of such a difference in the interviews which has to do, rather than with the number of people or the number of families sustaining the argument, with the quality of Tabascans' comments in this regard.[27]

Another remarkable finding is that in all interviews people assumed that the "ricos" were the proponents of the hypothetical closing of Radio Margaritas. Eight people discussed specific reasons why the ricos would like to see the station closed down.[28] Half of these reasons were related to the fact that ladinos are not fluent in indigenous languages; as a Maderan woman said, "For those who dare to say that the station should be closed down by the ricos' mandate, it's because they don't understand what we talk about over the radio. It's because they don't understand that they say that" (10m). A Maderan man pointed out the station's usefulness to the Tojolabal by stating: "I think they [the ricos] say that because they see that the radio is very useful to us and that's why they want to close it down" (23f). A Maderan woman was even more specific, arguing that XEVFS is useful to Tojolabals but not to the ladinos (13fs). Moreover, a Tabascan woman said that ladinos dislike indigenous people's participation in Radio Margaritas (3m), and a Maderan man stressed that ladinos would like to limit such participation: "I think that they say that so that the indigenous people will quit participating in the radio" (22f).

What lies at the bottom of these responses is the existing tension between indigenous people and ladinos. This tension goes back to the history of the virtual slavery of the Tojolabal and is present in multiple aspects of the interactions between these two peoples, but it seems to be particularly acute in relation to XEVFS. Tojolabals perceive Radio Margaritas as belonging to the Tojolabal sphere, and ladinos resent that the only radio station broadcasting from Margaritas City does not serve their interests and suit their taste. Thus the struggle for either maintaining or changing the status quo manifests itself in a struggle for communications resources: "We wouldn't like to see the ricos ending up with the station," stated a Maderan man (10f). And a Tabascan man put it even more explicitly:

I believe the ricos dislike the radio because they hear that now we the indigenous people talk, now it's the voice of the peasant, because when the ricos see that we're working with the radio, they see us as their enemies, I believe they think that way (2f).

The struggle for resources also takes place among indigenous peoples themselves. As I mentioned before, there is tension especially between the Tojolabal and the Tzeltal. These two groups share some common areas (e.g., Altamirano). Tzeltal people have immigrated to the Tojolabal region, and Tojolabals play a subordinate role in some of their own religious festivities which, oddly enough, are directed by Tzeltals.[29] I also pointed out how this tension manifests itself in the interviews. Confirming Cornejo and Luna's findings, five of the families pointed out XEVFS' programming in other indigenous languages as the least favorite,[30] and one of the few explicit suggestions given by interviewees was to diminish the air time for these languages so that the programing in Tojolabal can be expanded (4f). In addition, in the teacher's interview it was underscored that Tzeltal people complain because they cannot benefit from XEVFS in the same way that Tojolabals do. Despite this tension, only one Maderan man entertained the possibility that the Tzeltal might have suggested closing the station down (10f). Most interviewees felt that ladino people, rather than the Tzeltal, would threaten to seize Radio Margaritas.

Radio Comitán, the Ricos' Radio

Radio Comitán (XEUI) broadcasts only in Spanish, but it includes the Tojolabal in its target audiences. It airs avisos, and in addition to the popular ranchera and norteña music that characterize its format, it also transmits marimba music. INI's officials claim that XEUI has modified its programming since Radio Margaritas began broadcasting. This claim is probably true since XEUI has had to compete with the cultural offerings introduced by XEVFS. For 24 years XEUI was the only station transmitting from the Tojolabal region, and at present it attracts a sizable Tojolabal audience. Even in Tabasco, people acknowledge they like the music aired by XEUI: "To tell the truth, we're very accustomed to listen to the music aired by XEUI," said a Tabascan man (1f). Cornejo and Luna found that although XEVFS' listenership is greater than that of XEUI, 9 out of her 73 interviewees reported they prefer to listen to the latter.[31] I observed that particularly in Madero people tune to XEUI on a regular basis. A Maderan man said his family switches between XEVFS and XEUI: "Sometimes we switch stations, we listen for a while to Radio Comitán and then we return to Radio Margaritas" (16f). A further reason to believe the Tojolabal also listen to XEUI (as well as to other stations broadcasting in Spanish) is that while many of them understand at least some Spanish, hardly any of them understands Tzeltal, Tzotzil, or Mam, which are the other vernaculars of XEVFS' broadcasting. A Maderan woman (13fs) and a Tabascan man (18f) indicated that they turn the receiver off when programming in these languages is aired. Thus during the time slots that XEVFS broadcasts in these vernaculars, a segment of the Tojolabal audience, particularly that segment enjoying electric power, is likely to switch to XEUI.

But despite their likely consumption of XEUI's offerings, interviewees talked about XEUI as a media institution of the ladino sphere. They dealt with a number of interrelated reasons to explain their perception of XEUI as "the ricos' radio". They often pointed out that XEUI broadcasts only in Spanish: "Although we also listen to Radio Comitán," said a Maderan mother, "it's not the same as Radio Margaritas because they don't talk in Tojolabal as we're talking right now" (14m). They also argued that XEUI discourages Tojolabal participation: "In Radio Comitán everything has to be paid," argued a Tabascan young man, "and it doesn't give us the opportunity to participate with music, by contrast in Radio Margaritas everything is freely aired" (18f). And, like the young woman of the following quote notes, ten families underscored that XEUI charges for transmitting avisos:[32]

> If Radio Margaritas were closed, we are not going to be able to air our avisos, we are not even going to listen to the music, perhaps they air all of this in Radio Comitán, but that's a different thing, and besides we have to pay, in our own radio we don't have to pay for the services that it offers to us (2d).

Interviewees discussed XEUI and XEVFS side by side and used XEUI as a point of reference to explain how they felt about XEVFS. Many times this point of reference was explicitly mentioned, but many other times the comparison with XEUI was only implied. For instance, when interviewees said "we like Radio Margaritas because it doesn't charge us for sending avisos, or "we like Radio Margaritas because it airs saludos," they were making an implicit comparison with XEUI because this station charges for sending avisos and does not broadcast saludos.

Twelve families objected to one or to several aspects of XEUI.[33] Nine of them stated that XEUI charges a high price for airing avisos;[34] three complained that the station broadcasts only in Spanish;[35] four, interestingly, all of them Maderan families, pointed out that XEUI is located far away from their village;[36] and five objected to the lack of indigenous participation in XEUI.[37] Maderans were much more outspoken than Tabascans in their criticisms of XEUI; out of the 22 specific objections to XEUI 16 were raised by Maderans. Men, of course, also outnumber women in their criticisms to XEUI; only five of the 22 objections were raised by women (two by Tabascans and three by Maderans). Of course, given the fact that Maderan men travel often to Comitán City where XEUI is located, it is not surprising to find that they were the most critical of XEUI. But, what I want to highlight here is that Maderan men's dissatisfaction with the failure of the local ladino radio station to meet the Tojolabal's needs insinuates a complex correlation between gender and place of residence, on the one hand, and the Tojolabal's desires and expectations about the institutions of the dominant society on the other.

Interviewees' desires and expectations regarding Radio Margaritas reveal that they understand that INI sponsors and operates Radio Margaritas. They also clearly distinguish that the station is operated according to a non-commercial model and that its (stated) purpose is to serve indigenous people. As a Maderan lady put it, they gather that "the radio doesn't belong to a single person but to all the villages" (16m). Indeed, they feel that the Tojolabal either have or should have more control over Radio Margaritas than over other local radio stations, such as Radio Comitán; for instance, a Tabascan man stressed that when they send an aviso on Radio Margaritas, they decide how many times it should be broadcast (18f), and a Maderan man strongly objected the station's policy banning announcements publicizing festivals where non-traditional music is performed (20s). Nonetheless, for the fact that the station fails to provide mechanisms allowing indigenous villages direct input over policies, management, and programming, the type of control that indigenous people exert over the station resembles the flimsy leverage that consumers have over commercial media. A Maderan woman's remark, which was somehow breaking the rules of social interaction of the interviewing process, speaks for interviewees' sense of their dubious control over XEVFS. "Well," she said, "I have a question, I want to know if they [she referred to INI officials] are going to take into account what we say or not" (15m).

Notes

1. Like I mentioned earlier, I use a code to identify the families interviewed. The capital letter "F" followed by a number refers to one of the families, for example "F4" refers to family number four. Numbers followed by lowercase letters refer to family members. For instance, "6m" refers to the mother of family number six; "6f" refers to the father of the same family; and "6gf" to the grandfather. The complete code is presented in Chapter 2, page 27.

2. Mario Humberto Ruz, *Los Legítimos Hombres. Aproximación Antropológica al Grupo Tojolabal*, II (México: UNAM, 1982) 236-7.

3. Ruz 240.

4. Echeverría's administration was from 1970 to 1976.

5. Ruz 195.

6. Instituto Nacional de Indigenista, ¿Se Escuchan Nuestras Voces? XEVFS La Voz de la Frontera Sur, by Inés Cornejo and Silvia Luna, ts., internal document, México, 1991, 71-75.

7. There was only one mention (1f) in the interviews regarding news.

8. Robert J. Saunders, Jeremy Warford, and Bjorn Wellenius point out that "many

telecommunications professionals or development experts have observed, but have not well documented, individual cases in which specific benefits of improved communication have been associated with changes in telecommunications infrastructure." The authors group such benefits under four headings: (1) market information for buying and selling; (2) transport efficiency and regional development; (3) emergency security and isolation; and (4) coordination of international activity. *Telecommunications and Economic Development* (Baltimore, Maryland: International Bank for Reconstruction and Development/ The World Bank and Johns Hopkins UP, 1983) 19-24.

9. A number of researchers have explained the "linkage function" of the media. See for example Joseph R. Dominick, *The Dynamics of Mass Communication*, 3rd ed. (New York: McGraw-Hill, 1990) 39-41.

10. These four men were: 4f, 6f, 11f, and 21f.

11. Leif Lonsmann, "Community Radio. A Global Perspective," International Communication Association, Dublin, Ireland, 1990.

12. Question #20, 21, and 23 of the audience interview schedule.

13. Question #26 of the audience interview schedule.

14. Question #20 of the audience interview schedule.

15. Question #21 of the audience interview schedule.

16. 9f, 11f, 13d, 15m, 20f, 21m, 3f.

17. 1m, 2m, 6m, 14m, 21m.

18. 6m and 19m.

19. 10m and 23m.

20. F1, F2, F4, F6, F23.

21. F1, F2, F13, F21.

22. 14m and 7m.

23. Tabascan families referring to XEVFS as to "our radio" were: F1, F2, F3, F4, F5, F6, and F7. Maderan families were: F10, F15, F16, F19, F21, F22 and F23.

24. They were seven Tabascan men and two Tabascan women; seven Maderan men and three Maderan women.

25. These families were seven out of the nine Tabascan families (F1, F2, F3, F4, F6, F7, and F18), and seven of the twelve Maderan families (F11, F13, F16, F19, F20, F22 and F23).

26. Tabascan families were: F1, F2, F3, and F18; Maderan families were: F10, F14 and F16.

27. The 16 people talking about listening pleasures belong to 10 different families, 5 of which are Maderan, and 5 of which are Tabascan.

28. 3m, 7m, 13fs, 10m, 16f, 20f, 22f, 23f.

29. Ruz, 54, 223-232. It is also interesting to note that the lawyer employed in the CCI-Tojolabal was not a Tojolabal, but a Tzeltal.

30. F4, F10, F13, F19, F21.

31. Even though Cornejo and Luna's sample was composed not only of Tojolabals but also of Tzeltal, Tzotzil, and Spanish monolinguals, and the study does not provide responses by ethnic group, still the findings sound reasonable for Tojolabal villages.

32. F1, F2, F6, F11, F16, F18, F20, F21, F22, F23.

33. Please note that the categories that I used to group the remarks about XEUI

are not mutually exclusive.

34. These families were four Tabascan families: F1, F2, F6, and F18; and five Maderan families: F11, F16, F20, F21, and F23.

35. These families were three Maderan families: F10, F14, and F15.

36. These Maderan families were: F11, F13, F20, and F21.

37. These families were four Tabascan families: F1, F2, F6, and F18; and one Maderan family: F21.

10

Radio and Ethnodevelopment

You always have to look at the idea of tradition in terms of power. What is handed down to women as traditional is rarely in our favor. I don't mean that there aren't aspects of our indigenous culture that we will want to draw from, but even then, it should never be seen as a fixed and sacred thing. Just show me a time when tradition was "pure" and a-historical. Culture is not fixed in the past, unchanging and unchangeable. Tradition is constantly evolving.[1]

Radio Margaritas is part of INI's efforts championing cultural revivalism. Since its planning stage, the most transparent purpose of the station has been to change the attitude of indigenous audiences toward their own cultures. The network's overt ideology advocates the ethnodevelopmentalist idea maintaining that development can only be achieved through the revaluation of the ethnic group's culture. Because XEVFS was established in the Tojolabal region to counteract the modernizing pressures of Protestant sects, numerous aspects of the programming aim to revaluate old mores and traditions.

Tradition

Though it is difficult to assess the station's success regarding its ethnic revivalist crusade, I included in the interview schedule a set of questions inquiring into listeners' perceptions of such success. The issue was introduced by asking if the old mores of the Tojolabal are being lost. All families agreed on the loss of some traditions, and many interviewees pointed out specific customs that are no longer observed, such as the celebration of the old carnival and the use of the traditional Tojolabal costume. Several people, however, argued that important aspects of the Tojolabal tradition, like language, have been kept alive in the villages. As I expected, Tabascans were more prompt than Maderans to talk about living traditions. While 7 out of the 9 Tabascan families pointed out specific, traditional Tojolabal customs still observed in their villages, only 4 of the 12 Maderan families did so.[2]

The interview schedule also inquired about Radio Margaritas' contribution to the preservation of traditional practices. Informants eloquently spoke of the use of the station as a means to keep traditions alive. For instance, they said that Radio Margaritas helps them to preserve their customs by informing them where traditions are still being observed, and by serving as a forum for the reproduction of their customary practices. A young Tabascan man said: "The radio helps us to preserve our customs because it airs how other ejidos celebrate their festivals" (4s2).[3] And another Tabascan man argued for the continuing vitality of indigenous traditions by explaining that Tojolabal music is played in his village and moreover, that it is broadcast by Radio Margaritas:

> We think that our customs haven't been lost so much because we do things in the same way our ancestors used to, we don't want to lose their ways, we continue using tambor and carrizo and also in Radio Margaritas that [traditional Tojolabal music] is aired, and that's why we don't think that we are changing our customs (4f).

All families expressed a preoccupation with the loss of traditional ways, and many said that Radio Margaritas has contributed to the revalorization of the Tojolabal culture. Some of them even talked about a renewed interest in old customs furnished by the station: "Indigenous thought is being revived because we listen to it on the radio" (5mn). Interviewees highlighted four aspects of Radio Margaritas' efforts to preserve Tojolabal customs: broadcasting in the Tojolabal language, transmission of traditional Tojolabal music, programs on Tojolabal history, and persuasive talks about the value of traditional mores. Nonetheless, some interviewees ventured oblique criticisms about the scarcity of programs on Tojolabal history.

Loss of Tradition

The Tojolabal have experienced multiple pressures to assimilate into the dominant Mexican culture. Interviewees mentioned economic reasons ("we dress like ladinos to work in the city"), governmental assimilationist policies ("the children lean Spanish in school"), punitive measures from ladinos ("the patrones scold us when we practice our traditions"), the need to play a part in the macro political arena ("the first men to wear ladino pants were those who had to travel to Mexico City because of their political responsibilities"), and peer pressure ("we left the nahua [Tojolabal skirt] when we saw other fellow women doing so"). Interestingly enough, their comments show hegemony at work because they talked about the way they feel seduced by ladino culture: "To tell the truth now we want to dress in ladino fashion," said a highly educated Maderan.

Interviewees also described the pervasive influence of Protestant sects.

The Tojolabal have witnessed the destructive effects that Protestant sects can exert over indigenous cultures. Tabascans feel so strongly about this issue that they have banned these religious practices from the ejido, and Maderans isolate the few families (probably seven, I was told) who have converted to Pentecostal and Presbyterian sects. In the following excerpt, a Tabascan man eloquently narrates how traditions were lost because of the influence of Protestant sects. Though he recognizes the economic reasons to stop observing some festivities, he insisted Protestant sects were the main reason for the loss of these practices:

> Before we used to have the romerías, we also used to do the walks to the milpa to ask for water, we had parties, played the marimba and the tambor there in the milpa when people were going to the milpa to ask for water, when there was no water. But the day came when religions [he refers to Protestant sects] existed in the communities, and they told us that we shouldn't follow our traditions, they told us that there were no gods in the forest, neither in the water, and that there was only one god in the sky, and many people do believe it. Here in Colonia Tabasco there's no religion but when people hear people from other places saying that, people start saying that maybe that's true and they don't want to follow the traditions, but before it was very good the way our ancestors used to do it. Also because of the expenses that you have in the walks to the milpa, perhaps for that reason they're not done anymore, but for the most part when traditions were lost was when the religions came to our villages. Before, men and women were obliged to attend the dance every Saturday and the music for dancing was tambor music, and now with our radio's help we see traditions are being recovered, because in this place we didn't play the tambor anymore (1f).

As this quote shows, interviewees answered very positively to the question regarding XEVFS' contribution to the preservation of traditional Tojolabal practices. They are very aware of the potential of radio broadcasting to advocate a viewpoint, and they also argued that the station advances this end by disseminating the voice of ethnic revivalists: "The radio station is helping us to recuperate our traditions because it lets us know other villages' traditions, and the people who don't want to lose the traditions are helping us with their own thought" (1f).

Tojolabal Music

Interviewees also pointed out that by offering a forum for the reproduction of traditional music, XEVFS contributes to the destigmatizing of Tojolabal culture. However, since most Tojolabal music aired by XEVFS has almost ceased to be played in Tabasco and Madero, I believe that for Tabascans and Maderans the station's music acts more as part of a cultural revival than as a means to develop a new appreciation for a living cultural practice.

The profane instruments of the first settlers are no longer played either in Tabasco or in Madero. In Tabasco the violin has been substituted by the marimba sencilla and the guitar. "The instrument that we don't use anymore is the violin because the men who used to play it died, but before it was played here, now what we use is only marimba, and the tambor is also played" (4f). In Madero not even the marimba sencilla is used anymore. For their festivals Maderans hire professional musicians from out of town who play "the ricos' instrument," or marimba buena, as well as electronic instruments.

As many of the so-called traditional elements of the Tojolabal (e.g., their costume, violin, guitar), the marimba is an appropriation. When was the marimba appropriated by Tabascans and Maderans? Changes in Tojolabal music probably came about with the drastic transformation of Tojolabal society initiated by the Agrarian Reform. Before the establishment of ejidos, marimba was not played by the Tojolabal. In addition to tambor and carrizo, the profane music during the baldío[4] and the early times of the Tojolabal colonias (1940s and 1950s) included only violin and guitar. According to an elderly woman, marimba was not played in the newly established ejido Tabasco: "When my parents were alive, there was no marimba, only violin and guitar, people played those instruments and also the tambor" (4m). The grandfather of a Tabascan family still remembers how music was played during the baldío times:

> We only used to listen to violin and guitar music when we were working with the patrones, sometimes we celebrated the harvest and the workers used to get together and only in that way we used to make our hearts happy, but only with violin and guitar music, that's what we used to do when we were harvesting the milpas with the patrones (3gf).

Most Maderans interviewed remember marimba was already played in Madero when they were children. But the sample's oldest couple said the instruments played in the newly established ejido Madero were only tambor and carrizo. This elderly Maderan man said: "Many people from here listen to tambor and carrizo music because it is an old tradition, I like that kind of music a lot because that was the music played in Madero when I grew up and now I like to listen when it's aired over the radio" (19f). This couple, both over 60, are the children of the first settlers who came to Madero, in the early 1940s, from the finca Las Cruces.

When asked if Radio Margaritas plays marimba in the traditional way, interviewees, regardless of their and place of residence, tended to agree, though a 64 year-old Maderan woman disagreed: "The way of playing has been changed because before, they played marimba and men said verses, but the way I hear on the radio is not as it was before, but it has been changed a bit, the way we played marimba was very different to what is now aired in Radio Margaritas" (15m). The vast majority of Tabasco's and Madero's population lack first-hand knowledge about traditional Tojolabal music, but they have been listening to Radio Margaritas and use its programming as a model for traditional Tojolabal music. This use of the station's offerings permeated the interviews. Take for example how a Maderan man, using the station's broadcast as a point of reference, asserted that musical practices have changed in his village:

> What's played in Madero has changed because in Radio Margaritas the original indigenous music is aired, but here what we do in a festival is to hire a marimba, that's to say that now we hire the ricos' music instrument, it's not indigenous music anymore, the tradition has been changed (22f).

Likewise, informants indicated the use of the station as a means to search for cultural roots which, especially in the case of young Tojolabal men, seems to be a significant part of their on-going process of ethnic identity formation. Several young interviewees, despite their undoubtedly great interest in ladino musical genres, stated that they like Radio Margaritas music because it is their only way to hear how music was played by their ancestors. A young Tabascan suggested that the station might broadcast more traditional music:

> I would like for the tambor music, the marimba music, the violin and the carrizo music, I would like for this kind of music to be aired more, because many of us Tojolabal do not know how our ancestors played music, but if we listen to the music of these instruments, we are going to realize how music was played before. For example, here in Tabasco we didn't see how the violin was played, because in that time the marimba didn't exist, people used to dance with the violin, and I propose that the station air more of this kind of music so that we won't forget our ancestors' traditions (18f).

Tojolabal Language

In contrast with Tojolabal music, the Tojolabal language has persisted even in settings like Madero, where extensive pressures to assimilate into ladino society have existed.[5] "Some people say that our customs are being lost, but it's not true because our language has been preserved," eloquently argued a Tabascan man (2f). Through the process of colonization, however, Tojolabals came to regard their own language as inferior to Spanish. If, as Frantz Fanon says, to speak a language "means above all to assume a culture, to support the weight of a civilization,"[6] Radio Margaritas may play an empowering and liberating role because the station's broadcasting in Tojolabal may serve as a catalyst for changing the ethnic group's perception regarding their own language and in turn regarding their own culture.

The significance that XEVFS' broadcasting in vernaculars has for the

Tojolabal audience was quite clear in the interviews. In the section on community radio, I mentioned that several families stated that XEVFS is indeed the voice of the indigenous people because it broadcasts their voices and speech and its staff includes indigenous members. I also mentioned that one of the only two interviewees openly dissenting with this opinion argued that XEVFS' name is not in Tojolabal but in Spanish (18f). And I stressed how interviewees often pointed out that Radio Comitán, the ricos' radio, does not broadcast in Tojolabal. But there is perhaps nothing more powerful to illustrate the significance that the broadcasting in Tojolabal bears for villagers than a brief yet common remark made by interviewees: "We like it when the programs are aired in Tojolabal because we understand what they are telling us" (18f).

Even though I had no question specifically asking about language, there were 31 remarks about this topic in the interviews. The remarks on language deal with five issues: (1) the importance of the broadcasts in Tojolabal; (2) the bilingual or Tojolabal-Spanish broadcasting; (3) the broadcasting in Tojolabal as part of a larger social struggle; (4) the transmissions in Tzeltal, Tzotzil, and Mam, seen from a positive viewpoint; and (5) the same transmissions, seen from a negative viewpoint.[7] Some people briefly touched on one of these topics; others talked extensively on two or three of them.

I had expected that Tabascans, rather than Maderans, would talk more about language issues. But while only one Maderan family omitted these issues, there were two Tabascan families who overlooked them.[8] Proportionally, more Maderans talked about language. I had also expected that women and monolinguals would comment on the issues, yet there were far more remarks from bilinguals and from men.[9] Perhaps Maderans, bilinguals, and men, who are more intimately involved in a conflictual process of ethnic identity negotiation, are more sensitive about losing their mother tongue and are also more aware of the role that the mass media can play for preserving the Tojolabal language.

The importance of the broadcasts in Tojolabal was a common thread in most of the remarks on language. Interviewees emphasized that Radio Margaritas is the only radio station that many of the Tojolabal understand. Some interviewees pointed out that they only listen to XEVFS when the broadcasting is in Tojolabal, as this Tabascan woman said:

> We listen when it [the broadcasting] is in Tojolabal, but when Spanish is aired we don't understand because our parents didn't teach us how to speak Spanish, and that's why we don't know how, we don't understand Spanish, but when Tojolabal is spoken over the radio we understand everything (7m).

Some interviewees said they only listen when the broadcast is in Tojolabal though; others noted that even though they prefer this programming, they also listen to programming in Spanish, either because they (women in particular) have little control over the radio receiver or because several of Radio Margaritas' programs combine Spanish with vernaculars, for example the avisos and the saludos programs.

The ambivalent feelings of the Tojolabal toward Spanish were represented by interviewees' opinions about the station's broadcasting in Spanish. My interview schedule failed to address the subject, but nevertheless some interviewees touched on it. Two Tabascans and three Maderans stated bilingual broadcasting was acceptable, but two Tabascans and one Maderan talked about Spanish as the language of the oppressor, suggesting that the broadcasting in Tojolabal has become a part of the struggle between ladinos and Tojolabals. There is a remarkable illustration of this point in one of the replies to the hypothetical question about the closing of the station. A Maderan man interrupted the interviewer to say this:

> I'm sorry but I have to interrupt. But I learned that the ricos don't like Radio Margaritas, you see they don't understand Tojolabal, but we understand it very well and we want to listen to it, but they don't, they don't want to listen to it. At times when I go to work out of town, many Spanish speakers find fault when someone is listening to Radio Margaritas, what they like to listen to is Radio Comitán, why? Because they don't understand, as we're talking right now, and because they don't understand the radio broadcasting in Tojolabal, that's what they don't like, because they don't understand, but because we're from both places. We speak Spanish and Tojolabal and we understand them, but the ricos only speak Spanish, they don't understand Tojolabal (16f).

As for the broadcasting in Tzeltal, Tzotzil, and Man, there were also contradictory viewpoints. Tabascans tended to assert their identification with other ethnic groups and underscored these indigenous peoples' rights to have their languages broadcast over the radio. By contrast, Maderans tended to express a negative viewpoint. While there were six positive remarks about the transmissions in these vernaculars made by Tabascans, there was only one such remark made by a Maderan; by contrast, the interviews contained five negative remarks made by Maderans and only one negative remark made by a Tabascan. It is significant that one of the very few reasons to turn the radio off cited by interviewees was the broadcasting in these languages. This broadcasting was also one of the specific aspects of XEVFS' programing mentioned as less liked.[10] And it was the focus of one of the explicit suggestions advanced: to limit the air time in these languages so that the time for Tojolabal broadcasting can be expanded (4f). Behind these negative comments lie the quarrels, especially with Tzeltals, about resources. A Maderan man said: "I have heard that many people from the Tzeltal area say that Tojolabals, some communities, that we have the station very close and that that is something good for us" (10f).

Persuasive Talks About Tradition and Programs on Tojolabal History

Interviewees were very aware of Radio Margaritas' persuasive efforts to furnish the observance of indigenous traditions: "The government tells us to keep our old traditions, that's fine, I like what I listen to on the radio" (14m). All the families said that Radio Margaritas features persuasive talk shows on the need to preserve traditions, but how effective have these talk shows been? Compare a remark made by a Tabascan mother with a comment by a Maderan father. She said: "The radio tells us that we shouldn't stop practicing our customs and we also understand what it tells us" (7m). And he said: "The radio is telling us that it's better to observe the old customs, that we shouldn't lose them, but I see that little by little we have been changing for example our traditional costume" (9f).

A recurrent theme in the interviews is that Radio Margaritas' broadcasting has furnished the sense of shared traditions among Tojolabal villages. The Tojolabal have ceased to observe the religious pilgrimages or romerías that used to provide a means of keeping in touch with other villages. Today most of their contacts with other Tojolabals occur in Margaritas City and Comitán City, places where many Tojolabals are likely to hide their ethnic traits. In this context, Radio Margaritas has provided the villages with a new means for contact where traditional cultural practices are encouraged. Eight interviewees indicated that by broadcasting how other villages observe traditional practices, the station helps them to continue with their old mores.[11] Tabascans (men and women) and Maderan women were more likely to make this kind of remark than Maderan men. Since Tabascans and women are more traditional than Maderan men, the station may only contribute to invigorate living customs, or it may indeed help to reintroduce lost practices. Maderans often referred to the use of the traditional Tojolabal dress (which is an outdated practice in their village) by talking about the difficulty of reintroducing lost practices. The following quotes illustrate this point; the first is by a Maderan father, the second by a Maderan mother:

> They tell us in the radio that we shouldn't lose our traditions because I have heard that some people, those who have kept the traditions, tell us that we shouldn't stop observing our customs and the radio is helping us in this way, but I don't believe that the people from here [Madero] are going to, for instance, start wearing the traditional costume again, they are already accustomed to wearing [ladino style] dresses and pants (21f).

> When our mothers saw the way the rich people dressed, they learned it because before the poor were accustomed to use the regional costume, only those dressing in a different way were the rich, but when the women saw how the rich were dressed they learned that way and we learned too. Now as I see it, the regional costume is completely lost because our *planta*[12] [the essence of a person, of a people] has completely changed (10m).

These statements also suggest that, regardless of the persuasive efforts made through talk shows that aim at creating a positive opinion about certain practices, the station may contribute to preserve only those traditions having a strong aural dimension, such as language and music, because radio provides a space for their reproduction. The question remains about whether the station may have an impact, for instance, on the preservation of the declining Mam language. An even more crucial question is whether or not Radio Margaritas should allocate part of its limited and precious resources to broadcast classes of a declining language. As I show above, the broadcasts in other vernaculars, including Mam, were cited as one of the less liked aspects of the station's broadcasting.

The last point directly concerning Radio Margaritas' efforts to preserve traditions is the transmission of programs about Tojolabal history. As other INI's radio stations do, Radio Margaritas carefully selects which traditions to promote. Tojolabal music and language present no major challenge, but the Tojolabal history of oppression is another matter. If Radio Margaritas were to discuss the subject openly, it could stir up Tojolabal listeners and may provoke the local ladino elite. The station thus talks about Tojolabal history only indirectly and sparingly. Nonetheless, some of our interviewees said they appreciate any efforts to talk about the subject. A Maderan mother described how much she likes programs about the villages' history:

Interviewer: What do you like the most from Radio Margaritas' broadcasting?

Mother: Well, we like everything, for example when the radio airs tales about how much the [Tojolabal] people suffered during the baldío, and they tell us about how much our ancestors suffered, that's what we like.

Interviewer: Then you enjoy listening about traditions?

Mother: Yes because they tell us how it was before and also our traditions are kept alive by the radio, that's what we like. When our ancestors founded our village they had traditions, they [XEVFS] want to revalue those traditions now and we like that traditions be kept alive, in this way is more pretty to live in this world, because if we do not believe God's word, his orders, then our thought is not right, but like the government tell us to keep alive ancient traditions, that's right, I agree with what is said over the radio, because sometimes the grandparents tell us tales and it's very pretty what they tell us and we didn't see that but we listen to their tales over the radio (F14).

Likewise, a Tabascan father explained that when the station airs these programs, ladinos come to realize Tojolabal oppression (keep in mind that local ladinos dislike XEVFS and seldom listen to its broadcasts):

I think it is very good [that the radio airs talks about customs] because when talking about customs they tell us how our ancestors suffered with the patrones, of course, we didn't see it, we now live in the colonias, but for those who saw it, for example those who lived during the baldío, they broadcast that. They tell us what happened to them and in that way the ricos listen to them, so that they know how they used to mistreat our ancestors (2f).

On the other hand, a young Tabascan man spoke of the scarcity of such programs and youth's need to know and understand how it was to live during the baldío under conditions of virtual slavery:

The history of our ancestors should be aired there [over XEVFS] because we ourselves don't know how things happened before, because they tell us that the baldío existed then, but we didn't see it. I think that there are still some people in this community that still know that, but they may not want to go to the station. That's what I would like to listen to. That would be for us to have an idea of how our ancestors suffered, because they tell us that they lived as *baldíos* that's to say that they used to work with the patrones, it wasn't as it is now, that if one wants to work or not that's one's choice, one is not forced to work, before everything was by force, men and women (18f).

Instead of explaining interviewees' preoccupation with the loss of tradition by arguing for the compelling power of the media to impose an ideology, I contend rather that XEVFS has been successful in its efforts to revaluate the Tojolabal culture precisely because many Tojolabals had been engaged in their own ethnic revival struggle even before the introduction of the station. It is then in the merge of the station's ideology and the audience's craving for their own roots that the key of XEVFS' success lies. Yet I have to recognize XEVFS' power to set villagers' agendas. The station's emphasis on the preservation of tradition has probably had a lot to do with the way Tabascans and Maderans perceive the issue.

The last point I want to make is that, for the interviewees, reflecting on their history of exploitation implies considering their present oppression. The way in which they talked about the significance of the broadcast on Tojolabal traditions discloses their awareness of the relevance that the past has for the present, of the enormous explanatory power that history provides for understanding and changing current circumstances. One of the few open criticisms of Radio Margaritas refers precisely to the station's failure to discuss the present oppression of the Tojolabal and to situate this oppression in its historical context. A Tabascan man, who was somewhat drunk during the interview, ventured asking why Radio Margaritas fails to talk about the present oppression of the Tojolabal:

What I think is this: first God, thanks to him I'm fine, thanks to the *Padre Eterno*, [eternal father] listen: Couldn't the radio air this? The world has made our life hard, why are things so expensive? We, as poor, that's to say the indigenous people, why is the worth of our work so low? This is what I think, *Hermano*, [brother] listen, I'm telling you this seriously, it's true that we're very oppressed by the big landlords, why are we so oppressed? Would it be that God is never going to give us freedom? That's what I pray for, in this condition we ask for freedom, we as poor day after day we work like dogs and we don't get anything, that's how our life is (5f).

I had seen this 50-year-old man walking on the mountain trail and carrying a wood load bigger than himself. Reflecting on his disheartening words and his impoverished village I wonder what role development projects like the INI stations play in the transformation of an oppressive social system. I especially wonder this when the racist attitudes of the stations' ladino staff lead me to believe that they have come to view indigenous people's life and oppression as usual, normal reality, part of their cultures and their ethnicity.

Improving Living Conditions

The efforts of Radio Margaritas to improve the living conditions of the Tojolabal range from the global endeavor to bolster the group's self-esteem to programs specifically aiming to remedy health and agricultural problems. These efforts also include the foremost impact that the station has had on improving the information flow in the region. There was an overriding agreement among interviewees concerning the usefulness of XEVFS to the villages. For interviewees, "usefulness" carried several meanings referring to various aspects of the programming: it referred to the broadcasting of avisos and saludos and to the impact of broadcasting on local flows of information. It also referred to series on health and agriculture, and it alluded to the gratification of psychological needs and the preservation of traditions. Since I have already discussed many of these topics, in this section I will concentrate on XEVFS' series on health and agriculture, on the importance of the broadcasting of saludos, and on the station's contribution to solving immediate communication problems often related to health. Finally I will discuss how the Tojolabal may use Radio Margaritas to cope better with the almost imperceptible demands that the modern world has been imposing on the villages, such as punctuality.

The audience study on XEVFS by Cornejo and Luna included a question concerning the usefulness of Radio Margaritas: "What is the radio useful for to you?" Out of their 56 interviewees answering this question, 22 said the station provides companionship and distraction, about 15 pointed out that

XEVFS constitutes a feasible medium for fulfilling their telecommunications needs by allowing the audience to send avisos and saludos, 13 claimed it helps them find out about news and what goes on in other villages, and 2 indicated it offers a service to them by telling the time. Of the remaining 4, 2 failed to answer the question indicating perhaps that XEVFS is not useful to them at all, and the other 2 gave a number of answers, including the preservation of tradition and education. I should underline however that 37 of the 56 interviewees confronted with this question were Spanish monolinguals, and moreover that only 13 of the 19 interviewees who speak indigenous languages were Tojolabals.

Cornejo and Luna also found that, for indigenous interviewees, the broadcasting of avisos and saludos was more important than the companionship and distraction provided by XEVFS, and that finding out the time was as important as having information on news. In a closely related question posed by the same study, almost half of the 17 indigenous interviewees said XEVFS helps their communities by broadcasting avisos free of charge.[13] Aranda Bezaury and Valenzuela, in their research on the indigenous audience of XEZV found that most of their interviewees thought the station was useful for sending avisos.[14]

Radio Margaritas features only a limited number of programs dedicated to what has come to be regarded as the typical areas targeted by rural development efforts: education, health, and agriculture. Moreover, because both XEVFS and INI fail to originate media campaigns for development, no spots for such purposes are produced by the station. The few spots of this type are outside productions (*cápsulas*) done in Spanish by government agencies such as the National Council of Health (*Consejo Nacional de Salud*) and the government of the state of Chiapas. In a forum convened by Radio Margaritas (held on November 17, 1990), I observed how members of indigenous organizations specifically suggested that the station should broadcast more programming that aims at improving living conditions. "More about health and such things should be aired," said a member of one of these organizations. The results of my investigation also suggest that the station should allocate more resources to this type of programming.

Radio Margaritas only broadcasts two development series for the Tojolabal audience, though both are aired during prime time (see Chapter 6). *Nuestra Tierra* (our land) concentrates on agricultural issues and *La Voz de los Médicos* (the healers' voice) focuses on health topics. Both series feature interviews with Tojolabal people, often Tabascans and Maderans, and both are produced by young Maderan men working for XEVFS. *La Voz de los Médicos* is produced by one of my interviewers, Armando Alfaro. I had many reasons, therefore, to expect interviewees to talk about these two programs. And they did. Yet out of the 13 families speaking of programs related to development issues, only two men of one Tabascan family referred to

Nuestra Tierra by its name (F4). The rest of the interviewees spoke of "talks about health and/or agriculture" or described programs featuring talks and stories (*pláticas, historias*) where other fellow people discuss these issues.

Six out of the 9 Tabascan families and 7 out of the 12 Maderan families spoke of programs related to development issues.[15] I coded these remarks into 5 mutually exclusive categories ranging from specific to general comments. Since often a person would refer to development programming in a general fashion while also making a second specific comment (e.i., on the health or agriculture series), I discarded the former. There were 31 people, 17 Tabascans and 14 Maderans, stating remarks about these issues. Five of their remarks were about health and agriculture, 8 about health, 6 about agriculture, 8 about talks or talk shows, and 4 about exchange of indigenous expertise. Not surprisingly, the development issue most often discussed by interviewees was health.

Two-thirds of the remarks about development issues (20 of 31) were made by men, and proportionally, more Maderans mentioned these issues than Tabascans. In addition, interviewees speaking some Spanish mentioned these issues slightly more often than those monolingual in Tojolabal; only 12 of the remarks were made by monolinguals. It follows that those interviewees who tended to mention programming dealing with development issues were precisely those who also tended to be more acculturated into mainstream society: men, Maderans, and people with some proficiency in Spanish. On the other hand, women and Tabascans tended to be more specific in their comments; only 3 out of the 11 women and 5 out of the 17 Tabascans made general comments. The rest of them made extended remarks.

Health Problems and the Broadcasting of Avisos

I mentioned earlier that health was the single issue most frequently specified by people talking about programming for development. This finding, of course, is explained in part by reasons related to both the methodology of my research and XEVFS' programming, but it is also because of audience concerns and radio's potential for assisting in health-related problems. The Tojolabal suffer from ill health and, as several researchers have pointed out, the group "exhibits extreme preoccupation with disease."[16] Some interviewees displayed this preoccupation by making a direct reference to programs about health issues, but many others did so by explaining the advantage that XEVFS' avisos service offers when a family member becomes seriously ill.

Generally speaking, for people living in remote areas instantaneous communication does not have the importance that urban residents give to it, but quick means of telecommunication becomes extremely important for everyone when the health or the life of a loved one is at stake. By broadcasting avisos, radio stations assist isolated dwellers with those telecommunication problems that usually come with the ill health of a family member. Informants frequently claimed that XEVFS offers an indispensable service to the villages by broadcasting avisos. Just in response to the question about the hypothetical closing of XEVFS, roughly a third of the interviewees (19) argued that the station should continue operating because it is useful to the villages.[17] It should be noted however that all families indicated that XEVFS assists villagers in meeting various needs.

Series on Health Problems and Women's Concerns

Regarding the series *La Voz de los Médicos*, it is worth noting that despite the fact that it does not specifically target women (indeed the opposite may be argued), 8 of the 13 responses on health issues were made by women. This finding confirmed what a Tojolabal teacher had told me: "When there're programs talking about health care, mothers listen very carefully. For example they listen how to boil the water, how to feed their children." A Tabascan mother mirrors this remark by pointing out how much she likes this series: "The radio airs things that are interesting to us, for instance the programs on health are very useful to us and we really like how the radio airs them; it's when we realize how to be in better health" (5m). Other interviewees said that XEVFS assists the villages by broadcasting a series in which Tojolabal people with some medical expertise speak, for instance, of medicinal plants. Here is how a Tabascan man put it:

> We also like it when the radio talks about medicinal plants and tells us how to cure diseases, and also the way health extension workers talk to us because people's needs are plenty regarding diseases, and by means of the radio we exchange our experience about medicinal plants. I see that well because before nobody would help us, and if we needed a remedy for a sick person, we had to go far away to another community, like Margaritas City. There we used to get the remedies but now since there are health extension workers and they exchange their knowledge by means of the radio, that's very good because I believe they're telling us the truth because they do that kind of work (6f).

Two points should be highlighted regarding this response. One is the effective manner in which *La voz de los Médicos* promotes and coordinates with a development project sponsored by the Ministry of Health (*Secretaría de Salubridad y Asistencia, Programa Promotores de Salud*), and the other pertains to the issue of source credibility. This Tabascan personally knows several of the guest speakers on the program and trusts them. But cases like this may be more the exception than the rule. In the interview with Tojolabal teachers, they mentioned that villagers frequently question the authority of the speakers on this kind of programming. Though radio has the potential for conferring status and thus credibility to speakers, note how a Maderan father disclosed his distrust of the health series' guest speakers:

> Interviewer: What do you like the least about Radio Margaritas?
> Father: What I dislike are the healers because sometimes it's only lies they tell us, it's only to earn money.
> Interviewer: You dislike what they said?
> Father: I dislike it because we don't know them, they are strangers, and well, how are we going to know if it's true what they tell us? (16f).

What seems even more crucial is that such distrust may be an unintended effect of promoting popular participation because if ordinary people participate in the station, radio may lose much of its prestige status and in turn its persuasive power. Then convincing the audience to change its behavior, regarding for instance boiling the water, may become an even harder challenge for those agents implementing development projects.

Another challenge to the producers of health programs arises from the difficulty that lies in how to discuss in a public forum topics that have customarily been private matters. Women producing similar programs for another of the INI stations, XEZV, underlined this difficulty before, and they told me the story of an indigenous woman healer who agreed to participate in one of such programs, only to be seriously reprimanded by her fellow villagers. She received death threats for disclosing the village's most intimate domain. Other key informants also mentioned the issue, and in our interviews with Tojolabal listeners I also found a reference to the dilemma of how to address taboo topics in a medium which openly broadcasts its messages. Here is how a Maderan woman objected to the use of banned words in radio broadcasting:

> Interviewee: What do you like the least about Radio Margaritas?
> Mother: I don't like it when they use bad words and when that happens I better turn the radio off and stop listening.
> Interviewer: Do you remember in what program you heard these words?
> Mother: No, I don't remember, but as I said when I don't like it and I turn it off.
> Father: I think it's when they speak of healing because that's aired very clearly, it seems that there are some words that should be only whispered, they shouldn't utter them openly, because if they're said openly and the radio it's playing loudly the children listen and that's why they're becoming spoiled (F 11).

The suggestion advanced by this Maderan father, whispering taboo words, was exactly what the healer did over the microphone in XEZV, but of course the strategies of interpersonal communication to deal with secretive realms proved to be quite inadequate for radio broadcasting.

Women's role as keepers of tradition possess a further dilemma. Since numerous taboos pertain to sexuality and women's bodies, and quite often women see themselves as keepers of those traditions, the question is how to produce programs about women's concerns without alienating precisely the target audience. How to serve as a catalyst for the reflection on women's most intimate problems, their bodies, their sexuality, without threatening the foundation of traditional Tojolabal morality? How to speak publicly of what custom designates as secret? Radio Margaritas has yet to recognize these dilemmas. The station has so far not even properly dealt with more safe spheres of women's concerns, like domestic work. Because of the resignation of the only Tojolabal female employee (Candelaria Rodríguez, my research assistant), XEVFS stopped broadcasting the Tojolabal edition of the program *Nosotras las Mujeres* (we women) a few weeks before my fieldwork was conducted. The program addressed women's concerns, but apparently had failed to attract Tabascan and Maderan women. None of the women sampled commented on the program, though a Tabascan mother pointed out the station neglects women's home labor and its importance for the family's health: "Well as a woman I think the radio should talk about house chores, about how to clean the house because diseases come from there, and that may help us to take better care of the children (3m)."

The station's failure to produce development series targeting women may explain interviewees' responses regarding the usefulness of the station. Note that most of the interviewees specifying how XEVFS is useful to them were not women but men. These responses, however, may also be because of the logical connection between the idea of practical utility and avisos and the fact that the vast majority of senders of avisos are men.

Series on Agriculture and Exchange of Indigenous Expertise

Conversations with members of the audience make up the core of the station's series dedicated to development topics. Thus often when the interviewees talked about health and agricultural issues, they referred to these conversations and to the way in which XEVFS acts as a forum for the exchange of indigenous expertise. A frequent comment made by interviewees was that they like to listen to these programs because they are a way to exchange experiences with other villages. "Why do we say that what the radio offers to us is beneficial?," asked a Tabascan man, "because we find out about the work done by other villages, or when the indigenous healers' talk over the radio, we exchange experiences" (1f). Regarding agricultural expertise, another Tabascan said: "We listen to how other villages leave the [organic] waste on the land to feed it and that's useful to us because from that experience we learn how to do it, because the fertilizer is now very expensive, and that's why we like it and it's useful to us" (7f).

Only nine families, however, mentioned agricultural issues. There were eleven responses on the topic,[18] seven made by Tabascans and only two by women (Tabascan). Seven of these remarks were very brief; moreover, the two most lengthy comments actually criticized XEVFS' efforts in this respect. A Maderan man made an articulate suggestion:

> We like how the radio works, but only if the government could help us so that more talk shows about agriculture were aired, especially about how to fertilize the milpa, because for the people the most important thing is to work the land and if the government could help us in a joint effort with the radio, we could present petitions to request fertilizer, and that's what I think, that more talks on agriculture be aired (19f).

This man belongs to a local federation of indigenous organizations and sees that Radio Margaritas could play a more active role in assisting villagers with agricultural problems. Aware that such problems come not only from the lack of information, but especially from the lack of resources, he suggests that XEVFS should broadcast more programs on the topic, and that it also should play a more active role in assisting the Tojolabal to attain resources such as fertilizer. His suggestion resembles what has already been implemented in another station, XEZV. During my visit to XEZV I observed how this station's staff act as mediators between indigenous people and government agencies. As part of their daily work, XEZV's staff assists the locals with a variety of problems arising from the fact that indigenous people often lack the language and cultural proficiency to deal with mainstream society's institutions. I did not observe, however, this type of practical assistance in any other of the INI stations that I visited, including Radio Margaritas. The second criticism involved a suggestion to combine the broadcasting of programs for development with some efforts to organize the audience. A Maderan man, commenting on his own radio experience, stated:

> I haven't learned how people from other communities work, I haven't learned from the people exchanging experiences. What we could do is that at the time they're talking [over the radio], we should take notes on a notebook and later we would practice what they tell us and we will see what results we might get (16f).

Joint Efforts with Extension Workers and Support for Indigenous Organizations

In addition to specific programming about health and agriculture, Radio Margaritas' impact on improving the living conditions of its target audience includes joint efforts with extension workers and support for indigenous organizations. In contrast with interviewees' criticisms, I found that the

Tojolabal teachers spoke very positively about the series for development purposes. One of the teachers said:

> People are interested in this type of program, but we as teachers, we have more skills, we can take notes about the procedures, what purposes they are useful for, because also the peasants can't remember everything, it's heard and that's it, but we, since we're very interested, we pay more attention.

This comment touches on an effective use of radio for development, the broadcasting of special programs for extension workers. As do other INI stations, Radio Margaritas participates in joint efforts with the Ministry of Education and, customarily, the teachers employed by the latter work in the former. Unfortunately, during my fieldwork the station was not broadcasting any of the productions resulting from such joint efforts, but the teachers interviewed spoke of a former series produced by some of them and aired prior to my visit. The teachers argued that this series, focussing on INI's boarding centers, provided useful advice to extension workers who usually received little training for their jobs. The teachers also claimed that the station assists villagers by disseminating information about how to make the best of health resources sponsored by the government, and how to resist the abuse that some people make of similar resources, such as the rampant irresponsibility of rural teachers:

> Speaking about the teacher, the teacher has certain responsibilities but suppose the teacher doesn't do his work, then the father of a family and the people of a village through the radio have known what the obligations of a teacher are and how much people should demand, with that the radio is doing a lot for the people.

Regarding the support that XEVFS offers to indigenous organizations, a leader of one of these organizations pointed out that Radio Margaritas fails both to produce a series featuring indigenous organizations and to report regularly on their activities; he was actually proposing that the station consider these organizations as a news beat to be routinely covered.[19] Radio Margaritas, however, lacks the mechanisms for integrating indigenous organizations into any area of the project such as implementation and evaluation, not to mention planning and decision making. Two of the people who participated in my audience study and who are members of these organizations spoke of their concern regarding the station's potential. One of them said, "We talk about the radio when we attend the meeting of UNCAFAEXA, we're invited by the organizations from the region of Margaritas and in those conventions we talk about the radio" (19f). And the other was more explicit about the content of such talks: "We belong to an organization, it's a pity that not all people from Madero have joined this organization, I have been in this struggle for about 15 years and in many of our meetings we talk about the radio, we talk about how to be more united with it and help it to succeed" (21f).

Despite these shortcomings, the station does support indigenous organizations in various ways. It supports them by airing some of their important meetings and by broadcasting avisos to their members, and supports, as well as legitimizes, them by inviting their leaders to talk over the radio and by broadcasting at least some news about their activities. As a member of these organizations stated, he listens to XEVFS because it broadcasts their announcements:

> I listen to the radio because sometimes they air avisos from the UNKA of Comitán City and that's why we listen everyday to the radio, to see if there's an aviso, if they're calling us, because there are three federations, *Unión de Ejidos de Pueblos Tojolabales, Unión Tierra y Libertad*, and sometimes from those organizations they call us as members of those organizations and that's why we listen to the avisos aired by the radio, and we have also joined the federation *Yajk' achil b'ej*, and from those three federations we listen to avisos aired by the radio and that's why we listen (21f).

By broadcasting this type of avisos, Radio Margaritas provides the organizations with a telecommunications medium to reach their members. In sum, I should underscore that the major impact of the station on improving the living conditions of the Tojolabal has probably been precisely in the area of communication, by airing avisos. It is by broadcasting the announcements of indigenous organizations and by airing personal messages from the audience that the station has eased the villagers' communication difficulties. Since the broadcasting of avisos, far from being one of the intended uses of the INI stations, has been imposed by the audience itself, this finding corroborates the tremendous need for popular participation in media-based development projects. It is ironic, however, to see the way both some INI officials and some station staff members despise avisos, because while they unanimously recognize the importance that this service holds for the audience, they often argue that they "don't want to be a radio whose main purpose is to send avisos," that they "don't want to become a radio *avisera*."

Saludos and the Maintenance of Society

Though the broadcasting of saludos (greetings from the audience) lacks the immediate practicality of avisos programs, it has substantial implications for radio-based development projects. Approaching saludos from James Carey's ritual view of communication, I argue that saludos constitute one of those communication activities whose underlying function is not to transmit new information, but to maintain society.[20] From a more conventional view of communication, it can be argued that saludos function as lubrication for the channels of communication. In any case, saludos definitely contribute to improve Tojolabals' living conditions by strengthening social networks and by enhancing the villages' information flow. The broadcasting of saludos becomes even more relevant to the station's development efforts considering the kind of popular participation that this broadcasting has brought to the INI stations. Aranda Bezaury and Valenzuela report that they observed people listening very closely to the XEZV's program featuring saludos, which was the program most liked by their interviewees.[21]

Often my Tojolabal informants said Radio Margaritas is useful to them because it broadcast saludos. The station features a program (Monday trough Friday, 12:00-12:30 p.m.) in which roughly 35-40 letters with saludos are read every week day by a Tojolabal male announcer. In addition, most audience members talking over the station's microphone air saludos. Saludos thus constitute a prime form of audience participation.

In more than half of the interviews (11 of 21) there was at least one remark about saludos. Roughly a third of the interviewees mentioned saludos (13 of them were Tabascans, and 8 were Maderans; 14 were men, and 7 were women.)[22] I expected women to talk more about saludos because I think that greetings belong to the women's domain. I think this because in many societies women are in charge of ritual activities directed toward the maintenance of social networks, and also because greetings often involve personal and emotional issues. Although this finding contradicted my expectations, it offered further support to the hypothesis that the most frequent users of XEVFS are not women but men.

Perhaps because of my Western bias regarding the emotional realm, or maybe because, like music, saludos fail to convey new information, at first glance the broadcasting of saludos appears to be a trivial matter. But nothing could be farther from its actual function. In the same way that interviewees use music, they use saludos for psychological gratification: "It pleases us to listen when greetings for a member of our family are aired, that's what I like the most from Radio Margaritas," said a Tabascan mother (3m). Also like music, saludos make up for a considerable part of the ritual communication, to use Carey's term, that takes place in Radio Margaritas. It is interesting to remember here that ladinos who use XETAR for airing avisos seldom use this station for airing saludos.

We can see the link between the broadcasting of saludos and audience participation by observing the context for interviewees' remarks on saludos. They spoke of saludos when describing their listening preferences: "I like when the station airs marimba music and when it airs saludos" (11m). They also talked of saludos when talking about their visits to the station: "I have only gone to the station once, I went to deliver a saludo from my brother-in-law" (2f). And they mentioned saludos when commenting on the useful services offered to them by the station: "Oh yeah, the radio is useful to us, to air an urgent aviso to a family member and the saludos are useful too" (20f).

The broadcasting of saludos could be seen as a means to attract villagers to participate in programs for development, but I would like to emphasize that saludos, by themselves, accomplish a great deal. Saludos bring psychological gratification, help to lubricate communication channels, and contribute to the maintenance of social networks. This contribution is indeed much more than what numerous development programs have achieved. On the other hand, since the broadcasting of saludos seems innocuous and without any connection to issues of political power, nor to the struggle for resources, villages enjoy great freedom to air saludos on Radio Margaritas. Specific programs on health and agriculture could bring about very concrete improvements in the villagers' living condition if they were able to achieve, or perhaps I should say allowed to include, the kind of popular participation accomplished by the broadcasting of saludos.

Oblique Uses of Radio and Modern Living

Puzzled about rural migrants' fascination with television content that seems to be completely alien to their lives, Néstor García Canclini has suggested that they use television as a manners book on how to behave in the city.[23] Carlos Monsiváis made the same point long before in reference to Mexican cinema, saying that the cinema from 1930 to 1954 "manifests itself as a way of life, access door not to art nor to entertainment but to vital molds, [casts, models], to the possible variety or uniformity of behaviors [my translation]"[24] Jesús Martín Barbero extends Monsiváis's argument from the new urban population of Mexico to the same population of all Latin American countries during the 1940s, insisting that people went to the movies not to escape but to learn.[25] I have already discussed how young Tabascans appear to use the radio receiver as a signifier of modernity, which seems to be part of their strategy to deal with ladino society. Speaking more of deep structures and long-term changes, I would like to suggest that the Tojolabal may be using Radio Margaritas to adapt to modern conceptions of time and space.

XEVFS seems to have boosted Tojolabals' appropriation of radio, and this appropriation, along with the appropriation of other modern media of communication such as the automobile, has probably had a profound impact on the group's perception of time and space. The native experience of space most likely changed with the creation of radio practices, especially with the electronically mediated interaction made possible by the broadcasting of avisos. Further, this change may have influenced the group identity formation of Tojolabal villagers. Joshua Meyrowitz has argued that electronic media have permanently altered some aspects of group identity that are shaped by physical isolation.[26] This might especially be the case for sociological groups similar to Tabascans.

Likewise, the native perception of time was probably deeply modified by a new medium punctuating family life. Speaking of television, James Lull states that this medium "has the structural characteristic of being a behavior regulator. Television punctuates time and family activity such as mealtime, bedtime, choretime, homework periods, and a host of related activities and duties."[27] I observed that Tojolabal families use radio similarly to punctuate their activities.

But there is a paradox involved in this particular use of radio since XEVFS' programming has been structured according to a modern perception of time. Rather than adopting an approach to time in a way more akin to the the Tojolabal culture, such as long intervals, XEVFS divides time in short, clear-cut units of duration (30 minutes); and on top of that, it constantly tells the time in indigenous languages. By doing so, the station may be inadvertently assisting the Tojolabal in their struggle to develop cultural proficiency in the ladino society's ways. Despite my failure to include in my interview schedule an item specifically dealing with the station's broadcasting of the time, the topic was frequently introduced either by interviewers or interviewees.

As did INI's broadcasters, my interviewers recognized the importance of a subject that I had regarded as trivial. Interviewees referred to the transmission of the time as one of the useful services offered by the station: "The way the radio tells us what time it is is fine because we need to know it to go to work," said a Maderan woman (16m). And a lady who listens to XEVFS only through her neighbors' receiver said, "I like the way the radio is working, but because we have no radio [receiver] when my neighbor turns his radio off, even if something important is being aired or the time is told, we can't hear it" (19m). Here it is important to note that for many years, the radio stations operated by the Bolivian miners did nothing but transmit music and tell the time. Though certainly much of radio's potential was not put into use, the miners understood their families' need for music and for a clock.[28] "I only listen to the station to know what time it is," a Maya women replied to my question regarding her listening of XEPET.

Obviously, since a growing number of indigenous people no longer live in isolated villages, they have to adapt to modern conceptions of time and space to cope successfully with the ladino world. An interesting aspect of the impact of bilingual broadcasting was noted by a Maderan man who said that he was learning how to tell the time in Tojolabal from the bilingual broadcasting: "When they tell the time in Tojolabal, and they repeat it in Spanish, I look at my watch and that's how I have learned something about telling time in Tojolabal" (16f).

Let me finish with a hopeful note since, despite the poor attention that Radio Margaritas has paid to programming specifically targeting development problems, interviewees not only spoke enthusiastically about Radio Margaritas' performance, but also about its promise. Hopefully, local organized groups would push for playing a more active role in the implementation of the project. Thus hopefully, as some interviewees argued, "that radio station may really help the Tojolabal in the future" (6f).

Notes

1. Marieme, in Wendy Chapkis, *Beauty Secrets: Women and the Politics of Appearance* (Boston: South End Press, 1986) 72.

2. The Tabascan families talking about living traditions were F1, F4, F5, F6, F7, F17, and F18; the Maderan families were: F10, F11, F14, and F15.

3. I use a code to identify the families interviewed. This code is presented in Chapter 2, page 27.

4. As the reader may recall from Chapter 7, the "baldío times" were before the Agrarian Reform of the 1940s and 1950s.

5. Though the Tojolabal language is no longer spoken in numerous settlements (e.g., Cash, Progreso) whose residents, regardless of their obvious Tojolabal origin, do not consider themselves as Tojolabals anymore.

6. Frantz Fanon, *Black Skin, White Masks* (New York: Grove Press, 1967) 17-18.

7. The number of remarks about each of these five issues were ten remarks about the importance of the broadcasts in Tojolabal; five about the bilingual or Tojolabal-Spanish broadcasting; three about the broadcasting in Tojolabal as part of a larger social struggle; seven about the transmissions in other vernaculars seen from a positive viewpoint; and six about the same transmissions but seen from a negative viewpoint.

8. F3 and F5.

9. Twenty of these 31 remarks were made by men, and 22 were made by bilinguals.

10. The families expressing negative comments were F4, F10, F13, F19, F21.

11. 1f, 4f, 5mn, 7m, 17m, 18f, 11m, 14m.

12. The Spanish word used by my translator was *planta*, plant.

13. Instituto Nacional Indigenista, ¿Se Escuchan Nuestras Voces? XEVFS, La Voz de la Frontera Sur, by Inés Cornejo and Silvia Luna, ts., internal document, México, 1991, 71-81.

14. This research included three villages. The percentages for each village were 64, 65, and 41 percent. Josefina Aranda Bezaury and Verónica Valenzuela, "Investigación sobre la Presencia Radiofónica de la Voz de la Montaña en las Comunidades," unpublished essay, 1982, 39.

15. These Tabascan families were F1, F3, F4, F5, F6, and F7. Maderan families were F10, F11, F16, F19, F20, F21, and F22.

16. Luanna Furbee Losee, John S. Thomas, Harry Keith Lynch and Robert A. Benfer, "Tojolabal Maya Population Response to Stress," *The Tojolabal Maya: Ethnographic and Linguistic Approaches. Geoscience and Man 26*, eds. Mary Jill Brody and

John S. Thomas (Baton Rouge: Louisana State U, 1988) 23.

17. These interviewees were two Tabascan and three Maderan women (2d, 3dl, 11m, 13fs, 23m) and seven Tabascan and seven Maderan men (1mn, 1fb, 4f, 6s1, 6s2, 7f, 11f, 13f, 16f, 18f, 19f, 20f, 22f, 23f).

18. 3m, 3s1, 4f, 4s1, 6m, 7f, 11f, 15f 16f, 19f, 18f.

19. Forum at Radio Margaritas (November 17, 1990).

20. See James Carey, "A Cultural Approach to Communication," *Communication* 2 (1975): 1-22.

21. Aranda Bezaury and Valenzuela 49.

22. Interviewees mentioning saludos were 1f, 1gm, 1mn, 2f, 2dl, 3f, m, 3s1, 3s2, 5mn, 6s1, 6s2, 18m, 9f, 9m, 10f, 11f, 13f, 13fs, 16m, 20f.

23. Néstor García Canclini, "Culture and Power: The State of Research," trans. Philip Schlesinger, *Culture and Power*, ed. Paddy Scanell, Philip Schlesinger and Colin Sparks (London: Sage, 1992): 17-47.

24. Carlos Monsiváis, "Notas sobre la Cultura Mexicana en el Siglo XX," *Historia General de México* 4, 2nd. ed. (México: El Colegio de México, 1977) 435.

25. Jesús Martín Barbero, *De los Medios a las Mediaciones: Comunicación, Cultura y Hegemonía* (México: Gustavo Gili, 1987) 180.

26. Joshua Meyrowitz. *No Sense of Place: The Impact of Electronic Media on Social Behavior.* New York: Oxford UP, 1986.

27. James Lull, *Inside Family Viewing* (London: Routledge, 1990) 36.

28. Héctor Schmucler and Orlando Encinas, "Las Radios Mineras de Bolivia," *Comunicación y Cultura* 8 (1982): 69-88.

11

Outline of Radio Consumption Patterns

It is in the convergence of the multiple social uses to which participatory radio is put to where important boundaries of its social value are delineated. What follows is a picture, drawn with broad very strokes, of the patterns that I discern concerning audience uses of Radio Margaritas. Many of the patterns that I outline here, however, are far from being conclusive findings; the reader, then, needs to take into consideration the details and nuances that I have offered throughout the book.

Limitations to Exposure

Naturally, the first precondition for the emergence of social uses of participatory radio is exposure. Exposure to XEVFS is more limited than I initially thought. Three main factors account for this: economic constraints, restricted mobility of receivers, and the station's ineffective use of its potential prime time. Economic constraints reduce access to radio offerings because owning a working receiver can be prohibitively expensive for many Tojolabal families. Two of the families sampled had never had a receiver of their own, and five families had broken receivers (though three of them had a second working set). Thus, probably for most Tojolabal families the expense of consuming radio offerings can be costly, and despite the advantages of radio as a low-cost medium, economic considerations still constitute an important limitation to exposure to XEVFS' content.

The restricted mobility of receivers among the Tojolabal is a second limitation to exposure. Though most families have portable receivers, it is not a common practice to take the receiver to the work place, because receivers are a very valuable technology to be put to the hardships of the corn field. Also, since people have to walk to the corn field, taking the receiver with them becomes a burden; several interviewees mentioned they take the receiver only when they go to work to the nearby milpas. Another significant limitation to exposure, especially for women, springs from the preferred location for the receiver. I observed that rather than keeping the receiver in the kitchen, the place where women spend a great deal of time, villagers tend to keep it in the bedroom or house.

However, the chief limitation to exposure to XEVFS is the station's inadequate use of its potential prime time. I found that there is a mismatch between XEVFS' schedule and its listeners' routines, and I also found that XEVFS fails to put about 40 percent of its potential prime time to use. Tojolabals are more likely to listen to the radio during three basic slots: early morning, late afternoon, and Sunday. Given the daily routines of Tojolabal villages and the fact that AM radio waves travel farther during the early morning, there can be little doubt the station's potential audience during the early morning hours (4:00-7:00 a.m.) surpasses that of any other period. Yet XEVFS starts broadcasting not at 4:00 a.m. but at 5:30 a.m, failing to take advantage of half of this valuable, potential prime time. Furthermore, XEVFS fails to make the best of Sunday, another slot of its prime time. Since Tojolabals rest on Sundays, the station's potential audience is sizable during these days; however, on weekends XEVFS ends transmission at 3:00 p.m. One of the few open criticisms expressed by interviewees was of the early closing of transmissions on Sundays.

A related point was interviewees' negative remarks regarding broadcasting in Tzeltal, Tzotzil, and Mam. This broadcasting seems to be one of the least liked aspects of XEVFS' programming, even less liked than the broadcasting in Spanish. It was one of the few specific reasons given for turning the radio off or switching to the local commercial station, Radio Comitán. Apparently, interviewees lack a clear understanding of XEVFS' scheduling of languages spoken, and Tojolabals' uncertainty about when their language is transmitted has for them become a limitation to the availability of radio offerings.

Users and Consumers

Contrary to the opinion held by many members of the network's staff, those using the station the most, rather than being women, are in many cases young and adult men, because they have created a wider variety of radio uses than women. In places like Tabasco, men probably listen to the radio more than women, and men largely outnumber women as visitors to the station and as participants in programs. As development researchers often argue, those having more resources before the introduction of a project benefit the most from it. Tojolabal young and adult men tend to have more material resource (e.g., radio receivers), social resources (e.g., networks of friends from other places) and cultural resources (e.g., bilingualism) than Tojolabal women. On the other hand, one should not underestimate the democratizing effect that broadcasting in Tojolabal has probably had in local communication practices, an effect that, by enabling women to attain public knowledge, may well be empowering them.

Whereas when considering all kinds of uses of radio (listening, sending of avisos, etc.), gender turns out to be a clear indicator, gender by itself does not account for the consumption of Radio Margaritas' offerings; it has to be taken in combination with place of residence. I found that in Madero, women probably listen to radio more frequently than men, while in Tabasco the situation seems to reverse. Moreover, contrary to the general opinion among the network's staff regarding women as the heaviest consumers of radio, I contend that it is likely that Tojolabal women consume fewer radio offerings than Tojolabal men. This contention finds support not only in my audience study but also in the analysis of XEVFS' programming; Radio Margaritas' format, and to some extent the entire network's format, caters to a listenership composed of young adult and adult men.

As it is often the case with other populations, age is the clearest indicator of radio consumption among the Tojolabal. Regardless of their gender and place of residence, the elderly seldom listen to the radio. Likewise, the children show very little interest in radio, though I found a slight indication that Maderan children may listen more often than Tabascan children. Most of the Tojolabal consumers of radio in general, and of XEVFS' offerings in particular, are young and middle-age.

Place of residence largely determines the number and variety of radio uses, and it is also an indicator for the consumption of XEVFS' offerings. Tabascans use radio for a wide range of purposes that extend from symbolic uses to very practical ones. In contrast, Maderans use radio in a more limited fashion. This difference, I find, is only partially explained by the fact that Maderans have access to more means of communication and to more advanced technology than Tabascans. Station policies, such as refusing to transmit community announcements of Madero's festivals, also play a significant part in audience uses. Furthermore, since Tabasco embodies the ideal traditional Tojolabal culture promoted by the station, and Tabascans fit the implied reader of XEVFS' texts, it is not surprising that they tend to feel closer to XEVFS than Maderans. Hence, the modes of involvement of Tabascans and Maderans in the reception of XEVFS' broadcasting naturally differ. While most Tabascans probably feel reassured by XEVFS' ideology, some Maderans, especially those individuals highly acculturated, may feel even threatened by it.

Uses of Radio Margaritas' Music

Interviewees' use of the music programming of XEVFS mainly gravitates around the sense of social distinction and the building of group solidarity. Most interviewees insisted they prefer to listen to their own music on

XEVFS. This preference implies a twofold use of radio, to affiliate themselves with indigenous people and to distinguish themselves from ladinos. Their preference for their own music is also related to the use of radio for reproducing their culture. Interviewees said that they use XEVFS to find out how other Tojolabal communities play music, to gain an awareness of how other indigenous people express themselves through music, and to learn what, and where, traditions are kept alive. In this sense, they use Radio Margaritas as a source of social knowledge and also as a symbolic place of Tojolabal culture.

It is important, though, to note that my interview schedule only considered the music broadcast by XEVFS. Thus when interviewees said they prefer marimba, this does not mean that they dislike the popular genres aired by local commercial radio, since many Tojolabals consume this latter music. What it means is that they prefer traditional Tojolabal music over other genres broadcast by XEVFS, such as *nueva canción*, classic Mexican music, and the music of other ethnic groups.

Interviewees' remarks regarding music are insufficient to determine specific patterns of taste, but there is enough information on both villages to infer that Tabascans appreciate traditional and marimba music more than Maderans, and that XEVFS' playlist suits Tabascan better than Maderan taste. Radio Margaritas, by insisting on the traditional elements of Tojolabal society, is overlooking a large and growing sector of the Tojolabal audience, the sector that is more actively negotiating its ethnic identity and that perhaps needs to reaffirm its sense of belonging to the Tojolabal community the most.

Also, like most people around the world do, Tojolabals use music for recreation. The significance of such psychological gratification acquires a whole new meaning in the context of their material poverty, their multiple sources of stress, and their endangered cultural resources. Informants emphasized the pleasure derived from listening to XEVFS' music; they stated that XEVFS' music constitutes a prime source of entertainment and emotional release, and they said they used radio for companionship, family relaxation, conflict reduction, and relationship maintenance. When both Maderans and Tabascans are losing many of their traditional diversions, XEVFS has emerged as an alternative medium to enjoy the music traditionally produced by their people. On the other hand, as some interviewees pointed out, they also find pleasure in listening to ladino genres that many Tojolabals have already appropriated. And this is a pleasure that Radio Margaritas chooses to ignore.

Enhancing the Local Information Flow

A remarkable finding was the tremendous impact that Radio Margaritas has had on local information flow, and the democratizing effect that it may also have had on Tojolabal communication practices. Rather than being related to the station's news programs, this impact has to do with the broadcasting in Tojolabal and the transmission of avisos. I examined this impact at two levels, intravillage flows and external information flows. At the intravillage level, I posit that the broadcasting in Tojolabal has had a democratizing effect because it has introduced a new information source in the village, which has probably diminished the centrality of the ejidatarios network and, most importantly, has opened a channel for women, who traditionally have been excluded from this network.

Further, in combination with the automobile and the development of roads, XEVFS has made possible the emergence of a supernetwork of communication connecting indigenous villages with each other and with Margaritas City. The station has provided the infrastructure for this network by broadcasting programs with audience participation and especially by transmitting avisos and saludos free of charge.

Tojolabals use the network to speed up interpersonal communication, to ease the burden of village's messengers, to gather information from government agencies, to keep in touch with indigenous organizations, to find out how other fellow villagers live and work, and to develop a grasp of what goes on with both the Tojolabal people and the larger indigenous community. In short, they use XEVFS as a substitute for all the other telecommunication media (e.g., telephone, print media, post, and telegraph services) enjoyed by their ladino neighbors. I like to underscore that those people whose monolinguism has prevented them from using other channels have access to this communication network.

Radio Margaritas as Community Radio

Interviewees perceive XEVFS as belonging to the indigenous peoples' domain. They pointed out that the station encourages local participation by broadcasting in Tojolabal, by including indigenous people on the staff, and by reflecting the nuances of Tojolabal everyday life. Most revealing though was their frequent reference to XEVFS as "our radio" and to Radio Comitán as "the ricos' radio." By using the "us-them" opposition, interviewees fully expressed their perception of XEVFS as the radio station of the indigenous community.

As it probably happens in many rural areas, in the highlands of Chiapas radio listening is an especially useful consumer practice for positioning oneself and others in the social space. As a signifying practice, participation in XEVFS, even if it is only by consuming its cultural offerings, may reaffirm links of solidarity and may also furnish a sense of pride among the Tojolabal. Where listening to the ricos' radio may be, particularly for Tabascans, a practice somehow unfaithful to Tojolabal culture, listening to Radio Margaritas has come to be a legitimate, media-consuming practice for people like Tabascans and Maderans.

The extent to which Tojolabals view Radio Margaritas as belonging to the indigenous domain is disclosed in interviewees' responses to my hypothetical closing of the station. When confronted with such a hypothetical closing of XEVFS, interviewees reacted strongly, believing my speculative situation to be quite real and moreover a scheme planned by the ladinos. They also gave detailed descriptions of how they perceive the ladinos' hostile attitude toward XEVFS. And interviewees categorically maintained that the station should continue operating because it offers very useful services to the villages and its broadcasting has come to be an integral part of Tojolabal everyday life.

It seems that Tojolabals see XEVFS as a valuable communication resource to which they have access. One of the forms that this access takes is audience visits to the station. I found that visits to XEVFS occur according to two different cycles, a daily cycle (chiefly to send avisos and saludos) and an annual cycle (to attend the station's anniversary festival). The annual visits are explained by proximity, but the daily visits relate not just to proximity, but also to place of residence and gender. The general patterns that I discern are that women (especially Tabascan) seldom go to the station, and that Maderans and Tabascans have different reasons for visiting Radio Margaritas; Maderans attend the festival but seldom visit during the daily cycle, and Tabascans do the opposite.

However if interviewees offered numerous examples of access, their examples of control were meager. Only a handful of them risked questioning the station's policies, and the issue of XEVFS having a ladino general manager was discussed in the teachers' interview only because I brought it up. The families interviewed seemed to perceive no contradiction between XEVFS' sponsorship and its position in the indigenous peoples' domain; some interviewees even pointed out that it is precisely because INI sponsors the station that it pertains to the indigenous people. The explanation for these comments may lie in the point of comparison used to measure indigenous participation in XEVFS. I believe that rather than comparing the station with one of the resources over which the ejido has full control, interviewees were comparing XEVFS with local commercial radio, over which they have no control.

Traditions and the Reproduction of Culture and Society

The INI network advocates Paulo Freire's ideal of grassroots participation in development projects. Yet the stations, particularly Radio Margaritas, have made pointed efforts to use radio to persuade villagers to change their attitudes; these efforts indeed correspond more to the assumptions of the orthodox paradigm of development (see Appendix 1). Radio Margaritas has played a definitive role in sensitizing Tabascans and Maderans to the importance of revaluating two aspects of Tojolabal culture, language and music. All families voiced their concerns over the rapid loss of traditional ways, and many said they see a value in the station's efforts at preserving traditions. The broadcasting in Tojolabal was, of course, the chief reason behind numerous uses of the station. In addition to praising XEVFS' efforts to preserve Tojolabal language and music, interviewees also praised the station's persuasive talks on the value of reviving traditions. On the other hand, some interviewees objected to Radio Margaritas' meager broadcasts on the history of the exploitation of the Tojolabal.

I also gathered that interviewees use XEVFS' broadcasting as a point of reference and quite likely as a standard for traditional practices, such as music. They also use the station itself as a medium to advocate a cultural revivalist viewpoint, and as a place to find support for this viewpoint. All these uses of radio to preserve tradition are, of course, promoted by INI, but probably such promotion cannot, by itself, explain the search for a historical memory in which many of the Tojolabal seem to be engaged.

Interviewees' uses of XEVFS to satisfy the search for their roots may be seen as part of a broader use of radio for empowering ethnic minorities. The station indeed has become a forum for the reproduction of traditional cultural practices. Nonetheless, the mass media have the power not only to reproduce a way of life, but also to create the sense that a particular way of life is universal, natural, and legitimate. I argue that Radio Margaritas has been creating a romantic and populist image of Tojolabal culture and society, and that since not all Tojolabals live according to the way of life that XEVFS portrays, many of them probably hardly recognize themselves in the image of their ethnic group as is projected by Radio Margaritas. Thus many Maderans probably fail to gain the sense of empowerment that most Tabascans seem to derive from Radio Margaritas because, whereas Tabascans might feel that XEVFS validates their way of life, some, especially the most assimilated, Maderans might feel quite the opposite.

Improving Living Conditions

Radio Margaritas' major contribution to improving Tojolabals' living conditions has been to provide the infrastructure for expanding and enhancing their communication networks. This contribution includes all kinds of participatory programs, from those airing saludos to those featuring interviews with locals, but its keystone is solving immediate communication problems by broadcasting avisos.

With the exception of one family, interviewees were vague about XEVFS' programming directed at assisting villagers with the typical problems targeted by development projects (e.g., ill health, low agricultural productivity); more than half of them did not even mention this programming. But, despite the insufficient efforts made by XEVFS with respect to this kind of programming, all families insisted the station provides a variety of valuable services to the Tojolabal. These services range from the transmission of urgent avisos and saludos to general efforts at preserving traditions.

I confirmed my suspicion about the need for expanding the network's efforts regarding programs on health, education, and agriculture. Interviewees' remarks on this programming were vague, and only one family referred to one of XEVFS' series by name. Moreover, several interviewees specifically requested the expansion of programs on health and agriculture. I also found that there seems to be a slight positive correlation between the degree of acculturation into mainstream society and a person's interest in this type of programming. The people talking about these issues tended to be either Maderans, or Tabascan men who have some degree of bilingualism. This correlation also finds support in the remarks made by other acculturated Tojolabals (e.g., teachers and leaders of indigenous organizations) who insist on the value of this type of programming. The exception is the interest that women, who tend to be less acculturated in ladino ways, showed in health programs. This exception, of course, is likely to be explained by the traditional role of women as health providers.

Health is, not surprisingly, the single issue most frequently mentioned by people talking about programming on issues of development. Their comments shed light on the numerous challenges to producing programming targeting health problems, such as listeners' distrust and the addressing in public of concerns regarding intimate matters and private behavior. In addition, many positive remarks about avisos underscored the significance that this service has for alleviating the communications needs that accompany health problems. Since the Tojolabal suffer from ill health, Tabascans and Maderans naturally commended XEVFS' avisos service. For rural dwellers, who for the most part do not share urban residents' concern with access to rapid communication media, telecommunication becomes extremely important when the health of a loved one is at stake.

The last aspect of XEVFS' contribution to developing Tojolabals' communications that I think is important to emphasize is related not so much to the transmission of information as to the maintenance of social networks. This maintenance involves virtually all participatory programming, but it is particularly evident, first, in the airing of saludos, which helps maintain networks of family and friends, and second, in the broadcasting of affairs dealing with indigenous organizations, which may have strengthen larger networks, such as those among coffee producers.

12

Participation, Racism, and Social Uses

While numerous researchers believe that grassroots participation in development projects is indispensable to achieving sustainable development, most participatory radio stations in Latin America are not managed by grassroots organizations, but rather are sponsored by outside agents who limit the participation of the local people. These radio stations, however, immersed in a plethora of contradictions, are often the sites where popular communication practices thrive. Throughout the book, I have underscored the importance of looking at audiences' social uses of this type of radio, and I have also argued for a methodological approach which accounts for the complexity involved in the wide variety of radio practices created by rural minority populations.

In addition to restating my key points in this last chapter, here I elaborate on the role that racism plays in shaping the extent and quality of indigenous participation in the INI network. Then I discuss the theoretical and methodological implications that this research may have for the field of development communications, and since in the last instance this case study contains an evaluation of the INI network, I conclude with some specific recommendations for its stations. I hope my book will stimulate the discussion of the politics of race, class, and gender in development communications and will show the need to focus on practices and social uses to begin understanding the social value of participatory radio.

Indigenous Participation in the INI Network

The fundamental question about indigenous participation in the INI network is whether or not its sponsor, even occasionally, can act as a catalytic agent and thus play a positive role in indigenous people's development efforts. On the one hand, being a bureaucratic organization of the Mexican state, INI has a built-in structural bias toward keeping indigenous people in a disadvantaged position. But on the other hand, it is impossible for INI to have absolute control over its projects because it is far from being either a monolithic or an efficient institution. Because of inadequate funding, INI is ill-suited to control its projects effectively; the history of the network illustrates this point. INI's ability to carry out its legitimizing function for the Mexican state is fairly restricted, and in line with this, the network's ability to function as an ideological state apparatus, to use Louis Althusser's expression, is quite diminished.

But most importantly, operating concurrently with INI's inability to exert an absolute control over its projects are the everyday processes of resistance and accommodation involving indigenous people. Indigenous people are constantly striving to make the best of every rupture in the system, and often they find creative ways of asserting their needs. A case in point is the power that indigenous audiences have to direct the everyday activities of stations like XEZV through their uses of its resources.

Acting as brokers, indigenous staff members play a key role in this struggle. Though in numerous instances they in fact may unwillingly sustain the current hegemonic situation, there are also many ways in which the indigenous staff contributes to the creation of alternative practices. It is worth remarking that for many indigenous staffers the experience of working in an institution that at least gives lip service to participatory policies seems to trigger an awakening process, or in Paulo Freire's terms, a *conscientizaçao*.

On the other hand, INI network's hierarchic, racist, classist, and sexist practices unquestionably hinder the efforts to involve grassroots participation. As expected, indigenous participation in the stations' programming has been allowed only in those areas seen as "cultural," namely apolitical: music, storytelling, traditional health practices. The staff has faced tremendous constraints in producing programs that might be interpreted as "political," especially local news. Recounting his own train of thought when trying to envision a local newscast excluding all political matters, one staff member said that he came to the conclusion that INI officials were asking the station's staff to produce a sports newscast.

Even in XEZV, the most participatory of the stations, the reach of grassroots participation is limited to "cultural" matters. As one station worker expressed it: "The station encourages the people to participate through their music, stories, and traditional knowledge, but when they want to talk about their *reality*, the station stops them [emphasis mine]."

Hence the stations have indeed become sites of struggle for contradictory ideologies and for the opposed projects of diverse social subjects. While I want to emphasize the significance of everyday resistance practices, I do not mean to suggest that the network, and especially indigenous participation in the stations, offers no advantages to the sponsor. Given that the project has not only survived through three presidential administrations in a country where typically programs are terminated at the end of each administration, but has also undergone an unprecedented expansion during the early 1990s, it is fair to assume that the federal government has been getting something (probably securing indigenous consent to its rule) from this participatory institution. As the case of XENAC shows, supporting the present social order is the structural mandate around which the network revolves. Yet my study needed to situate the project in the web of national political negotiations between the government and the resistance movements of indigenous peoples to be able to pinpoint, specifically, the gains offered by the project to the government. I highlighted how the stations contribute to legitimize INI and its activities at the local level, strengthening in this way the federal government's position in its negotiations with state and municipal governments. I also briefly mentioned how XETAR made a direct contribution to the official party (PRI) during a moment of crisis. In the 1990s, when the party's popularity is markedly declining, the stations will probably be faced with less concealed demands from the party.

However, given that I had chosen to examine the micro level, I was not able to document the stations' contribution to its sponsor at the national level. This is certainly an area where further research is needed. This book focuses on what the everyday practices occurring at the production and consumption ends of the INI network reveal about the social value of a participatory radio project for its intended beneficiaries.

Unequal Participation: Project Beneficiaries

Some sectors of the indigenous community have benefitted more from the project than others. At Radio Margaritas, while the most traditional sector of the Tojolabal audience (e.g., the Tabascans) has received considerable attention, less-traditional sectors have been neglected. One frequent argument is that the former are needier than the latter, but it is worth examining this assumption more closely. In fact many people enjoy similar or even better living conditions in places like Tabasco than in places like Madero. But more to the point, it is important to ask: In greater need of what? In greater need of telecommunication resources? Probably. But perhaps not in greater need of self-esteem and skills for social organization. The fact that the single, organized group which has regularly produced its own programs (*Alcohólicos Anónimos*) comes from the mestizo sector indicates that the needs for psychological empowerment are plenty among members of the more acculturated sectors. And the low importance conferred on these programs by most of the staff speaks of the network's neglect of these sectors.

This neglect apparently emerges from a clear-cut conceptualization of "indigenous people" which, to state it once again, disregards ambiguities and ignores that ethnic identity formation is constantly negotiated.

Furthermore, this conceptualization conveniently excludes those who are most likely to attempt greater control over the project. Since the indigenous-mestizo sector is more skillful in dealing with the dominant society and its institutions, it is precisely from this sector that people with the cultural literacy necessary to occupy high positions in the network are most likely to come.

At another level, I also found several, poorly-served segments of the network's target audience: women of all ages, male children, elders, and teenagers. The profile of the typical station user is a young or adult male, and the network's programming caters primarily to this group. Since, like more acculturated sectors of the indigenous communities, male teenagers tend to be attracted to the mainstream society and its cultural forms (e.g., electronic music), their tastes and needs are ignored. Women, children, and elders who tend to be monolingual benefit greatly from vernacular broadcasts, but their specific needs are often overlooked. While there has been some effort to address women's interests, still many station practices and aspects of the programing prevent the network from achieving this goal. There has also been a concern for meeting children's needs, and sporadic efforts to support the staff of INI's boarding centers have been undertaken. Yet the stations have failed to take advantage of the tremendous opportunity that these boarding centers offer for educational programs addressing a captive audience. Lastly, concerning elders, there has been little attention to their particular problems, problems such as ageing diseases.

Along with the stations' failure to provide attractive radio offerings for these groups are elements pertaining to audience characteristics that impose severe constraints on radio consumption. Women, children, and elders often have limited access to radio reception technology. Women must also face gender-driven restrictions placed on them by tradition, restrictions against, for instance, public speaking and the production of music. The romantic view of indigenous cultures underlying many of the network's policies not only disregards gender oppression, but also ignores the contradictions and ambiguities existing internally in Mexican indigenous societies. As with many traditional societies, internally repressive practices exist, especially against women. Indeed, in many cases, these internally repressive practices—such as the veil in Algeria—often, and ironically, become the symbols of cultural resistance to colonialism. The network has to recognize, and not romanticize, these internally repressive practices.

Though I acknowledge the postmodern concerns about imposing researchers' cultural understandings and values on the social groups that they study, as a ladina feminist I believe that indigenous societies are not immune from the exploitative relations resulting from gender asymmetry and male privilege. Some indigenous female producers of the INI stations were perfectly aware of gender oppression and articulated their hope to use radio to challenge traditional ideologies and practices oppressing indigenous women; for example, a Náhuatl female producer said her program aims "to change the conception of indigenous women about themselves because most of these women do not see themselves as human beings." Thus examining the struggle among diverse gender ideologies existing within participatory stations and the consequences of these ideologies for participatory radio's impact in development is an important task for development communicators—as important as examining the politics of class, and race and ethnicity.

Racism

Assumptions about the inferiority of indigenous people are a crucial element of the network's ideology and constitute a formidable constraint to indigenous participation. Though it could be argued that these racist assumptions are the backbone of the network's ideology and practices, I would like to highlight only the two most salient manifestations of racism at the INI stations: the network's internal social space of positions and the romantic view of indigenous cultures held and promoted by the stations.

The most conspicuous manifestation of racism at the project is revealed by looking at the network's internal distribution of social positions. Though complying with participatory policies, about 70 percent of the staff is composed of members of ethnic groups. The highest positions are often held by ladinos; indigenous staffers are usually employed as disc jockeys, announcers, and producers; and mestizos tend to occupy the most disadvantaged positions (because linguistic competence in vernaculars becomes valuable symbolic capital inside the stations). The "glass ceiling" preventing indigenous staffers from reaching managerial levels at the network, results in outright inequality regarding monetary and other compensations (e.g., status in the local social arena), and most importantly, in a disparate sharing of control over the stations which duplicates, and therefore reinforces, the social inequality existing in Mexican society between ladinos and indigenous peoples.

Since just a handful of indigenous employees have reached managerial levels and only on rare occasions have they been allowed to play a part in matters related to the overall goals and scope of the network, the participation of the indigenous staff has either surreptitiously or only occasionally occurred in planning and decision-making processes. Indigenous control over the project, which is not argued for even in the network's documents, falls much short of what critical researchers stipulate for participatory projects. Further, my observation of Radio Margaritas' daily routines revealed that only the ladino general manager, and to a lesser extent the ladino program director, have the power to decide on a station's policies, goals, and the use of its resources.

I also found that the degree of autonomy enjoyed by indigenous staffers at the level of immediate production varies a great deal from one station to the other. At XEZV there is considerable elbow-room for indigenous staff, while at stations like XEVFS this control is confined to insignificant tasks; for instance, indigenous and mestizo personnel have very limited control over the work that they themselves produce and are constrained by certain irrational requirements, such as writing in Spanish (a second language that many of them use with great difficulty) the copy of radio programs to be aired in vernaculars. I observed a more vivid expression of the ladino control endured by some staffers at XEVFS when the ladino general manager scolded a Tzeltal staff member for presumably mispronouncing words in her own native tongue.

The limited extent of the indigenous staff's participation at the network illustrates how racism is experienced in this particular project and, in a broader sense, gives insights into how racism is experienced in Mexican society at large. Despite the fact that INI operates with the resources officially allocated to redress the condition of inequality between ladinos and indigenous people, the network's social space reaffirms this inequality and reinforces the ideology that nourishes it. If genuine participation is to occur in the network, it will require substantially more than just changes in the organizational structure of the network, though these changes are certainly necessary.

But, more than anything else, the prevailing attitudes among many staff members toward the limits of indigenous participation manifest the power of the dominant ideology to define what is and is not possible. The issue of the possibility of an indigenous person acting as station general manager attests to the network's racist ideology. I found that many indigenous staffers accept the current practice of appointing ladinos to this position as a natural, necessary reality. These attitudes mirror the widespread belief in Mexican society, and elsewhere, in the inferiority of indigenous people.

The second manifestation of racism that is crucial to underline is the network's romantic view of indigenous societies and cultures. This view guides multiple policies and everyday practices and sustains both glaring and veiled forms of racism. One of them is the indirect support given by the station to essentialist explanations for the material poverty of indigenous peoples. Such support is given by paying little attention to the context of oppression within which indigenous peoples live and have lived for centuries. A more glaring illustration of racist policies is the discrimination against acculturated sectors of indigenous societies and their cultural forms. And a veiled manifestation of racist attitudes is the network's representation of indigenous cultures constructed mainly by ladinos. In a broader sense, this means that the ladinos directing the network and its stations get to define the meaning of indigenous peoples' ethnic identities.

Take for instance how Radio Margaritas creates a representation of Tojolabal communities and their music. What lies behind the station's policies about music, and about many other matters, is a paternalistic and therefore racist attitude. This attitude is clearly evidenced by the station's banning of popular genres among Tojolabals, based on the ladino belief that this music corrupts indigenous people. Like many of their great grandparents in colonial times, the ladino staff takes on the task of enlightening peoples like the Tojolabal. Their enlightenment project is carried out by banning ranchera and norteña music and airing, instead, in addition to what they consider truly indigenous music, Edith Piaf, Mozart, and *nueva canción Latinoamericana*. Further, Radio Margaritas' efforts encouraging certain cultural expressions while discouraging others naturally limits audience's use of radio. For example, I saw that at XEVFS it is specifically prohibited to air announcements promoting festivals where non-traditional music will be performed. As one Tojolabal informant pointed out, regardless of the electronic music performed, the festivals are definitely a Tojolabal community affair.

The racism prevailing in the network is also evident in the meager resources allocated to programming targeting the improvement of living conditions vis-a-vis the extensive efforts made at preserving traditions. The current definition of priorities responds more to a conceptualization of indigenous peoples as exotic "others" than as fellow human beings. Critical anthropologists have long noted that this is a conceptualization that appreciates artifacts and practices more than the living people creating and transforming them.

Racism is also displayed by a careful selection of traditions that often ignores the fundamental fact of the enduring economic exploitation lived by Mexican ethnic minorities. The network has made a concrete effort to preserve and revaluate indigenous cultures; by providing a space for their reproduction, the network has probably made a contribution toward preserving and revaluating those traditions having both a strong aural dimension and an apparent non-political function, such as language and music. However, by carefully selecting only certain traditions and ignoring the context of oppression in which they were developed, the network has been promoting a romantic view of indigenous societies. Some of my Tojolabal informants strongly objected to the scarcity of programs dealing with past exploitation; for them, reflecting on historical exploitations helped to put present oppressions on the agenda. The challenge for the network, of course, is to discuss indigenous traditions in their context of oppression without provoking a local ladino elite who often threatens to close down the stations. I acknowledge this difficult challenge, but if the stations are going to become true catalysts for development, this challenge has to be confronted.

In brief, the network's working concept of indigenous peoples corresponds to a romantic view of their culture and society, and this view encompasses racist policies and practices. Despite such racism, however, indigenous people seem to be making the best of the resources provided by the stations, and using them not only in their survival strategies but also in the struggle against racism itself. Even limited participation in the radio network defies the racism of mainstream Mexican media where the near-total absence of indigenous faces and voices has been heretofore experienced as natural.

Collective Self-Esteem and Sustainable Development

It would be hard to maintain that the limited indigenous participation in the network fails to afford any power to the project's intended beneficiaries. As Denis Goulet might argue, this participation can be seen as strategic to the achievement of further ends, such as boosting indigenous people's collective self-esteem.[1] In the light of the Gramscian notion of hegemony, which posits that the ruling class rules not only by controlling economic and political matters but also by establishing its predominance over culture, this limited participation can enable significant resistance. Though examples abound of radio programs and production practices where commonsensical views are subtly disputed, it is probably vernacular broadcast that is contributing most to boosting indigenous peoples' self-esteem and, therefore, creating a new experience and consciousness of Indianness.

As with the transmission of local music, broadcasting in vernaculars is in itself a political act. To the extent that attitudes toward a mother tongue are related to individual and collective self-esteem, and to the extent that this broadcasting invites speakers of vernaculars to explore their attitudes toward minority and dominant languages, this may advance a process of psychological empowerment among indigenous peoples. This broadcasting is of paramount importance not only to the speakers of vernaculars, but also for the languages themselves, since one of the ways a language acquires new users is through speakers extending language use to new functions. Thus radio broadcasting in the vernacular may have a positive effect on the spread of vernaculars and may contribute to counteract their present decline and eventual disappearance.

Having discussed this possible outcome, I would like to raise a question concerning the need that ethnic minorities have for developing proficiency of a declining vernacular versus their need for learning Spanish, Mexico's lingua franca. As Ronald Wardhaugh has pointed out, learning the language of the colonizer might be the best surviving strategy for an oppressed group.[2] The broadcasting in vernaculars illustrates the significance of programming decisions and the need to involve indigenous people in planning and decision-making. I believe that, if given the option, many members of ethnic minorities would probably prefer the stations to air

Spanish language classes because Spanish is the language of opportunity. There is plenty of evidence showing that most indigenous people would like their children to be bilingual since proficiency in Spanish can provide them with an opportunity to better their living conditions. Hard-core positions against policies that tend to bring about any kind of assimilation should be measured against the desperate need ethnic minorities have for skills to improve their material conditions. As with many other programming decisions, language teaching is for me a question of allocating limited resources; the present programs aiming to rescue a declining language fail to make the best use of those limited resources.[3]

At the bottom of the language controversy lies the everlasting question of continuity and change. The network champions the idea that revaluating indigenous cultures is necessary for boosting collective self-esteem and constructing sustainable development. Still, granting the significance of continuity, the network has yet to recognize the importance of change. A Purépecha employed at XEPUR articulated the paradox confronted by many indigenous young people who have developed a second cultural proficiency to improve their living conditions but who are often accused by ladinos of selling out their Indianness. He once bluntly told me: "We the indigenous people also want to be middle class." His remark helps to foreground the assumptions of many INI-employed ladinos holding that indigenous people somehow become less indigenous (less "ethnic") when aspiring to, or even worse, enjoying the modern comforts enjoyed by ladinos.

The false dilemma between continuity and change underpinning many of the network's policies and practices may have contributed to the network's limited efforts specifically targeting the improvement of the material living standards of indigenous audiences. It is true that the INI network has made available radio resources so that people such as the Tojolabal can appropriate and refunctionalize a communication technology alien to their culture, but the efforts of stations like Radio Margaritas to assist indigenous peoples with appropriating other useful elements of modern living have been rather meager (despite this criticism, however, I am not suggesting that, within the constraints imposed by the network, stations like XEZV fail to assist its audiences to appropriate indispensable knowledge for achieving sustainable development).

The current orientation of the network, which has an almost-exclusionary emphasis on "culture," underestimates radio's potential by neglecting its capacity for building up knowledge; indigenous people are in great need of specific information to help them cope with their rapidly changing environment, specific information, for example, about the Mexican legal system, about the dangers of cigarette smoking, and about the preventive measures for diseases such as as AIDS and mange. By disregarding the value of specific programs for improving living conditions, this, almost-

exclusionary emphasis on culture offers support to the critics of the project
who insist that its underlying function is, as an ideological state apparatus,
to preserve the oppressive status quo.

Social Uses

To return once again to the question of how indigenous people cope and
even use the network's contradictions in imaginative ways, I should stress
the large variety of uses the stations and their broadcasts are put to by their
audiences. Dealing specifically with Radio Margaritas, I found a number of
uses that, though they are intertwined and occur simultaneously, can be
divided into two categories. In the first group are those uses in which
indigenous people act merely as listeners. This involves the use of broadcasts
for a variety of purposes, including those social uses occurring at the small
group level (i.e., those pointed out by James Lull, such as the punctuation
of family activities, communication facilitation, social learning, and
affiliation/avoidance[4]), but also involves uses taking place at the level of the
ethnic group, such as the consumption of Radio Margaritas' cultural
offerings as a social practice distinguishing indigenous people from ladinos
(and perhaps also from mestizos), and the symbolic use of the radio receiver
as a signifier of modernity. The second category is made up of all those uses
in which the Tojolabal community acts not only as a consumer of cultural
offerings but also as producer. This category involves the use of the station
as a telecommunication medium for transmitting information within their
social networks and for maintaining these networks; in a broader sense it
also includes the use of the station to maintain social institutions, such as
language, and to reproduce cultural expressions, such as music.

Situating Radio Margaritas in the context of the INI network, I would say
that audience uses of station resources are more limited at Radio Margaritas
than at other stations. Most visitors to XEVFS want either to send an aviso
or to deliver a letter for the write-in programs. I did not observe Tojolabals
using XEVFS in the rich variety of ways that indigenous people use other
INI stations. Very few visitors go with the intention of making recordings
of their music, as frequently occurs in XEPUR, nor did they very often go to
participate in programs. And, in contrast to what occurs at XEZV, Tojolabals
seldom visit XEVFS to get advice on dealing with mainstream society
institutions, nor to use the station's human or material resources (e.g., help
with translation, typing of documents). Every station is different, is operated
in a very different way, and broadcasts for populations with different
needs. I found that XEZV is probably the most participatory of the stations
and the one which seems to be assisting its audiences best. Two key reasons
account for this: the audience is in great need of the services that a
participatory radio station can provide, and, being the oldest station and

one with a low personnel turn-over, XEZV has accumulated precious staff expertise.

I also found that almost regardless of the particular way in which a station is operated, if its audiences have little need for the potential services offered, naturally the audience will create few uses. With its very low number of visitors, the case of XEPET in the Yucatan speaks for this. In many areas of the Yucatan, Maya can hardly be considered a minority language, and the local population has little need for using the station as a substitute for other telecommunication services. Contrariwise, I also found that the particular way in which a station is operated can seriously hamper the uses that are created, as is the case with XETAR in Chihuahua where audiences are mainly ladino. The extent to which a particular ethnic group benefits from a particular station depends on a combination of both the former's need for incorporating radio into their survival strategies and the latter's constraints on the emergence of social uses of radio.

Whereas indigenous participation in the network has been prevented from reaching the levels of planning and decision-making, the bottom line is that (with the exception of XETAR) the stations' audiences are predominantly indigenous people. The limited participation of indigenous listeners, users, and staff members is far from inconsequential. It appears to have brought about some concrete changes for improving the living conditions of ethnic minorities. For instance, the sending of avisos by indigenous organizations to their members may have facilitated greater participation in grassroots endeavors; the impact of the station in the information flow of traditional villages may have increased women's social knowledge, and this in turn may have stimulated women's participation in affairs of the local community; and, finally, the broadcasting in vernaculars may have bolstered the group's self-esteem and may have strengthened solidarity feelings and the sense of community. I came to the conclusion that despite the great constraints on indigenous participation in the network, ethnic groups like the Tojolabal do benefit from the project.

Implications for the Use of Radio-for-Development

The book's centerpiece is that ascertaining the social value of participatory radio requires examining ethnographically the concrete practices constructed by real people in specific projects. I have argued that research endeavors should focus on the matrix of interactions existing between participatory stations and their audiences. And I have pointed out that an adequate investigation of participatory radio has to incorporate the study of media institutions, the analysis of their cultural products, and the inquiry into consumption practices.

I have approached these issues, first, by relying on a definition of "participation" which is particularly attentive to issues of power and control and views participation as both a means and an end in itself, and second, by examining audience participation in the network from an interpretive and cultural perspective.

Since assessing the extent and quality of indigenous participation at the INI network is an evaluative task, I finish the book by emphasizing those elements that, I find, hinder the emergence of audience's social uses of the stations. The key point is utilizing the network's most valuable resource, accumulated expertise of senior staff members. As I have pointed out, newer stations like Radio Margaritas are repeating some of the mistakes made long ago by XEZV, the oldest station of the network. More than anything else, learning from the experience of other stations requires a substantial improvement in horizontal communication among stations. Horizontal communication could be improved with a constant rotation of personnel among stations and by making XEZV a center for the staff's continuing education. However, the staff should be wary of the fact that logistic problems related to the improvement of horizontal communication in the network do not constitute the main obstacle. The real obstacle may be an unwillingness, on the part of INI officials, to improve a communication process that may trigger a process of democratization and further *conscientizaçao* among staff members from different regions.

Another crucial point concerns delineating the network's goals more clearly. It is better to target and concentrate on just those ethnic groups likely to use station's resources fully, especially the avisos services. By targeting fewer groups, the difficulties involved in multilingual broadcasting will be reduced. This concentration is also important in programming matters. Concentrating human and material resources in a few programs, most of which can be adapted to different vernaculars, would lead to the accumulation of expertise and hopefully to better programs. The network must also focus more clearly on its objectives based on a precise understanding of the target audience's needs. Although this point may sound obvious, the case of XETAR, where the station is actually serving better local ladinos than indigenous people, underscores the detrimental consequences of blurred objectives.

Spatial considerations seem to shape a number of audience uses, and they should be fully integrated into the network's participatory goals. Four spatial elements are important: (1) the stations ought to be located in regions in great need of affordable telecommunications services (by broadcasting avisos the stations will provide a substitute for these services and the local people will participate in the numerous benefits derived from the broadcasting of avisos, such as improving information flow in their social networks); (2) the stations ought to be located in cities which are the center of the economic, political, and social activity of the region (villagers are much more likely to use the station's resources when instead of traveling for the sole purpose of visiting the station, they can visit it during their necessary trips to urban centers); (3) the stations should be located nearby the city's indigenous area to make the station's resources more accessible to those sectors of the indigenous population who at present are poorly served (elders and women with small children are more likely to visit the station if such visit represents only a minor effort); and (4) the stations ought to have a lobby where indigenous people can feel at home, and stations will always keep all doors open to visitors. To achieve indigenous audiences' involvement in the stations, keeping an open-doors policy is probably more effective than maintaining high radio production values.

As with spatial considerations, temporal concerns can have an encouraging or a restrictive influence on audience uses of the stations. The mismatch between a station's broadcasting schedule and its audience's daily routines (such as the one that I discuss in Chapter 8 with respect to XEVFS) can have devastating effects on the goals of the network. Consequently, the network must fully integrate its local broadcast scheduling to the daily routines of its target audience.

Finally, I would like to stress, once again, that the chief obstacle to indigenous participation in the network is the racist attitudes and assumptions held not only by ladino staffers but also by indigenous workers. These attitudes and assumptions prevent indigenous persons from reaching managerial levels in the network. They also inhibit the emergence of a more democratic distribution of allocative and operational control inside the stations. And they influence the stations' image of the ethnic groups. Such an image determines which sectors of the indigenous populations are either included or excluded from the target audience, and whose cultural expressions get promoted or not. Questioning the staff's racist assumptions is a prerequisite for accomplishing one of the network's basic objectives, which is helping to raise the self-esteem of historically oppressed ethnic groups. Though it is necessary for the ladino staff to question their racist assumptions, it is even more important for the indigenous and mestizo staff to become aware of how mainstream society's racist assumptions of inferiority and incompetence can be internalized and directed against themselves. Racial attitudes and assumptions are probably the greatest hindrance to the project's participatory goals.

The success of participatory radio largely depends on the best-fitting merger of audience's needs and station operation, and thus, research should address the interplay between production and consumption practices. To grasp how the poor cope with and even turn to their advantage the many contradictions present at participatory radio stations, it is necessary to examine the social practices taking place in participatory projects. By doing a case study of the INI radio network, I aimed to shed light on the possibilities and constraints facing popular participation in radio-based projects, as well as to offer some insight into the social uses of participatory radio constructed by ethnic minorities.

My research suggests that stations like Radio Margaritas are indeed sites where the meanings of indigenous cultural forms are struggled over, and that oppressed people like the Tojolabal seem to use their limited participation in these projects strategically to achieve further ends. At stations like Radio Margaritas existing tensions in majority-minority relations manifest themselves in ways which allow some rarely acquired power to the oppressed. Within the context of racist mainstream media such as the Mexican, where indigenous peoples have been customarily represented either as exotic primitives or criminals, this limited participation acquires tremendous significance.

Sadly, however, my research also revealed concealed, almost invisible, but nonetheless mighty obstacles to genuine grassroots involvement in participatory radio. Hopefully this and similar case studies in other participatory stations will help to understand how racism, classism, and sexism are experienced in this type of radio, and hopefully too, such insight will help to begin the long struggle against blunt and subtle forms of discrimination in the theory and practice of development communications.

Notes

1. Denis Goulet, "Participation in Development: New Avenues." World Development 17, 2 (1989): 165-178.

2. Ronald Wardhaugh, *Languages in Competition* (Oxford: Basil Blackwell, 1987).

3. To begin with, because effective radio language teaching requires a great deal of expertise and production time, the stations would have to allocate huge resources for this programming. Secondly, programs with high educational value merely aired on open broadcasting would be insufficient; they would need to be part of a broader campaign involving the audience in organized groups supported by print material. And thirdly, since none of the stations commands this level of resources, to allocate heavily to the teaching of declining vernaculars would waste precious resources, and would lead to a loss of listeners to competing stations.

4. James Lull, *Inside Family Viewing* (London: Routledge, 1990).

Appendixes

Appendix 1:
Conceptual Framework

Development communications is a hybrid area with a corpus of theoretical knowledge coming from two interdisciplinary fields, development studies and media research. During the last few years in these two fields, there has been a shift either toward the readers of media texts or toward the beneficiaries of development projects. While in development studies the need for the active participation of the intended beneficiaries in the projects has been underscored, in media studies reception processes have become the foci of much research. Because I was interested in looking at both the participation of minority ethnic groups inside of the INI stations and the social uses of radio created by indigenous audiences, my research was informed by the literature on participation in development and also by cultural studies, especially by a growing body of research on the ethnography of media consumption. In addition, since I was specifically looking at Mexican ethnic groups, I reviewed a number of investigations into the Latin American media experience and its relation to popular culture.

Concepts Drawn from Development Studies

Many development theorists and practitioners have come to the conclusion that without the participation of the intended beneficiaries, the success of any development project is unlikely. Reflecting on the collapse of the traditional paradigm of development, and the need for finding fresh approaches to the field's challenges, scholars have even posited to see participation as a new development paradigm.[1] As a result, interest in participation regained momentum in the late 1980s. Yet participation has always been a key concept in development communications. It is the goal of Daniel Lerner's model of modernity, as well as the core of Paulo Freire's *conscientização*, and it was also one of the main concerns in development circles during the late 1970s. Moreover, calls for local participation in development projects have been present in the vast majority of works in the field of development communications, from Wilbur Schramm's writings to recent publications.[2] However, participation is a very hazy term. Given its conceptual flexibility, using participation as a criterion to evaluate media-based development projects is quite problematic.

To establish the main connotations of participation, I begin with a review of the paradigms of development and include two theories that Latin American authors have constructed in response to the social inequality endured by indigenous peoples. Next, as an exploration of the most important sources of the critical (non-modernization) meaning ascribed to participation, I discuss the *Sarvodaya* Movement of Sri Lanka, Freire's thought, and some of the contributions of other critical authors. Then I give the specific conceptual definition of grassroots participation that I espouse, and risking an oversimplification of the topic, I present the "conceptual map" that I worked with when examining indigenous participation in the INI radio network. This conceptual map is based on the major recommendations offered by critical researchers.[3]

The point of departure for the book is a perspective on development that gives special emphasis to the political social question of power. Georgette Wang and Wimal Dissanayake offer a definition of development that is pertinent for my research. They view development as follows:

> a process of social change which has as its goal the improvement of the quality of life of all or the majority of the people without doing violence to the natural and cultural environment in which they exist, and which seeks to involve the majority of the people as closely as possible in this enterprise, making them the masters of their own destiny.[4]

It is important to note that development involves ethical decisions concerning what constitutes "the improvement of the quality of life." It implies crucial considerations of who is the most appropriate person to make decisions and what are the criteria for such decisions. I worked under the assumption that these two issues should be answered by the people directly affected by the changes occasioned by development efforts.

Paradigms of Development

Not all authors share the same understanding of how development theories came about, but most contend that there exists a basic opposition between the modernization paradigm and other approaches. An interpretation that I find very useful is the one made by Charles Wilber and Kenneth Jameson. The opposition in their work is between the modernization approach, or "orthodox paradigm," and what they call the "political-economy paradigm," which equates development with emancipation.[5] Wilber and Jameson stress that Western modes of thought are the common source of both paradigms, inasmuch as both imply a similar view of history as progress and a parallel analytical framework which consists of a theory of development and a plausible explanation for underdevelopment. The differences between the two paradigms have to do with the specific theories of development and underdevelopment which they espouse.

In the orthodox paradigm, historical development is conceived of almost as a natural and universal process, a unilineal series of stages toward economic growth (e.g., W. Rostow). Since the point of departure is the model of competitive market capitalism, it is believed that the forces of competition bring about a greater availability of goods and services. Underdevelopment is explained as a deviation from the normal course of history caused by non-rational behavior, such as peasants' traditional attitudes and government interference in the free working of markets. According to Wilber and Jameson, there are three main theories concerning how to eliminate underdevelopment: the laissez-faire approach, which either suggests that time will take care of the problem or insists on curtailing the role of government in the economy; the planning response, which asserts that the government should persuade the citizenry of the need for modernization and should counterbalance economic difficulties through planning; and the growth-with-equity approach, which, in contrast to the two prior theories, questions the success of postwar development and stresses the importance of political and social variables. This last approach argues that the implementation of conventional strategies has failed to bring about a "trickling down" of the benefits of economic growth to the poor and proposes the meeting of basic needs and a New International Economic Order. Although Wilber and Jameson insert this third approach in the orthodox paradigm, it draws on elements from the political economy paradigm. Like these authors say,"at this point the boundaries of the two paradigms become blurred."[6]

The political economy paradigm, according to Wilber and Jameson, includes two major schools of thought: dependency theory and what these authors call the Marxist approach. The *dependentistas'* theory of underdevelopment centers on relationships among countries and argues that the evolution of capitalism and the world market has been a twofold process which has dictated both underdevelopment in the periphery (Third-world countries) and development in the center (Europe and North America). Development and underdevelopment are then two interrelated expressions of the same process. Dependentistas maintain that the dependence of poor nations is perpetuated by the same twofold process that assures the development of the center. Dependency theory is essentially an explanation of underdevelopment and, as Wilber and Jameson say, lacks a clear theory of development. Nevertheless, many researchers working within the framework of dependency theory call for development policies directed toward self-reliance, such as breaking with an export-oriented economy, mobilizing own resources for own purposes, opening up domestic markets, and satisfying local needs;[7] they also call for strategies based on small-scale, participatory projects.[8]

For the school of thought that Wilber and Jameson refer to as the "Marxist approach to development," the locus of power and control of the economic surplus (which is the central issue in the political economy paradigm) resides in the internal class structure of nations which adopt a capitalist mode of production.[9] The advocates of this perspective criticize the assumption that all governments (especially those of Third World nations) want development since, they argue, the wealth and privileges of the ruling class would be threatened by promoting social and economic change. Many of the advocates of this school highlight not only issues of power and control, but also ethical values. On comparing the two paradigms, Wilber and Jameson say:

> Within the orthodox paradigm the most traditional laissez faire and planning economists focus on economic growth as the key to development, while the growth-with-equity economists concentrate on the distribution of the benefits of growth to the poor. Political economists are more concerned with the *nature of the process* by which economic growth is achieved. In addition, traditional economists look on people's values as means. Since the goal is growth, if people's values have to change in order to get growth, then society must effect that change. But for political economists, one goal is to enhance people's core values. Development becomes the means, not the end, for the end is to enhance people's values. Thus political economists such as Denis Goulet define development as "liberation."[10]

The political economy paradigm's emphasis on processes and values, and therefore culture, is a key point for the current debate on the role of participation in development. Such emphasis is a prerequisite for postulating that people's participation is necessary to raise living standards. Furthermore, processes, culture, and values are the cornerstone of the two sources that, I find, are best conceptually equipped to furnish the philosophical foundation for refining a development communications theory of participation. These two sources are Paulo Freire's pedagogy of the oppressed and the Sarvodaya Shramadana Movement of Sri Lanka. Both have influenced the work of Goulet, whose ideas guided my research.[11] I discuss these sources below, but before doing so, I turn to two theories that have been specifically constructed to address the social inequalities suffered by Latin American indigenous peoples.

Latin American Development Theories Regarding Indigenous Peoples. Reflecting on the oppression and poor living conditions of indigenous peoples, Latin American researchers have posited a theory of underdevelopment and also a theory of development.[12] One of these theories, internal colonialism, explains the historical reasons for the poverty and exploitation of indigenous populations; the other one, ethnodevelopment, puts forth specific principles on which to base strategies for improving these peoples' lives. Both theories were cast within a critical framework and share assumptions and goals with other alternative approaches to development.

Internal colonialism's essential trust is that at the same time that at the international level powerful nations impose neocolonial political and economic relations with Third World countries, the dominant or ladino group of a country like Mexico duplicates such relations of domination and exploitation at the intra-national level. One of the proponents of this theory, the Mexican sociologist Pablo González Casanova, argues that indigenous communities present all the characteristics of colonized societies, and that they are colonies within the national boundaries.[13] Indigenous people provide ladinos with a favorable supply of primary commodities and cheap labor, and also with an enduring market for the products of ladino industry and commerce.

Going beyond the class analysis of orthodox Marxism, the theory of internal colonialism looks at the intersections of class and race/ethnicity and posits that the internal relations of dominance within the complex class structure of developing countries are based not only on class differences, but also on racial/ethnic discrimination. This discrimination makes possible for ladinos to extract an economic surplus from indigenous people's labor and also to exclude them from participating in the civil and political life of the nation.

The second theory, ethnodevelopment, maintains that the social inequality endured by indigenous peoples is at least partially based on the cultural discrimination exerted by the ladino society upon minority ethnic groups; consequently, social inequality can only be diminished by destigmatizing indigenous cultural forms (like music) and cultural institutions (like language). Instead of seeing traditional practices and indigenous knowledge as backwards, the advocates of ethnodevelopment view them as valuable resources and argue that genuine development needs to be constructed upon the revaluation of the ethnic groups' cultures. Since these theorists insist on the right of ethnic groups to build their own futures based on their historical experiences and cultural resources, they call for local participation in development efforts. Rather than being imposed by ladino "experts," development projects must be designed and implemented by indigenous peoples themselves, within a process of growing autonomy and self-management.[14]

Hence this theory shares with other approaches, such as the "basic-needs" model, the idea that the only way to achieve development is via the self-organization and self-management of the poor. However, ethnodevelopment's political stance is different from most approaches because it contends that indigenous peoples' right to lead the processes of change in their societies implies the legitimation of ethnic groups as autonomous political entities.[15] The current participatory ideology of the INI network has borrowed some of the premises of ethnodevelopment but not its political stance.

Grassroots Participation

The meaning of the term "participation" in the orthodox paradigm derives, as Thomas Jacobson states, from both "American historical experience and political theory based on this experience."[16] Jacobson argues that in the American political system direct participation in the government is restricted, in practice, to voting and involvement in party politics.[17] Moreover, although the advocates of the orthodox paradigm championed political participation as well as economic growth, they sought to achieve participation of the representative sort, as opposed to direct involvement of all citizens in government. In the political economy paradigm, by contrast, "participation" means grassroots involvement. This kind of involvement is what I had in mind when assessing indigenous participation in the INI network.

The Sarvodaya Movement of Sri Lanka. Probably no other "approach" to development best embodies the model, advanced by those convinced that the key to redressing social inequality lies in popular participation, than the *Sarvodaya Shramadana* Movement of Sri Lanka. A humanist perspective which conceptualizes development as having multiple, interconnected dimensions, it puts the human being at its center and seeks to empower the people by a process of awareness-building in which their social, economic, political, cultural, moral, and spiritual potentialities are cultivated. The *Sarvodaya* movement is a grassroots effort that relies on Buddhist principles, which are important cultural resources of Sri Lankans; it has evolved into a mass movement reaching literally millions of people.[18] And moreover, after more than three decades of growth, the movement has formulated and implemented a complex, multi-stage strategy for achieving development through self-reliance, self-help, and community participation.

A key concept of the movement, *Shramadama*, means "the sharing of one's time, thought and effort for the awakening of all."[19] The practice of sharing, so crucial to assure participation of all people at both micro and macro social institutions, constitutes the leading activity for self-reliance and integrated community development. The process of spiritual awakening, understood as "the progressive reduction of one's greed, aversions and illusions and the development of beneficence, compassion, and wisdom,"[20] leads to psychological empowerment and liberation from manipulation.

The principles of sharing and awakening are also related to the *Sarvodaya* movement's view of the communication process. According to Wang and Dissanayake, in the Buddhist model of communication the "receiver" is given greater attention than in the Western, Aristotelian model. The purpose of communication in the Asian perspective is emphatic understanding and choice rather than intellectual influence and control. And in contrast to the top-down Western model, the Buddhist is a horizontal model with symmetrical relationships between "communicator" and "receiver."[21]

The philosophy of the *Sarvodaya* movement has influenced theorists, like Goulet, from whom I have borrowed many of the ideas to assess participation in the INI network. And, although it comes from a quite different civilization, several of its principles have a similar flavor to those of Freire's pedagogy of the oppressed, my fundamental source.

Paulo Freire's Conscientização. Freire's notion of *conscientização* is rooted in existentialist philosophy, especially that of Karl Jaspers and Jean-Paul Sartre. Both the analysis of the human being (vital for Jaspers) and the centrality of human choice (crucial for Sartre) constitute the core of the form of existentialism adopted by Freire. As a reaction to nineteenth century romanticism, existentialism holds that there is no such thing as an infinite force (reason, the absolute, spirit) manifesting itself through humanity, and that there is no transcendental order guaranteeing the final results of human actions. Human beings are a finite reality (subject to death) acting by themselves (fundamentally alone) and responsible for their own actions; human freedom is conditioned, limited by its particular circumstances.[22] These ideas are crucial to Freire's doctrine of *conscientização*, whose goal is the educatees' awareness of their own circumstances and their real choices. By substituting a naïve (in existentialist jargon, romantic) or magic (fatalistic) perception of reality with a critical awareness, people who were treated as mere objects become subjects of their social destinies. Freire explained his pedagogy for critical consciousness in this way: "We wanted to offer the people the means by which they could supersede their magic or naïve perception of reality by one that was predominantly critical, so that they could assume positions adequate to the dynamic climate of the transitions."[23]

Existentialist analysis uses dynamic relationships, particularly concerning the individual, as the instrument for describing and interpreting reality. The main interpretive category of this philosophy is "the possible." People's relationships to things around them are characterized by their possibilities for adapting things, through work, to their own needs. An individual's relationships with others consist of possibilities for collaboration, solidarity, communication, love, and friendship.[24] Consequently, Freire stated that humans are "beings of relationships."[25] Within the real limits of their own circumstances, people have the possibility of changing themselves and transforming their social conditions.[26] As a Catholic teacher working to improve adult literacy in Brazil, Freire came to the conclusion that any meaningful educational effort must be aimed at awakening critical consciousness. Following Jaspers, Freire argued that "dialogue creates a critical attitude" and proposed a method for development efforts based on dialogue as "a horizontal relationship between persons."[27]

When he posits his "pedagogy of the oppressed," Freire means to elaborate a theory which involves the oppressed actively. Freire observes that among the powerless "word" and "dialogue" have been replaced by a "culture of silence." Echoing Sartre, he asserts that traditional educational practices treat the oppressed as if they were objects, or mere recipients (Freire talks about "the digestive conception of knowledge," and Sartre about "banking education"). As such, they are deprived of their true ontological nature, which is being subjects. Freire asserts that authentic knowledge (or authentic development) can only be achieved when the oppressed "problematize," question "natural" reality, and become actively involved in their own education.

Development, for Freire, means liberation from all forms of oppression, freedom from social and economic domination, and emancipation from the culture of silence. Despite his severe critique of most developmental efforts (and to a certain extent despite his existentialist stance), Freire is an optimist. He believes his ideas provide the foundation for a new, humanist theory, which can guide the oppressed in their struggle for liberation. Furthermore, Freire ascribes a valuable role to the educator/extension worker, to help the people become subjects of history.[28] He asserts that only when the poor assume their ontological vocation as subjects of history and engage themselves in developmental efforts (seen as one of the multiple forms of the struggle for emancipation) can authentic development be attained.

Development Communications

Development communicators have proposed a number of explanations to and strategies for the particular area of the development phenomena which interests them by building upon the theories of development advanced by economists, political scientists, sociologists, and anthropologists. Along with the background provided by the latter, development communicators have also relied on specific models of the communication process. Early research in the field was done within the orthodox paradigm of development and relied on the first model of communication which, as critical authors remark, was mechanistic. Communication, as depicted in this model, is a system of message transmission, a one-way road from source to receiver. As Luis Ramiro Beltrán eloquently argues, the essential elements of the "vertical model" (who, what, to whom, and its persuasive aim) were established by Aristotle more than two thousands years ago, and they persisted so long because criticism of the model seldom attacked its foundation, which is, according to Beltrán, related to power."[29]

By the time the growth-with-equity approach and the political economy paradigm gained acceptance among development communicators, a new trend based on a questioning of the early model of communication had already emerged in the field, and media participation was no longer defined as passive reception of media messages. A review of the numerous ways in which the audience has been perceived by communication researchers would bring the participation controversy into sharpened focus. This is beyond the scope of this section, but I fully discuss it in the next section. What I wish to emphasize here is that most critical researchers in development communications work not only within a non-orthodox paradigm of development, but also with horizontal models of the communication process.

Participatory Communication in Development. The idea of popular participation was intensely discussed during the 1970s in Latin America and other regions of the Third World. A good example of this intellectual movement was the First Seminar on Participatory Communication sponsored by the *Centro Internacional de Estudios Superiores de Comunicación para América Latina* (CIESPAL) in 1978. In this seminar, participation was equated with liberation, and participatory communication was seen as both a means and an end; as Jeremy O'Sullivan Ryan and Mario Kaplún say:

> As a means towards a new model of development based on man's complete freedom from all forms of marginality and exploitation, and as an end because participatory communication can have very positive effects not only in creating a new awareness of one's condition, but also at the psychological and social-psychological levels.[30]

In other words, according to O'Sullivan Ryan and Kaplún, in the seminar it was stressed that "it is only meaningful to speak of participation if it is first understood as participation in political power."[31]

The CIESPAL 1978 Seminar's perspective is linked to the theory of marginality, which is itself closely related to the political economy paradigm of development. Authors like Boris Lima argue that the concept of marginality came about in opposition to the concept of participation, because people have a "marginal" social life when they are unable to participate in society either passively (as beneficiaries of public services, social security, and the like), or actively (by taking on tasks and responsibilities in support of the community and by conforming willingly to its values and mores).[32] O'Sullivan Ryan and Kaplún say that marginality "essentially refers to a situation in which large sections of a country's population do not participate in the social, cultural, economic and political activities of that country."[33]

By the 1970s then, Freire's "pedagogy of the oppressed" had become familiar to many development communicators, especially in Latin America.

Freire's thought, in conjunction with the closely related ideas of other thinkers and with the decline of the orthodox paradigm of development, inspired an interest in small-scale, grassroots projects, run for and by the beneficiaries. Media-based participatory projects, according to Robert Hornik, have included a strong element of consciousness-raising and have aimed to encourage political organization in poor communities.[34]

An interesting elaboration of Freire's thought has been made by Goulet who views participation as a development strategy. He states that participation can be used in social situations which are inserted in the broader context of a system based on a process of continuous negotiations among groups. Goulet's approach may be seen as a response to a crucial question posed by Shabbir Cheema: "Can we conceptualize popular participation as an independent variable in our efforts to understand the phenomenon of poverty?"[35] Goulet argues that participation "can fruitfully be understood as a moral incentive enabling hitherto excluded non-elites to negotiate new packages of material incentives."[36] The positive results that such a strategy may have, according to Goulet, are first to bring dignity to powerless people, thereby preventing government's treatment of them as instruments; second to promote the organization of the poor; and third to open a channel for local communities to macro arenas of decision-making.[37] Goulet's proposals include the fundamental premises of other critical views to development, the need for political organization of the poor, and the positive role played by indigenous cultures in development; for example, Goulet questions: "How can low-income peoples mobilize for 'development' without also creating new capacities for cultural and political self-affirmation?"[38]

Access, Participation, and Self-management. A UNESCO meeting held in Belgrade in 1977 was largely devoted to defining three terms that have been widely incorporated into the literature on participatory communication: access, participation, and self-management. According to a summary presented at the Belgrade meeting provided by O'Sullivan Ryan and Kaplún, "access" refers to a people's ability to use communication systems on two levels, designated as follows: choice (the right to receive desired programs, to have a wide range of materials available, and to transmit messages) and feedback (interaction between producers and receivers, direct participation of the audience in programs, the right to comment and criticize, and the means to keep in touch with the staff and administrator of media institutions). The word "participation" in this context alludes to the audience's involvement in production processes and in the management of communication systems; this kind of participation operates at three levels: production (availability of opportunities and resources to produce programs), decision-making (involvement in programming and management), and planning (formulation of policies and objectives). The term "self-management" is used to describe what UNESCO at the time regarded as the highest level of participation and therefore was chosen to stand for the full involvement of the people in media institutions and in communication policies. It is important to note that, as set forth at the Belgrade Meeting, the term participation may be applied only to representative participation (as in the orthodox paradigm of development). Self-management, on the other hand, was assigned a meaning closely resembling the way participation has been used by some of the advocates of the political economy paradigm.

Beltrán has further elaborated on the definitions proposed at the Belgrade Meeting. Beltrán points out that Lasswell had anticipated, in 1972, two contrasting models, which he labeled the "oligarchic model" and the "participatory model."[39] Beltrán also sets forth the basic elements of a "free and egalitarian," or horizontal, communication process; he talks about access, dialogue, and participation:

> *Access* is the effective exercise of the right to receive messages.
> *Dialogue* is the effective exercise of the right to concurrently receive and emit messages.
> *Participation* is the effective exercise of the right to emit messages.[40]

> Participation is the culmination of horizontal communication because without comparable opportunities to all persons to emit messages the process will remain governed by the few.

> *Self-management* ... is deemed the most advanced and wholistic form of participation since it allows the citizenry to decide on policy, plans, and actions [emphasis mine].[41]

In keeping with the resolutions adopted at the Belgrade Meeting, Beltrán attributed to self-management the sense of the highest level of participation. He differed with the definition of participation formulated at the Meeting in that he conceived of participation as the emission of messages, dismissing in this way the possible view of the concept as only representative participation.

Another Development Communications. Since, as it happened in development studies, the theoretical underpinnings of communication research have been in constant flux in the last two decades, it is no wonder that in the late 1980s the field was characterized as being in a state of confusion. John Lent rightly said:

> Confusion marks the status of development and communication projects and studies in the 1980s—confusion concerning which projects and approaches have been successful; confusion concerning the direction the research should take; confusion concerning what the concept really means.[42]

Though such a state of confusion persists in the 1990s, I believe that the most vigorous direction in the field has culture and grassroots participation at its center and has rejected the mechanistic model of communication. Wimal Dissanayake, for example, advocates a model of development communications which "emphasizes such elements as popular participation, grassroots development, integrated village development, use of appropriate technology, fulfillment of basic needs, productive use of local resources, and maintenance of the ecological balance."[43] In Dissanayake's model, social change is endogenously induced, and local culture is seen as a stimulus to development, rather than as an obstacle, as it was viewed in the orthodox paradigm.

Working Definition of Participation. The 1979 United Nations Research Institute for Social Development's (UNRISD) document "Inquiry into Participation" proposed to use the following working definition of participation:

> For the purpose of defining an adequate area of research *in a way that does not permit the evasion of the central issue of power* the definition proposed for this inquiry is: "the organized efforts to increase control over resources and regulative institutions in given social situations, on the part of groups and movements hitherto excluded from such control" [emphasis mine].[44]

UNRISD's document on participation "was circulated among some four hundred colleagues, social scientists, policy makers and activists," and a later edition of the document, which includes comments from 90 people, was published.[34] In this collective document, several interesting critiques of the definition were made. The two most relevant criticisms refer to the lack of an explicit purpose in the definition, and the failure to distinguish between participation as a goal and as a means (although the distinction is very clear in other parts of the document). Given that this dual nature of participation appears as the major constant in the literature (from the writings of Freire to the most recent publications), I expanded the definition offered by Pearse and Stiefel to encompass both participation as a means to achieve development, and participation as a goal in itself because participation empowers. Thus the working concept of participation that I used in the research of the INI network included the two following dimensions:

1. Participation as a means (equated to liberation):
The organized efforts to increase control over resources and institutions in given social situations, on the part of groups and movements hitherto excluded from such control, for the emancipatory purpose of achieving a better life, self-reliance, self-esteem, and freedom from servitude [expanded from UNRISD's document].[46]

2. Participation as a goal (equated to moral and psychological empowerment): The set of feelings, beliefs, and attitudes that accompany the sense of self-worth, on the part of groups and individuals historically regarded by a given society as being unable to cope effectively with situations concerning control over resources and institutions.

The need for a precise definition of the term participation and a set of guidelines to assess the extent and quality of participation in communication-for-development efforts has to do with the direct consequences that research on development communications can have for policy making. This need, along with the proliferation of participatory projects, calls for guidelines to evaluate participation in media-based development projects.

Goulet, who views participation as both "an instrument of development and a special mode thereof,"[47] establishes qualitative differences among different forms of participation, and in order to evaluate these forms, he presents a typology of participation envisioned along four axes. In Goulet's scheme, the first way to analyze participation is by understanding its dual character as both means and goal. Hence, participation may be an instrument, an end, or both. The second criterion for classifying participation is "the scope of the arena in which [participation] operates," either spatial (local, national) or sectorial (only in certain aspects of a given activity). Source, or originating agent, constitutes the third basis for distinguishing among forms of participation; this can be introduced from above, generated from below, or "catalytically promoted by a third agent" (whose primary interest is empowering the people). The last axis for the analysis is temporal, the moment at which participation is introduced (diagnosis, planning, and implementation). The impact that participation may have in development depends on both its quality and the extent to which it is linked to political activity in the macro arena. Following Goulet's criteria, the purest form of participation would be the offspring of a grassroots action that is introduced at the initiation of such effort, and having a broad scope, is seen not only as a means, but also as an end.[48]

In the remaining part of this section I present a scheme or conceptual map which is chiefly guided by Goulet's work and which synthesizes the recommendations proposed by critical researchers. This is the scheme that guided my assessment of indigenous participation in the INI radio stations. Though I present this scheme to offer the reader a sense of my own stance regarding evaluation research on participatory projects, I have to stress my wariness about the use of these abstractions. They oversimplify social reality and fail to account for the inherent ambiguity and contradiction of both bureaucratic organizational practices and popular cultural practices. The worst side of these schemes is that they tend to suggest that all the manifestations of phenomena as complex and elusive as meaningful participation can be quantifiable, or at least clearly identifiable.

A Conceptual Map for Assessing Participation. The chart presented in Figure A.1 is composed of nine variables (rows) with four levels of what might be called "desirability" (columns) each. Variables are rated according to the extent of their desirability in a development project. The criteria for desirability correspond to the expected impact on development. When a certain characteristic is listed under the "non-desirable" heading, it means that I believe its real impact will be detrimental for development.

The difference between categories in the first two variables, Scope and Reach, may be only one of degree. The underlying assumption is that the scope of participation can, and should, expand from micro to macro arenas. However, participation is not desirable when such an expansion is not expected and even much less when it is prevented. The first variable, Scope, refers to the social arenas where participation may take place. Reach designates the socio-political aspects in which participation may occur.[49] Goulet refers to reach when he says that "participation may be confined sectorially, as when school teachers are given freedom to shape the curriculum in collegial fashion, but not the budgets of their respective departments."[50] It is assumed that people will be allowed to play a part in matters not perceived as directly related to control, especially political control.

Origin refers to the agent or sponsor who initiates a project. Outside agents (such as international organizations, missionaries, and militants) may be catalysts or catalytic agents when their actions play a part in grassroots efforts of communities to carry out salutary projects. Authentic participation in projects sponsored by the government has been seen as more difficult to achieve than participation in projects sponsored by other outside agents, such as the Catholic Church and non-government organizations from European countries. As early as the late 1970s, authors like Dean Jamison and Emile McAnany were warning that "participating with the government may contain serious dangers of co-optation by the power holders who are inclined to short-term solutions."[51]

Purpose refers to the gains that a program potentially offers. Ideally, the purpose of a project is for powerless groups to achieve control over the resources and institutions which affect their lives. On the other hand, projects whose only objective is to solve immediate problems (first level) have been seen as counterproductive by critical researchers, because their paternalistic approach tends to promote a passive attitude among the powerless. Nonetheless, I should underline that acceptable, or even desirable, results might be produced when efforts to solve immediate problems are combined with the information and knowledge with which to promote self-reliance and organizational skills among the intended beneficiaries.

The last three columns pertaining to the fifth variable, Who Participates,

FIGURE A.1 Conceptual Map for Assessing Participation in Media-based Projects

Levels of desirability	Non-desirable	Acceptable	Desirable	Highly desirable
Scope of participation	Only inside project	Some immediate micro-arenas	Local macro-arenas	Macro-arenas
Reach of participation	Only in matters not related to control	In matters allowing limited control	In political aspects	In all aspects
Origin of the project	Outside agent	Catalytic agent	Local groups with limited aims	Grassroots movement
Purpose	Only to solve immediate problems	To provide knowledge and information for self-reliance	To promote skills for social organization	To achieve control over resources and institutions
Who participates	Elites/ powerless, isolated individuals	Powerless, non-organized groups	Powerless, organized groups	Grassroots movement
Reasons for participation	Coerced by authorities	Economic pressure	Social pressure from peers	Willing choice
Participation as a stategy to achieve	Mobilization	Participation in co-related projects	Organization in micro-arenas	Organization in macro-arenas
Results of participation	System-maintaining	Toward system-transforming	System-transforming in micro-arenas	System-transforming in macro-arenas

classify powerless groups according to their level of social organization. Critical researchers suggest that participation on the part of powerless, isolated individuals is inadequate because it does not lead to participation in macro arenas. Reason for Participation registers the motives members of developing communities have for cooperating on a project; these can range from coercion to willing choice. Because of the widespread acceptance in the field of the need for grassroots participation, development agencies sometimes use coercive measures to induce participation. This coerced participation is clearly undesirable. On the other hand, participation may be desirable when it is motivated by social pressure from peers because peer pressure is often a by-product of organization.

Participation as Strategy makes the distinction between mass mobilization, which is promoted or imposed by power elites at the macro level, and authentic grassroots organization, which is free from manipulation and co-optation. Many authors have warned against manipulated participation, arguing that projects that depend upon manipulated participation in the initial stages face the problem of sustaining local participation later on. The two intermediate levels are participation in co-related development programs and organization in micro arenas. The former is seen as acceptable because it may lead to integrated development, and the later is considered desirable since it relies on grassroots organization. Finally, the outcomes of participatory projects are classified under the variable Results according to whether or not these outcomes are system-maintaining, which is non-desirable, or system-transforming, which should be the goal of a participatory development project.

Participation and Empowerment

In brief, I understand participation in the sense of direct involvement of the intended beneficiaries in all arenas of the development work. Like critical researchers, I also regard participation in media processes, and especially in political processes, as the goal of development efforts. Media participation presupposes the self-management of media institutions by grassroots organizations, because participation should be defined in relation to issues of power and control. Also like critical researchers, I espouse a conceptualization of participation in two senses. First participation is a means of achieving development: a better life, self-reliance, self-esteem, and freedom from servitude. In this sense participation is equated with liberation. Second, I understand participation implies moral and psychological empowerment, and as such it is an end in itself. It was crucial for me to keep in mind this last sense of the term when I was analyzing indigenous participation in the INI network.

In the remaining part of this appendix I introduce the theoretical and methodological insights, which I used in this book, coming from cultural studies to media.

Concepts from Cultural Studies

In addition to the insights regarding popular participation in development offered by critical authors, I was guided in this investigation by the main thrusts of contemporary cultural studies. Cultural studies might well be defined as a general approach to the inquiry into cultural practices, cultural products, and meanings seen in their social contexts. As Ron Lembo remarks, this approach comprises various perspectives, yet one can distinguish "at least five working assumptions" shared by researchers operating within this conceptual framework. The following, five working assumptions, listed by Lembo, were indeed pivotal for my own investigation:

(1) society is divided into dominant and subordinate groups that differ in terms of their access to social power; (2) dominant groups assert their power in cultural as well as in political and economic domains; (3) cultural meanings are linked to the social structure and, consequently, to power relations, and such meanings can only be understood if the history of the social structure and power relations is made explicit; (4) the creation of cultural meanings by those who use the media is relatively autonomous from the institutional production of media objects; (5) this relative autonomy in the creation of meanings in media use can serve as a basis for oppositional politics.[52]

Marxism is the grand theory sustaining these working assumptions, and more specifically, the cultural Marxism of Antonio Gramsci that has reoriented Marxism away from its crude economic determinism. In this second part of this appendix, I briefly review the fundamental concepts sustaining my investigation of a mass media institution and the circuits of production and consumption of its products. I start by reviewing a number of key ideas of the Gramscian thought, then I introduce the reader to the influential work of British cultural studies and summarize Pierre Bourdieu's theory of cultural consumption. All of this material is followed by a more detailed exposition of reception studies, the specific strand of cultural studies where I found the method, with its inherent epistemological grounds, for my own audience research. Importantly though, since I recognize that a Third World, radio-based development project differs vastly from the usual object of study of reception analyses (typically television viewing in the developed world), I include in this appendix an outline of the thought-provoking work by Latin American scholars concerning mass media and popular culture. This line of research influenced the blueprint of my investigation to a great extent; especially inspiring was the pioneering work on people's radio done by the Peruvian researcher Rosa María Alfaro. Finally, to give the reader a sense of how investigations dealing with my specific topic have been conducted in the past, I conclude this appendix with a brief survey on Latin American participatory stations.

Gramsci's Legacy to the Study of Culture

Cultural studies have been nourished by several sources of the Marxian philosophy, yet a number of Marxist concepts coming from the thought of Antonio Gramsci have been pivotal to much of the research done under the umbrella of cultural studies. These ideas include Gramsci's vision of the organic intellectual, his theory of hegemony, and his conceptualization of ideology. An organic intellectual himself, Gramsci was an activist who suffered imprisonment and torture by the Fascist regime for his political involvement with the Italian revolutionary movement. He struggled against elite rule to try to realize a participatory society regulated by the principles of self-government and popular control.

Whereas one of Marxism's greatest contributions to social theory has been its insistence on those enduring factors structuring the social world (mode of production, class struggle), Gramsci's contribution lies in his emphasis on human consciousness and human agency. He privileged the role played by human will and subjectivity in history and highlighted the need to consider conscious intentions and subjective meanings in the analysis of social life.

Gramsci's thought has been vital to critical cultural researchers because it offers a way of systematically inquiring into the workings of the superstructural sphere, an area which had been hitherto neglected by Marxism. Gramsci posited that in addition to the coercive apparatuses of the state (political superstructure), the moral and intellectual leadership of the institutions of the civil society (ideological superstructure) help to sustain capitalist societies by creating and recreating the dominant ideology. The ruling class retains its hegemonic power by getting society's ideological apparatuses to generate social consent to its rule. He was interested in finding out how the institutions of the civil society serve to secure the supremacy of the elite. Thus his theory of hegemony proposes that the ruling class governs not just by grounding its superiority in economic matters, but also by establishing a widespread belief in its moral and intellectual leadership; it rules by molding, through the church, the school, and the media, the attitudes and convictions of the members of subordinated classes.

Gramsci understood hegemony as the way in which the ruling class struggles to establish and maintain its dominance not just by force, but by achieving consensus through a combination of moral and intellectual leadership and via the formation of alliances and compromises among diverse social groups. Consensus is produced and reproduced in the interweaving of social relations, institutions, and intellectual creations. But hegemony is never total, and to win continually popular consent to its dominance, the ruling class requires the cooperation of a cast of intellectuals, who are the manufacturers of consent (for Gramsci these included teachers, clerics, artists, journalists, political leaders, civil servants, and so on).

Ideology for Gramsci is a conception of the world, yet it is also a site, a terrain where meanings and understandings are negotiated and where people's consciousness are struggled over.[53] Gramsci argued that in the same way the ruling class requires the cooperation of those he called "traditional intellectuals" to protect its interests, the working class needs "organic intellectuals" to struggle on its behalf on the cultural front. Hence Gramsci saw the efforts of organic intellectuals as having a key role in revolutionary strategy. He thought that to bring about social change, the political practice of the proletariat must include organic intellectuals who in a "war of positions" would eventually capture the institutions of the civil society. The Gramscian concept of hegemony became a cornerstone of critical cultural studies because, as Joseph Femia says, it "was not just a tool of historical and social analysis; it was also a guiding concept for political practice."[54] And it is this possibility of integrating research with meaningful political practice which is so critical to British cultural studies.

British Cultural Studies

Stuart Hall's 1986 essay "Cultural Studies: Two Paradigms" delineates succinctly the historical development and the various currents of thought that have contributed to shape the problematic of British cultural studies and to redefine its boundaries.[55] This essay offers, I feel, the best synthesis of the approach not only because it was written by one the doyens of British cultural studies (and a former director of the Center for Contemporary Cultural Studies at the University of Birmingham), but also because it brilliantly recounts how various lines of thought have intersected in this approach. These influences, some of which are seemingly at odds with each other, have furnished cultural studies with an elaborate theoretical base from which to undertake critical analyses of culture. Hall's work itself is a good example of the multiple, conceptual intersections converging in this approach.

In his essay, Hall argues that there have been two paradigms in cultural studies, the culturalist and the structuralist. He traces the origin of the culturalist paradigm to the work done in the 1950s and 1960s by Richard Hoggart, E. P. Thompson, and Raymond Williams, and he maintains that this "dominant paradigm of cultural studies" revolves around a novel, and in many ways distinct, more anthropological conceptualization of "culture." The emphasis on ideas and the high/low culture distinction of the previous debate on culture was discarded in favor of a set of notions to think and analyze popular culture: working class cultural forms viewed as texts that can be read; culture understood as "ordinary" social practices, as "a whole way of life"; and human agency, consciousness, and lived experience as significant elements in the making of history. Also important was the challenge to economic determinism and to the literal understanding of the base/superstructure metaphor. In Hall's words, culture was conceptualized as:

> interwoven with all social practices; and those practices, in turn, as a common form of human activity: sensuous human praxis, the activity through which

men and women make history... as *both* the meanings and values which arise amongst distinctive social groups and classes, on the basis of their given historical conditions and relationships, through which they 'handle' and respond to the conditions of existence; *and* as the lived traditions and practices through which those 'understandings' are expressed and in which they are embodied.[56]

While the culturalist paradigm stressed the dynamic role played by human agency and the creative and transformative potential of lived practices, the structuralist or linguistic paradigm insisted on the part played by fixed elements (language/ideology, cognitive unconscious categories, socio-economic frameworks) in structuring human experience and action. Hall identifies two main influences in this latter paradigm, Louis Althusser and Claude Levi-Strauss. From Althusser cultural studies took on an emphasis on the key notions of ideology and over-determination; and from Levi-Strauss, it incorporated the anthropological appropriation of Saussurean linguistics for analyzing culture and society. Hall also points out what he views as the strengths of structuralism: its emphasis on determinate conditions, its view of society as a whole, "its decentering of 'experience' and its seminal work in elaborating the neglected category of 'ideology.'"[57] As for the strengths of culturalism, Hall indicates that it is the particular way in which this paradigm incorporates crucial elements of Gramsci's thought that contribute most to its endurance.

Even though Hall does not explicitly mention it, his own contribution to mass media studies is substantial. His encoding/decoding model offered a fresh approach to the processes of mass media production and reception, an approach emphasizing the constructed and polysemic nature of media messages and the social and political contexts in which the processes of encoding and decoding messages take place. Rejecting the contemporaneous North American media model's conceptualization of the audience as passive receivers, Hall suggested that audience members may read a media message either from a dominant-hegemonic position (and thereby accept the preferred meaning encoded in such message), or they may construct a negotiated, or even an oppositional, reading of the same message. Further, Hall proposed to look at those non-dominant readings as openings for a political and ideological analysis of underlying social forces and structures. Graeme Turner rightly points out that the significance of Hall's model goes beyond the linguistic implications of the possibility of an encoding/decoding mismatch between writer/producer and reader. Hall's main contribution has to do with his emphasis on analyzing people's decodings of media messages to explore broader social and cultural issues: "the encoding/decoding model defined media texts as moments when the larger social and political structures within the culture are exposed for analysis."[58]

One of the limitations of the model, acknowledged by Hall himself, is that it describes hypothetical decoding positions rather than actual sociological groups.[59] This shortcoming makes the application of the model quite difficult. However, Hall's point about the relationship linking decoding positions to socio-economic, structural differences among audience members (class positions) definitely has helped to move the discussion to a promising zone, that of the study of cultural consumption. In the next section I review a quite elaborate proposal for analyzing the consumption of cultural products, including mass media texts and technologies.

Bourdieu's Theory of Cultural Consumption

The theory of cultural consumption of the French sociologist Pierre Bourdieu has provided researchers with a rich framework to analyze cultural practices and their social value. Bourdieu set himself to ascertain the principles and workings of "the economy of cultural practices." His use of the term "economy" is key to understanding his work since one of his central concepts is the notion of symbolic "capital." In addition to wealth or economic capital, social subjects (consciously or unconsciously) procure artistic and other cultural goods and acquire cultural competences. This symbolic capital helps to position and differentiate subjects in the social world.

Combining the tools of empirical, quantitative, sociological research with the theoretical sophistication of the Marxian social critique, Bourdieu analyzes issues that have been frequently mystified, such as taste, aesthetic judgment, and the meaning of artistic products. His theory contends that people's preferences for given cultural goods and the particular manner in which they are used is to a great extent determined by social position (mainly by education and social origin).[60] Taste, Bourdieu argues, is produced by social conditions. Yet taste and consuming practices serve to constitute social positions and to distinguish an individual from those belonging to other social classes or even from people situated within the same class, but holding more or less symbolic capital. In essence, art and cultural consumption are not innocent; they play an important part in social inequality. According to Bourdieu, they "are predisposed, consciously and deliberately or not, to fulfill a social function of legitimating social differences."[61]

Like the literary critics who suggested that we should shift from a text-centered perspective to one that looks closely at "the role of the reader," Bourdieu offers a model which focuses not just on the cultural product but especially on the practices occurring in the realm of consumption and social uses. He says that "most products only derive their social value from the social use that is made of them."[62] However, if some strands of the reader-oriented criticism and similar approaches to popular culture have celebrated the freedom of readers to "produce" their own readings,[63] Bourdieu has insisted on the power of societal structures to limit consumers' latitude. The structures organizing aesthetic preferences and cultural practices are the "systems of dispositions characteristic of the different classes and class fractions" that Bourdieu calls the "habitus."[64] The habitus of a given social group has been constituted by the social and economic conditions in which the group has been raised, and its distinctive signs (or "tastes") can be observed in the life-style that the group's specific habitus has developed.

Bourdieu's theory of cultural consumption, I believe, can greatly enhance the understanding of the social value of participatory media because it pays attention to the constraints imposed by social structures on the emergence of participatory uses of these media. In my investigation of the INI network, Bourdieu's concepts have helped me to interpret, for example, certain uses of the radio stations and their products as means of legitimizing social differences and establishing social distinctions.

Since the bulk of indigenous participation in the INI network is realized in the consumption of its cultural offerings, I was particularly interested in looking at the way indigenous people use the INI network's radio resources and products. I also wanted to use an interpretive method which would allow me to give voice to indigenous audiences' interpretations of these offerings; consequently, I decided to follow closely the methodological suggestions from a growing body of research focusing on reception processes that has come to be known as either ethnography of media consumption or reception studies.[65] I turn to these investigations in the next section.

Reception Studies

Those who have conducted reception studies (e.g., Dorothy Hobson, David Morley, Charlotte Brunsdon, Stuart Hall, Ien Ang, Klaus Bruhn Jensen, James Lull, Tamar Liebes, Elihu Katz, Angela McRobbie, Janice Radway, Andrea Press) may or may not consider themselves culturalists, but all of them have focussed on the medium-audience nexus. Most of these investigations are either an outgrowth of the Birmingham School (e.g., Morley) or share its central premises (e.g., Radway), though others were developed within the framework of uses and gratifications research (e.g., Lull). Authors like Shaun Moores have warned about the difficulty of a convergence of both approaches because the uses and gratifications approach, blind to issues of power and ideology, fails to link individual uses of media to societal structures and larger sociological issues.[66] Though in general I agree with Moores' concerns, I found the work of James Lull (who, as Moores remarks, "writes in the language of the functionalist school"[67]) quite useful for my audience study because it provided me with a typology of micro uses of media that helped me begin to make sense of my data (I discuss Lull's work below).

However, most of the conceptual underpinnings of my audience study indeed came from the audience research done by members of the Center for Contemporary Cultural Studies. This Birmingham group, drawing on Gramsci and on traditions of literary analysis, have examined mass media texts while paying greater attention to the audience and to the social contexts where meanings are constructed; the focus is on the real experience of people and their relationships with media products. With a positive view of the manner by which people decode/read/use products of mass culture, this group of researchers attempt to understand the role of these products in society, especially in deviant or oppositional groups.

By and large, the foci of the Birmingham school's applied research has been either on the cultural products themselves (Screen theory) or on the uses of these products by popular audiences (ethnography of reception). John Fiske distinguishes two methodological strategies of cultural studies. One comes from semiotic and structuralist textual analysis; the other,

> derives from ethnography and requires us to study the meanings that the fans of Madonna actually *do* (or appear to) make of her. This [strategy] involves listening to them [fans], reading the letters they write to fan magazines, or observing their behavior at home or in public. The fans' words or behavior are not, of course, empirical facts that speak for themselves; they are, rather, texts that need 'reading' theoretically in just the same way as the 'texts from Madonna' do.[68]

Elaborating on the encoding/decoding model, the Birmingham group has carried out a number of ethnographies of media consumption, many of them focusing on television viewing and combining in-depth interviewing with observation in naturalistic settings. For example, they have looked at how television viewing affects other family activities, such as structuring the temporal experience of family life and facilitating/obstructing interpersonal communication among family members.

I borrowed heavily from one of these ethnographies, David Morley's *Family Television: Cultural Power and Domestic Leisure.*[69] Arguing from a similar position as Radway, who in her investigation of romance readers found that the meaning of the act of reading was at least as important as the meaning that women constructed from the novels, Morley concentrated on the act of watching television. His study, thus, focuses on the uses of television and the dynamics of those uses within the context of family politics; gender relations and family politics were especially important for this research. Sadly, it was not until I finished the fieldwork that I discovered Dorothy Hobson's *Crossroads: The Drama of a Soap Opera,*[70] a wonderful study which influenced Morley's *Family Television*. I say sadly because in her work, Hobson did exactly what I have done, namely, investigate a media phenomenon in its three moments: production, text, and consumption.

Reception studies are concerned with the interplay between the communication system, as an institutional expression of social structures and the audience's media experience. Nordic authors like Bruhn Klaus Jensen assert that within reception analysis there is a convergence of empirical research with neo-Marxist approaches. While reception studies are interdisciplinary and eclectic, most of them do share certain key concepts set forth by critical approaches to media. Important here are Gramsci's discussions of hegemony, ideology, and consensus. The authors of reception studies appreciate the relative independence of ideology (from the economic base) and respect ideology's mechanisms of signification, expression, and consent creation, without, however, adopting the extreme Althusserian/ Screen Theory position which argues that ideology and its mystification are all-embracing. Rather, following Gramsci's position, mass media and their products are seen as sites of ideological struggle. Authors of reception studies would stress that it is mass-mediated meanings which are struggled over.

Reception studies have also relied upon theses and methods of analyzing messages proposed by semiotically-oriented structuralists (Roland Barthes, Umberto Eco) whose main concern is with the formal qualities of media discourse and with the systems and processes of signification and representation. However, where someone like Barthes or Eco might apply these semiotics methods to texts alone, the practitioners of reception studies would be more concerned to apply these methods to the interpretation of interview data.

It is often said that this approach aims to build a theory of reception that is both critical and empirical. On the one hand, reception studies' point of departure is a critical view of the mass media (based largely on Marxist and neo-Marxist approaches). On the other hand, they share the basic goal of mainstream North American research, which has been to collect empirical evidence about the audience. North American research in the post-war period concentrated on the measurable effects of media on individuals (attributed to direct media exposure) and to a lesser extent, on the changes generated in society attributable to the presence and activities of mass media institutions and their products. This research contributed with an enormous number of empirical investigations to the study of audiences, but later it was strongly criticized.

Criticisms came not only from Marxists and neo-Marxists[71] but also from some empirically-oriented researchers working from within the effects tradition. Marxists and neo-Marxists challenged the entire effects research's paradigm as American liberal-pluralist sociological theory at its worst, as a theory willing to banish questions of conflict and power, and as a theory wiling to presume a functional role for media in a society assumed to have once-and-for-all "achieved" a conflict-free normative consensus. The empirically-oriented insiders, rather than concentrating on media effects on attitudes and opinions, questioned the effects tradition's assumption that the mass media merely and innocently mirror reality and turned to examine how media productively structure and restructure cognitions and perceptions.[72]

Despite the criticisms and the theoretical distance between the effects tradition and reception studies, the latter has a link with one branch of the former, the uses and gratifications school of research. Traditionally, gratificationists have allowed a more active role for the audience than the effects tradition, by stressing that people differentially select and use media to satisfy felt needs. Significantly, gratificationists have also recognized the mediating role played by a person's initiative to select media channel and content in the emergence of patterns of media use.

Thus the uses and gratifications school acknowledged the mediating role of social and psychological factors in mitigating mechanistic media effects and viewed media use as motivated behavior. Additionally, the school recognized that the audience is capable of articulating their own needs and motivations for media consumption, asserting, thereby, that self-reported accounts of media behavior can provide accurate and significant information about media use.

Reception studies share the basic aim of uses and gratifications (i.e., understanding audience media use and its focus on media consumption). Yet they differ from the gratificationists' approach in theory and methodology. In the uses and gratifications model, the individual is the unit of analysis and this individual's self-report is taken in the sample survey format. Reception studies, on the contrary, place the individual in a wider social context. They maintain that the unit of analysis should be the group (a family, a subculture, the residents of a nursing home, etc.), and data gathering techniques should include in-depth interviewing and observation in naturalistic settings. They also claim that small samples, if qualitatively rich, need not hinder the explanatory potential of the analysis. Importantly, in contrast with uses and gratifications analyses, which too-often take verbal accounts at face-value and fail to view them as texts themselves needing interpretation in light of contextual and observational data, reception studies make the interpretation of the interview transcripts a crucial analytical procedure.

The audience is conceptualized as groups of people sharing strategies of understanding (interpretive communities), and media are seen as arenas of ideological struggle where consent is won or lost. The results of these investigations are often ethnographic case studies of social groups and institutions. Three main areas of social use have been suggested: (1) "media use that defines subcultures, (2) "media use as 'frames' for understanding life concerns and experiences," (3) "media use as constitutive of ongoing social interactions and relationships," and (4) "media use as influencing the development of expressive competence."[73]

Some authors of reception studies acknowledge their link to the school of uses and gratificationists, but they have distanced themselves from its individualistic and behavioral orientation by introducing an emphasis on the "social" uses of media. James Lull, for example, states: "I consider my own work to be positioned somewhere between communication studies [quantitative scientific approach] and cultural studies."[74]

Lull's typology of social uses of television was quite helpful for my research. Lull points out that even though "it is somehow arbitrary to distinguish between the personal and interpersonal uses of television," his "inventory and explication of the uses of television...focus directly on their communicative value as social resources."[75] He classifies uses of television in the home into two types: structural and relational. Structural uses include two following subgroups: (1) environmental (background noise, companionship, entertainment) and (2) regulative uses (punctuation of time and activity, talk patterns). Relational uses involve four subgroups: (1) communication facilitation (experience illustration, common ground, conversational entrance, anxiety reduction, agenda for talk, value clarification); (2) affiliation/avoidance (physical, verbal contact/neglect, family solidarity, family relaxant, conflict reduction, relationship maintenance); (3) social learning (decision-making, behavior modeling, problem-solving, value transmission, legitimization, information dissemination, substitute schooling); and (4) competence/dominance (role enactment, role reinforcement, substitute role portrayal, intellectual validation, authority exercise, gatekeeping, argument facilitation).[76]

Lull's typology is a comprehensive one, and I kept it in mind when exploring the social uses of the INI radio stations. However, participatory radio differs greatly from television viewing, which is the typical object of study of reception analysis. Since the beneficiaries of participatory radio projects not only participate in reception but also in production processes, I found it was necessary to modify Lull's typology by incorporating several kinds of uses which account for practices related to, for example, the promotion of ethnic pride, the reproduction of cultural forms, and the utilization of the radio stations as a substitute for telephone and other media. I present specific suggestions, in Chapter 1, about the kind of uses of participatory radio that can be added to those heretofore proposed. It is also important to emphasize that, though I paid attention to both individual and family uses, I was especially concerned with the uses of a larger group, the ethnic community. In the next section I discuss the current research of Latin American authors who, like other authors of reception studies, have also focused on reception processes but have paid closer attention to the social uses of mass media developed by populations more akin to the indigenous peoples using the INI radio stations.

Latin American Media Research

In Latin America, the way of conceptualizing the audience has moved away from the idea of extremely powerful media to an emerging model that takes into account processes of negotiation of meaning, appropriation of technology, and re-functionalization of media and their messages. A major characteristic of Latin American communication research is the attention given to the question of power. One may trace the evolution of communication research in the region by analyzing how the conceptualization of power has evolved in different approaches. Most of the research done during the 1960s and 70s focused either on media structures or on media texts, while audiences were conceptualized as passive individuals. Even studies on the ideological effects of cultural products, such as *telenovelas* or comic strips (done along the line of research initiated by Armand Mattelart), were essentially text-centered and did not recognize the active role of the reader. During the 1970s, then, there was a view of power as something concrete and localized in media ownership and production capacity. In the 1980s, however, power was conceptualized as something diffuse and abstract, as something relating, as Foucault put it, to occupying a "strategic position." Since researchers no longer support the theory of direct ideological manipulation, concentrating on media institutions and texts became less popular. Researchers' interest shifted to describing the subtle and complex ways in which consent and resistance emerge and are interwoven.

By the mid 1980s, the interest in *cultura popular* was already thriving in Latin American communication research.[77] One leading figure, Jesús Martín Barbero, has emphasized the need to investigate mass-mediated communication processes from a perspective sensitive to interpreting subjects and to processes of mediations. He states that these processes should be examined as an articulation between communication practices and social movements.[78] Mediations are often defined as the multiplicity of subjects, processes, institutions, and cultural matrices that filter hegemonic messages and interact with their reception. Or, as Robert White puts it, mediations are "the points of articulation and interaction between the processes of media production on the one hand and the daily routine of media use in the context of family, community and nation."[79]

Like culturalists, Latin American researchers focus on people's media experience. They also share with cultural studies a view of the relation of audiences to mass culture that is less pessimistic than the Frankfurt School's.

The culturalists' point concerning the ways in which popular audiences use and integrate mass media products into their culture has been highlighted especially well by Latin Americans. Nestor García Canclini, for instance, has stressed the need to examine how media products may help subaltern classes cope with modern life; he has suggested that television may serve as a *manual de urbanidad* (etiquette book) for peasants new to the cities, operating as a kind of "users manual" to provide advice on unfamiliar urban ways of dressing, eating, and expressing oneself.[80]

They also like the culturalists adopt Gramsci's concept of hegemony and the view of mass media as an arena of ideological struggle where consent is either won or lost. Martin Barbero, for instance, says that Gramsci's concept of hegemony makes it possible both to see cultural products as strategic sites of struggle over meaning and to view the audience as playing an active role in the politics of meaning.[81] Since the consumption of mass media products is here viewed as central, the study of audiences is itself placed within the broader analysis of consumption, though the broader analysis of Latin American consumption patterns has yet to be elaborated.

Further stressing processes of negotiation of meaning, the audience is often viewed as a social group with multiple options of interacting with media texts. One of the key concepts for understanding this view of the audience is "reading." Reading is seen as a site where meanings are negotiated and where the cultural creativity of the subaltern classes is expressed.[82] It is often argued by these Latin American scholars that the reading of mass media texts is above all a collective activity among popular audiences. The places and the ways in which those readings occur play an important part in the reception of media messages. Luis Alberto Romero, for example, talks of *ámbitos* (a concept similar to that of interpretive communities) and argues that in a given ámbito messages are re-elaborated, commented upon, discussed, and incorporated or rejected, according to the group's collective experience.[83] Martín Barbero also highlights this point by asserting that for the popular classes, reception is an oral process in which the group collectively gives a "rhythm" to the reading, while the text serves only as a point of departure for the display of collective memory.[84]

Concerning radio listening, there is an important group of empirical investigations in which radio is understood in terms of cultural reproduction and as a public space where the struggle over cultural hegemony occurs. Critical in this discussion is radio's role in the cultural reproduction and mediated representation of different social, class, and ethnic groups, plus its role in the discursive struggle to define the nation and its ethnic composition.

In her pioneer work on radio practices, Rosa María Alfaro combines concepts from both Bourdieu's social reproduction theory and Gramsci's concept of hegemony. She maintains that in Peru the popular sectors have started a process of cultural revaluation and alternative construction of meaning inside commercial radio. Her research cast light on how peasants manage to use commercial radio to meet their own collective needs, such as promoting a sense of sharing a larger social reality and helping to reproduce and defend their cultural roots. She sees popular communications as texts in which social relations and processes of exploitation and hegemonic construction can be read from "the point of view of the oppressed."

In her interesting study of low-income women's use of radio melodrama, Alfaro maintains that this genre, by reproducing specific linkages between personal drama and collective life, has become a vital feminine popular discourse, one helping create alternative solutions to familiar, local, and public problems. Alfaro concludes that via the collective reception and discussion of melodramas, poor women are using popular communication as a means for self-education and creating a new feminism. Thus the author views popular communication as providing a moral incentive for social change.[85] This view of popular communication resembles, interestingly enough, the conceptualization of participation proposed by Denis Goulet, who strongly advocates an alternative paradigm of development.[86]

In an early piece, Javier Albó stressed the importance of alternative radio practices in Bolivian commercial radio. Albó examined radio programs produced in commercial stations by ex-campesinos and broadcast in their vernacular languages. These new immigrants to the cities would buy broadcast time at commercial stations and then seek funding from small merchants and their working class listeners in exchange for paid announcements (avisos) and music dedications (saludos). The programs became very popular in Bolivia during the 1970s, even in big cities. According to Albó, programs prepared by ex-campesinos not only have an alternative content, but also work with a very different style, which is repetitive, very personal, and composed using a concrete language; the native listener thus assimilates emotionally the whole broadcasting style more than specific contents. On these grounds, Albó contends that regardless of the intended ideological (integration of the peasantry to consumer society) and commercial functions of these programs, their implicit functions are beneficial to the popular sectors because they bolster indigenous creativity, they become a channel of expression for culturally oppressed groups, and they promote solidarity among indigenous people by fostering ethnic identity.[87]

In addition to this handful of investigations, some authors have dealt briefly with the appropriation of modern communication media by indigenous ethnic groups, but their investigations have not specifically addressed the reception issues. Catharine Good Eshelman, for example, briefly described the social importance of cassette-players among the Nahuas,[88] and García Canclini commented briefly on the use of cassette-players among the Purépechas (also called Tarascos), a group served by the INI station, XEPUR.[89]

As White correctly suggests, even though the trend in Latin American media research has borrowed heavily from European thinkers, especially Gramsci, Bourdieu, Foucault, and members of the Birmingham School, Latin American researchers' involvement with grassroots movements, coupled with their long standing commitment to the democratization of communication policies, has resulted in certain theoretical orientation characterized by a preoccupation to democratize communication resources and society.[90] This orientation has allowed them to move beyond the effects paradigm and beyond the examination of individual readings of media texts to focus more on the way subaltern groups interact with, interpret, resist, and sometimes even use available media in their survival strategies.

It is following this line of thought that I have examined radio practices and indigenous participation taking place in the INI radio network. Because I was unable to find the conceptual and methodological insights needed for the research in the existing literature on participatory radio, I turned to cultural approaches to mass media. To offer a general idea of how the typical research on Latin American participatory/community-oriented radio stations has been conducted, I finish this appendix by briefly discussing a number of studies on these stations.

The Research on Latin American Participatory Radio

In many Third World countries the end of the colonial era and the recent resurgence of ethnic groups from within the modern state have been accompanied with the rise of numerous community radio stations broadcasting for minority audiences. This type of radio broadcasting has prospered considerably in Latin America. Despite their similarities, Latin American community-oriented stations differ greatly in their degree of popular participation. Self-managed stations have been the mass media outlet of popular organizations and frequently have been organized around subaltern groups' political resistance; whereas some of them have operated as clandestine stations (e.g., the Salvadorean Radio Venceremos), others have operated more or less within the state's legal framework (e.g., the Bolivian miners' radio and the Mexican Radio Ayuntamiento Popular de Juchitán). Stations allowing only limited degrees of audience participation have generally been funded and operated by the state, international agencies, or religious organizations, such as the Catholic Church, the Baha'i Faith, or one of several Protestant denominations. Typically, the stated purpose of these latter stations has been quite narrowly framed as being concerned with "improving living conditions." Seldom, if ever, have they gone beyond their stated purpose to question openly the political and economic structures that shape local "living conditions."

The research on Latin American participatory stations can be divided in a general fashion into two broad categories: one composed of studies done from the traditional perspective of development communications,[91] and another including works that narrate or review specific radio experiences from the point of view of counter-hegemonic media.[92] In the first category the purpose of the analysis is scientific evaluation, while in the second category the study is chiefly a historiographic effort to record alternative communication. Most of the studies fail to understand radio as a communication medium in which social practices are constructed, and most importantly, they fail to consider fully reception processes. I should note that several of these studies were undertaken at least a decade ago, when most research in development communications was done within the orthodox paradigm of development and often centered on the analysis of media institutions and their products, failing to look at reception processes. Thus the current concerns with popular participation and negotiation of meanings are beyond the scope of the research done at the time.

For those authors who view participatory radio stations from the traditional perspective of development communications, the crucial point is to determine the extent to which radio is "effective" for a certain development program. They examine design and implementation strategies, then try to identify the difficulties and obstacles that prevent the project's maximum utilization, and suggest corrective measures. Ultimately, they hope to understand the limits of the medium in promoting development.

By contrast, for those authors concerned with alternative media, what is critical is establishing the possibility of counter-hegemonic media institutions. The issue of power is a key concern for these authors, but their conceptualization of power in society is based on a Manichaean opposition between dominance and resistance. Often they neglect to examine the intricate and complex relations existing between elites and popular classes, including forms of adaptation, negotiation, co-optation, and alliance. A consequence of this Manichaean opposition and of this neglect of the complex interactions between those with power and those resisting it is that these authors frequently argue that self-managed stations are, by their very nature, conducive to social change, while those with different institutional arrangements (such as commercial radio or stations sponsored by outside agents) are regarded as incapable of generating any systemic change. As a result of this overemphasis on issues of ownership and allocative control, as important as they are, those popular communication practices taking place inside stations with less than fully democratic institutional structures have been neglected. The authors of these studies often assume that media texts are monosemic and that the audience is composed of passive "receivers."

In short, in most of the research on Latin American community-oriented stations, there is no model for examining the radio practices of subaltern groups and the social value of participatory radio. Although many of the studies discuss, some extensively, the issue of local participation, the priority given to media institutions and texts, and the neglect of media consumption makes any analysis of popular communication practices and their articulation with multiple aspects of social reality very difficult.[93]

How much we overcome the limiting perspective that reduces the phenomenon of people's radio to just the analysis of media structures depends on our openness to account for the socio-political context in which community-oriented stations operate. This context has, for the most part, prevented the emergence of truly autonomous and self-managed radio stations, yet it has allowed simultaneously the growth of popular communication practices around community-oriented stations sponsored by outside agents, and in countries like Peru and Bolivia, inside commercial systems. It is in this framework that the vast majority of popular participatory radio practices take place in Latin America. And it is only by recognizing that participatory practices have been created in stations with diverse institutional structures that we, as development communicators, might be able to cast light on the social value of participatory radio.

Notes

1. Thomas Jacobson, "Modernization and Post-modernization Approaches to Participatory Communication for Development," Unpublished essay, 1989, 1.

2. See for example Wilbur Schramm, *Mass Media and National Development* (Stanford: Stanford University Press, 1964) 119.

3. Here I use the adjective "critical" to refer to all those authors who are critical of the post-war modernization paradigm of development. It includes authors who work within the framework of the political economy paradigm, but it is not limited to them.

4. Georgette Wang and Wimal Dissanayake, "Culture, Development, and Change: Some Explorative Observations," *Continuity and Change in Communication Systems: An Asian Perspective*, eds. Georgette Wang and Wimal Dissanayake (Norwood, NJ: Ablex, 1984) 5.

5. Charles Wilber and Kenneth Jameson, "Paradigms of Economic Development and Beyond," *The Political Economy of Development and Underdevelopment*, ed. Wilber K. Charles, 3rd ed. (New York: Random House, 1984) 4-14.

6. Wilber and Jameson 13. Other authors view the growth-with-equity approach as a different paradigm altogether. See for example Uma Narula and W. Barnett Pearce, *Development as Communication* (Carbondale and Edwardsville: Southern Illinois UP, 1986).

7. Dieter Senghaas, "The Case of Autarchy," *Development* 2/3 (1980): 17-22.

8. Michael Lofchie and Stephen K. Commins, "Food Deficits and Agricultural Policies in Tropical Africa," *The Political Economy of Development and Underdevelopment*, ed. Charles K. Wilber, 3rd ed. (New York: Random House, 1984) 222-41.

9. James H. Weaver and Marguerite Berger, "The Marxist Critique of Dependency Theory: An Introduction," *The Political Economy of Development and Underdevelopment*, ed. Wilber K. Charles, 3rd ed. (New York: Random House, 1984) 45-64.

10. Wilber and Jameson 13.

11. Denis Goulet, *The Cruel Choice: A New Concept in the Theory of Development* (New York: Atheneum, 1978).

12. For an overview and analysis of the Latin American contribution to development studies, see Cristóbal Kay, *Latin American Theories of Development and Underdevelopment* (London: Routhledge, 1989).

13. Pablo González Casanova, *La Democracia en México* 17th ed. (México: Era, 1987) 104.

14. Guillermo Bonfil Batalla, comp."Declaración de San José sobre el Etnocidio y el Etnodesarrollo," *América Latina: Etnodesarrollo y Etnocidio* (San José, Costa Rica: Ediciones FLACSO, 1982) 24.

15. Bonfil Batalla, *Etnodesarrollo*, 142; Salomón Nahmad Sittón, "Indoamérica y Educación: ¿Etnocidio o Etnodesarrollo?," *México Pluricultural. De la Castellanización a la Educación Indígena Bilingüe y Bicultural* (SEP), eds. Patricia Scalon Arlene and Juan Lezama Morfin (México: Editorial Porrúa, 1982) 21-42.

16. Jacobson 3.

17. Jacobson 4.

18. According to A. T. Ariyaratne, the movement was active in 8,000 villages, reaching nearly three million people; A. T. Ariyaratne, "Beyond Development Communication," *Rethinking Development Communication*, eds. Neville Jayaweera and Sarath Amunugama (Singapore: AMIC, 1987) 243.

19. Ariyaratne 239.

20. Ariyaratne 241-42.

21. Wimal Dissanayake, "A Buddhist Approach to Development," *Continuity and Change in Communication Systems: An Asian Perspective*, eds. Georgette Wang and Wimal Dissanayake (Norwood, NJ: Ablex, 1984) 39-52.

22. Nicola Abbagnano, *Diccionario de Filosofía*, trans. Alfredo N. Galleti, 2nd Spanish ed. (México: Fondo de Cultura Económica, 1974) 490-4.

23. Paulo Freire, *Education for Critical Consciousness* (New York: Seasbury Press, 1973) 44-5.

24. Abbagnano 490-4.

25. Freire 136.

26. Freire *48*.

27. Freire, 45.

28. Freire 44-5.

29. Luis Ramiro Beltrán, "A Farewell to Aristotle: 'Horizontal' Communication," *Communication* 5 (1980): 5-41.

30. Jeremiah O'Sullivan Ryan and Mario Kaplún, "Communication Methods to Promote Grass-roots Participation," *Communication and Society* 6 (n.d.): 11.

31. O'Sullivan Ryan et al. 4.

32. Boris A. Lima, *Exploración Tèorica de la Participación* (Buenos Aires: Humanitas, 1988) 27.

33. O'Sullivan Ryan et al. 6.

34. Robert C. Hornik, *Development Communications. Information, Agriculture, and Nutrition in the Third World* (New York: Longman, 1988) xii.

35. Quoted in United Nations Research Institute for Social Development, *Inquiry into Participation: A Research Approach*, by Andrew Pearse and Matthias Stiefel, 79/

c/14. (Geneva: United Nations, May 1979) n. pag.

36. Denis Goulet, "Participation in Development: New Avenues," *World Development* 17/2 (1989): 172.

37. Goulet "Participation."

38. Denis Goulet, *The Cruel Choice* 16.

39. Beltrán 27-28.

40. Beltrán 31.

41. Beltrán 33.

42. John Lent, "Devcom: A View from the United States," *Rethinking Development Communications*, eds. Neville Jayaweera and Sarath Amunugama (Singapore: AMIC, 1987) 20.

43. Wimal Dissanayake, "Development and Communication: An Interpretive Approach," International Communication Association Convention, San Francisco, 28 May, 1989, 4.

44. United Nations Research Institute for Social Development, n.pag.

45. United Nations Research Institute for Social Development, n.pag.

46. United Nations Research Institute for Social Development, n.pag.

47. Goulet, "Participation" 172.

48. Goulet, "Participation."

49. Neither the variable "Scope" nor "Reach" indicate geographical territory.

50. Goulet, "Participation" 166.

51. Dean T. Jamison and Emile McAnany, *Radio for Education and Development* (Beverly Hills: Sage, 1978) 91.

52. Ron Lembo, "Is There Culture After Cultural Studies?," *Audiences and Cultural Reception*, eds. Jon Cruz and Justine Lewis (Boulder, CO: Westview, 1994) 34.

53. As opposed to Gramsci, Althusser views media in terms of "ideological state apparatuses" which exert a deliberate and pervasive cultural influence on subaltern classes to assure the reproduction of capitalism. Although Althusser's ideas regarding media's domination have not been dropped from the current debate (e.g., some of the advocates of hegemony theory), the debate has definitely moved closer to the Gramscian notions of sites of ideological struggle.

54. Joseph V. Femia, *Gramsci's Political Thought* (New York: Oxford UP, 1987) 50.

55. Stuart Hall, "Cultural Studies: Two Paradigms," *Media Culture and Society. A Critical Reader*, eds. Richard Collins, James Curran, Nicholas Garnham, Paddy Scannell, Philip Schlesinger and Colin Sparks (London: Sage 1986) 33-48.

56. Hall, "Two Paradigms" 39.

57. Hall, "Two Paradigms" 43-45.

58. Graeme Turner, *British Cultural Studies* (New York: Routledge: 1992) 94.

59. Stuart Hall, "Reflections upon the Encoding/Decoding Model: An Interview with Stuart Hall," *Viewing, Reading, Listening*, eds. Jon Cruz and Justin Lewis (Boulder, CO: Westview, 1994) 255-56.

60. Pierre Bourdieu, *Distinction, A Social Critique of the Judgement of Taste*, trans. Richard Nice (Cambridge: Harvard UP, 1984) 13.

61. Bourdieu 7.

62. Bourdieu 21.

63. For an example on this perspective, see John Fiske, "Moments of Television:

Neither the Text nor the Audience," *Remote Control*, 2nd ed., eds. Ellen Seiter, Hans Borchers, Gabriele Kreutzner, and Eva-Maria Warth (New York: Routledge, 1991) 56-78.

64. Bourdieu 6.

65. Other terms often employed to refer to this line of research are "qualitative audience research," "reception studies," and "social semiotics."

66. Shaun Moores, *Interpreting Audiences* (London: Sage, 1993) 7.

67. Moores 35.

68. John Fiske, "British Cultural Studies and Television." *Channels of Discourse*, ed. Robert C. Allen (Chapel Hill: U of North Carolina Press, 1988) 272.

69. David Morley, *Family Television: Cultural Power and Domestic Leisure* (London: Routledge, 1988).

70. Dorothy Hobson, *Crossroads: The Drama of a Soap Opera* (London: Methuen, 1982).

71. According to Denis McQuail, Marxist approaches to the media include, in addition to British cultural studies, four main currents: the Frankfurt School, political-economy theory, structuralist analyses, and hegemony theory, *Mass Communication Theory* (London: Sage, 1984) 59-64.

72. New hypotheses emerged regarding the long-term effects of media which see effects not as particular behavioral changes but as the structuration and restructuration of cognitions and perceptions. These hypotheses assert that media define or construct reality rather than just reflect it. Among them are, for example, M. McCombs and D. L. Shaw's idea of the "agenda setting" role played by media, E. Noelle-Neumann's thesis regarding opinion forming ("spiral of silence"), and G. Gerbner's cultivation theory. McQuail 175-211.

73. Thomas R. Lindlof and Timothy P. Meyer, "Mediated Communication as Ways of Seeing, Acting, and Constructing Culture: The Tools and Foundations of Qualitative Research," *Natural Audiences*, ed. Thomas R. Lindlof (Norwood, NJ: Ablex, 1987) 13-14.

74. James Lull, *Inside Family Viewing* (London: Routledge, 1990) 20.

75. Lull 35.

76. Lull 36. The author presents these uses in a chart.

77. Readers not familiar with the Spanish language may need to realize that the Spanish *"cultura popular"* has a different connotation from the English "popular culture." Because of the history of colonization and the multiethnic composition of Latin American nations, the Spanish adjective *"popular"* (e.g., *"sectores populares"*) has been often used to refer to peasant populations composed either of indigenous people or of mestizos with strong links to indigenous cultures. More recently, authors have been using the term *"sectores populares urbanos."* In any case, a point of contention in the discussion has been the kind of mass communication products and practices that can be considered genuine popular cultural forms.

78. Jesús Martín Barbero *De los Medios a las Mediaciones: Comunicación, Cultura y Hegemonía* (Barcelona: Gustavo Gilli, 1987) 1.

79. Robert White, "The Latin American Contribution to Communication Theory," ts. Centro Interdisciplinare Sulla Communicazione Sociale, La Universidad Gregoriana, Roma, 16.

80. Néstor García Canclini, "Cultura Transnacional y Culturas Populares: Bases

Teórico-Metodológicas para la Investigación," (Lima: IPAL, 1985). 38-39.

81. Martín Barbero, *De los Medios* 85.

82. Martín Barbero, *De los Medios*.

83. Luis Alberto Romero, "Los Sectores Populares Urbanos como Sujetos Históricos," ts., U de Buenos Aires, 18-19.

84. Martín Barbero, *De los Medios* 115.

85. Rosa María Alfaro, "La Pugna por la Hegemonía en la Radio Peruana," *Diálogos* 18 (1987): 62-73.

86. Goulet, *Participation in Development*.

87. Javier Albó, *Idiomas, Escuelas y Radios en Bolivia* (La Paz: Centro de Investigación y Promoción del Campesinado, 1977).

88. Catharine Good Eshelman, *Haciendo la Lucha. Arte y Comercio Nahuas de Guerrero* (México: Fondo de Cultura Económica, 1988) 63-65.

89. Néstor García Canclini, *Las Culturas Populares en el Capitalismo* (México: Nueva Imagen, 1986) 85-86.

90. White 15-16.

91. The assumptions of this perspective, typical of the literature published in the 1970s, are still found in recent publications; see for example: Stephan F. Brumberg, "Colombia: A Multimedia Rural Education Program," *Education for Rural Development*, eds. Manzoor Ahmed and Philip H. Coombs (New York: Praeger: 1975) 1-60, and other case studies in the same volume; Sylvia Schmelkes de Sotelo, "The Radio Schools of the Tarahumara, Mexico: an Evaluation," *Radio for Education and Development: Case Studies*, eds. Peter Spain, Dean T. Jamison and Emile McAnany, Vol. 1 World Bank Staff Working Paper No. 266 (Washington: World Bank, 1977); Asociación Latinoamericana de Educación Radiofónica, *Análisis de los Sistemas de Educación Radiofónica* (Quito: ALER, 1982); Jeremiah O'Sullivan Ryan, *Radio Occidente. El Pueblo Dialoga con el Pueblo* (Quito: ALER, 1987); and Kurt John Hein, *Radio Bahá'í, Ecuador. A Bahá'í Development Project*, (Oxford: George Ronald, 1988). In addition, one may include in this category general works on development communications in Latin America, such as Dean T. Jamison and Emile McAnany, *Radio for Education and Development* (Beverly Hills: Sage, 1978).

92. For example Alfonso Gamucio Dagron, "El Papel Político de las Radios Mineras. Un Documento para su Historia," *Comunicación y Cultura* 8 (1982): 89-99; Antonio Oseguera, "Una Experiencia de Comunicación Educativa para el Desarrollo Rural," *Comunicación y Cultura* 8 (1982): 33-38; Jorge Villalobos Gryzbowics, and Felipe Espinosa Torres, *Huayacocotla y Teocelo* (México: Fomento Cultural y Educativo, 1987).

93. Perhaps an exception to this general pattern is the research of Alan O'Connor who has examined indigenous radio in Ecuador and Bolivia from a cultural studies perspective. His work is more akin to the research done by Alfaro. However, his articles lack the "thick description" that, I find, is necessary to be able to connect, for example, issues of ideology to specific social practices. See Alan O'Connor, "Indigenous Radio in Ecuador: Issues of Institution, Cultural Form and Hegemony," International Communication Association, San Francisco, 1989; and Alan O'Connor, "The Bolivian Miners' Radios in the Late 1980s," Union for Democratic Communications, New York, 1989.

Appendix 2:
Interview Schedules

Focus Groups Interview Schedule

1. When you were children and used to live in small villages, can you recall how people used to find out about the things going on in the village? Also can you tell us how villagers found out about events happening in other places?

2. How do you find out about things going on in the village and other places now? Do you feel the radio station has integrated, substituted or reinforced the forms of communication you have just mentioned?

3. Tell us about one or two conversations which you have had about the station (e.g., its programming, coverage) that have impressed you. These conversations may include one in which you participated or one that you overheard.

4. Which do you think are the three most important programs for the local people (*espacios*) broadcast by the station?

5. Do you think that the so-called "national culture" (Spanish) has imposed a kind of cultural domination on the local indigenous peoples. And, if you believe this is so, in which ways has the station contributed to counteract this process of cultural domination?

6. Do you think that the station is really a participatory medium? Describe what you would consider participatory and non-participatory aspects of the station. (This question tends to elicit mainly participatory aspects. When this happen I used the following commentary to encourage the group to talk about non-participatory aspects: "Most of you said that this station is a participatory medium, however, I sometimes wonder about your opinion because the station's institutional structure seems authoritarian and the local people, including you, play a very limited role in the most important aspects of planning and decision making.")

7. If you could change one or two things regarding the way in which the station operates, in order to make this more open and more sensible

to the needs of the local ethnic groups, what would you change?

8. You know that there is a lot of talk about transferring of INI's functions directly to the ethnic groups (e.g., Warman's 1989 document). What do you think will happen if they transfer the operation of this station to the indigenous peoples? What do you think would be the positive and negative consequences of such an act? What are the obstacles for such transferring? Do you see any intermediate solution for this problems?

9. Tell us what you think are the positive and negative sides of having a member of the ethnic groups as director of this station.

Audience Interview Schedule

1. How many people are in this family?
2. Are all of them present now?
3. Here at your home, how many radio receivers do you have?
4. How many do you use?
5. Where are they?
6. If they operate with batteries, how often do you put new batteries in your sets? (Is it a major expense? Is it an insignificant expense?)
7. How long have you lived in this village?
8. What do you do for a living?
8.1. If peasant:
   Do you work your own land?
   Do you hire people to work for you? How often?
   Do you work for someone else? (Agriculture) How often?
   Do you combine agricultural work with other non-agricultural work?
9. What do you do to get some cash?
10. Do you own animals?
9.1. if yes: how many of which kind?
11. Which family members are attending school?
12. Which family members know how to read and write?
13. Which family members speak Spanish?
14. Do all family members speak Tojolabal?

Part Two

15. At what time do you listen to Radio Margaritas? Is there any time of the day or any day of the week that you prefer listening to Radio Margaritas?
16. Who in the family listens to Radio Margaritas the most? Who listens the least?
17. Who usually turns on the radio receiver? Has any member of the family his or her own receiver?

18. Please describe the things you like the most of Radio Margaritas' broadcasts. (Prompt: The music? Which kind of music? When they speak indigenous languages? When they talk about traditional medicine? The news?)

19. Tell us about the things that you like the least from Radio Margaritas broadcasts.

20. Have you ever visited Radio Margaritas? Do you know any person that has gone to Radio Margaritas? Had you ever thought about visiting Radio Margaritas?

21. What do you know about Radio Margaritas anniversary festival? Have you ever attended one of these festivals? Do you know someone who has attended them? What have you heard about this festivals?

22. Tell us about one or two conversations which you have had about Radio Margaritas that have impressed you. This conversations may include one in which you participated or one that you overheard.

23. Radio Margaritas says that it is "the Voice of the Southern Border." Do you think that the station is *really* the voice of your people? Do they broadcast things that are interesting for you and your community? Do they talk about the things you and the people from Tabasco/Madero and other Tojolabal villages want to hear about it?

24. If you could change one or two things about Radio Margaritas in order to make the radio station more open and more sensitive to the needs of the indigenous peoples, what would you change?

25. What kind of things would you like Radio Margaritas to play? (Prompt: Would you like the station to play different music? Would you broadcast what kind of programs? Would you broadcast more hours? Would you have announcers speaking Tojolabal most of the time? Would you improve the technical quality?)

26. Some people do not like Radio Margaritas and they would like the station to be closed, what do you think about this? Do you agree with them or do you prefer that Radio Margaritas continue broadcasting?

27. When you were children, can you recall how people used to find out about the things going on in the village? Also can you tell us how villagers found out about events happening in other places?

28. How do you find out about thinks going on in the village and other places now? Do you feel the radio station has integrated, substituted or reinforced the forms of communication you have just mentioned?

29. When you were children, can you recall if people used to play music to entertain themselves? Which kind of music?

30. Are people still playing this type of music? Do you feel Radio Margaritas has integrated, substituted or reinforced the music and activities you have just mentioned?

31. Do you think that the people around here do things in ways that are more similar to the way ladinos *(ricos)* live than to the way your grandparents used to live? Do you think that the traditional mores of Tojolabals are being lost? And, if you believe this is so, in which ways has Radio Margaritas contributed to reinforce these traditions?

FIGURE A.2 Sample of the Audience Study

Family	Village	Number of interviewees	Interviewees	Interviewer's gender
F1	Tabasco	6	f, m, gm, fb, mn, fn	Man
F2	Tabasco	4	f, m, d, dl	Man
F3	Tabasco	6	f, m, gf, s1, s2, dl	Man
F4	Tabasco	4	f, m, s1, s2	Man
F5	Tabasco	4	f, m, mn, fn	Man
F6	Tabasco	5	f, m, s	Woman
F7	Tabasco	3	f, m, fb	Woman
F9	Madero	2	f, m	Woman
F10	Madero	2	f, m	Woman
F11	Madero	2	f, m	Man
F13	Madero	2	f, fs	Man
F14	Madero	1	m	Man
F15	Madero	2	f, m	Woman
F16	Madero	2	f, m	Woman
F17	Tabasco	2	f, m	Woman
F18	Tabasco	2	f, m	Woman
F19	Madero	2	f, m	Woman
F20	Madero	2	f, s	Woman
F21	Madero	2	f, m	Woman
F22	Madero	2	f, m	Woman
F23	Madero	2	f, m	Woman

Code: f=father, m=mother, s=son, d=daughter, gf=grandfather,
gm=grandmother, dl=daughter-in-law, fb=father's brother, fs=father's sister,
mn=male neighbor, fn=female neighbor

References

Abbagnano, Nicola. *Diccionario de Filosofía*. Trans. Afredo N. Galleti. 2nd. Spanish ed. México: Fondo de Cultura Económica, 1974.

Ahued, Eduardo. "El Archivo Etnográfico Audiovisual." Instituto Nacional Indigenista, *Instituto Nacional Indigenista: 40 Años*. México: Instituto Nacional Indigenista, 1988. 540-545.

Albó, Javier. *Idiomas, Escuelas y Radios en Bolivia*. La Paz: Centro de Investigación y Promoción del Campesinado, 1977.

Aguirre Beltrán, Gonzalo. "Derrumbe de Paradigmas." Seminario Permanente Sobre Indigenismo. Jalapa, Veracruz, CIESAS Del Golfo, March 30, 1990.

Alfaro, Rosa María. "La Pugna por la Hegemonía Cultural en la Radio Peruana." *Diá-logos* 18 (1987): 62-73.

—. "Modelos Radiales y Proceso de Popularización de la Radio Limeña." Unpublished essay, 1984.

Aranda Bezaury, Josefina and Verónica Valenzuela. "Investigación sobre la Presencia Radiofónica de la Voz de la Montaña en las Comunidades." Unpublished essay. 1982.

Arce Quintanilla, Oscar. "Del Indigenismo a la Indianidad. Cincuenta Años de Indigenismo Continental." *Instituto Nacional Indigenista: 40 Años*. Ed. Instituto Nacional Indigenista. México: Instituto Nacional Indigenista, 1988. 105-120.

Ariyaratne, A. T. "Beyond Development Communication." *Rethinking Development Communication*. Eds. Neville Jayaweera and Sarath Amunugama. Singapore: AMIC, 1987. 239-251.

Asociación Latinoamericana de Educación Radiofónica. *Análisis de los Sistemas de Educación Radiofónica*. Series investigaciones I. Quito: ALER, 1982.

Bartolomé, Miguel and Alicia Barabas. Forward. *Zapotec Struggles*. By Bartolomé and Barabas. Howard Campbell, Leight Binford, Miguel Bartolomé, and Alicia Barabas, eds. Washington: Smithsonian Institution Press, 1993. xi-xv.

Beltrán, Luis Ramiro. "A Farewell to Aristotle: 'Horizontal' Communication." *Communication*, 5 (1980): 5-41.

Bonfil Batalla, Guillermo. "Lo Propio y lo Ajeno. Una Aproximación al Problema del Control Cultural." *La Cultura Popular*. 5th. ed. Comp. Adolfo Colombres. México: Premiá, 1987. 79-86.

—. *México Profundo. Una Civilización Negada*. México: Secretaría de Educación Pública, 1987.

—, ed. *Utopia y Revolución: El Pensamiento Contemporáneo de los Indios en América Latina.* 2nd ed. México: Editorial Nueva Imagen, 1988.

—, comp. *América Latina: Etnodesarrollo y Etnocidio.* San José, Costa Rica: Ediciones FLACSO, 1982.

Bourdieu, Pierre. *Distinction. A Social Critique of the Judgement of Taste.* Trans. Richard Nice. Cambridge: Harvard UP, 1984.

Brody, Mary Jill. "Discourse Processes of Highlighting in Tojolabal Maya Morphosyntax." Diss. Washington U, 1982.

—. "Discourse Genres in Tojolabal." *The Tojolabal Maya: Ethnographic and Linguistic Approaches. Geoscience and Man* 26. Eds. Mary Jill Brody and John S. Thomas. Baton Rouge: Louisiana State U, 1988. 55-63.

— and John S. Thomas, eds. *The Tojolabal Maya: Ethnographic and Linguistic Approaches. Geoscience and Man* 26. Baton Rouge: Louisiana State U, 1988.

Browne, Donald R. "Aboriginal Radio in Australia: From Dreamtime to Primetime?" *Journal of Communication* 40.1 (1990): 111-120.

Brumberg, Stephan F. "Colombia: A Multimedia Rural Education Program." *Education for Rural Development.* Eds. Ahmed Manzoor and Philip H. Coombs. New York: Praeger, 1975. 1-60.

Cabrera, Lucas Rosendo. "El Mensaje y la Imaginación del Radioescucha." Unpublished essay, 1989.

Campbell, Howard, Leight Binford, Miguel Bartolomé, and Alicia Barabas, eds. *Zapotec Struggles.* Washington: Smithsonian Institution Press, 1993.

Campos, Teresa. "El Sistema Médico de los Tojolabales." *Los Legítimos Hombres. Aproximación Antropológica al Mundo Tojolabal.* Ed. Mario Humberto Ruz. México: UNAM, 1983. 195-223.

Carey, James W. "A Cultural Approach to Communication." *Communication,* 2 (1975): 1-22.

Castañeda Peñabronce, Odilón. "Las Lenguas Indígenas en la XEZV." XEZV Foro. Tlapa, Guerrero, México, March, 1989.

Castañón Gamboa, Fernando. "Panorama Histórico de las Comunicaciones en Chiapas." *Lecturas Chiapanecas* 2. Ed. Cuauhtémoc López Sánchez. México: Editorial Porrúa y Gobierno del Estado de Chiapas, 1988. 279-328.

Chapkis, Wendy. *Beauty Secrets. Women and the Politics of Appearance.* Boston: South End Press, 1986.

Colombres, Adolfo, ed. *La Cultura Popular.* México: Premiá, 1987.

—. *La Hora del Bárbaro.* 2nd edition. México: Premiá, 1984.

Comisión del Río Balsas. Dirección de Información y Comunicación Social. "Anteproyecto para la Instalación de una Radiodifusora en Tlapa, Guerrero." Internal document. ts. n.d.

Consejo Consultivo del Programa Nacional de Solidaridad. *El Combate a la Pobreza.* México: El Nacional, 1990.

Cornejo, Inés. "La Voz de la Mixteca y la Comunidad Receptora de la Mixteca Oaxaqueña." M.A. Thesis, U Iberoamericana, 1990.

Cruz Merino, Fernando. "Mejoramiento de Transmisión y Calidad Noticiera." XEZV Foro. Tlapa, Guerrero, México, March, 1989.

Cruz Tito, Filomena. "La Mujer Indígena y la Voz de la Montaña." XEZV Foro. Tlapa, Guerrero, México, March, 1989.

Dagron, Alfonso Gumucio. "El Papel Político de las Radios Mineras. Un Documento para su Historia." *Comunicación y Cultura* 8 (1982): 89-99.

Díaz Bordenave, Juan E. *¿Qué es Comunicación Rural? Necesidad y Reto en América Latina.* México: Carrasquilla Editores, 1987.

—. *Communication and Rural Development.* Belgium: UNESCO, 1977.

Dissanayake, Wimal. "Development and Communication: An Interpretive Approach." International Communication Association Convention. San Francisco, 28 May, 1989.

—. "A Buddist Approach to Development. *Continuity and Change in Communication Systems: An Asian Perspective.* Eds. Georgette Wang and Wimal Dissanayake. Norwood, NJ: Ablex, 1984. 39-52.

Dodson, Michael. "Failed Development and the Rise of Religious Fundamentalism in Central America." Unpublished essay, 1990.

Dominick, Joseph, R. *The Dynamics of Mass Communication.* 3rd ed. New York: McGraw-Hill, 1990.

"El Comandante Marcos, al Periódico *L'Unita:*" Mejor Morir Combatiendo que Morir de Disentería,'" *Proceso*, 10 Jan. 1994: 8-9.

Encinas, Valverde, Orlando. "Radio Mezquital: Posibilidades de Comunicación Popular." *Comunicación y Cultura* 8 (1982): 19-31.

Espinoza, Luis. "Lenguas y Dialectos de las Diversas Tribus que Pueblan el Estado de Chiapas y Lugares Donde se Hablan." *Lecturas Chiapanecas* 2. Ed. Cuauhtémoc López Sánchez. México: Editorial Porrúa y Gobierno del Estado de Chiapas, 1988. 123-126.

Esteva Gustavo. *La Batalla en el México Rural.* 6th ed. México: Siglo XXI, 1987.

Estrada, Marta Patricia. "XENAC." Unpublished essay, 1990.

Fanon, Frantz. *Black Skin, White Masks.* New York: Grove Press, 1967.

Femia, Joseph V. *Gramsci's Political Tought.* New York: Oxford UP, 1987.

Flores, Ana Lydia. "Prioridad en Comunidades Indígenas de Eloxochitán, el Aprendizaje del Español." *El Universal* 15 July 1990, 2.

Fiske, John. "British Cultural Studies and Television." *Channels of Discourse.* Ed. Robert C. Allen. Chapel Hill, U of North Carolina Press, 1988. 254-289.

—. "Moments of Television: Neither the Text nor the Audience." *Remote Control.* 2nd ed. Eds. Ellen Seiter, Hans Borchers, Gabriele Kreutzner, and Eva-Maria Warth. New York: Routledge, 1991. 56-78.

Freire, Paulo. *Education for Critical Consciousness.* New York: Seasbury Press, 1973.

—. *Pedagogía del Oprimido.* Trans. Jorge Mellado. 36th ed. México: Siglo XXI,1987.

—. *La Educación como Práctica de la Libertad.* México: Siglo XXI, 1971.

Fuego, Emilio. "Una Estación de Radio en el Lugar de los Espantos." Unpublished essay, 1986.

Furbee Losee, Louanna. *The Correct Language: Tojolabal. A Grammar with Ethnographic Notes.* New York: Garland Publishing, 1976.

—. "To Ask one Holy Thing: Petition as a Tojolabal Maya Speech Genre." *The Tojolabal Maya: Ethnographic and Linguistic Approaches. Geoscience and Man 26.* Eds. Mary Jill Brody and John S. Thomas. Baton Rouge: Louisiana State U, 1988. 39-53.

— and John S. Thomas, Harry Keith Lynch, Robert A. Benfer. "Tojolabal Maya Population Response to Stress." *The Tojolabal Maya: Ethnographic and Linguistic*

Approaches. Geoscience and Man 26. Eds. Mary Jill Brody and John S. Thomas. Baton Rouge: Louisiana State U, 1988. 17-27.

García Canclini, Néstor. "Culture and Power: The State of Research." Trans. Philip Schlesinger. *Culture and Power.* Eds. Paddy Scanell, Philip Schlesinger and Colin Sparks. London: Sage, 1992. 17-47.

—. *Las Culturas Populares en el Capitalismo.* 3rd ed. México: Nueva Imagen, 1986.

—. "Cultura Transnacional y Culturas Populares: Bases Metodológicas para la Investigación," Lima: IPAL, 1985. 38-39.

Geertz, Clifford. *The Interpretation of Cultures.* New York: Basic Books, 1973.

Giménez, Gilberto. "Sectas, Religión y Pueblo." *El Nacional* 21 Sept. 1989, Suppl. Política, 3-5.

Gobierno del Estado de Chiapas. *Las Margaritas. Memorias Municipales.* Tuxtla Gutiérrez: 1988.

Good Eshelman, Catharine. *Haciendo la Lucha. Arte y Comercio Nahuas de Guerrero.* México: Fondo de Cultura Económica, 1988.

González Casanova, Pablo. *La Democracia en México.* 17th ed. México: Era, 1987.

Goulet, Denis. "International Ethics and Human Rights." *Alternatives* 17 (1992): 231-246.

—. "Participation in Development: New Avenues." *World Development* 17, 2 (1989): 165-178.

—. *Mexico: Development Strategies for the Future.* Notre Dame: U of Notre Dame Press, 1983.

—. *The Cruel Choice: A New Concept in the Theory of Development.* New York: Atheneum, 1978.

Gramsci, Antonio. *La Formación de los Intelectuales.* Trad. Angel González Vega. México: Grijalbo, 1967.

—. *Antología.* Trans. and comp. Manuel Sacristán. 11th ed. México: Siglo XXI, 1988.

Hacer la Radio a Diario. Memoria del II Seminario-Taller Sobre Radiodifusión en Regiones Indígenas en América Latina. 10-15 de agosto. Villahermosa, Tabasco, México: Instituto Indigenista Interamericano, 1987.

Hall, Stuart. "Reflections upon the Encoding/Decoding Model: An Interview with Stuart Hall." *Viewing, Reading, Listening.* Eds. Jon Cruz and Justin Lewis. Boulder, CO: Westview, 1994. 253-74.

—. "Cultural Studies: Two Paradigms." *Media, Culture and Society. A Critical Reader.* Eds. Richard Collins, James Curran, Nicholas Garnham, Paddy Scannell, Philip Schlesinger and Colin Sparks. London: Sage, 1986. 33-48.

Harding, Sandra. *The Science Question in Feminism.* Ithaca: Cornell UP, 1986.

Hein, Kurt John. *Radio Bahá'í, Ecuador. A Bahá'í Development Project.* Oxford: George Ronald, 1988.

Hernández Moreno, Jorge and Alba Guzmán. "Trayectoria y Proyección de la Educación Bilingüe y Bicultural en México." *México Pluricultural. De la Castellanización a la Educación Indígena Bilingüe y Bicultural,* (SEP). Eds. Patricia Scalon Arlene and Juan Lezama Morfin. México: Editorial Porrúa, 1982. 83-95.

Hernández, Severo. "El Instituto Nacional Indigenista y la Educación Bilingüe y Bicultural." *México Pluricultural. De la Castellanización a la Educación Indígena Bilingüe y Bicultural.* (SEP). Eds. Patricia Scalon Arlene and Juan Lezama Morfin. México: Editorial Porrúa, 1982. 63-76.

Herrera, Emerenciana. "La Mujer Indigena." XEZV La Voz de la Montaña. XEZV Foro. Tlapa, Guerrero, México, March, 1989.

Hobson, Dorothy. *Crossroads: The Drama of a Soap Opera.* London: Methuen, 1982.

Hornik, Robert C. *Development Communication. Information, Agriculture and Nutrition in the Third World.* New York: Longman, 1988.

Instituto Mexicano del Seguro Social. IMSS-Solidaridad, Unidad Médica Regional Número 56. Internal document, ts. México, 1989.

Instituto Nacional de Estadística, Geografía e Informática. Dirección Regional Sur, Chiapas, Oaxaca y Tabasco. Coordinación Censal Estatal Chiapas. *Boletín Informativo 2* (cifras preliminares), 1990.

Instituto Nacional Indigenista. "Plan de Acción Radiofónica para la Montaña de Guerrero." By Mario Chagoya Landín, Jorge Ramírez, José M. Ramos Rodríguez, and Maripaz Valenzuela. México: Internal document, ts. México, 1991.

—. "¿Se Escuchan Nuestras Voces? XEVFS, La Voz de la Frontera Sur." By Inés Cornejo and Silvia Luna. Internal document, ts. México, 1991.

—. "La Radio Indigenista." *Perfiles del Cuadrante. Experiencias de la Radio.* By María Antonieta Rebeil Corella, Alma Rosa Alva de la Selva and Ignacio Rodríguez Zárate. México: Trillas, 1989. 85-96.

—. "Perfil de Programación Tipo." Internal document, ts. México, 1989.

—. "Políticas y Tareas Indigenistas 1989-1994." Reunión del Consejo Directivo. Internal document, ts. México, 24 May, 1989.

—. *Instituto Nacional Indigenista: 40 Años.* México: Instituto Nacional Indigenista, 1988.

—. "Informe de Entrega. Departamento de Radio" (annex 6). Internal document, ts. México, Nov. 1988.

—. "Lenguas Indígenas de México y Radiodifusión Cultural." Asamblea Anual 1988, VII Simposio de AMLA. México, 10 June, 1988.

—. "Cartas del Auditorio." Internal document, ts. México, 1988.

—. "Planes de Trabajo 1989 de las Radiodifusoras del Instituto Nacional Indigenista." "Informe de Entrega. Departamento de Radio" (annex 6). Internal document, ts. México, Nov. 1988.

—. "Diagnósticos de las Radiodifusoras del Instituto Nacional Indigenista." By Teresa Niehus. Internal document, ts. México,1988.

—. "Dos Años del 'Reportero Serrano.' La Experiencia de un Noticiero Regional." Internal document, ts, México, 1987.

—. "El Presidente Miguel de la Madrid Definió la Política Indigenista," *Documentos,* 1, 1, México: Instituto Nacional Indigenista, 1984.

—. "La Música Indígena en las Estaciones Radiodifusoras del Instituto Nacional Indigenista." *México Indígena.* January-February, 1985: 38-39.

—. XEPET. "Informe." By Filemón Ku Che, internal document, ts. 9 Feb. 1990.

—. XEPET. "Informe." By Filemón Ku Che, internal document, ts. 8 May 1990.

—. XEZV. "Informe." Internal document, ts. 12 July 1989.

Jacobson, Thomas. "Modernization and Post-modernization Approaches to Participatory Communication for Development." Unpublished essay. State U of New York at Buffalo, 1989.

Jamison, T. Dean and Emile McAnany. *Radio for Education and Development.* Beverly Hills: Sage, 1978.

Kay, Cristóbal. *Latin American Theories of Development and Underdevelopment*. London: Routhledge, 1989.

Kleinsteuber, Hans, J. and Urte Sonnenberg. "Beyond Public Service and Private Profit: International Experience with Non-commercial Local Radio." *European Journal of Communication* 5(1990): 87-106.

Krueger, Richard A. *Focus Groups. A Practical Guide for Applied Research*. Newbury Park: Sage, 1988.

Kuncar, G. Lozada F. "Las Voces del Coraje: Radios Mineras de Bolivia." *Chasqui*, CIESPAL, April-June (1984): 52-57.

"La Tribu Yaqui Expulsó al INI de su Territorio." *La Jornada* 20 Sept. 1990: 1.

Larios Tolentino, Juan. "A Cuarenta Años. Experiencias y Aportaciones del Instituto Nacional Indigenista." *Instituto Nacional Indigenista: 40 Años*. México: Instituto Nacional Indigenista, 1988. 181-207.

—. "El INI a Cuarenta Años de su Fundación." *México Indígena*, Número Extraordinario, Otoño (1988): 7-9.

Lembo, Ron. "Is There Culture After Cultural Studies?" *Audiences and Cultural Reception*. Eds. Jon Cruz and Justine Lewis. Boulder, CO: Westview, 1994. 33-54.

Lenkersdorf, Carlos. "B'omak'umal Tojol Ab'al-kastiya." *Diccionario Tojolabal-Español*. Comitán, Chiapas: Carlos Lenkersdorf, 1979.

Lent, John. "Devcom: A View from the United States." *Rethinking Development Communication*. Eds. Neville Jayaweera and Sarath Amunugama. Singapore: AMIC, 1987. 20-37.

Lerner, Daniel. *The Passing of Traditional Society: Modernizing the Middle East*. New York: Free Press, 1958.

Lewis, P. M. "Community Radio: The Montreal Conference and After." *Media, Culture and Society* 6 (1984): 137-150.

"Ley que Crea el Instituto Nacional Indigenista." *Diario Oficial* 4 Dec., 1948.

Lima, Boris, A. *Exploración Téorica de la Participación*. Buenos Aires: Humanitas, 1988.

Limón Aguirre, Eduardo and José Manuel Ramos Rodríguez. "Indigenismo y Radiodifusión." *México Indígena* 66, supplement. (1982).

Lindlof, R. Thomas and Timothy P. Meyer, "Mediated Communication as Ways of Seeing, Acting, and Constructing Culture: The Tools and Foundations of Qualitative Research." *Natural Audiences: Qualitative Research of Media Uses and Effects*. Ed. Thomas R. Lindlof. Norwood, NJ: Ablex, 1987. 1-30.

Lofchie, Michael, F. and Stephen K. Commins. "Food Deficits and Agricultural Policies in Tropical Africa." *The Political Economy of Development and Underdevelopment*. Ed. Wilber Charles K. 3rd. ed. New York: Random House, 1984. 222-41.

Lomelí González, Arturo. *Algunas Costumbres y Tradiciones del Mundo Tojolabal*. Chiapas: Gobierno del Estado, 1988.

Lønsmann, Leif. "Community Radio. A Global Perspective." International Communication Association, Dublin, Ireland, June 1990.

López Nelio, Daniel. Interview. *Zapotec Struggles*. Eds. Howard Campbell, Leight Binford, Miguel Bartolomé and Alicia Barabas. Washington: Smithsonian Institution Press, 1993. 233-235.

Lull, James. *Inside Family Viewing*. London: Routledge, 1990.

Martínez A., Silvina. "Nosotras las Mujeres." XEZV La Voz de la Montaña. XEZV Foro. Tlapa, Guerrero, México, March, 1989.

Martín Barbero, Jesús. "Repossessing Culture. The Quest of Popular Movements in Latin America." *Media Development* 2 (1989): 21-24.

—. *De los Medios a las Mediaciones: Comunicación, Cultura y Hegemonía.* México: Gustavo Gilli, 1987.

Masferrer Kan, Elio. "La Proyección del Instituto Nacional Indigenista en América." *Instituto Nacional Indigenista: 40 Años.* Ed. Instituto Nacional Indigenista. México: Instituto Nacional Indigenista, 1988. 208-20.

McAnany , Emile, ed. *Communication in the Rural Third World,* New York: Prager, 1980.

—. *Radio's Role in Development: Five Strategies of Use.* Washington: Clearing House on Development Communication, Information Bulletin Number Four, 1973.

McQuail, Denis. *Mass Communication Theory.* London: Sage, 1984.

—, Jay G. Blumler and Brown, J. R. "The Television Audience: A Revised Perspective." *Sociology of Mass Communication.* Ed. Denis McQuail. Harmondsworth, England: Penguin, 1972.

Meyrowitz, Joshua. *No Sense of Place: The Impact of Electronic Media on Social Behavior.* New York: Oxford UP, 1986.

Melgarejo, Félix Dircio. "¿Cúal es la Verdera Cara de la Voz de la Montaña ante los Desastres de la Naturaleza?" Unpublished essay, 1989.

Mejía Piñeros, María Consuelo and Sergio Sarmiento Silva. *La Lucha Indígena: Un Reto a la Ortodoxia.* México: Siglo XXI, 1987.

Monsiváis, Carlos. "Notas Sobre la Cultura Mexicana en el Siglo XX." *Historia General de México,* 4. 2nd ed. Ed. El Colegio de México. México: El Colegio de México, 1977. 303-476.

Montagú, Roberta. "La Ranchería de Yocnahab. Primer Libro de Notas." *Los Legítimos Hombres. Aproximación Antropológica al Mundo Tojolabal,* IV. Ed. Mario Humberto Ruz. México: UNAM, 1986. 126-236.

Moores, Shaun. *Interpreting Audiences.* London: Sage, 1993.

Morales, Oscar. "La Radio Comercial Regional: Anatomía de un Poder." *Perfiles del Cuadrante.* Eds. María Antonieta Rebeil Corella, Alma Rosa De La Selva and Ignacio Rodríguez Zárate. México: Editorial Trillas, 1989. 55-62.

Moreno Estrada, Alberto."Nuestros Pueblos." XEZV La Voz de la Montaña. XEZV Foro. Tlapa, Guerrero, México, March, 1989.

Morley, David. *Family Television: Cultural Power and Domestic Leisure.* London: Routledge, 1988.

Murdock, Graham. "Large Corporations and the Control of the Communications Industries." *Culture, Society and the Media.* Eds. Michael Gurevitch, Tony Bennett, James Curran and Janet Woollacott. London: Metheun, 1982.

Nahmad Sittón, Salomón. "Indoamérica y Educación: ¿Etnocidio o Etnodesarrollo?" *México Pluricultural. De la Castellanización a la Educación Indígena Bilingüe y Bicultural,* (SEP). Ed. Patricia Scalon Arlene and Juan Lezama Morfin. México: Editorial Porrúa, 1982. 21-42.

Narula Uma and W. Barnett Pearce. *Development as Communication.* Carbondale and Edwardsville: Southern Illinois UP, 1986.

O'Connor, Alan. "The Bolivian Miners' Radio in the Late 1980s." Annual Conference of the Union for Democratic Communications. New York, NY, 26-29 October, 1989.

—. "Indigenous Radio in Ecuador: Issues of Institution, Cultural Form and Hegemony." Intercultural/Development Communication Division. International Communication Association, 1989.

Oseguera, Antonio. "Una Experiencia de Comunicación Educativa para el Desarrollo Rural." *Comunicación y Cultura* 8 (1982): 33-38.

O'Sullivan Ryan, Jeremiah. *Radio Occidente. El Pueblo Dialoga con el Pueblo.* Quito: ALER, 1987.

— and Mario Kaplún. *Communications Methods to Promote Grass-Roots Participation.* Communication and Society 6. Paris: UNESCO, n.d.

Ortiz, Montealegre, Reyna. "La Mujer Indígena y la Radio." "XEZV La Voz de la Montaña." XEZV Foro. Tlapa, Guerrero, México, March, 1989.

Pantoja Segura, Ubaldo. "Programa Resonancias." "XEZV La Voz de la Montaña." XEZV Foro. Tlapa, Guerrero, México, March, 1989.

Pareja, Reynaldo. "Radio Sutatenza: Notas para su Historia." *Comunicación y Cultura* 8 (1982): 39-44.

Perea de la Cabada, Roberto. "El Instituto Nacional Indigenista y las Radios Indigenistas." IV Encuentro Nacional del CONEICC. Colima, March, 1986. 119-129.

Pérez, Matilde. "Al Terror que Imponen Caciques y Pistoleros se Suma el de Judiciales." *La Jornada,* July 31, 1990. 3.

Plascencia, Carlos. "La Presencia de la Radio." *México Indígena,* Número Extraordinario, Otoño (1988): 37-41.

—. "La Radiodifusión Indigenista." Unpublished essay, 1986.

Pozas, Ricardo and Isabel H. de Pozas. *Los Indios en las Clases Sociales de México.* 13th ed. México: Siglo XXI, 1984.

Quezada, Edmundo. "Radio Estatal Regional: Entre el Centralismo y la Expresión Local." *Perfiles del Cuadrante. Experiencias de la Radio.* Eds. María Antonieta Rebeil Corella, Alma Rosa Alva de la Selva and Ignacio Rodríguez Zárate. México: Trillas, 1989. 63-79.

Radway, Janice A. *Reading the Romance.* 2nd. ed. Chapel Hill: U of North Carolina Press, 1991.

Ramos Rodríguez, José Manuel. Interview. By Carlos Plascencia. Audiotape, 1989. México City.

Ramos, Villarruel Miguel. "Trazos Indigenistas en la Política Educativa." *México Pluricultural. De la Castellanización a la Educación Indígena Bilingüe y Bicultural.* (SEP). Eds. Patricia Scalon Arlene and Juan Lezama Morfin. México: Editorial Porrúa, 1982. 46-57.

Real, Michael, R. *Super Media. A Cultural Studies Approach.* Newbury Park: Sage, 1989.

Reissner, Raúl. "El Indio de los Diccionarios." *Comunicación y Cultura* 14 (1985): 5-33.

Romero, Luis Alberto. "Los Sectores Populares Urbanos como Sujetos Históricos." Unpublished essay, U de Buenos Aires, March, 1988.

Ríos, Diana. "KUT 90.5 FM: A Case Study of Public Radio Disc Jockeys." Unpublished essay, 1989.

Rubin, Jeffrey W. "COCEI Against the State: A Political History of Juchitán." *Zapotec Struggles.* Eds. Howard Campbell, Leight Binford, Miguel Bartolomé and Alicia

Barabas. Washington: Smithsonian Institution Press, 1993. 157-175.

Ruz, Mario Humberto. *Los Legítimos Hombres. Aproximación Antropológica al Grupo Tojolabal*, II, México: UNAM, 1982.

Santiago, Blanca. "El Camino Andado. XETLA La Voz de la Mixteca." Memoria del II Seminario Taller sobre Radiodifusión en Regiones Indígenas de América Latina. Villa Hermosa, Tabasco, México, 10-15 August, 1987.

Saunders, Robert J., Jeremy J. Warford and Bjorn Wellenius. *Telecommunications and Economic Development*. Baltimore, Maryland: International Bank for Reconstruction and Development/ The Word Bank and Johns Hopkins UP, 1983.

Schmelkes de Sotelo, Sylvia. "The Radio Schools of the Tarahumara, México: an Evaluation." *Radio for Education and Development: Case Studies*. Eds. Peter Spain, Dean T. Jamison and Emile G. McAnany. Vol. 1. World Bank Staff Working Paper No. 266. Washington: World Bank, 1977.

Schmucler, Héctor and Orlanda, Encinas. "Las Radios Mineras de Bolivia" (Entrevista con Jorge Mancilla Romero). *Comunicación y Cultura* 8 (1982): 69-88.

Schramm, Wilbur. *Mass Media and National Development*. Stanford: Stanford UP, 1964.

Schroder, Christian. "Convergence of Antagonistic Traditions? The Case of Audience Research." *European Journal of Communication* 2 (1987): 7-31.

Secretaría de la Reforma Agraria. Resolución Presidencial. April 8, 1969.

Senghaas, Dieter. "The Case of Autarchy." *Development* 2/3 (1980): 17-22.

Serrano Serna, Alfonso. "Sistema Radifónico como Apoyo a los Programas Educativos Aplicados en el Medio Indígena." *México Pluricultural. De la Castellanización a la Educación Indígena Bilingüe y Bicultural* (SEP). Eds. Patricia Scalon Arlene and Juan Lezama Morfin. México: Editorial Porrúa, 1982. 235-250.

Servaes, Jan. "Development Theory and Communication Policy: Power to the People!" *European Journal of Communication* 1 (1986): 203-29.

Sesín, Saide. "Una Tradición Arrancada Produce Vacío." *UnoMásUno* 4 Jan. 1989: 28.

Simpson Grinberg, Máximo. "Trends in Alternative Communication Research in Latin America." *Communicacion in Latin American Society: Trends in Critical Research 1960-1985*. Eds. Rita Arwood and Emile McAnany. Madison: U of Wisconsin Press, 1986. 165-189.

Sjoberg, Gideon, Norma Williams, Ted Vaughan, and Andrée F. Sjoberg. "The Case Study Approach in Social Research." *A Case for the Case Study*. Eds. Joe R. Feagin, Anthony M. Orum, and Gideon Sjoberg. Chapel Hill: U of North Carolina Press, 1991. 27-79.

Spradley, James P. *The Ethnographic Interview*. New York: Holt, Rinehart and Winston, 1979.

Stavenhagen, Rodolfo. *Problemas Etnicos y Campesinos*. México: Instituto Nacional Indigenista/Secretaría de Educación Pública, 1989.

Thomas, John Stephen. *Determinants of Political Leadership in a Tojolabal Maya Community*. Diss. Columbia, U of Missouri, 1978.

— and Mary Jill Brody "The Tojolabal Maya: Ethnographic and Linguistic Approaches." *The Tojolabal Maya: Ethnographic and Linguistic Approaches. Geoscience and Man* 26. Eds. Mary Jill Brody and John S. Thomas. Baton Rouge: Louisiana State U, 1988. 1-9.

— and Michael Robbins. "The Limits to Growth in a Tojolabal Maya Ejido." *The*

Tojolabal Maya: Ethnographic and Linguistic Approaches. Geoscience and Man 26. Eds. Mary Jill Brody and John S. Thomas. Baton Rouge: Louisiana State U, 1988. 9-16.

— and Michael Robbins. "The Use of Settlement Pattern Features to Determine Status Differences in a Tojolabal Community. *The Tojolabal Maya: Ethnographic and Linguistic Approaches. Geoscience and Man* 26. Eds. Mary Jill Brody and John S. Thomas. Baton Rouge: Louisiana State U, 1988. 29-38.

Toledo Tello, Sonia. "Estudio de la Organización Social del Grupo Tojolabal." Unpublished essay.

Toussaint Alcaraz, Florence. *Recuento de Medios Fronterizos*. México: Fundación Manuel Buendía, 1990.

Turner, Graeme. *British Cultural Studies*. New York: Routledge, 1992.

United Nations Research Institute for Social Development. *Inquiry into Participation: A Research Approach*. By Andrew Pearse and Matthias Stiefel. 79/c/14. Geneva: United Nations, May 1979. n. pag.

—. *Debater's Comments on "Inquiry into Participation: a Research Approach."* Ed. Selina Cohen. 1980. Geneva: United Nations.

Urías, Luis. "La Radio como Educación y como Conciencia Nacional." COPLADE meeting, Wachóchi, March 24, 1983.

Valdéz, Luz María. *El Perfil Demográfico de los Indios Mexicanos*. México: Siglo XXI, 1988.

Vargas, Lucila. "The Social Uses of Radio by Ethnic Minorities in Mexico. Diss. U of Texas at Austin, 1992.

—. "KAZI, The Voice of Austin." Unpublished essay, 1989.

—. "The Radio Broadcasting of Messages from the Audience." MA thesis. U of Texas at Austin, 1987.

Villalobos Grzybowics, Jorge, and Felipe Espinosa Torres. *Huayacocotla y Teocelo. Camino Hacia la Emisora Horizontal*. México: Fomento Cultural y Educativo. A. C., 1987.

Villegas Ortega, Raúl and Jonathan Molinet Malpica. "El Instituto Nacional Indigenista." *Instituto Nacional Indigenista: 40 Años*. México: Instituto Nacional Indigenista, 1988. 519-539.

Vivó, Jorge A. "Geografía Lingüística y Política de Chiapas y Secuencia Histórica de sus Pobladores." Cuauhtémoc López Sánchez, ed. *Lecturas Chiapanecas* 1. México: Editorial Porrúa y Gobierno del Estado de Chiapas, 1988. 127-163.

Wang, Georgette and Wimal Dissanayake. "Culture, Development, and Change: Some Explorative Observations," *Continuity and Change in Communication Systems: An Asian Perspective*. Eds. Georgette Wang, and Wimal Dissanayake. Norwood, NJ: Ablex, 1984. 3-20.

Wardhaugh, Ronald. *Languages in Competition*. Oxford: Basil Blackwell, 1987.

Weaver, James, H. and Marguerite Berger. "The Marxist Critique of Dependency Theory: An Introduction." *The Political Economy of Development and Underdevelopment*. Ed. Charles K. Wilber. 3rd. ed. New York: Random House, 1984. 45-64.

White, John Standridge. "Lexican and Cognitive Aspects of Tojolabal Semantics." Diss. U of Texas at Austin, 1979.

White, Robert. "Communications Strategies for Social Change: National Television Versus Local Public Radio." *World Communications: A Handbook*. Eds. George Gerbner and Marsha Siefert. New York: Longman, 1984.

—. "The Latin American Contribution to Communication Theory." Unpublished essay. Centro Interdisciplinare Sulla Communicazione Sociale. Roma: La Universidad Gregoriana, 1989.

Wilber, Charles and Kenneth Jameson. "Paradigms of Economic Development and Beyond." *The Political Economy of Development and Underdevelopment*. Ed. Wilber K. Charles. 3rd. ed. New York: Random House, 1984. 4-25.

About the Book and Author

Combining concepts and methods from critical cultural studies with the Freirean approach to development, Lucila Vargas examines the social value of participatory radio and the possibilities and constraints that participatory radio stations hold for improving the living conditions and the sense of self-esteem of the poor in Mexico. This book provides an ethnographic account of the social uses of radio created by several Mexican ethnic minorities by examining the matrix of interactions between a government-sponsored participatory radio network and its indigenous audiences.

Vargas specifically emphasizes how and why the politics of race, ethnicity, class, and gender shape the extent and quality of people's participation in development efforts, and she also considers the larger issue of the way subaltern ethnic groups appropriate and refunctionalize modern mass technology. This inquiry leads to a method for analyzing the cultural subtleties and social intricacies of the practices that emerge from participatory radio.

Through a thorough investigation of two Tojolabal Maya communities in the highlands of Chiapas, Mexico, Vargas reveals the conflicts and challenging contradictions typical of many participatory radio stations. She finds that despite the rampant racism against indigenous peoples prevalent at the radio stations, groups like the Tojolabal Maya have found creative ways to make the best of the communication resources that this participatory project has made available to them.

Lucila Vargas teaches in the school of Journalism and Mass Communication at the University of North Carolina–Chapel Hill.